TRACING THE THREADS

SOCIETY OF BIBLICAL LITERATURE

EARLY JUDAISM AND ITS LITERATURE

Number 06

TRACING THE THREADS
Studies in the Vitality of Jewish Pseudepigrapha

edited by
John C. Reeves

TRACING THE THREADS

Studies in the Vitality of
Jewish Pseudepigrapha

edited by
John C. Reeves

Scholars Press
Atlanta, Georgia

TRACING THE THREADS
Studies in the Vitality of Jewish Pseudepigrapha

edited by
John C. Reeves

© 1994
Society of Biblical Literature

Library of Congress Cataloging-in-Publication Data
Tracing the threads : studies in the vitality of Jewish pseudepigrapha /
    [edited] by John C. Reeves.
        p.   cm. — (Early Judaism and its literature ; no. 06)
    Includes bibliographical references and indexes.
    ISBN 1-55540-994-6. — ISBN 1-55540-995-4 (pbk.)
    1. Apocryphal books (Old Testament) — Influence. 2. Rabbinical literature—History and
criticism. I. Reeves, John C. II. Series.
BS1700.T73   1994
229'.9106—dc20   94-25032
                                                         CIP

Printed in the United States of America
on acid-free paper

TABLE OF CONTENTS

PREFACE

The past two decades have witnessed a remarkable surge of interest in Jewish pseudepigraphical literature, popularly designated "Old Testament Pseudepigrapha." There are several factors nurturing this interest. The recent (and, in the case of the former, continued) publication of the Qumran and Nag Hammadi manuscript finds, both of which feature texts attributed to biblical figures, has awakened interest in the rich intellectual and literary currents flowing through Second Temple and Late Antique Judaism, spurring scholars to make new assessments of the date, provenance, and cultural influence of previously known pseudepigrapha. The fact that some of the newly found texts are hitherto unparalleled in the surviving corpus of pseudepigraphic works has heightened scholarly excitement and activity. Another reason for renewed attention can be traced to the stimulative projects sponsored by the Society of Biblical Literature Pseudepigrapha Group. In addition to holding annual public forums and presentations, the Group has supervised the publication of inexpensive textual editions (the Texts and Translations series) as well as collections of interpretive essays. Finally, the recent publication of the two-volume Charlesworth anthology (along with his useful bibliography), together with the synchronous release of Sparks' Oxford compilation, has made English-language versions of these texts readily available to a new generation of scholars.

The present volume, a solicited collection of essays, seeks to advance and stimulate the study of the "afterlife" of Jewish pseudepigrapha by presenting some considerations of their employment in a variety of temporally subsequent texts and contexts.

These latter include, but are by no means limited to, the literatures of Judaism, Christianity, Gnostic communities, and Islam. The ten essays comprising this volume might be conveniently grouped under three categories of discourse. Four present programmatic statements on the methodological issues involved in the identification and analysis of Jewish pseudepigrapha surfacing in these later contexts (the contributions of Kister, Urowitz-Freudenstein, Kraft, and Wasserstrom). Three provide focused studies of select pseudepigraphical sources found in one author, work, school, or textual tradition (Adler, Himmelfarb, and Reeves). The final three trace a particular pseudepigraphical motif (or set of motifs) through an assortment of textual and confessional traditions (Visotzky, Bowley, and Dalley).

Hence the title for this collaborative effort: *Tracing the Threads*, where the "threads" refer to the persistent survival (or in some cases rediscovery) of Second Temple and Late Antique Jewish pseudepigraphic texts and traditions among the respective literary corpora of an astonishing diversity of religious communities, while the "tracing" alludes to the modern recognition and study of this textual vitality, repeatedly exemplified in the present contributions. It is my hope that the contents of this volume will enhance the current discussions about ancient intertextuality, and spur others to engage in this exciting work.

Most of the abbreviations employed in the essays and the endnotes should be readily intelligible to students of the discipline; in cases of doubt, the guidelines of the *Journal of Biblical Literature* (107 [1988] 583-96) should be consulted. Moreover, a brief supplemental list of abbreviations for works or journals not contained in the *JBL* list is included herein. Treatises of Philo are cited in accordance with the abbreviations listed in the Loeb Classical Library edition of his works (10.xxxv-xxxvi).

I would like to express publicly my profound appreciation and admiration to each of my collaborators for their willingness to participate in this enterprise and the intellectual acumen displayed in their contributions. I especially thank Bill Adler: it was he who initially suggested the idea for such a volume to me, and who secured a place for it in the Early Judaism and its Literature series. Special gratitude is also due the Research and Publications Committee of the Society of Biblical Literature and the Winthrop University Research Council for contributing financial support to the preparation of the manuscript for publication.

John C. Reeves
Winthrop University

SUPPLEMENTAL ABBREVIATIONS

CMC   *Cologne Mani Codex*

CSHB   *Corpus Scriptorum Historiae Byzantinae* (Bonn:
                Weber, 1828-97)

EI   *The Encyclopaedia of Islam* (Leiden: Brill, 1913-38)

EI²   *The Encyclopaedia of Islam*, new edition (Leiden:
                Brill, 1960-)

EJMI   *Early Judaism and its Modern Interpreters* (ed.
                R.A. Kraft and G.W.E. Nickelsburg; Atlanta:
                Scholars Press, 1986)

Finkelstein   *Sifre Devarim* (ed. L. Finkelstein; reprinted, New
                York: Jewish Theological Seminary of America,
                1969)

Horowitz-Rabin *Mekhilta de-Rabbi Yishmael* (ed. H.S. Horowitz and
                I.A. Rabin; reprinted, Jerusalem: Wahrmann, 1970)

Kephalaia   *Manichäische Handschriften der Staatlichen Museen
                Berlin, Band 1: Kephalaia, 1. Hälfte* (ed. H.J.
                Polotsky and A. Böhlig; Stuttgart, 1934-1940); *2.
                Hälfte (Lfg. 11/12)* (Stuttgart, 1966)

Margolioth   *Sefer ha-Bahir* (ed. R. Margolioth; Jerusalem, 1951)

Psalm-Book   *Manichaean Manuscripts in the Chester Beatty
                Collection, vol. II: A Manichaean Psalm-Book, pt.
                II* (ed. C.R.C. Allberry; Stuttgart, 1938)

Theodor-Albeck *Midrash Bereshit Rabba* (3 vols.; ed. J. Theodor and H.
                Albeck; reprinted, Jerusalem: Wahrmann, 1965)

ZPE   *Zeitschrift für Papyrologie und Epigraphik*

OBSERVATIONS ON ASPECTS OF EXEGESIS, TRADITION, AND THEOLOGY IN MIDRASH, PSEUDEPIGRAPHA, AND OTHER JEWISH WRITINGS

Menahem Kister
Hebrew University, Jerusalem

To my mother

Study of the aggadic material in rabbinic literature (Talmud and Midrash collections) and of the Apocrypha and Pseudepigrapha makes increasingly clear the linkage between these two literatures. Notwithstanding all the external differences between them, we find in them not only similar contents, but also common exegetical materials that can be discerned behind the non-exegetical cloak of narrative or of poetic expression.[1] In fact, the work of uncovering the extensive exegetical and midrashic material embedded in apocryphal writings and in Qumran literature is only just beginning.[2] In some instances, we can attempt to reconstruct a complete commentary to a biblical verse (or to a cluster of verses) on the basis of a particular expression borrowed from the biblical source for use in apocryphal or Qumran texts. I have studied elsewhere several examples of this phenomenon.[3]

1

1. Let us take as an example the following verses from Ben Sira (Sir 35 [32]:1-5, not preserved in the Hebrew Geniza fragments):

> He that keeps the law multiplies offerings,
> He that heeds the commandments sacrifices a peace-
>   offering.
> He that does works of charity offers fine flour,
> And he that does mercy sacrifices a thank-offering.
> A thing well-pleasing to the Lord is to avoid
>   wickedness,
> And a propitiation to avoid what is wrong.
> Appear not empty before the Lord
> For all these are for the sake of commandment.
> The offering of the righteous makes the altar fat[4]
> And its sweet savour (comes) before the Most High.

The verse "Appear not empty (Gr. κενός, Heb. ריקם) before the Lord, for all these are for the sake of commandment (Heb. מצוה)," which is not entirely clear in its context, becomes more intelligible when we note that the biblical verses "None shall appear before Me empty" (Exod 23:15, 34:20, and similarly Deut 16:16) are rendered in Palestinian Targum traditions (*Frg. Tg.* Exod 34:20; *Tg. Neof.* Exod 23:15 [margin], 34:20 [margin], Deut 16:16; *Tg. Ps.-J.* Deut 16:16) as "My people, the Children of Israel, you may not appear before the Lord your God empty of any מצוה." Ben Sira assumed his readers would be familiar with the midrashic interpretation of these verses that is preserved for us in the Targum traditions. Therefore we learn from this biblical reference in Ben Sira both how to interpret the verse in Ben Sira and the relatively early age of this interpretation of the biblical verse.[5]

2. It sometimes happens that exegetical material found in rabbinic literature turns up in the body of one of the ancient versions of a biblical book. Thus, for example, R. Nehorai deduces (*m. Nazir* 9:5) that Samuel was a Nazirite. This is stated explicitly in an ancient fragment of Samuel from Qumran, and it is found in Ben Sira as well.[6] It has already been demonstrated that at times a variant reading in the

biblical text can be shown to be hiding in a rabbinic midrash, ostensibly referring to the Masoretic text.[7]

We encounter in *b. Sanh.* 105b a short, puzzling disagreement among early Amoraim: "'And the Lord put a דבר ("saying/thing") in Balaam's mouth' (Num 23:5). R. El'azar said 'angel'; R. Yonathan said 'a hook.'" (According to the parallels in the *Tanḥuma*, the Sages who disagree are the Tannaim R. Eli'ezer and R. Yehoshua). The latter Sage's comment is clear: according to his interpretation, דבר in the verse is a real physical object, like a hook or bit placed in the mouth of an animal.[8] But what is the meaning of R. El'azar's comment? Is it, too, an interpretation of the word דבר?[9] (The parallel passages in *Tanḥuma* state, "R. Eli'ezer says: 'an angel was speaking.'")[10] If we consult the Samaritan version of the biblical verse, as well as a version found in a Qumran biblical fragment,[11] we find: "And the angel of the Lord put a דבר in Balaam's mouth." As in other cases, it is difficult to determine whether the variant text and R. El'azar's comment are based on the same tradition -- if so, quite an ancient one -- or whether, alternatively, R. El'azar's comment is a remnant of this ancient reading of the biblical verse and its interpretation.

3. There are instances in which an early interpretation of a biblical verse embedded in the narrative context of one of the apocryphal books is found again only in late collections of midrash. Thus, for example, in *T. Zeb.* 3:2 we read: "They took his [i.e., Joseph's] price and bought sandals for themselves, their wives, and their children." As has been noted,[12] this narrative detail is derived from Amos 2:6:

> Thus says the Lord:
> For three transgressions of Israel,
> For four, I will not revoke it:
> Because they have sold the righteous for silver
> And the needy for a pair of sandals.

The "righteous" person in this verse is identified as Joseph, since the righteous one is depicted by Amos as being "sold for silver," and "righteous" is a standard epithet for Joseph in apocryphal and rabbinic literature.[13] This verse contains a certain exegetical difficulty, but the aggadah at hand does not set out to solve it. One can assume, after all, that the author of the aggadah was not unaware of the verse's twin: "We will buy the poor for silver, the needy for a pair of sandals" (Amos 8:6). No doubt these two verses, using identical language, make the same point. The latter verse, however, cannot be related in its context to the sale of Joseph. Yet that did not prevent the early exegetes, whose innovations were employed as early as in the *Testament of Zebulun*, from making precisely that connection. Hence we have an aggadah based on a midrash which in turn deals with an exegetical difficulty, even though the midrash is not the product of an attempt to come to grips with that difficulty. This early aggadah about the purchase of sandals recurs explicitly in late Talmudic sources, at times accompanied by the verse from Amos (*Tanḥuma, Vayyeshev* §2 = *Pirqe R. El.* 38; *Tg. Ps.-J.* Gen 37:28).[14] A reference to this interpretation of the verse (without citing the related story) can also be found in another source in *Tanḥuma*[15] and in *'Aggadat Berešit*.[16]

The *Testament of Zebulun* also explains why the profit from the sale of Joseph was used to buy sandals: "[They] bought sandals for themselves, their wives, and their children [saying], 'we will not use the money which is the price of our brother's blood for eating, but we will trample it underfoot in response to his having said he would rule over us. Let us see what becomes of his dreams!'" From the moment it attains narrative form, the midrashic connection drawn between Joseph's sale and the purchase of sandals almost inevitably takes on realistic and psychological features. (Is this related to Amos 2:7: "You who trample the heads of the poor into the dust of the ground"? In any case, the process of interpretation does not stem from this verse). It is interesting to note that R. David Luria (d. 1855) in his commentary to *Pirqe de R. Eli'ezer* makes precisely the same point as the *Testament of Zebulun*: "'to buy sandals for themselves' -- the simple meaning of this seems to be that they regarded him as self-aggrandizing and seeking power over them, and therefore they sold him as a slave to humble him. With the money they bought sandals to wear underfoot, as a sign that he deserved to dwell near the dust while alive." (chap. 38 n.77). The subsequent verses of the *Testament of Zebulun* contain a rather strange homily on the sandals in Amos 2:6 as a symbol of the *ḥalitzah* ceremony. Is this just a further development of the story, or is it another, more problematic, midrash on the same verse?[17]

In *'Aggadat Berešit*[18] we read: "And afterwards they sold him four times, as it is written: "For three transgressions of Israel, for four I will not revoke it." It could be assumed that this aggadah stems from an expansion of the exegesis of this verse. However, when we compare it to *Gen. Rab.* 83.22 (ed. Theodor-Albeck 1028), it becomes clear that we have here a different midrash which the redactor of *'Aggadat Berešit* skillfully managed to graft on to the continuation of the verse from Amos. We may note at this point the frequent difficulty of determining whether a biblical verse is the actual origin of a given midrash; that is to say, its formal basis. This problem will concern us again in the remainder of this study.

If we examine the context of the biblical verse (Amos 2:6) cited above, we will find that the exegesis of "righteous one" (צדיק) as referring to Joseph involves seeing the sale of Joseph as a sin for which the entire nation was punished for many generations.[19] This connection finds no explicit expression in midrashic literature until the late *Midrash of the Ten Martyrs*,[20] but traces of such a midrash on Amos can be found as early as the liturgical poetry of Yose ben Yose, the first *payṭan* known to us by name, who lived not long after the peak period of midrashic creativity (fifth century CE?).[21] It is not impossible that this homily on the sin of the brothers' sale of Joseph is part of an exegetical conception that formed the basis for the early tradition (i.e., antedating the *Testament of Zebulun*), and perhaps this very tendency was one of the theological motives underlying the identification of the accusation "for they have sold the righteous for silver" with the sale of Joseph.

4. The phenomenon of traditions found in apocryphal books reappearing centuries later in late midrashim is not rare. One must ask, then, whether the absence of such a tradition in the interim literature is

a chance occurrence, or whether perhaps the tradition has been deliberately suppressed by "mainstream Judaism."[22] In my view, there is generally no evidence for the latter position.[23] Let us take as an example the ancient tradition that Abraham came to recognize the existence of one God through observation of the heavens[24] or of natural phenomena in general[25] that is found in writings of the Second Temple period (Josephus, *Ant.* 1.155-157; *Apoc. Abr.* 7; cf. *Jub.* 12:16ff.), but which is known to us in this form[26] only in late midrashim.[27] A *piyyuṭ* by Yose ben Yose, however, clearly reflects a detailed version of this midrash.[28] This early *payṭan*, the sources for whose poems can usually be found in extant midrashim from the early period, belongs without a doubt to "mainstream Judaism," and he composed his works in a period not far removed from the redaction of the classical midrashim.

5. Perhaps the most well-known aggadah in rabbinic literature that owes its existence to a midrash is the one about Abraham being rescued from the furnace into which he had been thrown by Nimrod. This aggadah is based, of course, on reading the word אור in the phrase אור כשדים ("Ur of the Chaldeans") to mean "fire."[29] According to *Jub.* 12:12-15, Abraham set fire to "the house of the idols." The *Apocalypse of Abraham* (chap. 8) reports that a fire descended from the heavens upon the house of Abraham's father (a pagan priest) after Abraham had been told to leave.[30] According to *Biblical Antiquities* (chap. 6) and rabbinic sources (*Gen. Rab.* 38.13 and parallel texts; *Tg. Neof.* Gen 11:28, 31; 15:7; cf. also Samaritan traditions[31]), Abraham was thrown into fire and saved from it by God. In these traditions, אור כשדים is not a toponym but rather simply "the fire [of the Chaldeans]."[32] The report that Haran died באור כשדים (Gen 11:28) was interpreted as describing the manner of death ("by fire") and not its place (*Jub.* 12:14, rabbinic literature, and Samaritan sources).[33] God's statement to Abraham, "I am the Lord who brought you out of אור כשדים" (Gen 15:7) is thus taken as a report of his deliverance from fire. According to *Jubilees*, however, Abraham is not saved from a fire, but rather (as noted above) sets the house of the idols on fire. We may therefore

consider the possibility that *Jubilees* intentionally assigns Abraham a more active role.

The exegetical element is distinctly dominant in this tradition. It is clear, however, that even in this case the exegetical element by itself did not shape the various versions of the tradition. Forms and themes of this tradition vary from version to version and from period to period (Abraham as setting fire to the shrine of the idols, Abraham as a martyr).[34] It is these shifting themes that gave life to the legend and made it so popular in Jewish sources.

6. No one doubts the existence of traditions in which the exegetical element is merely an *asmakhta*; that is, a prooftext that serves after the fact as a basis in the biblical text for an independently generated idea. This is the case, for example, in the midrashic similarity of Moses and Ezra, derived from biblical verses which can scarcely serve as prooftexts (*t. Sanh.* 4.7 and parallel sources). It is a distant reflection of the image of Ezra as a second Moses, giving the Torah to Israel, found in 4 Ezra 14:3-6, 36-47.[35]

We thus face two different challenges. The first is to identify and reconstruct the midrashic foundation of some passages in the Pseudepigrapha. A second, independent problem is to try to determine whether the passage is engendered primarily by exegetical motives and then takes on narrative coloration, or, alternatively, originates as narrative having its own aims (narrative, theological, etc.) with the exegetical element being secondary. This second question is never easy to answer, and is indeed sometimes impossible to answer. Posing it, though, and attempting to find an answer may enrich our research and lead us to make more precise distinctions. Even if we succeed in locating the exegetical point upon which the tradition was built, this still does not mean that the origin of the story is in fact exegetical. These complicated theoretical considerations I shall now demonstrate by an example.

7. In the biblical narrative formula "and it happened after those דברים," the word דברים is rendered by ῥήματα ("words") in the

Septuagint and ממלליא in the Samaritan Targum.[36] This is probably to be attributed simply to the translation techniques. It is however a good point of departure for the midrashic interpretation of the Hebrew word דברים in these verses as meaning "words, speech." Indeed, several midrashim interpret this formula to signify some unreported speech (supplied by the midrash) taking place before the events recounted in the biblical text immediately after this formula.[37] In *Gen. Rab.* 55.4 (Theodor-Albeck 587) we read:

'אחר הדברים האלה [והאלהים נסה את אברהם]' הרהורי דברים היו שם. מי הרהר?
אברהם אמר שמחתי ושימחתי את הכל ולא הפרשתי לקב″ה לא פר ולא איל ולא אחד. אמר לו
הקב″ה: על מנת שנאמר לך שתקריב לי את בנך ולא תעכב. על דעתיה דרבי לעזר דאמר
'אלהים -- והאלהים' -- הוא ובית דינו -- מלאכי השרת אמרו אברהם זה שמח ושימח את
הכל ולא הפריש לקב″ה לא פר ולא איל. אמר להם הקב″ה: על מנת שנאמר לו שיקריב לי
את בנו ולא יעכב. אומות העולם אמרו אברהם זה שמח ושימח את הכל ולא הפריש לקב″ה
לא פר ולא איל ולא אחד. אמר להם הקב″ה: על מנת שנאמר לו שיקריב לי את בנו ולא יעכב.

> 'It came to pass after these דברים [that God (והאלהים) tested Abraham]' (Gen 22:1).
> A. Certain thoughts (הרהורי דברים) took place there. Who thought them? Abraham. He thought: I myself rejoiced and I caused everybody to rejoice, but I did not set aside for the Holy One a single bull or a single ram. The Holy One said to him: Even if I were to say to you 'sacrifice your son to Me,' you would not be slow [to do so].
> B. In accord with the opinion of R. Eleazar, who said that wherever Scripture says והאלהים (cf. the text of Gen 22:1) it refers to both Him and His heavenly court, the ministering angels were the ones who said: This man, Abraham, has rejoiced and caused everybody to rejoice, but he has not set aside for the Holy One even a bull or a ram. The Holy One said to them: Even if I were to say to him, 'sacrifice your son to Me,' he would not be slow [to do so].
> C. The nations of the world were those who said: This man, Abraham, has rejoiced and caused everybody to rejoice, but he has not set aside for the Holy One even a bull or a ram. The Holy One said to them: Even if I were to say to him, 'sacrifice your son to Me,' he would not be slow [to do so].

One gets the impression that section B is a learned combination, from a relatively late date, of R. Eleazar's rule that והאלהים refers to the heavenly retinue alongside the regular interpretive formula on דברים: "thoughts took place previously." Fortunately it can be shown that this is not the case. *b. Sanh.* 89b reads:

> 'After these דברים, God tested Abraham' -- R. Yohanan said in the name of R. Yose ben Zimra: after Satan's words (דבריו של שטן) ... Satan said before the Lord: Master of the Universe, You have bestowed upon this old man offspring at the age of one hundred years. Of all the feasts he has prepared, he had not even a turtledove or a young bird to sacrifice to You. He replied: All he did was for his son, but if I were to say to him, 'sacrifice your son to Me,' he would immediately sacrifice him. Immediately then 'God tested Abraham ....'

The two reports about either Satan (*Bavli*) or the angels (*Genesis Rabbah*) speaking ill of Abraham are clearly two versions of the same tradition. The version in the *Bavli* has, as has been noted, a parallel in *Jub.* 17:15-18:1:

> And it came to pass in the seventh week, in its first year, in the first month, in that jubilee, on the twelfth of that month, that there were words in heaven concerning Abraham that he was faithful in everything which was told him, and he loved the Lord and was faithful in all affliction. And Prince Mastema came and said before God: Behold, Abraham loves Isaac, his son, and he is more pleased with him than everything. Tell him to offer him (as) a burnt-offering upon the altar. And you will know whether he is faithful in everything in which you test him. And the Lord was aware that Abraham was faithful because he tested him ... and his soul was not impatient. And he was not slow to act because he was faithful and a lover of the Lord. And the Lord said to him: 'Take your beloved son ....'

It should be stressed that we have here not only a close topical parallel to the aggadah in the passage of the *Bavli* cited above (and evidence for its antiquity),[38] but also an implicit interpretation of the words "after these דברים" that is in the same form as the midrash preserved in the *Bavli* and *Genesis Rabbah*. The same biblical phrase underlies the phrase in *Jubilees* (i.e., "there were words in heaven"), "words" being a rendering of דברים.[39] Recognition of this fact is crucial even for establishing the correct reading in *Jubilees*. The editors of *Jubilees* note that there are manuscripts of the Ethiopic translation that read "there was a voice/word in heaven," while others read "there were voices/words in heaven." In light of what has been noted above, there can be no doubt that the plural reading is to be preferred, and the phrase should be translated "there were words (דברים) in heaven."[40] These observations are no less important for establishing the antiquity of this line of exegesis of דברים. Apparently the situation in *Jubilees* is shaped by the opening scene of the book of Job. What is apparent in *Jubilees* is even more clearly evident in the legends of the binding of Isaac in rabbinic literature (cf. *b. Sanh.* 89b; *Gen. Rab.* 56.4 [Theodor-Albeck 599]) wherein verses from Job are placed in the mouths of Satan and of Abraham. Here, however, in contrast to the case above, there is no midrash being performed on the Job verses, but rather there seems to be an echo of the frame story from the book of Job in a new literary creation.[41]

The replacement of Satan by the ministering angels in the *Genesis Rabbah* version seems to be secondary, but *Bib. Ant.* 32:1-4 proves its antiquity:

> And He gave him (i.e., Abraham) a son at the end of his old age, and took him out of a sterile womb. And all the angels were jealous of him, and the worshipping hosts envied him. And it happened, when they were jealous of him, God said to him: 'Kill the fruit of your belly to Me ....' And when he had offered the son upon the altar ... the Most Powerful hastened and sent forth His voice from on high saying: 'You shall not slay your son ... for now I have shown [you?] to reveal you to those who do not know you, and have shut the mouth of those who are always speaking evil against you.'[42]

The motif of the angels' struggle against humankind and their envy of humankind is familiar to us from rabbinic sources, but to my

knowledge it is rare in apocryphal literature.[43] Yet here this motif
takes control of the story, and the ministering angels entirely displace
Satan.[44] We should note one important point: the accusations raised
against Abraham by the angels or by Satan in both *Genesis Rabbah*
and the *Bavli* are not at all identical to the general criticism of
Abraham in *Jubilees* or, apparently, in *Biblical Antiquities*. The reason
for the specific accusations made in *Genesis Rabbah* ("Of all the feasts
he prepared, he had not even a bull or a ram to sacrifice to You") is
actually an attempt to relate the setting of Genesis 22 ("And it
happened after these things [דברים]") to the preceding story dealing with
Isaac (Gen 21:8). The author of this midrash was dissatisfied with the
lack of grounding for the phrase "these things (דברים)" in a specific
antecedent in the biblical text itself, and preferred to attribute such an
antecedent even though the resulting midrash exhibits a slightly petty
character.[45]

The binding of Isaac (and the trial of Abraham) is connected
with angelic arguments in an interesting Tannaitic source, *t. Soṭa* 6.5
(ed. Lieberman, pp. 184-85):

> At that time [of the Song at the Sea], the ministering angels
> looked, the same angels who had denounced [humankind]
> before the Holy One at the time when He created Adam,
> and said to Him: Master of the Universe, 'What is man that
> you are mindful of him,' etc. (Ps 8:5). At that time, the
> Holy One said to the ministering angels: Come and see the
> song that My children are reciting before Me. They too,
> when they saw this, sang. And what song did they sing?
> 'O Lord, our Lord, how majestic is Your name throughout
> the earth. From the mouths of infants and sucklings, etc.
> O Lord, our Lord, [how majestic is Your name throughout
> the earth.]' (Ps 8:2-10). R. Shim'on ben Menasya says: This
> section of Scripture [i.e., Psalm 8] is about the binding [of
> Isaac].

The core of R. Shim'on ben Menasya's exegesis is undoubtedly
the verse from Psalm 8 quoted above: "From the mouths of infants
and sucklings You have founded strength on account of Your foes, to
put an end (להשבית) to the enemy and avenger." The "infants and
sucklings" are equated with Isaac. It may be that he is indicating that

in the binding of Isaac "enemy and avenger" met their end, just as in *Biblical Antiquities* God "has shut the mouth of those who are always speaking evil against Abraham."

Ps 8:5 ("What is man that You are mindful of him") is often interpreted in midrash as a statement of angels opposed to the creation of man.[46] If R. Shim'on ben Menasya's statement has linked the angels' argument at the time of creation with the binding of Isaac, that is a sophisticated midrashic conflation of two traditions. This combination is found in a developed form in a midrash (of unknown source) in *Yalquṭ Shim'oni* 96:[47]

> The Holy One said to the ministering angels: Had I listened to you when you said, 'What is man that You are mindful of him,' would Abraham, who glorifies Me in My world, exist? The Attribute of Justice said to the Holy One: All the tests to which You have put him have been about his property. Test him by [damage to] his body. Tell him to sacrifice his son to You. Immediately, He said to him: 'Take your son ....'

This source begins with the ministering angels and concludes with the Attribute of Justice. The angels and the Attribute of Justice interchange in many traditions. Here the direction of development is clear: from angels to the abstraction of the "Attribute of Justice."[48] Note that this midrash is closely related to Job: God takes pride in His faithful servant, but that servant's faith is called into question ("All the tests to which you have put him have been about his property. Test him by [damage to] his body"). These words are not at all appropriate for Abraham's trials, most of which did not involve his property. Moreover, the binding of Isaac did not put Abraham himself at physical risk. This sentence stems from Job 2:5, and in this way it is actually the late source, *Yalquṭ Shim'oni*, that is more similar to *Jubilees* than are the traditions preserved in the *Bavli* and in *Genesis Rabbah.*[49]

An ancient *'abodah piyyuṭ* (apparently from the sixth century) based upon the midrash of R. Shim'on ben Menasya confirms our reconstruction of it from the terse language of the *Tosefta*. The

piyyut, to be published by Y. Yahalom, begins with the words אז באין כל
There we read in connection with a description of the binding of
Isaac:[50]

> You took pains to show the affection of the one who loves
> You [i.e., Abraham], in order to make Your name majestic
> among those [i.e., the angels] who had said 'What is man
> [that you are mindful of him]?' The angels were agitated
> and the Arielites became weakened when they saw the one
> who sacrificed [i.e., Abraham] rejoicing and the sacrificed
> one [i.e., Isaac] glad. Your [....] (?) You made known in the
> great council of angels when You have demonstrated that
> You have not created Adam in vain, as it is written: 'O
> Lord, our Lord, [how majestic is Your name throughout
> the earth.]'

Unlike the rest of the sources (including *Biblical Antiquities* and
Yalqut Shim'oni 96), here the only question under discussion is the
creation of the world. There is no attack on Abraham's personal
qualities. Of course, one could see this as only a difference in nuance
(since Abraham's positive traits are a justification for the creation of
humankind), but nonetheless, the content of the tradition changes
markedly.

Another source that develops the material in the *Tosefta* is
Canticles Zuta, and it is instructive precisely for its distancing from the
kernel of this aggadah:

> On what [Scriptural] basis can one claim that two songs
> were sung by the ministering angels, one at the binding of
> Isaac and the other at [the crossing of] the sea? At the
> binding of Isaac they sang before the King of Kings: 'O
> Lord, our Lord, how majestic is Your name throughout the
> earth!' That gives us one song, at the binding of Isaac.
> And one [was sung] at [the crossing of] the sea, as it is
> written: 'From the mouths of infants and sucklings You
> have founded strength.' Therefore it is said 'the song of
> songs,' teaching that these two songs were sung by the
> heavenly angels.

In this text the force of the angels' envy has been blunted,[51] and
the two conflicting approaches of the *Tosefta* have been unified.

Perhaps this can be seen as the conclusion of the stage of a "pure midrashic" attitude to the biblical verses, in this case at the expense of the content of the former components.

Let us return now to the passage cited above from *Genesis Rabbah*. It is clear that the three traditions (marked as A, B and C) interpret דברים here as "sayings" or "thoughts" (הרהורי דברים). Moreover, all of them use exactly the same wording. C seems to be a secondary version of B formulated after the angels accusing Abraham were identified with the Angels of the Nations. But the dialogue ("words") between the angels and God in B becomes simply the reflection of Abraham himself in A. Thus a wonderful, daring innovation has been created. The test is for the sake of the one being tested; the intent is not just to reveal his faithfulness to others, but to prove to the one undergoing the trial just how great is his faith. If we examine it carefully, this midrash shifts the focus of the trial from the theocentric to the anthropocentric domain, and from what is external to what is personal and internal.[52] Yet there is a distinct impression that the phrasing of version A is dependent to a significant extent on exegetical conventions and borrowings from earlier midrashim: A uses B on the one hand, and employs the usual midrashic convention to interpret דברים as "thoughts" of a certain biblical hero on the other hand. The midrash, as we have it, is a result of a "parallelogram of forces" of exegesis, redaction, and theology. Is it possible to determine which one of these factors was dominant in the formation of the midrash? Unfortunately, as in most cases, this essential question remains without a decisive answer. Remaining conscious of this dilemma, however, may prevent us from overestimating the theological component in itself.

We have seen that the phrase "there were words in heaven" reflects a midrash of the biblical verse "and it happened to be after these דברים." It is evident, however, from the very nature of this midrash that it is not drawn from the biblical text but instead reads into that text, by means of an exegetical device, new ideas and motifs. The exegesis is in this instance not the source of the midrashic unit; it is its external garb. The complex relationship among conscious theological innovation, casual mutation of tradition, exegetical elements, and biblical reflection (the implicit reference to Job) is clearly evident in this example. The mutual contribution of the study of Pseudepigrapha and rabbinic literature for understanding the development of ancient traditions is well illustrated by this complicated case.

8. Frequently we can derive a great deal of benefit from comparing two sets of sources, in the Midrash and in the Pseudepigrapha, that are related to a given biblical text.

Origen reports that the work known as the "Prayer of Joseph" was in use by Jews at the beginning of the Amoraic period.[53] Two sections of this work are extant. One of them is a short sentence in which Jacob says, "For I have read in the tablets of heaven all that will befall you and your sons." This fragment has a neat parallel (noted by Milik) in the Aramaic "Testament of Jacob," a small fragment of which was preserved at Qumran.[54] According to these testaments, Jacob revealed to his sons what would happen to them at the end of days. These traditions are evidently related to Gen 49:1: "And Jacob called his sons and said, 'Come together that I may tell you what is to befall you at the end of days.'" The words "the end of days" were interpreted eschatologically, even though no eschatological prophecy is present in the biblical text. Those "Testaments of Jacob" which display an eschatological interest (the fragment from Qumran as well as the fragment from the "Prayer of Joseph") fill in what is missing in the Bible, as do some of the rabbinic Sages. Others explain that Jacob intended to reveal the eschaton, but at the last moment changed his mind (*Gen. Rab.* 98[99].2; Theodor-Albeck 1251). Against the background of the eschatological literature that stemmed from the verse, one can appreciate the full weight and the polemical nature of this rabbinic exegesis.

In the second, longer fragment of the "Prayer of Joseph" we read:[55]

> I, Jacob, who am speaking to you, am also Israel, an angel
> of God ... but I, Jacob, whom men call Jacob, but whose

name is Israel, am he whom God called Israel, which
means 'a man seeing God,' because I am the firstborn of
every living thing to whom God gives life.

Later, in a description of Jacob's struggle with the angel, it is
emphasized that Israel is the highest angel of all whose very name is
even above them all.[56]   No doubt what is said here gives a
personalized, mythic form to the idea that the Jewish people, embodied
in the figure of Jacob, are superior even to the angels and have a role
at the head of the divine world.[57] This importance of the People of
Israel is recounted also in several midrashim to the personality of the
biblical hero Jacob.[58] Peculiar to this work however is the exalted
heavenly image accorded the biblical character, one that is beyond the
bounds of the human.[59] As was pointed out, it appears that in this text
Jacob is speaking to his sons before his death,[60] just as in the other
fragment of the "Prayer of Joseph." Thus it is appropriate to compare
the first sentence of this fragment with what is stated in *Genesis
Rabbah*: "'[Assemble and hearken, O sons of Jacob]; Hearken to (אֶל)
Israel your father' (Gen 49:2) .... R. Pinḥas said: Israel your father is an
אֵל ("god"); just as the Holy One creates worlds, so does your father
create worlds, and just as the Holy One allots worlds, so does your
father allot worlds" (*Gen. Rab.* 98[99].3; Theodor-Albeck 1252). In
other midrashic sayings of the same Sage, verses are intepreted with
reference to Jacob in such a way as to portray him as "creator of all
things."[61] It may be that what is stated in the "Prayer of Joseph" is
related to the phrasing of Gen 49:2 as well,[62] but this remains mere
speculation. What is important is the fact that we have before us two
comparable texts dealing with precisely the same situation in the Bible
(Jacob's words before his death). It is interesting that the wording of
the midrash is even bolder than that of the apocryphal fragment ("a
god" versus "an angel"; "firstborn of the creatures created by God"
versus "creator of worlds"). In the mouths of the Sages, these were
apparently no more than hyperbole, but it may be that these images
are rooted in mythic conceptions that were prevalent among Jewish
circles. In any case, the boundary is blurred: poetic imagery may
become myth as easily as myth may become mere imagery.

Appendices

1. As was pointed out above (cf. n.24), the tradition about Abraham's discovery of God through observation of the heavens is related to the aggadah about Abraham as astrologer. From Josephus (as well as from the context in Eupolemus and Artapanus)[63] it appears that the description of Abraham as an astrologer is the result of an attempt to "Judaize" a non-Jewish hero (cf. Berossus quoted by Josephus), and it is apparently motivated by an apologetic thrust.[64] The ancient legends that make use of the image of Abraham as astrologer in order to discredit astrology developed, it seems, after the image of Abraham as astrologer was already firmly implanted in tradition (see Philo,[65] rabbinic literature,[66] and *Jub.* 12:16-21).[67] It would appear that all these traditions refer either to Gen 15:7 (Philo, *Jubilees*) or Gen 15:5 (rabbinic literature), and constitute in fact a common midrashic tradition.[68] Late pagan authors (Vettius Valens, Firmicus Maternus, and, most notably, the emperor Julian)[69] also made use of the ancient image of Abraham as astrologer. This image, which was originally created in order to "Judaize" the pagan tradition, was employed by these authors to make Abraham into a pagan.[70] There is no doubt that the starting point here is not exegesis (even though this is the external form of some of the legends), but a raging polemic.

2. The following example attests to a similar process in the development of an ancient tradition. In *Genesis Rabbah* R. Aḥa says that Abraham addressed God before the destruction of Sodom: "You swore an oath that You would never again bring a flood upon the world. If You mean to get around that oath by claiming that You are bringing a flood of fire, not a flood of water, You have not upheld the oath'" (*Gen. Rab.* 49.9; Theodor-Albeck 511). "Flood of fire" refers to the destruction of the people of Sodom. A tradition in the *Tosefta* confirms this: "'and never again shall there be a flood' (Gen 9:11) -- R. Meir said: There will be no flood of water, but there will be a flood of fire and of sulphur, like the one He brought on the Sodomites, as it is

written: 'And the Lord rained upon Sodom ....' (Gen 19:24)" (*t. Ta'an.*
2[3].13; ed. Lieberman p. 335).[71] Philo, too, hints that the destruction
of Sodom is a "flood of fire." He states that Genesis tells of "how fire
and water wrought great destruction of what is on earth" (*Abr.* 1). In
another place he writes that "fire and water fell upon them, so that, as
the times revolved, some perished by deluge, others were consumed by
conflagration," and the destruction of Sodom is referred to specifically
further on (*Mos.* ii 53-64). In a third, less explicit, reference Philo says
that people forgot about the Sabbath because of the consecutive
destructions they suffered by fire and water (*Mos.* ii 263).[72] Gnostic
texts reveal the same tradition, considering the destruction of Sodom as
"the flood of fire," regarded as a universal calamity.[73] It has already
been demonstrated that the concept of a flood of water and a flood of
fire was common in the Hellenistic Near East.[74] This concept is
expressed by Berossus, and Plato attributes it to Egyptian sources
(*Timaeus* 21e-22e).[75] Plato's *Timaeus* is no doubt the source of the
idea of the cessation of Sabbath observance due to the floods, which
Philo has employed for his own purposes.[76] This identification of the
Hellenistic "flood of fire" with the destruction of Sodom ignores the
fact that the destruction of Sodom was not a universal disaster like the
Flood.[77] Surprisingly, traces of this problematic identification of the
destruction of Sodom with the pagan concept of the "flood of fire" are
found (albeit in a rather blurred form) in the midrashic sayings cited
above. The identification alluded to in these sayings is not a remnant
of popular belief, but is rather a learned attempt to put a biblical event
within the framework of pagan concepts (as is demonstrated by
Philo).[78] In this sense, there is a perfect parallel here to the traditions
of Abraham the astrologer. In the literature of the Sages,
characteristically, these ancient traditions, although blurred and blotted
out, are pegged to biblical verses (both in *Genesis Rabbah* and in the
Tosefta). Actually the very fact of presenting the material as the
result of exegetical play removes some of their sting. The same may
be said of the midrashim about Jacob and Ezra that were treated
above.

In this case too a pagan polemicist turned the debate on its head. Celsus argued that the story of the destruction of Sodom was but a "misunderstanding" of the doctrines and myths of Greeks and barbarians.[79] It is quite possible that Celsus was making use here of the aforementioned identification of the destruction of Sodom, which he may have found in a Christian or a Judeo-Hellenistic source.

Other references to the "flood of fire" can be found in a famous tradition of Josephus and in the *Life of Adam and Eve*.[80] It may well be that the "flood of fire" mentioned in these sources refers to the time of the eschaton,[81] but such an interpretation is not beyond doubt.[82] In any case, these two instances demonstrate that sometimes underlying the traditions of rabbinic midrash are products of a different, earlier era reflecting an ancient Hellenistic heritage, one almost unrecognizable when hidden behind the veil of a putatively innocent tradition.

3. To the mythic image of Jacob we should perhaps append the ancient tradition that the antecedent of the pronoun in the clause מלאכי אלהים עולים ויורדים בו ("angels of God were going up and down on it/him" [Gen 28:12]) is Jacob, not the ladder (*Gen. Rab.* 68.12; Theodor-Albeck 787). The editor of *Genesis Rabbah* found this tradition problematic, and explains that the real intent of the saying is quite different.[83] As scholars have noted,[84] John 1:51 is based upon this same interpretation of Gen 28:12: "you shall see Heaven open wide, and God's angels ascending and descending upon the Son of Man."[85] If we were to have to understand what is said in the Christian source in light of the text of the Hebrew Bible that underlies it, we would explain that the later source rests upon a mystical midrash on Jacob's dream.[86] Such a midrash, describing the Son of Man as a mythical heavenly figure, seems possible in the special mystic atmosphere of the Gospel of John, but very strange and improper in the context of rabbinic midrashim as we know them. Yet it seems to me that the original saying known to us from *Genesis Rabbah* should be explained by that same daring and mystical interpretation, although it is doubtful whether those who transmitted the tradition recorded in *Genesis*

Rabbah understood its full meaning. No less than the surprising proximity we find between certain traditions preserved in the midrash and ancient, mythic traditions, we must also take notice of the great distance between such traditions and the religious content of the midrashim of rabbinic literature.[87]

Postscript (to #7 above)

4Q225 (PsJub[a]) is most illuminating for our discussion of the role of the angels in the binding of Isaac as reflected in the Pseudepigrapha and rabbinic literature.[88] This fragment preserves the tradition, quoted above from *Jubilees*, that Prince Mastema accused Abraham because of Isaac. *Jubilees*, however, has many additional details not found in the concise version of this fragment. One of these details is the implicit reference to Gen 22:1. On the other hand, according to this fragment, at the moment of the 'Aqedah the "angels of holiness" were weeping (בוכים),[89] while other angels (probably "the angels of Ma[stema]") were joyous. It seems that Prince Mastema, according to this tradition, had a host of angels on his side. This may shed new light on the parallel traditions attributing the charges against Abraham to Satan or to jealous angels. A striking parallel to the Qumran fragment is found in *Gen. Rab.* 56.5 (Theodor-Albeck 600) where the weeping of the ministering angels is described, along with a report of God's binding of the Princes of the Nations (who are equivalent to the "bad angels" in the fragment).[90] Indeed, 4Q225 ii 13 reads: "And Prince Mastema was bound (אסור)," possibly referring to his being bound at the time of the 'Aqedah. But even without taking into account the last dubious detail, the Qumran fragment demonstrates the antiquity of this Amoraic midrash. Remarkably, it seems that the ancient tradition was more dualistic than the present midrash in *Genesis Rabbah*.[91] The midrash in *Genesis Rabbah* is ostensibly based on problematic biblical prooftexts, but they may well be secondary. As we have seen, the two motifs -- the accusations of the angels and their weeping -- are juxtaposed in some sources (see above, n.50). The most ancient evidence for such a juxtaposition is provided by 4Q225.

1 Y. Heinemann (*Darkhei ha-Aggadah* [Jerusalem: Magnes & Massada, 1953/4] 176) states: "There is no sign, then, of the methods of rabbinic explication in the two books which we have surveyed [*Testaments of the Twelve Patriarchs* and *Jubilees* - M.K.], and the same is true of all the Apocrypha and Pseudepigrapha." Since the last of the Pseudepigrapha were written at about the same time in which the midrashic traditions were originating, this points, in Heinemann's view, to an essential difference between these two genres. However, the more one looks closely at the Apocrypha and Pseudepigrapha, the more one discovers that in this aspect the difference between them and rabbinic literature is only in the shape given to ancient exegetical material (see the next note).

2 Cf. G.B. Sarfatti, "Notes on the Genesis Apocryphon," *Tarbiz* 28 (1958/9) 257 (Hebrew). See especially J.L. Kugel, *In Potiphar's House: The Interpretive Life of Biblical Texts* (New York: HarperCollins, 1990), and the theses presented at the end of the book (pp. 247-70).

3 M. Kister, "Biblical Phrases and Hidden Biblical Interpretations and Pesharim," *The Dead Sea Scrolls: Forty Years of Research* (ed. D. Dimant and U. Rappaport; Jerusalem and Leiden: Magnes Press and Brill, 1992) 27-39.

4 "Makes the altar fat" in the Greek text is a translation of the Hebrew ידשן מזבח. This phrase appears only in Num 4:13, where it means "take away the ashes." Ben Sira had in mind Ps 20:4 (יזכר כל מנחתיך ועולתך ידשנה) meaning that the sacrifice is burnt to ashes as a sign that it is accepted. The reconstructed Hebrew should be translated therefore: "The sacrifice of the righteous is accepted by the Lord."

5 On the interpretation of this passage in the Targum, cf. S. Abramson, "Four Notes on Halakhic Midrashim," *Sinai* 74 (1973/4) 12 (Hebrew); *contra* S. Lieberman, *Tosefta ki-Fshuṭah* (New York: Jewish Theological Seminary of America, 1961/2) 5.1279.

6 F.M. Cross, "A New Qumran Fragment to the Original Hebrew Underlying the Septuagint," *BASOR* 132 (1953) 15-26; Sir 46:13. Cf. recently Z. Talshir, "The Septuagint Version of Kings," *Tarbiz* 60 (1990/1) 205 n.72 (Hebrew). With the discovery of the genre "biblical paraphrases" at Qumran, which occupy a position between the biblical text itself and the "rewritten Bible," the distance between textual tradition and commentary at the end of the Second Temple period becomes smaller, at least in some circles. Cf. E. Tov, "The Textual Status of 4Q364-367," *The Madrid Qumran Congress: Proceedings of the International Congress on the Dead Sea Scrolls, Madrid 18-21 March, 1991* (2 vols.; ed. J. Trebolle Barrera and L. Vegas Montaner; Leiden: Brill, 1992) 1.49-52.

7 Cf., e.g., D. Rosenthal, "On the Sages' Treatment of Biblical Variants," *I.L. Seeligmann Memorial Volume* (Jerusalem: A. Rubinstein, 1982/3) 407-408 (Hebrew) on the various ways of explaining the similarity between the words of R. Eliezer in *m. B. Qam.* 4:9 and the Septuagint version of Exod 21:29; U. Cassuto, *A Commentary on the Book of Genesis* (2 vols.; Jerusalem: Magnes, 1961-64) 2.177 on the versions of Deut 32:8.

8   In *Tanḥuma* the same idea is expressed in a nearby passage: שעקם את פיו ופקמו
(*Tanḥuma, Balak* §12); שנתן כלבוס בפי בהמה ופוקמה (ibid. §13).   J.N. Epstein
(*Introduction to the Text of the Mishnah* [Tel Aviv: Magnes & Devir, 1962] 104
n.1 [Hebrew]) supports the reading פקס and explains it on the basis of the Arabic
verb *faqasa*, meaning "to break by force," but this is less appropriate here. S.
Lieberman (*Tosefta ki-Fshuṭah* 3.297 n.52) tries to validate both readings. It
appears worthwhile to consider preferring the reading פקם found in a number of
sources (cf. Epstein and Lieberman cited above) and comparing it to the Arabic
verb *faqama*, used to describe leading an animal with a muzzle and reins, and to
the Arabic noun *afqam*, which means "crooked-mouthed" or "crooked-jawed," as
has been suggested by J. Levy, *Wörterbuch über die Talmudim und Midrashim*
(Berlin-Wien: Harz, 1924) 90.

9   This is how the dispute was interpreted in a "*Tanḥuma*" midrash cited in
Yalquṭ Shim'oni Num sect. 765, where it is stated that "דבר [in the biblical verse]
means an angel." This identification of דבר and "angel" is discussed by S.
Lieberman, *Greek in Jewish Palestine* (New York: The Jewish Theological
Seminary of America, 1942) 167 n.48 (who refers in this connection to λόγος
meaning an angel in Philo), but in light of our argument, it seems that this
apparent identification of דבר and "angel" came into being only in this late
secondary version of the midrash.

10   *Tanḥuma, Balak* §12; *Tanḥuma Buber, Balak* §16 (ed. S. Buber 2.141).
Immediately following there is a difficult textual problem in the various versions
of *Tanḥuma.* Cf. Buber's n.103 *ad loc.*

11   According to a lecture by Nathan Jastram (at the international conference on
the Dead Sea Scrolls at Escorial in 1991), 4QNum[b] reads: [וימצא] מל[אך אלוהי]ם [אל
ב]לעם (Num 23:4).

12   R.H. Charles, *The Testaments of the Twelve Patriarchs* (London: A. & C.
Black, 1908) 113.

13   L. Ginzberg, *The Legends of the Jews* (7 vols.; Philadelphia: Jewish
Publication Society of America, 1909-38) 5.324-25.

14   There is reason to suspect interdependence between these two sources. In
Pirqe de-R. Eli'ezer, the verse from Amos is cited as a prooftext.

15   *Tanḥuma Buber, Noah* §4: "And Joseph, since he provided sustenance for the
people for seven years, is called צדיק as it is written: 'Because they have sold the
righteous (צדיק) for silver.'"

16   '*Ag. Ber.* (72) 73 (*Agadath Bereschith: Midraschische Auslegungen zum
ersten Buche Mosis* [ed. S. Buber; Cracow: J. Fischer, 1902] 142).

17   Perhaps the author interpreted "for a pair of sandals" (בעבור נעלים) to mean
"because they removed his sandal" (i.e., they wanted to kill him, as he explains).
Or perhaps the Hebrew word בעבור itself is taken to refer to the removal of the
sandal?

18   Cf. n.16 above.

19   This conception is early. On the goat sacrificed on the Day of Atonement
and on the Day of Atonement itself as related to the great sin of selling Joseph,
cf. *Jub.* 34:18-19. See also n.21 below.

20   G. Reeg, *Die Geschichte von den zehn Martyrern* (Tübingen: Mohr, 1985)
12*-13*. The story in question is mentioned there explicitly.

21 Cf. his *piyyut* אזכיר גבורות line 160 in *Piyyutey Yose ben Yose* (ed. A. Mirsky; [Jerusalem: Bialik Institute, 1976/7] 154): "Atonement will be made for the sin of the house of Jacob by this [i.e., through the cloak of the High Priest], for those who sold a righteous man because of a coat of many colors" (מוכרי צדיק על כתונת פסים). The verse from Amos is hinted at here. In his *piyyut* אתה כוננת line 98 (ed. Mirsky 186), Yose ben Yose addresses the same topic more abstrusely: ויסיר דאגת כתונת הפסים ("He removes the concern about the coat of many colors"). A parallel text in the Palestinian Talmud states "The cloak made atonement for those who wore garments of mixed wool and linen (כלאים). Some say: for people guilty of bloodshed, as it is written (Gen 37:31), 'They dipped the coat in blood.'" (*y. Yoma* 7:5, 44b). The cited verse refers, of course, to the sale of Joseph, but the atonement according to this passage in the Palestinian Talmud is not for the sale of Joseph in itself, but for bloodshed in every generation. Yose ben Yose, or a tradition he relies on, apparently related the atonement of the cloak of the High Priest to the sale of Joseph. Cf. also n.19 above.

22 D. Flusser, *Judaism and the Origins of Christianity* (Jerusalem: Magnes, 1988) 645-53.

23 This does not mean that the preference of one editor or another is not one of the factors in this process. In cases where the weight of the theological factor was particularly heavy (e.g., the Enoch traditions), there is room to consider the possibility that ancient traditions have been rejected by the "mainstream Judaism" of the classical Midrashim.

24 It appears to me that this ancient tradition is related, at its core, to the description of Abraham as an astrologer (cf. Appendix 1 below). In *Jubilees*, as in Philo (*Questions and Answers on Genesis* 3.1 [LCL; ed. R. Marcus; Cambridge: Harvard University Press, 1961] 174-75), recognition of the Divine is related to astrology. *Jubilees* distinguishes between Abraham's revolt against idol worship (12:1-4) and his observation that "all the signs of the stars and the signs of the sun and the moon are all in the hand of the Lord" (12:17). Only after this experience does Abraham say, "You alone are God to me ... and I have chosen You and Your kingship" (12:19); i.e., he accepts pure monotheism (cf. Flusser, *Judaism and the Origins of Christianity* 653, citing Brad Young). Only after this insight was God revealed to Abraham in the command "Go forth" (Gen 12:1). Actually, these are two sides of an age-old anti-pagan polemic: denial of the validity of gods as idols coupled with observation of the heavens while asking "Who created these?" (Isa 40:19-26). For different attitudes to idolatry and to the worship of heavenly bodies or of natural forces in Hellenistic Judaism, contrast Wis 13:1-9 with vv. 10ff. Those who worship natural forces are but one step away from monotheism in this view (cf. vv. 1-7, 9). Cf. D. Winston, *The Wisdom of Solomon* (AB 43; New York: Doubleday, 1979) 253-56. On Wis 13:4 cf. M. Kister, "A Contribution to the Interpretation of Ben Sira," *Tarbiz* 59 (1989/90) 358-60 (Hebrew). It is interesting to note that in the Qur'ān as well (6:73-79) the abandonment of the worship of statues is set apart from the ultimate recognition of God. According to the Qur'ān, Abraham deduced the existence of God from observing the sun and moon. Cf. also Qur'ān 37:82(88): "And he observed the stars," referring apparently to our subject. Cf. n.28 below.

25   *Apoc. Abr.* 7.
26   But cf. *Gen. Rab.* 38.13 (Theodor-Albeck 363-64) on the dispute between Abraham and Nimrod.
27   *Midrash ha-Gadol* to Genesis (ed. Margulies 210); J. Mann, *The Bible as Read and Preached in the Old Synagogue. Volume 1: The Palestinian Triennial Cycle: Genesis and Exodus* (Cincinnati, 1940; reprinted, New York: Ktav, 1971) 60 (Hebrew), where there is printed a Geniza fragment of a work that preserved a long quotation from this midrash. Cf. also the commentary to *Gen. Rab.* attributed to Rashi at *Gen. Rab.* 39.1. In *Midrash ha-Gadol* and in the Geniza fragment, the following parable is cited: "To what may this be compared? To one who was walking along the way and saw a great, exceptionally high castle. He looked up and saw red woolen garments laid upon the roof. Then he saw white linen garments. The man said, 'There is surely someone in this castle. For if there were no one in the castle, how is it that those garments are taken in and these put out?' When the owner of the castle saw how he was concerned about this, he said to him, 'Do not be concerned, I am the owner of the castle.'" On the other hand, *Gen. Rab.* (39.1; Theodor-Albeck 365) cites a parable of R. Yitzhak (it is integrated secondarily into a *petiḥa* bearing R. Yitzhak's name): "This is like a person travelling from place to place, and seeing one castle on fire he said: Would you say that this castle has no owner? The owner looked out and said, 'I am the owner of this castle.'" Contrary to the external similarity between these two parables, the ideational difference between them looms large. In *Genesis Rabbah* the theological emphasis has shifted from the observation of nature to what is human and historical, from rational corroboration of the existence of one God (which however requires divine revelation for its accomplishment) to amazement at the way the world is directed, which only revelation can uncover.
28   The *piyyuṭ* אזכיר גבורות lines 80-84 (ed. Mirsky 137-38) reads: [אברהם] חשב להבין סוד מפעלות המתנהגות בשוטר ומושל. חזותו מרוצת שואף וזורח שש כגבור בצאתו וחלש בבואו. חלוני שחק אשר בקדמה וימה אשר בם תנזר לבנה יום יום. חצי ברקים ודוהר כוכבים רצים ושבים ואיש לא נעדר. חכם סוג לב ושכל מאליו ושח אדון לאלה אחריו ארוצה "He [i.e., Abraham] sought to understand the secret of creations that act as following a ruler. When he saw the sun setting and rising, going out eager as a warrior and returning weak, and the windows of the sky in the east and in the west, in which the moon daily leaps, and lightning arrows and the brilliance of the stars running and returning, and no one is absent; the confused one became wise, gained insight by himself, and said: 'These have a master; I will follow [lit.: run after] Him.'" The phrase חכם סוג סוג לב ושכל מאליו is based on *Gen. Rab.* 95.3 (Theodor-Albeck 1189; note that this section is not original to *Genesis Rabbah*, but comes from *Tanḥuma*): "R. Levi said: He [Abraham] learned Torah by himself, as it is written: 'The confused man is sated from his own ways, and a good man by himself'" (a reading of Prov 14:14). For the phrase אדון לאלה, Mirsky compares *Midrash ha-Gadol* to Genesis (Margulies 205). The end of the last quoted line hints at Cant 1:4: משכני אחריך נרוצה. There was apparently a midrash that took this verse to refer to Abraham, because Yannai also brings this verse as a prooftext (ונאמר) in a *piyyuṭ* on Gen 12:1. Cf. Z.M. Rabinovitz, *The Liturgical Poems of R. Yannai* (2 vols.; Jerusalem: Bialik Institute, 1984/5) 1.122 (Hebrew).

It should be noted that the previous verse (Cant 1:3) is taken to refer to Abraham in *Gen. Rab.* 39.2 (Theodor-Albeck 366; cf. also p. 123). See also Yose ben Yose's *piyyuṭ* אתה כוננת line 55 (ed. Mirsky 180): נטש מגוריו ונמשך אחריך which is based on the same verse. See also *The Pizmonim of the Anonymus* (ed. E. Fleischer; Jerusalem: The Israel Academy of Sciences and Humanities, 1974) 82 (Hebrew), where Abraham is called ראש לנמשכים "first among the followers (of God)." Cf. also *Cant. Rab.* on עלמות אהבוך (Cant 1:3) and מישרים אהבוך (1:4), and *Gen. Rab.* 48.6 (Theodor-Albeck 481). It seems therefore that there was a midrash that read Cant 1:3-4 as referring to Abraham. Perhaps we can roughly reconstruct it as follows: when Abraham left his father's house, his good name became well-known throughout the world, and he was attracted to the Holy One and followed the Holy One to the land which He showed him (חדריו in the biblical verse).

[29] The component אור bothered early biblical exegetes, and several interpretations were offered for it. The Septuagint renders it not by transcription but by translation, using the word χώρα. *Jub.* 11:3 preserves a tradition that Ur of the Chaldeans was founded by a man named Ur son of Kesed. According to *Bib. Ant.* 4:16, people used to observe the stars using astrology (thus כשדים) and sacrifice their children in fire (thus אור) -- an oblique explanation of the origin of the name of the city.

[30] In keeping with the language of Gen 12:1. This comes after Abraham requested that God reveal himself, and follows the discovery of His existence by observing nature.

[31] See n.33 below.

[32] In *Jubilees* the two interpretations of אור כשדים, as a toponym and as meaning "fire," have been combined. See *Jub.* 11:3; 12:12-15.

[33] Z. Ben-Hayyim, "The Book of Asatir," *Tarbiz* 14 (1942/3) 119 (chap. 5): "And Nimrod took him and threw him into the fire, because he said that the world has a God. And when Haran was insolent toward Abraham, saying that he was a sorcerer, the fire came and consumed him. And Haran died during the lifetime of his father Terah in אור כשדים." Cf. also *y. Ber.* 9, 14b, and S. Lieberman, "Persecution of the Jewish Religion," *Salo Baron Jubilee Volume* (3 vols.; Jerusalem: The American Academy for Jewish Research, 1974/5) 3.221 n.68 (Hebrew). On the date of the Book of Asatir, cf. Ben-Hayyim, "The Book of Asatir" 102-112.

[34] Included at times in these descriptions are reflections of other biblical stories, such as the rescue of Hananiah, Mishael, and Azariah from the fire, for which the midrash explicitly employs Abraham as a prototype. Cf. *Gen. Rab.* 39.3 (Theodor-Albeck 367) and 44.13 (ibid. 435). Cf. Heinemann, *Darkhei ha-Aggadah* 24; G. Vermes, *Scripture and Tradition in Judaism* (Leiden: Brill, 1961) 88-89. On the rescue of Abraham from death by fire, cf. *Bib. Ant.* 38:3. In any case, we cannot state with certainty when the tradition of the martyrology of Abraham begins. It may be quite early. Compare E.E. Urbach, *The World of the Sages* (Jerusalem: Magnes, 1988) 448 (Hebrew); Vermes, *Scripture and Tradition* 90.

[35] The precise connection between the two traditions is not entirely clear. 4 Ezra indicates that the whole nation forgot the Torah, and that through divine

inspiration Ezra gave it to Israel once again. That source also states, without any emphasis, that the script underwent a miraculous change (4 Ezra 14:42). This latter fact is stated with clarity in Talmudic literature (where it is also sometimes related to biblical verses in a midrashic way). Undoubtedly this detail reflects historical facts which cannot be inferred from the biblical account. What is the nature of the legendary tradition that the Torah was forgotten and given once again by Ezra? A Talmudic account reports "At first the Torah was given to Israel ... it was once again given to them in the time of Ezra ..." (*b. Sanh.* 21b), and another states "Ezra would have been worthy of having the Torah be given by him" (*t. Sanh.* 4.7 and parallel texts). All these, to judge from the plain meaning of the words, reflect a similar picture to the one in 4 Ezra, even if the context in which they occur in Talmudic literature is different and much more restrained. We may assume that both 4 Ezra and the Talmudic traditions are making use of an ancient tradition. Perhaps we should conjecture that the tradition recorded in 4 Ezra is primary precisely because of the theological difficulty involved (that the Torah was forgotten by Israel, and the Torah, as we know it, was that given a second time by Ezra). For a description of Ezra as the last figure in the canonization of the Hebrew Bible, cf. also *'Abot R. Nat.* B 37 (ed. Schechter 98). Alternatively, "the 'would have been worthy' of the Sages becomes 'had the honor of' in 4 Ezra" (D. Rokeah, *Judaism and Christianity in Pagan Polemics* [Jerusalem: Dinur Center, 1991] 173 n.308 [Hebrew]).

36   Aramaic פתגמא, פתגמיא in Jewish Targumim and Peshitta exhibits both meanings of Hebrew דבר.

37   In addition to the references in n.51 below, cf. *b. Sanh.* 102a: "'After this דבר, Jeroboam did not turn back from his evil way' -- What does it mean 'after'? This means after the Holy One grabbed him by his clothes and said 'Repent' ...." The locus of this midrash is undoubtedly the term דבר, which is interpreted to mean "a heavenly word," or conversation between God and Jeroboam.

38   The *Bavli* is often given to the literary development and reshaping of its older Palestinian sources. Cf. recently S. Friedman, "On the Historical Aggadah in the Babylonian Talmud," *Saul Lieberman Memorial Volume* (ed. S. Friedman; New York and Jerusalem: Jewish Theological Seminary, 1993) 119-64. But in this case the tradition in *Jubilees* provides evidence for the antiquity of the version of the aggadah, which is preserved only in the Babylonian Talmud. Therefore there is no basis for suspicion of later reshaping.

39   In Ethiopic *qālāt*, which is the most semantically appropriate rendering of Hebrew דברים (I am grateful to Mr. Amnon Shapira for assistance in interpreting the Ethiopic text). Indeed, this same word is used to translate מלתא of the Aramaic version of *1 Enoch*. Cf. J.T. Milik, *The Books of Enoch: Aramaic Fragments of Qumrân Cave 4* (Oxford: Clarendon, 1976) 383, but also קלה, ibid. 391. There is also the word ܡܠܐ for *qāl* in a Syriac fragment of *Jub.* 12:17; cf. J.C. VanderKam, *The Book of Jubilees: A Critical Text* (2 vols.; Louvain: E. Peeters, 1989) 2.71. While it is true that one meaning of this Ethiopic word is "voices," its connection to biblical דברים would indicate that in this context it is not to be understood as "voice" or "voices," as Charles, VanderKam, Littmann, and Berger have all rendered it. Cf. R.H. Charles, *The Book of Jubilees* (London: A. & C. Black, 1902) 120; E. Littmann, "Das Buch der Jubiläen," *Die*

Apokryphen und Pseudepigraphen des Alten Testament (2 vols.; ed. E. Kautzsch; Tübingen: Mohr, 1900) 2.71; K. Berger, *Das Buch der Jubiläen* (JSHRZ 2.3; Gütersloh: Gerd Mohn, 1981); O.S. Wintermute, "Jubilees," *OTP* 2.90; VanderKam, *Jubilees* 2.71.

40 This is the reading preferred by Wintermute, Littmann, Charles, and VanderKam (the first of whom translates it as "words," the latter three rendering it as "voices"), as against the Hebrew translation of M. Goldman (see A. Kahana, *ha-Sefarim ha-Ḥiṣoniyyim* [2 vols. in 4; Tel Aviv: Maqorot, 1936-37]) who employs the singular רבד, and Berger's German translation ("eine Stimme"). Berger states the textual problem the most clearly, and tries to decide between versions by using rabbinic literature, but without apparent success.

41 Cf. Heinemann, *Darkhei ha-Aggadah* 24.

42 The parallel to *Genesis Rabbah* is cited by D.J. Harrington in his translation; cf. *OTP* 2.345. The last sentence of the passage may be compared to the early *piyyuṭ* cited below in n.50.

43 On this motif, cf. P. Schäfer, *Rivalität zwischen Engeln und Menschen* (Berlin: W. de Gruyter, 1975) 223-24. The passage from *Biblical Antiquities* escaped Schäfer's notice. Is the object of the angels' envy the friendship between the Holy One and His beloved, Abraham? Or is it perhaps envy of the son given to him? Our source is not explicit on this point. The envy of the gods is a decidedly mythic motif. An angel's envy of a mortal, stated in clearly mythic terms, can be found in a small fragment of the "Prayer of Joseph," and is treated at the end of the present essay.

44 I do not share Schäfer's view (*Rivalität* 223) that the evil angel or Satan is merely the representative of the angels in general. "The angels" are part of the divine world, and so may represent an aspect of the Godhead (e.g., the transcendent aspect), while the Satanic angel struggles against God. Therefore we must ascribe important significance to this shift in the tradition, certainly since it affects its later transmission. Cf. also n.48 below. For a combination of the two motifs (the opposition of the angels and the envy of the Devil), see *Pirqe R. El.* 13 (beginning).

45 Cf. M. Friedmann, *Seder Eliahu Rabba* (Wien: Achiasaf, 1902) 45.

46 *Gen. Rab.* 8.6 (Theodor-Albeck 60-61) and parallel sources. Cf. also Ginzberg, *Legends* 5.69-70 n.12.

47 The commentary *Minḥat Bikkurim* to the *Tosefta* cites this midrash from *Yalquṭ Shim'oni*. Referring to this commentary, S. Lieberman (*Tosefta ki-Fshuṭah* 8.669) writes: "but there is no reference there [in this midrash] at all that the ministering angels recited a song." The source in *Yalquṭ Shim'oni* is also cited by Ginzberg, *Legends* 5.248 n.228 (although the *Tosefta* is not cited there). On the surface, it would seem that the same midrash is to be found in *Tanḥuma, Vayyera* §18: the angels who say "What is man that You have been mindful of him?" are juxtaposed with Abraham and Isaac. But in fact this is only a fraction of a long midrash (which does not refer exclusively to Abraham and Isaac) that appears in *Midrash Tehillim* 8:7 (ed. S. Buber 78), and therefore, despite the appearance of similarity, it has no direct relationship with the matter at hand.

48 Cf. the differing opinion of E.E. Urbach, *Ḥazal -- Pirqei Emunot ve-De'ot* (Jerusalem: Magnes, 1970/1) 406-407 (= idem, *The Sages: Their Concepts and*

Beliefs [Jerusalem: Magnes, 1975] 461), where the author speaks of "the process of the concretization of the Attribute of Justice (Heb.: עיצומה) and its replacement by angels" (the English translation is very inaccurate at this point). On the other hand, cf. Schäfer, *Rivalität* 222.

49 In fact, in *Mekhilta de-R. Yishma'el* as well (ed. Horowitz-Rabin 120-121), which tells of the angels' song at the time of the crossing of the Sea of Reeds, the element of struggle with the angels is absent -- that element which is the central focus of the *Tosefta* text.

50 The Hebrew text: ריעות אוהבך שקדת להראות להאדיר שמך באומרי מה אנוש רעשו אלים ורפו אראלים בשורם זוביח דין ונזבח שמיח [...] בסוד רבה הודעתה בהראותך ללו ריק יצרתה אדם כב״ מי אדונינו I am grateful to Prof. Yahalom for permission to cite here these stiches of the poem. The phrase להאדיר שמך alludes to Ps 8:10. The words רפו אראלים echo Isa 38:7, which are taken by *Gen. Rab.* 56.5 (Theodor-Albeck 600) to refer to the ministering angels who at the time of the binding of Isaac requested mercy for the child and cried over him. The poet juxtaposed these two midrashim. Cf. also a similar juxtaposition in the late *Midrash Vayyosha'*: "The Holy One said to the ministering angels: 'Have you seen Abraham who loves Me, how he professes My unity in this world? Had I listened to you when you said 'What is man that You are mindful of him?', who would have professed My unity in this world like Abraham?'" Immediately afterwards the ministering angels are begging for Isaac. In a midrash of unknown source found in *Midrash ha-Gadol* to Genesis (ed. Margulies 354-55), these two motifs are united in one aggadah.

51 *Aggadat Shir ha-shirim* (ed. S. Schechter; Cambridge: [s.n.], 1896) 10. Cf. *Gen. Rab.* 44.5 (Theodor-Albeck 428); 47.3 (ibid. 614); 87.4 (ibid. 1063); *Esth. Rab.* 7.4; and cf. *Pesiq. R.* 3 (ed. M. Friedmann 10b): "and Jacob, too, when his time came to die and Joseph heard he was ill, began to think things (דברים) in his heart. R. Eliezer says: He thought about three things; R. Shmuel bar Nahman says: five." It is clear from the context that this is a midrash on Gen 48:1: "After these דברים, Joseph was told 'Your father is ill.'" Here too, then, "thoughts" take the place of "After these דברים" in the biblical text, although the biblical phrase that is the locus of the midrash has been excised. *Qoh. Rab.* 9.7 contains a dialogue between Sarah and Satan, as well as thoughts of Abraham after the '*Aqedah*, all of which are in fact a midrash on the phrase "after these דברים" in Gen 22:20, although this verse is not cited. Cf. *Tg. Ps.-J.* to this verse.

52 It should be noted that Abraham's doubts are not about his readiness to give himself to the Holy One, which could have given a special sense to Abraham's trial in the theological setting described here (cf. the dispute between Isaac and Ishmael, *Gen. Rab.* 55.4 [Theodor-Albeck 588]), but instead Abraham denounces himself over one relatively marginal issue, which this midrash borrows from the earlier midrash (B).

53 It is referred to by Origen in his commentary to the Gospel of John as "an apocryphon that the Jews use nowadays." This shows that the text was in use in certain Jewish circles in 231 CE.

54 J.T. Milik, "Ecrits préesséniens de Qumrân," *Qumrân: sa piété, sa théologie et son milieu* (ed. M. Delcor; Paris: Duculot, 1978) 104. As Milik noted, this testament is referred to in *Jub.* 32:21.

55 On this work, see the exhaustive article by J.Z. Smith, "The Prayer of Joseph," *Religions in Antiquity: Essays in Memory of Erwin Ramsdell Goodenough* (ed. J. Neusner; Leiden: Brill, 1970) 253-94. (The similarity noted further on in the present article was not mentioned by Smith). In this article, Smith cites a great deal of parallel material to the motifs of the "Prayer of Joseph"; but with respect to rabbinic literature, a sizeable amount of irrelevant material is also included, and the discussion is not always focused.

56 For important parallels in Philo and Gnostic writings, cf. Smith's summary in his "The Prayer of Joseph" 260-64, 267-68.

57 Cf. P. Schäfer, "Competition between Angel and Human in the Apocryphal Prayer of Joseph and Rabbinic Literature," *Proceedings of the Sixth World Congress of Jewish Studies* (4 vols.; Jerusalem: World Union of Jewish Studies, 1973) 3.515-51 (Hebrew). Cf. also the story of Hillel the Elder, which expresses most clearly the tension between the status of Israel and the status of the angels in rabbinic thought: *y. Sukk.* 5.3; *b. Sukk.* 55b; and parallel texts.

58 There are quite a few midrashim on this theme. Cf. *Tanhuma, Bamidbar* §19: "The Holy One said to Jacob: Jacob, you are very dear to Me. Why? I placed your image on My throne, so to speak (כביכול), and by your name the angels praise Me, saying 'Blessed is the Lord, God of Israel, from eternity to eternity.'" A midrash along these lines underlies Yose ben Yose's *piyyuṭ* אספר גדולות line 19 (ed. Mirsky 202): יקר שמו למעלה וכיחש לו שר "His name is dear above, and a Prince (i.e., an angel) was submitted to him"; the first hemistich borrows from 1 Sam 18:30: ויקר שמו מאד . Cf. also the *piyyuṭ* אזכיר גבורות by Yose ben Yose line 97 (ed. Mirsky 141), and Rabinovitz, *Liturgical Poems of R. Yannai* 1.169. Cf. also *Tanḥuma, Qedoshim* §2, which nicely expresses the inseparable link between the people of Israel and the historical figure Jacob (discernable in rabbinic literature in the phrase ישראל סבא). This is only one example among many. (Cf., e.g., *Gen. Rab.* 68.12 (Theodor-Albeck 788). The comments by Smith in "The Prayer of Joseph" [pp. 263-64] are incorrect). Another interesting example of the presentation of Joseph at Qumran is reflected in E. Schuller, "A Text About Jacob," *RevQ* 14 (1990) 349-76. "Joseph" in this text means the tribe of Joseph, but it is referred to in this early fragment in a very personified way.

59 Smith, "The Prayer of Joseph" 260-65, 293 cites some non-Jewish sources wherein Israel (Jacob) is at least an angel. Philo mentions (*Conf.* 146) "Israel" once as a name for the Logos; see Smith, pp. 267ff.

60 Smith, "The Prayer of Joseph" 255-56.

61 *Lev. Rab.* 36.4 (ed. Margulies 846): "R. Pinḥas, in the name of R. Reuben, said: The Holy One said to the world: O My world, My world, I will tell you who created you, I will tell you who formed you; Jacob created you, Israel formed you, as it is written: '[he] that created you, Jacob, and he who formed you, Israel' (Isa 43:1)." *Tanḥuma Buber, Toledot* §11 (Buber 1.132): "'May God give you ....' (Gen 27:28) ... Jacob is a partner to his Creator in all things. R. Pinḥas bar Hama the Priest said in the name of R. Reuben: See what is written: 'The lot of Jacob is not like them, for he is the creator of all things.' (Jer 10:16) ... And how do we know that the righteous are partners with the Holy One when He creates a form ...?" Note that "Jacob" at the end had already become "the righteous." Both

sources have already been cited by Albeck in his commentary to *Gen. Rab.* It should be noted that the exegesis of *Gen. Rab.* may be related to the midrash on Jer 10:16 "the lot of Jacob is not like them" (לא כאלה חלק יעקב) referring to lots alloted by Jacob, and to the phrase at the end of this verse: "the creator of all things" (= "creates worlds"). Cf. also Jerome's explanation of the name "Israel" when interpreting Gen 32:29: "sed vocabitur nomen tuum princeps [Heb. שר] cum Deo [Heb. עם אלהים], hoc est, Israel." (*Liber Hebraicarum Quaestionum in Genesim* 32:28, cited by Smith, "The Prayer of Joseph" 264). Compare this explanation to *Gen. Rab.* 78.3 (Theodor-Albeck 921), which explains the same verse: "You are the one whose image is engraved on high." The commentators on the midrash explain: "because you were a prince with God, your image is engraved on high," exactly as in Jerome's tradition!

62 Note that "Jacob" is juxtaposed with "God of Israel" in this verse. Ginzberg (*Legends* 5.313 n.282) and Urbach (*Ḥazal* 149-50 [= *The Sages* 171-72]) cite a midrashic saying similar to the "Prayer of Joseph": "[Jacob] said: You are God in the upper world, and I am god in the lower world." (*Gen. Rab.* 79.8; Theodor-Albeck 949). It should be stressed that this passage follows closely upon Jacob's victory over the angel. This saying is apparently the occasion for the critical comment of R. Huna in the name of R. Shim'on ben Lakish (ibid. 950), although the main focus of this comment is on the words ויקרא לו . Cf. *t. Meg.* 3[4].21 (ed. Lieberman 359). Ginzberg cites *Sifre* Deut §355 (ed. Finkelstein 422); *Gen. Rab.* 77.1 (Theodor-Albeck 910), where we find a midrash on Deut 33:26 אין כאל ישרון ("There is none like God, [O] Jeshurun") identifying Jeshurun with God. However, in their present form, these midrashim are intended as non-literal rhetoric about the people Israel, not the person Jacob, as is evident from their contexts. This is an instructive example of how a bold idea becomes in a Tannaitic midrash stock phraseology. Ginzberg's conjecture (*Legends* 5.275 n.35) about the origin of the legend of "Jacob the god" does not withstand critique; cf. Smith, "The Prayer of Joseph," 261, 293.

63 Cf. *OTP* 2.880, 897; Josephus, *Ant.* 1.158; 1.166-68. And cf. M. Stern, *Greek and Latin Authors on Jews and Judaism* (3 vols.; Jerusalem: The Israel Academy of Sciences and Humanities, 1974-84) 2.173.

64 Abraham transmitting Enoch's astrological knowledge to Egypt is found in the *Genesis Apocryphon* (J.A. Fitzmyer, *The Genesis Apocryphon* [2d ed.; Rome: Pontifical Biblical Institute, 1971] 118). See also the Jewish Orphic hymn reproduced in *OTP* 2.799. A similar identification of Abraham with a (presumably non-Jewish) cult-hero occurs in *Jub.* 11:11-24. On analogous identifications of biblical heroes with Egyptian gods, cf. S. Lieberman, *Hellenism in Jewish Palestine* (New York: The Jewish Theological Seminary of America, 1950) 137-39. See also G. Mussies, "The Interpretatio Judaica of Sarapis," *Studies in Hellenistic Religions* (EPRO 78; ed. M.J. Vermaseren; Leiden: Brill, 1979) 189-214 (I owe this reference to Dr. D. Satran. Some details and considerations in this article concerning Talmudic sources should be revised). Regarding ancient Palestinian tradition, see also D. Flusser and S. Amorai-Stark, "The Goddess Thermuthis, Moses and Artapanos," *Jewish Studies Quarterly* (forthcoming).

65 *Abr.* 15; *Questions and Answers on Genesis* 3.1. A polemic against astrology

without explicit reference to Abraham but which is perhaps related to him can be found in *Sib. Or.* 3.218ff.

[66] See *Gen. Rab.* 44.12 and the parallel sources listed there. Cf. also Ginzberg, *Legends* 5.227 n.108; Lieberman, *Tosefta ki-Fshuṭah* 8.985-86.

[67] In the Book of Asatir, a relatively late Samaritan work (cf. Ben-Hayyim, "Book of Asatir" 105-112), there is a connection made between Abraham's sojourn in Egypt and astrology. A sorcerer from Antiochia who was an expert in "The Book of Signs" wanted to denounce Abraham before Pharaoh, but Abraham "at once looked heavenward in prayer," prayed, and was saved (chap. 6; ed. Ben-Hayyim 119). This tradition seems to be almost the opposite of the tradition of the early Samaritan Eupolemus and seems shaped by an anti-astrological polemic.

[68] For the aggadah about Abraham being lifted up above the heavens and there being commanded to count the stars (which is related to these verses), cf. *Apoc. Abr.* 19:2-3; 21:1; *Bib. Ant.* 18:5. In the *Apocalypse of Abraham*, however, this tradition is unrelated to astrology. It is not impossible, therefore, that the aggadah in rabbinic literature is a conflation of two legends. It should be noted that according to Philo and *Jubilees*, astrology stands in opposition to monotheism. The converse opinion can be found in the Jewish Orphic hymn cited in n.64 above, where astrology leads to monotheistic belief. Cf. also n.24 above.

[69] Cf. Stern, *Greek and Latin Authors* 2.173-75, 492-94, 527, 544. It should be noted that the earliest works cite astrological writings attributed to Abraham. For Jewish elements in astrology, cf. Suetonius, *Life of Nero* 40.

[70] Especially Julian, who interpreted Gen 15:5 in a midrashic manner. Cf. R. Levi's opinion in Gen. Rab. 42.12 (Theodor-Albeck 432), and especially *Midrash Zuta al Shir ha-shirim, Rut, Ekah, we-Qohelet* ... (ed. S. Buber; Vilna: Romm, 1925) 2. See also Rokeah, *Pagan Polemics* 242-43 n.207. Could Julian have found such a midrash in a Jewish source? For a similar phenomenon, see most recently D. Flusser, "The Dead of Massada in the Eyes of Their Contemporaries," *Jews and Judaism in the Second Temple, Mishnah and Talmud Periods: Studies in Honour of S. Safrai* (Jerusalem: Y. Ben Zvi, 1992) 143-45 (Hebrew). Cf. also G. Alon, *Studies in Jewish History* (2 vols.; Jerusalem: Hakibbutz Hameuhad, 1970) 2.314 (Hebrew).

[71] For different readings of the name of the Sage quoted, see the variant readings recorded in *Tosefta* manuscripts and Lieberman, *Tosefta ki-Fshuṭah* 5.1097.

[72] See n.76 below.

[73] G. Stroumsa, *Another Seed: Studies in Gnostic Mythology* (Leiden: Brill, 1984) 106-111.

[74] Cf. A.F.J. Klijn, *Seth in Jewish, Christian and Gnostic Literature* (Leiden: Brill, 1977) 121-24.

[75] Berossus links the periodic floods of water and of fire with the position of the stars. This concept may form the background for some rabbinic sources wherein the Flood is correlated with a certain position of the stars (cf. *S. 'Olam Rab.* 4 and its parallels). Another tradition states that the stars were not active at all during the Flood (*Gen. Rab.* 34.11; Theodor-Albeck 323). See also the late

astronomical passage in *Midrash ha-Gadol* to Genesis (ed. Margulies 168-69).
[76] Philo's German translator seems to have had this in mind despite the lack of an explicit reference to Plato. This point escaped L. Ginzberg, "Flood of Fire," *On Halakha and Aggada* (Tel Aviv: Devir, 1960) 205 (Hebrew). Ginzberg is correct in saying that Philo solves a theological problem about forgetting the sanctity of Shabbat; the tools to reach this solution were however borrowed from non-Jewish sources. Philo's comment that the reason for the lapse is "the sequence of destructions that befell them by fire and by water" (διὰ τὰς ἐν ὕδατι καὶ πυρὶ γενομένας συνεχεῖς καὶ ἐπαλλήλους φθοράς) is not consonant with the biblical account of world history, but is in keeping with pagan concepts. His comment in *Mos.* ii 53 (ὡς καιρῶν περιόδοις) is also to be interpreted in the light of a non-Jewish background, even though those floods are identified there with the biblical Flood and the story of Sodom.
[77] See, e.g., F.H. Colson, *Philo with an English Translation* (LCL; Cambridge: Harvard University Press, 1935) 6.4 note a.
[78] Ginzberg ("Flood of Fire" 217) emphasizes the "popular" nature of this tradition. My analysis of its development differs markedly from Ginzberg's, and leads to very different conclusions. Cf. also ibid., 205-19, 292-94.
[79] Book 4 §11-21 (*apud* Stern, *Greek and Latin Authors* 2.277).
[80] Josephus, *Ant.* 1.70-71; *Adam and Eve* 48:3-50:2 (*OTP* 2.292). Cf. also Klijn (n.74 *supra*); Lieberman (n.71 *supra*). It would seem that a similar tradition forms the background to the statement attributed to the generation of the Flood in *b. Sanh.* 108b: "A flood of what? If it is a flood of fire, we have one thing .... but if it is a flood of water ...." This tradition is best understood in light of the prophetic statement (of Adam or Eve) contained in Josephus and *Adam and Eve* mentioned above. Since the people of that generation knew of the likelihood of a flood of water or of fire, they chose not only to preserve their wise sayings (as in those sources), but to develop also the means of countering both fire and water, which could save their lives in time of danger. Thus this rabbinic aggadah not only alludes to "a flood of fire," but also refers to a tradition of Adam's prophecy that is unknown to us explicitly from rabbinic sources.
[81] On judgment by fire at the end of days in the Qumran sect and its religious context, cf. D. Flusser, *Jewish Sources in Early Christianity* (Tel Aviv: Sifriyyat Po'alim, 1979) 97-102 (Hebrew).
[82] Is it not possible, for instance, that here too the destruction of Sodom was meant (notwithstanding the universal nature of the two floods in this prophecy; cf. Philo and the Gnostic texts in nn.73 and 76 *supra*)?
[83] *Gen. Rab.* 68.12 (Theodor-Albeck 787-88): "The statement that they go up and down the ladder is not problematic. The statement that they go up and down Jacob means they were bringing things up on him and bringing things down on him, sporting (?) with him, leaping on him, scoffing at him." The wording of the interpretation of the statement that the angels "go up and down Jacob" is apparently inspired by *Gen. Rab.* 68.13 (ibid. 790). It is impossible to reconcile the original statement itself (that of R. Hiyya or R. Yannai) with this explanation, the intent of which is quite different. By such an interpretation the original tradition could become a part of rabbinic literature.
[84] Cf. H. Odeberg, *The Fourth Gospel* (Uppsala: Almqvist & Wiksell, 1929) 33-

42. Cf. also Smith, "The Prayer of Joseph" 285-87. The latter comments "[the] interpretation of *bw* as *by'kb* implies a mystical growth of Jacob to cosmic size." Smith (as well as the other scholars who have dealt with this midrash) was unaware of the various layers to this passage in *Gen. Rab.* He can also be criticized for the interpretation he gives some midrashim (cf. p. 285 nn.2-3; p. 286 n.4), and for citing some irrevelant midrashim (p. 287 n.1).

85 Greek ἐπί, literally "on," but in Hebrew (or in Aramaic) the preposition was undoubtedly ב as in Genesis. (Does this indicate that the heavenly figure contains angels within itself? Similar ideas are found in Gnostic systems and in the Logos of Philo, which contains divine forces -- but not in the Midrash!). In any case, the translation "for Jacob" proposed by Kugel (*In Potiphar's House* 114) seems unlikely to me in light of these parallels, as well as difficult to support linguistically. Further on (*Gen. Rab.* 69.3; Theodor-Albeck 792) the same sages (R. Hiyya and R. Yannai) disagree over the interpretation of והנה יי נצב עליו ("and the Lord was standing over him/it" [Gen 28:13]). Here the ambiguity ("over it" or "over him") is indeed present in the text (there, too, the redactor of *Gen. Rab.* explains the interpretation "over Jacob" in a way which probably does not match the original intent of the Sage who offered it). Indeed, it is not impossible that the ambiguity in Gen 28:13 is what brought about the midrash of the angels going up and down Jacob in Gen 28:12. In light of the evidence from John, however, we know that this midrash is in any case very early; were we to judge only on the basis of the midrashic material, we could have offered the conjecture that our midrash (on the angels) is a transfer of the Sages' disagreement about the later verse to the earlier one. This is a very common phenomenon in *Genesis Rabbah.* We may also have to ask ourselves what is the weight of exegetical play, especially when the ideas it raises seem strange in the context of midrash. But the parallel in John keeps us from arriving at any simple solution, and makes us face the fact that the statement in *Genesis Rabbah* is a remnant of an early puzzling midrash.

86 A midrash about Jacob "set on the ground, and his head reached to the sky"? Any reconstruction would be speculative and likely to mislead.

87 The common midrash about "Jacob's image (איקונין)" engraved on high is also related to the heavenly image of Jacob. Cf. Smith, "The Prayer of Joseph" 284. (The sources in his n.2 are mostly late or irrelevant). Cf. also Urbach, *Ḥazal* 150 (= *The Sages* 171). See also the end of n.61 above. In my view, one should not assume that the idea of Jacob's image being located in Heaven came about through the exegesis of a particular verse. Kugel (*In Potiphar's House* 113ff.) claims that the source of the idea of "Jacob's image" above is in Jacob's dream and in the midrash discussed here, even though the midrashim cite other verses for support. (The support brought by *Gen. Rab.* 68.12 [Theodor-Albeck 788] from Isa 49:3 must be understood in light of the usage of the root פאר in Isa 44:13). In fact, however, the idea of Jacob's image on high needs no exegetical basis. Once the idea exists, it can easily be woven into the dramatic story of angels going up and down between earthly and heavenly figures. There is no reason to connect the heavenly image of Jacob with Joseph's vision of Jacob's image (cf. Kugel, *In Potiphar's House* 113ff.). It is interesting to adduce the early Aramaic *piyyuṭ* ארכין יי שמיא לסיני (cf. Joseph Heinemann, *'Iyyunei Tefillah*

[Jerusalem: Magnes, 1980/1] 150). In this work, God says to Moses: "Don't be small in your own sight, Moses, for you do not know how beloved you are to Me. I endure forever, and I created your image before I created the height and the depth." The conception that Moses was in God's mind to be created (*excogitavit et invenit me*) and was prepared (*praeparatus sum*) since Creation to be a mediator at the giving of the Torah can be found in *As. Mos.* 1:14. Cf. J. Sermonetta, "The Liturgy of Sicilian Jews," *M.D. Cassutto Memorial Volume* (Jerusalem: Magnes, 1983/4) 191 n.106 (Hebrew). My thanks go to Prof. Y. Yahalom for this last reference. With regard to the text of *As. Mos.*, compare *Gen. Rab.* 30.8 (Theodor-Albeck 274) and its parallel texts: "'And Moses was'

(ומשה היה Exod 3:1) -- prepared as redeemer." The Aramaic *piyyuṭ* speaks of an image of Moses in the context of a struggle between him and the angels. It appears that the concept is transferred from Jacob's image, which this *piyyuṭ* says stood erect before Moses (line 15). Jacob's struggle with the angels is alluded to in line 2 as well.

88 PAM 42.361. I am grateful to Professor J.C. VanderKam, to whom this fragment has been assigned, for allowing me to discuss its contents.

89 This is the right reading (rather than בימים).

90 An example of traditions replacing "Satan" by "ministering angels" and "nations of the world" (perhaps through the identification of the latter with the "Angels of the Nations") is provided by *Gen. Rab.* 55.4 (Theodor-Albeck 587), as noted above.

91 It should be noted that "the angels of peace" mentioned in Isa 33:7 (upon which *Genesis Rabbah* is based) could be opposed to Mastema quite naturally (cf. "the angel of peace" as opposed to "Satan and his spirits" in *T. Dan* 6:5; *T. Asher* 6:6; *T. Benj.* 6:1). But 4Q225 has "holy angels," and does not allude to the verse from Isaiah.

PSEUDEPIGRAPHIC SUPPORT OF PSEUDEPIGRAPHICAL SOURCES: THE CASE OF *PIRQE DE RABBI ELIEZER*

Anna Urowitz-Freudenstein
The Jewish Theological Seminary

Pirqe de Rabbi Eliezer (henceforth *PRE*) is a midrash that is a retelling of the Bible in Hebrew, from "the beginning" until the death of Miriam. It is readily datable to the ninth century.[1]

Gerald Friedlander's translation of *PRE* into English (*Pirke De Rabbi Eliezer* [London: Kegan Paul, Trench, Trübner and Co., 1916]) was particularly exciting in that it made the text more accessible to the English reader. In his introduction, he deemed this midrash a pseudepigraphic work. Although he was not the first to state that the book was not written by the author to whom it is traditionally attributed (R. Eliezer ben Hyrcanus of the first century CE), he was the first to label it rabbinic "pseudepigrapha." Categorizing *PRE* in this novel way should not seem unusual considering the milieu in which Friedlander prepared his translation. His work immediately followed upon the first publication of the monumental collection edited by R.H. Charles entitled *The Apocrypha and Pseudepigrapha of the Old Testament in English* (2 vols.; Oxford: Clarendon, 1913).

Friedlander however took his characterization one step further. He not only called *PRE* pseudepigraphic. He also believed that it had

35

been influenced by apocryphal and pseudepigraphical writings. He
wrote in his introduction:

> There seems to be reasonable ground for assuming that the
> author of our book was acquainted not only with Jubilees,
> but also with the pseudepigraphic Books of Enoch
> (Ethiopic and Slavonic), and very probably with the
> Testaments of the XII Patriarchs, [and other related works]
> or with the sources of these books.[2]

Friedlander documents what he claims to be the influences of these
works in his introduction and footnotes. They are considerable enough
that *PRE* is still understood to be a midrash that exhibits "knowledge
of the pseudepigrapha."[3]   Current scholarly opinion has accepted
Friedlander's hypothesis regarding these apocryphal and
pseudepigraphical influences on *PRE*.   However, a careful reading of
its text, with attention given to the corpus of rabbinic sources extant
prior to the composition of *PRE*, suggests that these sources in fact
provide ample background for almost all of the material extant in
PRE, without having to invoke dependence upon apocryphal or
pseudepigraphical works.

    This essay will show that Friedlander's hypothesis regarding the
apocryphal and pseudepigraphical influences on *PRE* is not valid.[4]   This
will be accomplished by a fresh analysis of his data while relying upon
critical texts where available.   The analysis will focus upon
Friedlander's alleged parallels from *Jubilees* and *1 Enoch* to *PRE*
(which amount to more than one hundred examples).   Some of these
correspondences are problematic in that they stem from texts written
in different languages and therefore linguistic clues cannot be utilized.
Another problem involves the reconstruction of the reasoning
involved in Friedlander's determination of some of his "parallels."   This
is complicated by the fact that the alleged "parallels" are usually also
found elsewhere in earlier rabbinic literature, or are of the sort that
may be easily deduced from the observation of natural phenomena,
appeals to common knowledge, or the careful reading of the Bible
itself. With these issues in mind, it becomes increasingly difficult to
prove exactly how the author of *PRE* was influenced. Thus the points

that Friedlander thought were indications that *PRE* was influenced by the Apocrypha and Pseudepigrapha may actually suggest derivations from more conventional Jewish sources, such as the Bible, earlier midrashim, Talmudic material, and a Jewish understanding of the natural order of the world.

Among Friedlander's parallels between *PRE* and apocryphal and pseudepigraphical literature are many that appear valid,[5] but which are not of much worth because of their parallels to material in other genres of literature. In other words, if a passage in *PRE* parallels apocryphal and pseudepigraphical literature but simultaneously possesses a Scriptural parallel, one should assume from a methodological standpoint that the connection rightfully belongs with the latter, not because Scripture is chronologically prior, but because it is considered holy by *PRE* and quoted as such elsewhere in it. A similar argument may be made for rabbinic literature. If a passage in *PRE* occurs in an earlier rabbinic work and in a non-rabbinic work (such as apocryphal and pseudepigraphical literature), then since *PRE* itself is rabbinic and obviously reflects rabbinic texts, the parallel to rabbinic material is the more valid one.

Scriptural Parallels[6]

There are many straightforward parallels between *PRE* and Apocrypha and Pseudepigrapha that are also firmly based in Scripture. The points that all three share must derive then from the one that not only is the oldest, but the one from which the other two self-consciously draw. Therefore it must be assumed that *PRE* derived such material from its understanding of Scripture, rather than from a knowledge of apocryphal and pseudepigraphical literature.

Importance of circumcision	*PRE* §29 (pp. 203ff.; 212ff.)	*Jub.* 15:11ff., 33ff.	Gen 17:10-14
Azazel	*PRE* §46 (p. 363)	*1 Enoch* 10:4	Lev 16:8
Throne of Sapphire	*PRE* §4 (p. 23)	*1 Enoch* 18:8	Ezek 1:26
Heavenly tree	*PRE* §51 (p. 418)	*1 Enoch* 25:5	Ezek 47:12

It had been good for them if they had not been born	*PRE* §15 (pp. 104ff.)	*1 Enoch* 38:2	Job 3:3; Jer 20:14[7]
Four presences around the Lord of Spirits	*PRE* §4 (pp. 22ff.)	*1 Enoch* 40:2	Ezek 1:5
Transformation of heaven and earth	*PRE* §51 (pp. 410ff.)	*1 Enoch* 45:4-5	Isa 65:17; 66:22
Gold and silver will not save you	*PRE* §34 (pp. 256ff.)	*1 Enoch* 52:7	Zeph 1:18
Isaac's oath to the Philistines	*PRE* §36 (p. 278)	*Jub.* 24:25	Gen 26:28-31
Fire of evil	*PRE* §15 (p. 103)	*1 Enoch* 54:6	Ps 140:11
Light on the face of the holy	*PRE* §2 (p. 7)	*1 Enoch* 38:4	Exod 34:35; Qoh 8:1
Fighting among themselves	*PRE* §9 (p. 62)	*1 Enoch* 56:7	2 Chr 15:6
Sand as border of the sea	*PRE* §5 (pp. 27-28)	*1 Enoch* 69:18; 101:6	Jer 5:22
New creation in the future	*PRE* §51 (p. 411)	*1 Enoch* 72:1	Isa 65:17
Relationship of water and earth	*PRE* §12 (p. 87)	*1 Enoch* 60:22	Gen 2:5-6
Detailed description of the Chariot (*Merkavah*)	*PRE* §4	*1 Enoch* 14:9ff	Ezek 1
Earth returns what was entrusted to it	*PRE* §34 (p. 258)	*1 Enoch* 51:1	Isa 10:3[8]

Of these parallels identified by Friedlander to apocryphal and pseudepigraphical literature, but which are really biblical "parallels" or references, there is a particularly interesting subset. These are passages within *PRE* that are not *PRE* at all, but rather quotations from the Bible. They are

Firmament	*PRE* §4 (p. 21)	*1 Enoch* 18:5	Ezek 1:22
Description of the north	*PRE* §3 (p. 17)	*1 Enoch* 34:3	Jer 1:14
God's works worthy of praise	*PRE* §2 (pp. 8ff.)	*1 Enoch* 36:4	Ps 145:4
Trisagion	*PRE* §4 (p. 26)	*1 Enoch* 39:12	Isa 6:3

Pledge: 'as long as heaven is above the earth'	*PRE* §23 (p. 172)	*1 Enoch* 55:2	Deut 11:21
Power of heavens will have light sevenfold	*PRE* §51 (p. 412)	*1 Enoch* 91:16	Isa 30:26

It is very unclear why these examples were singled out by Friedlander as part of his proof that the *PRE* is dependent upon apocryphal and pseudepigraphical literature. They simply prove that *PRE* quotes Scripture, and that apocryphal and pseudepigraphical literature also deals with Scriptural issues. However, these two points were neither in question nor the focus of the subject at hand.

Parallels in Rabbinic Literature

Some of the *PRE* parallels that Friedlander argues are based upon Apocrypha and Pseudepigrapha can also be traced to rabbinic literature.[9] While it is true that the Apocrypha and Pseudepigrapha are often older than the (redacted) rabbinic texts, one cannot necessarily argue that their temporal priority gives them greater weight. Since *PRE* certainly has other passages "borrowed" from earlier rabbinic literature,[10] it may be assumed that such three-way parallels (*PRE*, Apocrypha and Pseudepigrapha, rabbinic literature) derive from rabbinic literature. Following is a chart of the straightforward correspondences listed by Friedlander with their rabbinic parallels.

Ten trials of Abraham	*PRE* §26 (pp. 187ff.)	*Jub.* 17:17; 19:8	*m. 'Abot* 5:4
Abraham spoke Hebrew	*PRE* §26 (p. 188)	*Jub.* 12:26	*Gen. Rab.* 42.8
Restrictions on eating food with non-Jews	*PRE* §29 (p. 208); §38 (p. 301)	*Jub.* 22:16	*m. 'Abod. Zar.* 2:6; *m. Šeb.* 8:9
Law as older than creation	*PRE* (not cited)	*Jub.* 2:33	*Gen. Rab.* 1.1
Messiah named before the creation of the sun	*PRE* §3 (p. 12)	*1 Enoch* 48:2,3	*b. Sanh.* 98b
Description of the South	*PRE* §3 (p. 17)	*1 Enoch* 36:1	*b. B. Bat.* 25a

Sun is opposite the moon	*PRE* §8 (p. 44)	*1 Enoch* 41:7	*b. Roš. Haš.* 23b
Seventy nations of the world	*PRE* §11 (p. 67)	*1 Enoch* 89:59	*b. Sukk.* 55b
Waters from heaven are masculine, waters from beneath the earth are feminine	*PRE* §23 (p. 167)	*1 Enoch* 54:8	*y. Ber.* 9.2, 65b[11]
Eyeshadow as adornment that leads to straying	*PRE* §22 (p. 160)	*1 Enoch* 8:1,2	*b. Šabb.* 62b[12]
'The world to come'	*PRE* §16 (p. 112)	*1 Enoch* 71:15	*m. 'Abot* 2:7
Windows for the sun	*PRE* §6 (pp. 37ff.)	*1 Enoch* 72:3	*y. Roš. Haš.* 2:5, 58a
Satan at the sacrifice of Isaac	*PRE* §31 (p. 228); §32 (p. 233)	*Jub.* 18:9,12	*b. Sanh.* 89b

In addition to these parallels, there are others cited by Friedlander which are more complicated but which are also included in this category. These involve quotations that describe biblical characters in the book of Genesis observing the festivals and commandments that were later given formally to the Israelite nation. These parallels as presented by Friedlander are not one-to-one correspondences. He lists the examples of Adam and Isaac observing Passover in *PRE* (pp. 153, 236), and tries to equate these instances with those of Noah and Isaac and Ishmael observing Shavuot (Pentecost) in *Jubilees* (6:17ff.; 22:1). He cites four places in *PRE* concerning such observance of commandments. Two of these may be ignored for methodological reasons.[13] The remaining two however have rabbinic parallels. They are

Adam ends Sabbath with ritual of *havdalah*	*PRE* §20 (pp. 145ff.)	*Gen. Rab.* 11.2
Adam is married under a marriage canopy	*PRE* §12 (pp. 89ff.)	*Gen. Rab.* 18.1

The parallels offered by Friedlander to these two midrashim are from *Jubilees*. However, the citations there neither describe Adam's activities on Saturday night nor his marriage. They instead portray early biblical figures offering ritual sacrifices. While these stories might be examples of early biblical characters observing the Israelite religion, they are not really parallel to the cited *PRE* passages. This phenomenon of inexact parallelism actually pervades Friedlander's list of alleged parallels and will be analyzed in more detail below.

Friedlander's list of alleged parallels is especially difficult to interpret because it is just that -- a list lacking the detailed arguments required for each point that he wishes to make. His lists of parallels consist of a catchword or phrase cited from a pseudepigraphical book. The passage that is being compared from *PRE* is then quoted by using the relevant page number from his particular edition. In order for one to really understand each suggested parallel, both sources must be carefully studied. Unfortunately, when one situates the alleged parallel within its original context, the "parallelism" is not always apparent. In fact it may be difficult to categorize them as parallels at all. Certainly they share something in common like a word or an idea. However, Friedlander's efforts seem to be a case of "parallelomania," which Sandmel defined as "... that extravagance among scholars which first overdoes the similarity in passages and then proceeds to describe source and derivation as if implying literary connection flowing in an inevitable or predetermined direction."[14] Nevertheless, there are so many of these "loose parallels" presented by Friedlander that rather than simply dismiss them and therefore ignore his scholarship, we will instead consider the possible value of his cumulative evidence by re-examining them here. In order to show that *PRE* did not have to rely on the Apocrypha and Pseudepigrapha, other more conventional sources are suggested. These Scriptural or rabbinic sources may not be exact parallels to the *PRE* texts, but they may be seen as their sources or inspiration. In these cases precise parallels are not necessary in order to refute Friedlander's hypothesis, as his alleged parallels are not exact either.

Loose Parallels That Refer To Scripture

There are numerous parallels suggested by Friedlander that are not direct parallels, even though they share a kernel of an idea. However, this kernel of an idea can also sometimes be found in Scripture.

1. *PRE* (§9 [p. 61]; §29 [p. 212]) and *Jub.* 21:17 both stress the duty of covering blood with dust. However, each of these sources deals with a different ritual situation. The first one in *PRE* is an example of the commandment of covering shed blood with dust as outlined in Lev 17:13-14. The second one in *PRE* teaches that the blood of a circumcision is to be covered with dust.[15] The *Jubilees* verse does not describe either of these rituals. It discusses the burial of the blood of a sacrifice. While this idea probably stems from the above mentioned biblical verses, it was not commanded in rabbinic law (see *m. Ḥul.* 6:1).

2. The importance of the new moon is supposedly paralleled in *PRE* §51 (p. 410) and *Jub.* 6:23-29. In fact, while this *PRE* text is concerned with all new months, the *Jubilees* citation emphasizes the beginnings of four specific new months out of the year as important. Scripture certainly understands new months as special, and assigns for them ritual sacrifices (see Num 28:11-15).

3. *PRE* §23 (p. 171) and *Jub.* 6:3 both speak of a sacrifice offered by Noah. Both sources describe this offering, but the descriptions are not parallel. The idea behind both of them, that Noah presented a sacrifice, is found in Gen 8:20.

4. *PRE* and *1 Enoch* are claimed to be parallel in their treatments of the Leviathan,[16] the Behemoth,[17] and the four quarters of the world.[18] In fact both works do discuss these topics, but in very different ways. These topics are also extant in Scripture,[19] and the authors of these later works obviously interpreted them in different ways.

5. Friedlander tries to compare the "measuring of righteousness" in *PRE* §51 (pp. 416ff.) with *1 Enoch* 70:3. In *PRE* this phrase explains

Ezek 47:1-6, wherein occurs a description of the measuring of the depth of water into which the prophet is led. The verse in *1 Enoch* describes angels measuring a place for Enoch and others in heaven.[20]

6. Friedlander claims that both *PRE* §51 (p. 418) and *1 Enoch* 67:8 discuss waters for the healing of the body. However, the *1 Enoch* text describes a river of fire which heals or punishes the spirit, while the *PRE* passage describes a future river (of water) that will heal sick people, and it is furthermore connected to Ezek 47:8-9, which is quoted as a prooftext.

7. *PRE* §25 (p. 181) and *1 Enoch* 65:7 both treat the origin of silver. However, the *1 Enoch* citation (as may be seen from the verse that follows it) claims that silver does not come from a mine. This stands in opposition to the *PRE* text that quotes from Job 28:1: "Surely there is a mine for silver ...."

8. Angels reviving people that have seen or heard God are allegedly paralleled in *PRE* and *1 Enoch*. It is clear that the described incidents are based ultimately on the concerns of the children of Israel who in Exod 20:19 request "... let not God speak with us lest we die." *PRE* §41 (p. 325) tells the midrash of the children of Israel dying when they heard the voice of God at Mt. Sinai and how they were revived by God's word. There are some angels present in this midrash, but they do not do the reviving. However, in a completely different situation in *1 Enoch* 60:3-4, it is Enoch who collapses after seeing the heavenly court, and an angel is sent to revive him.

9. *PRE* and *1 Enoch* both use the terms "ends of the earth" (*PRE* §3 [p. 16]; *1 Enoch* 33:2) and "ends of the heaven" (*PRE* §3 [p. 16]; *1 Enoch* 71:4). Each text, though, uses the terms differently, and the terms themselves are biblical in origin.[21]

10. The image of "seven mountains" appears in both *PRE* and *1 Enoch*. *PRE* §10 (p. 71) refers to the seven mountains upon which Jerusalem is situated. In *1 Enoch* 32:1 mountains are mentioned, but without reference to the number seven or to Jerusalem, and elsewhere in *1 Enoch* (77:4) there are seven mountains described as part of a "mystical geography."[22] The seven mountains of *PRE*, which do not

exactly correspond with those of *1 Enoch*, do have precedent in Scripture.[23]

11. An attempt is made to parallel *PRE* §51 (pp. 411-12) and *1 Enoch* 25:6. However the only thing they have in common is an assertion of a life free of pain. This life as depicted in *1 Enoch* occurs in this world and is experienced only by the elect. The description in *PRE* applies to the future and is not as limited. Further, it is Scripturally based upon Isa 65:19.

12. Noah's inheritance to his sons, as in *PRE* §10 (p. 68) and *Jub.* 8:10-30, is another parallel claimed by Friedlander.[24] The parallel in itself is problematic. The allocation of lands in each text is different. While this precise inheritance is not mentioned in the Bible, the idea that the land was divided up among different nations who are named for Noah's descendants can be found in Genesis 10 and Deut 32:8.

Loose Parallels That Refer to Rabbinic Literature

There are a number of examples of Friedlander's "parallels" that are also present in earlier rabbinic literature.

1. Moses's interactions with angels in *PRE* §46 (pp. 361-62) are paralleled in *Jubilees* (chap. 1; 10:12-13). However, in *PRE* Moses argues with the angels about the ownership of the Torah, but in *Jubilees*, he is a passive receiver of history. A gift of tablets to Moses from the angels is also mentioned here. This story is much closer to a similar account in *b. Šabb.* 88b-89a than to the description of Noah receiving angelic instructions in *Jubilees* 10, which is the parallel offered by Friedlander.

2. The premundane activities described in *PRE* §3 (p. 11) and *1 Enoch* 39:11 are listed as parallels. They both do talk about things before creation, but the *PRE* passage discusses creations, and the *1 Enoch* piece discusses knowledge. There is a closer rabbinic parallel that is cited by Friedlander himself (*b. Pesaḥ.* 54a and *b. Ned.* 39b).

3. The term "to pass down" is used in *PRE* §8 (p. 52-53) and in *1 Enoch* 82:1. Each however describes "passing down" different things.

The idea of "passing things down" is one of the underlying principles of rabbinic Judaism and is articulated at the beginning of *m. 'Abot*.

4. Friedlander draws parallels among the foundation stone of *PRE* §10 (p. 71),[25] the cornerstone of the earth (*1 Enoch* 18:2), and the middle of the earth (*1 Enoch* 26:1). In fact, this foundation stone is already mentioned in *b. Yoma* 54b.

5. *PRE* §48 (p. 379) and *1 Enoch* 62:2 are seen as parallel because they both describe words that are lethal. Unfortunately, these examples are very different, as the first one describes the word of Moses, and the second one the word of God. Friedlander himself indicates an earlier midrash in *Lev. Rab.* 32.4 that is similar to the one in *PRE*.[26]

6. Seven bodies of water are mentioned in *PRE* §18 (p. 140) and in *1 Enoch* 77:5. The *1 Enoch* source mentions seven rivers, while the *PRE* citation speaks of seven seas, an idea already found in *b. B. Bat.* 74b.[27]

7. An alleged parallel that humanity is created exactly like the angels is very tenuous. All the references compare humans and angels, but in very different ways. There are two *PRE* citations. The first (§12 [p. 85]) compares Adam's leisure in the garden to that of an angel. Yet Adam is compared to an angel in a number of places in rabbinic literature, including *Gen. Rab.* 8.11. The second citation compares Moses's appearance at birth to that of an angel and is paralleled in *b. Soṭa* 12a. In *1 Enoch* 69:11, humans as they were first created, pure and without sin, are compared to angels. A similar idea is expressed in *Gen. Rab.* 21.5. Similarly, Friedlander tries to parallel *PRE* §46 (p. 364) and *Jub.* 2:17-21 in their comparison of Israelites and angels. However, the circumstances in both texts vary. The former passage discusses specific actions on Yom Kippur, while the latter text states that both angels and Israelites observe the Sabbath. There is yet another alleged parallel concerning Israel and angels and their common observance of the Sabbath. *PRE* §18 (p. 138) discusses the merits of the recital of the benediction over wine on the Sabbath, which will lead to increased days in this world and in the next. In *Jub.* 2:21,30 Israel's election is justified on the grounds that they may celebrate each Sabbath

concurrent with the angels' celebration in heaven. This happens weekly, and is not only a reward after death, as was explained in *PRE*. These last two examples of parallels are not parallels at all.

8. Both *PRE* §22 (p. 161) and *1 Enoch* 7:1-5 offer slightly different descriptions of the violent actions of the Giants. A similar idea is also found in *Gen. Rab.* 26.7.

9. Black, red, and white are given as the colors of Noah's children (*PRE* §23 [pp. 172-73]; *1 Enoch* 89:9). There are only two colors in the *PRE* source: black (Shem and Ham) and white. The colors in *PRE* are not surprising, as they are familiar skin tones. The blackness of Ham is also described in *Gen. Rab.* 36.7. The colors of the other sons may be learned from biblical context. The blackness of Shem, if he is understood as the ancestor of the Israelites (*Gen. Rab.* 36.6), may have echoes in Cant 1:4, and Japhet's whiteness could have been assumed based on the skin color of at least one of his well-known descendants, Greece (see Gen 10:4).

10. The connection among "the children of God," heaven, and angels is claimed by Friedlander to be discussed in *PRE* §22 (p. 161) and *1 Enoch* (6:2; 106:5). While these parallels are not direct, this idea is present in rabbinic literature.[28] Closely related to this is the topic of fallen angels (*PRE* §§7, 13, 22, 27 [pp. 46, 92, 160, 194]; *1 Enoch* 12:4; 15:3). While this issue is not fully developed in earlier rabbinic literature, it is nevertheless present there and in related works.[29]

11. Four angels are mentioned in *PRE* §3 (p. 22) and in *1 Enoch* 9:1. The list in *PRE* reads Michael, Gabriel, Uriel, and Raphael, while the list in *1 Enoch* is Michael, Sariel, Raphael, and Gabriel. Black claims that this is an unusual usage of Sariel. He writes: "In all other lists, in the versions and rabbinical sources, while the order of the names varies, Michael, Gabriel and Raphael remain constant, but Sariel is replaced by Uriel ...."[30] Therefore the *PRE* citation is more closely aligned with rabbinic texts than with *1 Enoch*.

12. Verbal reaction from the earth and its inhabitants before the Flood is found both in *PRE* and *1 Enoch*. However, in *1 Enoch* (8:4; 9:2-3, 10) the inhabitants of the earth cry up to heaven because of the violence and bloodshed that they are experiencing, but the cries in

PRE §22 (p. 162) are threats shouted against heaven should the Flood come. The *PRE* midrash is very similar to one contained in *b. Sanh.* 108b.

Different Types of Parallels

There are some parallels offered by Friedlander that may rely upon a different type of source: that of the contemporary, popular understanding of the world, especially astronomy. For instance, *PRE* §6 (p. 31) and *1 Enoch* (72:37; 78:3) claim that the sun and the moon are of equal size. However, the writer of *PRE* did not have to read *1 Enoch* in order to acquire this information, as it was "common knowledge in ancient astronomy."[31] Similarly, the "day of the full moon" mentioned both in *PRE* §7 (pp. 50-51) and *1 Enoch* 78:13 must be the day of the month when the moon is full. In the lunar calendar this day falls in the middle of the month, as is described in *PRE* and all other astronomical literature.[32] The idea of the sun ascending on a chariot, present in *PRE* §6 (p. 40) and *1 Enoch* 72:5, is not one that would have been believed by the scientists of the day, but is one rooted since Hellenistic times in popular mythology.[33]

Some of the parallels offered by Friedlander are also attested within texts such as the Septuagint and the Dead Sea Scrolls. It is often difficult or even impossible to trace the sources used by rabbinic texts, especially if it is discovered that an idea existed in more than one early text. This problem was solved above by deciding that some texts were far more likely to be used as sources than others (i.e., a preference for biblical and rabbinic literature over Apocrypha and Pseudepigrapha). The issues here are not as obvious. However, since these forms of literature were just as prior to *PRE* as Apocrypha and Pseudepigrapha were, and at least as potentially accessible to the writer of *PRE*, they will be considered here as valid alternate parallels to *PRE*.

The expression "since the creation of the world" is found in *PRE* §52 (p. 420) and in *1 Enoch* 71:15. Black claims that this usage is paralleled in the Qumran *Thanksgiving Hymns* (1QH 13:10).[34]

Similarly he parallels the oath formulation of *PRE* §38 (p. 293) and *1 Enoch* 6:4 to Deut 13:15(16) and Num 21:3 in the Septuagint.[35]

There are two alleged parallels which may also be found in the Targumim. There is a direct parallel between *PRE* §37 (pp. 283-84) and *Jub.* 32:2ff. regarding the choice of Levi as a tithe devoted to God, a motif which may also be found in *Tg. Ps.-J.* Gen 32:25. The parallel claimed by Friedlander concerning a protest against nakedness in *PRE* §22 (p. 160) and *Jubilees* (3:31; 7:20) is not as direct. However, the *PRE* text is paralleled in *Tg. Ps.-J.* Gen 6:2. The Targumim do not fall into the same category as the rabbinic literature discussed in the bulk of this paper since their final redaction probably did not occur until a time concurrent with or after the composition of *PRE*. Most scholars believe, however, that the Targumim do contain more ancient material.[36]

Similar problems concern the dating of *Hekhalot* literature. Nevertheless, it is the only other literature before or close to the time of *PRE* which includes the usage of the title שר (chief? prince?) for Sammael,[37] which is also found in *PRE* §8 (p. 92). Friedlander suggests that this title is a parallel to that of "Prince Mastema" as found in *Jubilees* (17:16; 48:2). Moreover, the title of שר is given to other heavenly beings who have control over the nations of the earth in early rabbinic literature.[38]

Non-Parallels

Some of Friedlander's "parallels" are simply empty. They may share a theme or even a word but essentially treat different ideas. There are a number of examples of this phenomenon.

1. *PRE* §46 (p. 363) and *Jub.* 10:8-11 both discuss the power that Sammael/Mastema has over the world. In *Jubilees*, Mastema asks for power, but is willing to settle for control over only one-tenth of the world. In *PRE* Sammael wields much more power. He has power over all of the nations except Israel, and even over Israel one day a year, on Yom Kippur.

2. In *PRE* §4 (p. 23) there is a reference to the fact that there are seven angels who were created first. This is not elaborated further. *1 Enoch* 20:2-8 names and describes seven different angels who watch, but does not describe their creation. It is not at all clear that these are parallel sources.

3. *PRE* §14 (p. 98) explains that the cloud of glory covered Adam. However, *1 Enoch* 62:15 depicts the resurrected dead who will be clothed in garments of glory.[39]

4. Friedlander claims that *PRE* (§13 [pp. 94ff.]; §21 [pp. 150ff.]) and *1 Enoch* 69:6 both describe Eve going astray. However, whereas *PRE* provides narrative details, the *1 Enoch* verse only mentions that Eve was led astray, without describing how (except for the inclusion of an angel named Gadre'el, who is not mentioned in *PRE* at all).

5. Both *PRE* §6 (p. 34) and *1 Enoch* (72:3; 75:1) describe "leaders of the stars." They have however very different functions. While the ones in *PRE* begin and complete each solar month, those in *1 Enoch* are positioned with the sun and the moon and are appointed to rule over all creation, among other things.

6. *PRE* §3 (p. 9) and *1 Enoch* 93:11 are also compared. However, the former passage discusses the inability of humans to praise God with language adequate for the task, while the latter one states that humanity cannot hear the voice of God because of God's greatness.

7. Another example of Friedlander's parallels concerns brothers who die together. However, this only describes the brothers mentioned in *1 Enoch* 100:1. In *PRE* §30 (p. 220), there is a description of brothers separating.

Conclusion

Friedlander's assertion that " ... we must illustrate Rabbinical literature by the teaching of the Apocrypha and Pseudepigrapha" is still true today.[40] However, his work detailing the allegedly strong connections between *PRE* and Apocrypha and Pseudepigrapha, in light of the research presented here,[41] should be seen as a "false writing" itself. Of the parallels that he drew, a small number can no longer be considered valid due to advances that have been made in critical textual scholarship. Others cannot be used because they are not clear parallels, and no justifications were offered for them. Nevertheless, the vast majority of the parallels suggested by Friedlander are similar enough to warrant examination. Most of these consist of a word or idea which is found in *PRE* as well as in a work of the Apocrypha and Pseudepigrapha. However, none of these words or ideas are unique to these literary corpora. Most can be found in earlier rabbinic texts or even the Bible itself, works with which the author of *PRE*, a rabbinic midrash, was certainly familiar. Certainly there are a small number of examples that do not fit as neatly into this scheme. However, even these ideas were available to the redactor of *PRE* in forms other than the actual books of *Jubilees* and *1 Enoch*. Therefore, even though the majority of Friedlander's parallels analyzed in this paper are in fact extant in works of the Apocrypha and Pseudepigrapha, they are also readily available in the works more conventionally quoted and drawn upon by rabbinic writers. It is these that must be seen as the influences upon *PRE*.[42]

---

[1]   H.L. Strack and G. Stemberger, *Introduction to the Talmud and Midrash* (Edinburgh: T. & T. Clark, 1991) 356-57.
[2]   Gerald Friedlander, *Pirke De Rabbi Eliezer* (London: Kegan Paul, Trench, Trübner and Co., 1916) xxii.
[3]   Strack-Stemberger 357.
[4]   I am not the first to propose this criticism, as may be seen in a review of Friedlander's book written just one year after its publication: "On the whole, it seems to me that Mr. Friedlander overrates the influence of the book of Jubilees on our author ... It is quite conceivable that a man imbued with the midrashic spirit could have written these *Chapters* [*PRE*] without having seen any part of the apocryphal and pseudepigraphic literature." (B. Halper, "Recent Hebraica and Judaica [including review of Friedlander's *PRE*]," *JQR* n.s. 8 [1917-18] 481). Halper continues this criticism by disproving three of Friedlander's examples. However, this criticism was obviously not considered and/or accepted by the academic world, for as shown above, Friedlander's original hypothesis regarding apocryphal and pseudepigraphical influences on *PRE* still persists. It should also be noted that H. Albeck claims (in the notes to his translation of L. Zunz's *Die gottesdienstlichen Vorträge der Juden* [*Ha-derashot be-yisrael* (Jerusalem: Bialik Institute, 1954) 136-40]) to have discovered a connection between *PRE*

and the Apocrypha and Pseudepigrapha, even before Friedlander's work came to his attention. He discredits Friedlander's efforts, but as the means of proving his version of the theory he cites examples of parallel passages, much as Friedlander does. Since therefore his examples from *Jubilees* and *1 Enoch* are very similar to Friedlander's, they too may be seen as encompassed within the general framework of this paper.

5   There are a number of parallels offered by Friedlander that can no longer be considered valid because they do not exist in the critical editions published after Friedlander's translation. They are (where * represents the section not extant in a critical edition): a. "Remember you for good" -- *PRE* §1 (p. 2*) and *1 Enoch* 104:1; b. Israel is subject to God -- *PRE* §24 (p. 177*) and *Jub.* 15:30-32; c. Books of the living -- *PRE* §15 (p. 104*) and *1 Enoch* 47:3; d. Resurrection of those devoured by fishes and beasts -- *PRE* §33 (p. 249*) and *1 Enoch* 61:5; e. Sinners have no ransom -- *PRE* §34 (p. 256), §51 (p. 416), and *1 Enoch* 98:9*. The critical editions I refer to are James C. Vanderkam, *The Book of Jubilees* (CSCO Scriptores Aethiopici 87-88; Louvain: E. Peeters, 1989); Matthew Black, *The Book of Enoch or 1 Enoch* (Leiden: Brill, 1985); Michael Higger, "Pirke Rabbi Eliezer," *Horeb* 8 (1944) 82-119; 9 (1946) 94-165; 10 (1948) 185-294 (Hebrew).

6   Where more than one rabbinic/Scriptural parallel is available, I cite usually only the one that is the most appropriate for the sake of brevity. For ease of reference, all *PRE* references are cited according to the chapter enumeration of Luria's edition and the corresponding pages of the Friedlander translation.

7   Black (*Enoch* 195) claims that this idea was a commonplace in the ancient world. He cites examples from a number of works (*2 Apoc. Bar.* 10:6; 4 Ezra 4:12; *2 Enoch* 41:2; Matt 26:24) in addition to these verses.

8   Rabbi David Luria (*Pirke Rabbi Eliezer haGadol* [reprinted, New York: Om Publishing Co., 1946] 80b) suggests this Scriptural parallel based on its usage of the same Hebrew root.

9   However, one seemingly important parallel concerning the angelology and demonology in *PRE* and *Jubilees* cannot be further investigated here because Friedlander does not offer any example citations.

10   See the extensive notes in Friedlander and the commentary of Luria.

11   Friedlander cites this passage in his notes to this portion of *PRE*.

12   Friedlander also cites *Tg. Yer.* to Gen 6:2 as a parallel.

13   The first (*PRE* §21 [p. 154]) uses a midrash about Cain and Abel in order to explain the commandment of *shaatnez* (combining wool and linen; see Lev 19:19). It does not however describe them observing this commandment. The second (PRE §19 [p. 142]) is not extant in the critical edition.

14   Samuel Sandmel, "Parallelomania," *JBL* 81 (1962) 3.

15   While this is not commanded in the Bible, there was a tradition to do so in some areas. Friedlander discusses this in his note on p. 212.

16   *PRE* §9 (pp. 63ff.), §10 (p. 70); *1 Enoch* 60:7.

17   *PRE* §11 (pp. 75ff.); *1 Enoch* 60:8.

18   *PRE* §3 (p. 17); *1 Enoch* 77:1-3.

19   For Leviathan, see Isa 27:1; Behemoth, Job 40:15; the four quarters of the world, Gen 28:14.

20   Black (*Enoch* 231) claims that it is based on Zech 2:1ff.

21 For "ends of the earth," see Isa 40:28; for "ends of the heaven," see Deut 4:32.

22 Black, *Enoch* 407.

23 Friedlander 71 n.6.

24 According to L. Ginzberg (*The Legends of the Jews* [7 vols.; Philadelphia: Jewish Publication Society, 1909-38] 5.193), there is no parallel to this idea in rabbinic literature. He claims to understand this *PRE* text differently, and makes it apply to the distribution of the earth to seventy angels and not to the sons of Noah. See idem, *Die Haggada bei den Kirchenvätern und in der apokryphischen Litteratur* (Berlin: S. Calvary & Co., 1900) 88. However, Ginzberg here seems to distort this passage of *PRE* by making it correspond with another passage in the next chapter of *PRE*, thereby changing its meaning.

25 The reference to *PRE* §35 (p. 266) also cited here is not found in the critical edition.

26 Friedlander 379.

27 Mentioned by Friedlander 140 n.8.

28 E.E. Urbach, *The Sages: Their Concepts and Beliefs* (reprinted, Jerusalem: Magnes Press, 1985) 147 (Hebrew). For other similar interpretations of this term, see also Philip S. Alexander, "Jewish Aramaic Translations of Hebrew Scriptures," *Mikra* (CRINT; ed. M.J. Mulder; Philadelphia: Fortress Press, 1988) 245.

29 See Urbach above and Ginzberg, *Legends* 5.169-171 n.10.

30 Black, *Enoch* 129.

31 O. Neugebauer *apud* Black, *Enoch* 396 n.12.

32 Another alleged astronomical parallel in *PRE* (p. 322) and *1 Enoch* 72:14 concerns the phenomenon described there of the day as double the length of the night. This citation in *1 Enoch* is from the section of the book known as "The Astronomical Chapters" and is part of a technical discussion of the calendar. According to Charles (R.H. Charles, *The Book of Enoch* [2d ed.; Oxford: Clarendon, 1912] 153 n.8) this astronomical phenomenon can only occur at 49 degrees latitude. The reference in *PRE* discusses many miraculous features surrounding the revelation at Sinai, including a claim that the day was double the length of the night. However, Mt. Sinai lies at approximately 30 degrees latitude, thereby preventing these particular lengths of day and night from occurring naturally. Therefore, this expression of time must be simply another example of the described miracles at Mt. Sinai, a situation very different from the one presented in *1 Enoch*. Also, as the revelation at Sinai is believed to have occurred close to the time of the summer solstice, the daylight hours would have been quite long and may have prompted even further exaggeration as to their length.

33 See Ovid, *Metamorphoses I-IV* (ed. D.E. Hill; Oak Park, Illinois: Bolchazy-Carducci Publishers Inc., 1985) 2.53 lines 100-112. Also note here a parallel to "Eastern gates" as in *PRE* §6 (p. 37) and *1 Enoch* 72:2. Compare also the concept of the sun setting into a river of fire in *PRE* §51 (p. 412), *1 Enoch* 17:5, and Homer, *Odyssey* 10.513. Note that this is not necessarily the same river of fire beneath the throne of God mentioned in *PRE* §4 (p. 25) and Dan 7:10.

34 Black, *Enoch* 211.

35 Ibid. 116-17.

36 See Alexander, "Jewish Aramaic Translations" (cited above). It should be noted that there is an opinion that claims that *Tg. Pseudo-Jonathan* relied upon *PRE* for certain materials. This was recently described by Avigdor Shinan, *The Embroidered Targum* (Jerusalem: Magnes Press, 1992) 176-85 (Hebrew). However, although Shinan claims that *Tg. Pseudo-Jonathan* was redacted after *PRE*, he considers it a product of the eighth century (ibid. 193-99), a date which is earlier than the one customarily assigned to *PRE* (cf. n.1 above).

37 *Konkordanz zur Hekhalot-Literatur* (2 vols.; ed. P. Schäfer; Tübingen: J.C.B. Mohr [Paul Siebeck], 1986-88) 2.485.

38 See for example *Lev. Rab.* 21.4.

39 Black (*Enoch* 237) compares this to Isa 61:10: " ... For He has clothed me with garments of triumph .... "

40 Friedlander liii.

41 That is, using the examples from *Jubilees* and *1 Enoch* as indicative of the rest of the apocryphal and pseudepigraphical literature used by Friedlander.

42 I would like to take this opportunity to thank Dr. Burton Visotzky for his helpful comments and encouragement.

THE PSEUDEPIGRAPHA IN CHRISTIANITY

Robert A. Kraft
University of Pennsylvania

In the autumn of 1975, I was asked to prepare a paper for the 1976 annual meeting of the Studiorum Novi Testamenti Societas (SNTS) at Duke University on "The Christianity of the Pseudepigrapha," a topic closely related to my sabbatical project for 1975/76. After struggling with this assignment from a variety of perspectives, I finally decided to modify the title to "Christianity and the so-called Jewish Pseudepigrapha," or more concisely, "The Pseudepigrapha in Christianity." Thus I have chosen to deal less with precise details *within* particular pseudepigrapha, and more with questions of *methodology* that arise in the study of these writings.[1]

I must confess at the outset that I am relatively unhappy about some of the directions that twentieth-century scholarship has been traveling in the study of this rather amorphous collection of writings that have been preserved to the modern period primarily by Christian efforts, but that are attributed to or closely identified with various heroes and heroines of pre-Christian Jewish tradition. Not that I think many of the conclusions reached in pseudepigrapha scholarship are necessarily wrong; on the contrary, I believe that much modern work is of great scholarly significance and suspect that most of the conclusions are relatively accurate. By and large, these "pseudepigraphical" writings ought to be examined for any light they may be able to throw on the pre-rabbinic Jewish situation. Certainly we need to use all available help to illuminate that shadowy period! Nevertheless, I am unhappy about the relatively uncontrolled and hasty approach pursued by most scholars in sifting these materials for clues regarding Judaism. I am convinced that there is also a great deal to learn about Christianity from careful study of the "pseudepigrapha," and that in most instances it is premature to distill from these writings information about pre-rabbinic Judaism before they are thoroughly examined for their significance as witnesses to Christian interest and activities.[2]

Problem Areas

In a nutshell, my discontent centers on the following areas of study which seem to me to be inadequately pursued in much current investigation of the pseudepigrapha:

1. *Comparative Linguistic Analysis.* -- Little if any systematic attention has been given to how the vocabulary and syntax employed in the preserved manuscripts and forms of a given pseudepigraphon relate to vocabulary and syntax found in other writings from approximately the same time in the same language. As we all know, languages change over the years and often display local variations. To what extent is it possible to classify the Greek of a particular pseudepigraphon as Hellenistic Egyptian, or as early Byzantine from Antioch, or perhaps even as early modern? What post-Hellenistic linguistic features recur in various Greek pseudepigrapha? What is the history of transmission and translation of these materials into such languages as Latin, Coptic, Syriac, Arabic, Ethiopic, Armenian, and Old Slavic, to mention only the most obvious? What can be learned about the most recent stages of development in a writing by careful attention to these linguistic matters?[3]

I see this as an avenue for discovering more precisely *who* was interested in these materials at what periods. Is it possible to identify in time and space schools of revisors or translators? Insofar as details of linguistic analysis are difficult to convey satisfactorily in an oral presentation, I will not elaborate on these matters here. But this approach will be facilitated considerably by the increase in relevant linguistic tools such as Lampe's *Patristic Greek Lexicon*,[4] Gignac's new *Grammar of Greek Papyri*,[5] the various concordances and lexicons in preparation covering such materials as Philo, Josephus, and the Greek pseudepigrapha themselves, not to mention the ambitious computer-based Thesaurus Linguae Graece (TLG) project or the proposed Septuagint lexicon.[6] Methods such as R.A. Martin's "syntactical analysis" of Greek translated from Hebrew or Aramaic also should prove helpful when adapted for use with the Greek pseudepigrapha.[7] I am less familiar with the resources available for work in other relevant eastern Christian languages, but suspect that the situation there is less encouraging.

2. A second, closely related area of concern is *The Role of the Pseudepigrapha in Christian Thought*. -- Why was a particular writing preserved and transmitted? By whom? For whom? How was the writing understood and interpreted? With what other writings was it associated? What can we learn about Christianity from each document, and especially about non-Latin and non-Greek Christianity? In what follows, I intend to explore this approach in greater detail.

3. A third problem area is the *Formulation of Satisfactory Hypotheses Regarding Origins and Transmission of Pseudepigrapha*. If a writing has been preserved only by Christians, as is normally true for the pseudepigrapha, how strong is the possibility that the writing actually was compiled in its preserved form(s) by a Christian? To what extent is it possible that some or all of the supposedly Jewish contents are actually Christian in origin? What are suitable criteria for distinguishing "Jewish" from "Christian" elements? Is it possible that Christians appropriated the document or some of its Jewish contents from Jews in the medieval/Byzantine period? What do we know of Jewish-Christian contacts after 135 CE?[8] What do we know of Christian writing and reading habits during the first millennium of Christian existence? What are acceptable criteria for the identification of "glosses," "interpolations," "redactions," and "recensions," and how do

these types of literary activity differ from each other?[9]   Who translated these materials from one language to another, for what reasons, and under what conditions? Again, a more detailed look at crucial aspects of this problem area will follow.

In short, there seems to be a wide spectrum of important issues on which little attention has been focused and for which little precise information is presently available. These are issues of primary importance that require close examination before a suitably careful and consistent use can be made of "pseudepigrapha" for purposes of reconstructing pre-Christian, or at least pre-rabbinic, Judaism. Recent developments in the study of Christian and Jewish history and literature offer promising rewards in this regard. I have already mentioned some of the more helpful tools for linguistic study. The fantastic increase in the number of known manuscripts and, through inexpensive mail-order microfilms, in their accessibility, will hopefully lead to significant new insights about the literature that is already well known as well as providing access to hitherto little-known or unknown writings and traditions.[10] Current interest in the relationships between emerging orthodoxy and its heterodox competitors in both Christian and Jewish settings[11] also provides a healthy context for reexamining the various pseudepigrapha, and the growing awareness among students of religious history of the possible value of insights and approaches drawn from anthropological-sociological studies should not be ignored (I think especially of studies of so-called "millennial/millenarian movements" in various times and places, as this may apply to the production and use of various apocalyptic writings).[12]

Contemporary Use of the Term "Pseudepigrapha"

The term "pseudepigrapha" is not a precise term in contemporary scholarly usage. It has become useful primarily by default, and against the theological background of the discussion of the Old Testament canon among Christians. Especially in the Byzantine Greek church, the traditional term for the literature with which we are concerned was "apocrypha," as distinct from "canonical" and "ecclesiastical" literature recommended for use in Christian churches. But modern Protestant scholarship came to restrict the term "apocrypha," used with reference to Jewish literature, to those particular writings or portions of writings accepted as "deutero-canonical" by Roman Catholics (with some ambiguity regarding Prayer of Manasseh and 4 Ezra/2 Esdras) but not included among the classical Jewish canonical scriptures. Thus some other term was needed to designate works attributed to or associated with revered persons of pre-Christian Jewish tradition that were considered neither canonical nor "apocryphal" in the limited sense of "Old Testament Apocrypha." The term "pseudepigrapha" has come to serve this function in relation to ostensibly Jewish material, although the more traditional sense of the term "apocrypha" has been retained by most scholars in dealing with so-called "New Testament Apocrypha" (not "pseudepigrapha"!).

The exact range of items included as "pseudepigrapha" also varies considerably.[13] The standard older editions of E. Kautzsch (1900) and R.H. Charles (1913) agree in employing the term in a very restricted sense for about a dozen or so writings including the *Epistle of Aristeas*, 4 Ezra, and the *Psalms of Solomon*. Charles even published Pirke Avot (*m. 'Abot*), Aḥiqar, and the Zadokite Fragments (CD) among the pseudepigrapha. At the opposite end of the scale, with regards to inclusiveness, is P. Riessler's German edition (1928) of some sixty-one allegedly "non-canonical ancient Jewish writings" other than Philo and Josephus. Judging from such contemporary projects as the Pseudepigrapha Veteris Testamenti Graece, edited by A.-M. Denis and M. de Jonge, or M. Philonenko's *Textes et études* ... series, or the history of H.F.D. Sparks' long-awaited British edition (see its preface!), or J.H. Charlesworth's ambitious Duke-Doubleday edition, or the work of the SBL Pseudepigrapha Group, the inclusive use of the term now predominates. Although I am not particularly fond of the term "pseudepigrapha," I also employ it in a radically inclusive sense to indicate writings attributed to or associated with persons known primarily from Jewish scriptural tradition, and a few other similar writings such as the *Sibylline Oracles* (as an example of "pagan" prophecy).[14]

Modern Methodologies in Studying Pseudepigrapha

Not all scholars are methodologically self-conscious. There is often a tendency to be overawed by the results achieved by scholarly giants of past generations, without careful reevaluation of their operating procedures and presuppositions. We build on "the assured results of critical scholarship" without consistently analyzing how those results emerged. And many of us shy away from detailed work with the preserved texts themselves -- I mean the actual manuscripts or facsimiles thereof -- relying instead on whatever printed editions are conveniently available. Thus we and our students are too often unaware of the extremely complicated and often tenuous processes by which suspicions have been turned into hypotheses and hypotheses into "assured results" which become enshrined as foundation stones for further investigations.

In the modern investigation of "pseudepigrapha," the strong desire to throw light on a relatively obscure period of Jewish history which was believed to be of great significance for early Christian studies played an important role. The earliest pioneers of pseudepigrapha study tended to be understandably cautious in attributing hitherto unattested works to Jewish authorship, but were relatively quick to identify newly recovered writings with titles found in ancient lists. M.R. James is perhaps a good example of caution in the former regard -- he seldom attached the unqualified adjective "Jewish" to the numerous pseudepigraphic texts he helped to rescue for scholarly investigation. Other influential scholars, however, including some well-versed in Jewish traditions like Louis Ginzberg or Kaufmann Kohler, argued strongly for the Jewish origin of numerous traditions and sections in the pseudepigrapha.[15] Riessler represents this latter perspective. It is worth noting how important the argument from parallel passages was in these earlier investigations. M.R. James would list page after page of alleged verbal reminiscences of New Testament writings, with the conclusion that the writing being examined had made use of the New Testament and thus was Christian in its present form. In contrast, Ginzberg would list at length the parallels to known rabbinic Jewish traditions and conclude that the basic core of the writing was Jewish.

We have, hopefully, come a long way in our critical awareness if not in our actual practice from simple "parallelomania" as Samuel Sandmel has dubbed it.[16] Most of us no longer assume that virtually any phrase that appears in New Testament literature necessarily originated there. We have become more aware of diversity within pre-Christian Judaism including the presence there of emphases on faith, on special knowledge, and on imminent eschatological salvation, among other things. Now Qumran has supplied good examples of even such seemingly Christian ideas as the divine sonship of God's eschatological agent, appropriation of God's promised new covenant, eschatological asceticism, and the religious importance of baptisms and special meals.[17] We have also become more aware of diversity in early Christianity, which exhibits a broad spectrum of beliefs and attitudes ranging from a relatively conservative and cultic Jewish sort of Christianity to a highly philosophical and/or mystical dualistic gnostic Christianity.[18]

In the study of the pseudepigrapha, realization of pre-rabbinic Jewish pluralism has played a much more influential role than recognition of early Christian pluralism. Perhaps this is only natural. After all, most Christianity built on a Jewish base and introduced relatively little that could be called uniquely Christian beyond specific references to Jesus of Nazareth and other personages or events of specifically Christian history, or the trinitarian God-language that arose in classical Christian circles and became standardized by the fourth century. For the most part, Christians appropriated Jewish scriptures and traditions, Jewish liturgical language, Jewish eschatological hopes, Jewish ethical ideals, and many Jewish practices. Reflecting such a setting, most Christian writings contain apparently "Jewish" elements and aspects, as is obvious to any contemporary New Testament student. The problem comes in attempting to place a label on such materials. At what point do I describe an originally Jewish ethical tract that has been adopted and perhaps also adapted by Christians as

"Christian" rather than "Jewish"? And if a Christian author who has been trained to think about religious life and conduct in ethical terms that derive from Judaism now writes an ethical treatise based on that author's own views -- not simply copying an older tract -- is the author not writing a Christian work, even though it may have all the characteristics of a Jewish work?

This methodological problem is perhaps best illustrated by quoting some actual operating procedures of earlier scholars. In his 1893 history of ancient Christian literature, Adolf Harnack includes a valuable, pioneering section entitled "Jewish Literature Appropriated, and Sometimes Reworked, by Christians."[19] Harnack argues that Christians sometimes imitated the style of older Jewish forgeries, thus making it impossible any longer to distinguish Jewish from Christian elements. In this connection, Harnack suggests that the investigator will seldom err if the following rule is observed: "Whatever is not clearly Christian is Jewish"![20] L.S.A. Wells enunciates a similar philosophy in his study of the Adam-Eve materials in Charles' *Pseudepigrapha* volume: "The complete absence of references, direct or indirect, to Christian notions of Incarnation, Redemption, even of Christian higher moral teaching, would make it impossible to assign to most of the work a Christian origin."[21]

Dissenting voices were also heard occasionally, but were clearly in the minority. I have already alluded to the cautious approach taken by M.R. James. Similarly, F.C. Burkitt's 1913 Schweich Lectures provide a good example. Burkitt is explicitly critical of the tendency to proclaim as "Jewish" virtually any writing that is not overtly Christian. Regarding Slavonic (i.e., *2*) *Enoch*, he writes

> I do not know that a Christian romance of Enoch need
> differ very much from a Jewish romance of Enoch. And ...
> the whole question of the channels by which rare and
> curious literature found their [*sic*] way into Slavonic
> requires fresh and independent investigation.[22]

According to the Harnack-Wells approach, a pseudepigraphon would be considered Jewish until proven otherwise; Burkitt would reverse the situation and put the onus of proof on those claiming Jewish origin.

Although I am emotionally disposed towards a position like that of Harnack-Wells, it is clear to me that the James-Burkitt approach is methodologically more defensible. Except in rare instances where Jewish fragments or clear early patristic usage renders the Jewish origin or location of a writing virtually beyond dispute (as with the "Old Testament" deutero-canonical writings, some form of Aḥiqar, *1 Enoch, Epistle of Aristeas*), the preserved pseudepigrapha are known only from relatively late Christian manuscripts of various sorts. Clearly the pseudepigrapha, including those of demonstrable Jewish origin, have had a long association with Christianity and deserve more than passing attention in that context. Once their setting in Christianity has been recognized more clearly, it may be possible to pose more carefully the questions of origin and early transmission.

Attitudes to the Pseudepigrapha in Pre-Modern Christianity

On the whole, the pseudepigrapha were viewed as a threat by leaders of classical Christianity, Greek and Latin, from about the mid-fourth century through at least the ninth. The gradual standardization of Christianity that was achieved in the internal battles against heterodoxy and the external achievement of official recognition in the Roman worlds (west and east) exhibited itself in the formation of an exclusive Christian scriptural canon. Aspects of the problem were recognized already in the late second century. Irenaeus rails against the Marcosians for "introducing an innumerable number of apocrypha and of counterfeit writings which they themselves created to amaze the foolish who do not understand the true writings" (*Adv. haer.* 1.20.1). Perhaps around the same time, or not too much later, the author of the Muratorian canon rejects compositions associated with various heterodox groups including "those who composed a new book of Psalms for Marcion."

To what extent these early testimonies had allegedly Jewish writings in view is not clear. But the principle of opposition to unacceptable heterodox writings is quite plain, and is continued even more explicitly in later authors. According to Athanasius, who writes from Alexandria at a time when Christianity had successfully withstood the attempts of the emperor Julian ("the apostate"!) to revive old Roman "paganism" and is about to be proclaimed as *the* official religion of the Roman empire, the "apocryphal" books (that is, our "Jewish" pseudepigrapha, among others) are a "device of heretics" who compose them at will and assign them ancient dates to mislead the simple. Athanasius speaks with disdain of books ascribed to Enoch, and apocryphal books of Isaiah and Moses. Similar negative attitudes are found in such other later fourth-century authors as Epiphanius, Cyril of Jerusalem, the compiler of the *Apostolic Constitutions*, Rufinus, and Jerome, while the prohibition of pseudepigrapha is buttressed with more extensive lists of titles in such later sources as the pseudo-Athanasian *Synopsis* (sixth century?), the *Decretum Gelasianum* (sixth century?), the so-called *Catalogue of the 60 Canonical Books* (sixth/seventh century?), the *Stichometry of Nicephorus* (ninth century), and elsewhere.[23] Among the writings to be avoided are those associated with the names of Adam, Enoch, Lamech, Abraham and the Patriarchs, Joseph, Eldad and Modad, Jambres and Mambres, Job, Moses, David, Solomon, Elijah, Isaiah, Baruch, Zephaniah, Zechariah, Habakkuk, Ezekiel, Daniel, Ezra, the Sibyl, and various angels. One list even refers to a "book of the giant named Og who is said by the heretics to have fought with a dragon after the flood" (*Decretum Gelasianum*)!

Not all the preserved notices are equally negative. In the second century, Justin Martyr accuses the Jews of excising certain passages from their scriptures in order to counter their use by Christians, including a passage attributed to Ezra (*Dial. c. Tryph.* 72) and a reference to Isaiah's death by means of a wooden saw (*Dial. c. Tryph.* 120).[24] In Justin's view, of course, the excised materials are not "pseudepigrapha" (as they become for us!) but authentic scripture. Justin also refers with favor to various Greek philosophical authors such as "the Sibyl and Hystaspes" (*1 Apol.* 20). Even more striking is the practice of Clement of Alexandria at the end of the second century, who shows an extremely wide acquaintance with a great variety of writings, Jewish, Christian, and "pagan," as well as with

"Jewish scriptures" in a strict sense.[25] He is less concerned with what writings people use than with how they use the writings, including scripture (*Strom.* 6.15.124.3). Indeed, he believes that the scriptures are filled with mysteries that can only properly be understood by the true Christian gnostic whose life is in accord with the apostolic tradition. And non-scriptural literature also contains valuable material when understood properly; that is, "gnostically." Clement cites "Paul" as exhorting his readers to "take also the Hellenic books, read the Sibyl ... and take Hystaspes to read ..." (*Strom.* 6.5.43.1). Elsewhere Clement quotes material attributed to "Enoch" (*Eclog. Proph.* 2.1), to "the prophecy of Ham" (*Strom.* 6.6.53.5, indirectly, from Isidore's *Exegetica of the Prophet Parchor*),[26] to a non-canonical revelation by "Sofonia [Zephaniah] the prophet" (*Strom.* 5.11.77.2), and refers to Moses' "assumption" (*Adumbratio in Ep. Iudae* 9 and *Strom.* 1.23.153.1 -- at least referring to the event, if not the name of a writing). In none of these passages, nor in numerous other references to what are now non-canonical Christian materials does Clement apologize or show discomfort about his use of such sources.

The situation is recognizably different when we examine the evidence from Origen, who inherits Clement's openness and exposure to a wide variety of sources but who also betrays some revealing reticence in using non-canonical sources. At least in the later part of his life, when he worked in Caesarea on the *Hexapla*, he was in first-hand contact with Jewish informants and traditions.[27] For him, the Jewish scriptural canon was fairly well defined as is evident from his work on the *Hexapla*, his preserved list of canonical books, and his "exegetical" writings (scholia, homilies, commentaries). Nevertheless, he does not forsake the sympathetic use of extra-canonical, presumably Jewish, works and traditions, although he sometimes prefaces such with words like "if anyone accepts such a writing" -- so with reference to a passage about angels disputing at Abraham's death (*Hom. in Luc.* 35), to a long quotation from the "Prayer of Joseph" (*Comm. in Joh.* 2.31 [25]), and to an "Isaiah apocryphon" about the death of the prophet (*Comm. in Matt.* 13:57; 23:37). Elsewhere he also shows knowledge of the book or books of *Enoch* (*c. Cels.* 5.54-55), of

Joseph-Asenath materials (*in Genesim* 41:45-46), of a book of Jannes and Mambres (*Comm. in Matt.* 23:37; 27:9), and of an apocryphon of Elijah or of Jeremiah (*Comm. in Matt.* 27:9), among other non-canonical references. Thus Origen stands in personal tension between a relatively firm, exclusivistic view of scripture that apparently was present in some of the churches (and/or perhaps in the Jewish circles) with which he was in contact and the relatively less restrictive attitudes of his predecessor Clement.

A couple of decades earlier, in North Africa, Tertullian had revealed similar reticence in citing the book of *Enoch* regarding fallen angels, in full recognition that some Christians rejected it because it was not included by the Jews in their scripture (*Cult. fem.* 2-3). Around the middle of the third century, Origen's pupil Dionysius (bishop of Alexandria ca. 247-264) admits to having read "*both* the compositions *and* the traditions of the heretics" despite a warning from one of the presbyters that he would thereby injure his soul. However, in a vision God instructed Dionysius to read everything at hand so as to be able to test and prove everything, and thus he was able to refute heresy all the more powerfully (Eusebius, *Hist. eccl.* 7.7.1-3; cf. 7.24).

Even at the end of the fourth century (Filaster of Brescia) or as late as the eighth century (John of Damascus) we still hear faint ecclesiastical voices arguing, in the same vein as Clement, Origen, and Dionysius, that enlightened Christians can profit from any and all available literature. But for the most part, the orthodox spokesmen of whom we know throughout this period were violently opposed to the pseudepigrapha, associating such writings with heterodox groups and even accusing the heretics of having forged some, if not all, of this material.

Alleged Heterodox Christian Transmitters of Pseudepigrapha

Some of the orthodox Christian sources attempt to identify specific heterodox groups which produced, or at least used, allegedly Jewish pseudepigraphical writings. Other heterodox groups are also described in terms that suggest an openness to such literature. In the earliest period, apart from amorphous Jewish Christian outlooks for which wide use of Jewish materials would be fully expected, we hear of Elkesaites (early second century) with their special traditions and their "Book of Elksai."[28] Some decades later Basilides is said to have had a special psalter,[29] and the second-century Montanist apocalyptic orientation appears to be well suited to the use of pseudepigraphic apocalyptic writings (Tertullian argues for accepting *Enoch* as scripture, perhaps even before his Montanist alignment). Irenaeus accuses the followers of Mark the gnostic of using and of forging apocrypha (*Adv. haer.* 1.20.1) in the late second century. About the same time, Lucian of Samosata satirically describes the temporarily converted Peregrinus as having authored many books for his Christian associates (*Peregr.* 11). Passing reference is perhaps appropriate here to the relatively obscure Melchizedekian Christians[30] and to the reputed Syrian rhapsodist Bardaisan.[31]

In the third century, Mani *consciously* selected "the writings, wisdom, apocalypses, parables and psalms of all the previous religions" for use in his Manichaean super-religion.[32] His background seems to include close contacts with Elkesaites and Marcionites, at the very least. Unfortunately, the extent to which our allegedly Jewish pseudepigrapha might have been used among Manichaeans is presently unknown.[33] According to the Coptic text of Athanasius' famous Easter letter of 367, unspecified apocryphal works also were used by the Meletian sect, which sometimes was closely identified with the Arians. A few decades later, Epiphanius names a great many books allegedly used by heretical groups: the Borborite gnostics use books in the name of Ialdabaoth and of Seth as well as an apocalypse of Adam and various books attributed to Mary and the apostles (*Pan.* 26.8.1); other gnostics use a Gospel of Eve (26.2.6ff.) and a book of Noriah, wife of Noah (26.1.3-4); the Sethians write books in the name of great men such as Seth, or his offspring called Allogenes, or Abraham (an apocalypse), or Moses (39.5.1); the Archontics create "apocrypha" with such names as the Small and Great Symphonia or the Ascent of Isaiah or books in the name of Seth (40.2.1; 40.7.4). Also from the late fourth century we hear of the Priscillians in Spain who used

apocryphal-pseudepigraphical books associated with prophets such as
Adam, Seth, Enoch, Noah, Abraham, Isaac, Jacob, and others, and who
were accused of Manichaeism and of magic.[34] Some of their views
seem to have survived among the medieval Cathari (and Albigenses?).

Resurgence of Interest in Pseudepigrapha in Christian Circles

Very few Greek manuscripts of allegedly Jewish pseudepigrapha
have survived from the period prior to the ninth century.[35] To what
extent this is a reflection of official orthodox hostility, or even
censorship, or is simply due to the general paucity of materials that
have survived from that period is difficult to determine. In any event,
from the tenth century onward there is a growing flood of Jewish
pseudepigraphical materials in Greek, especially those which deal with
the lives and deaths of ancient righteous persons.[36] From the
fourteenth century onward, various apocalyptic pseudepigrapha
manuscripts appear in Greek, including both the popular reward-
punishment scenes of the afterlife (as in Dante's *Commedia*)[37] and the
more cosmic surveys of the mysteries of past and future history.
Again, it may be simply due to coincidence that the preserved
manuscripts are so late in date, but at least this information provides a
starting point for further investigation. The main point I wish to make
here is that by the later Byzantine period, the orthodox Greek
transcribers readily transmitted and used pseudepigraphical materials.
The primary justification seems to be an avid interest in martyrology
and hagiographic narrative.[38] Greek liturgical practice provided a
framework for this by stipulating specific dates on which to
commemorate the saints and martyrs of the Christian tradition --
including pre-Christian Jewish notables. As nearly as I can determine,
the Christian Latin manuscript tradition shows much less sustained
interest in the Jewish pseudepigraphical materials in the late medieval
period, although some noteworthy Latin manuscripts or fragments
dating from the sixth century (*Jubilees*, [*Assumption of*] *Moses*,
Ascension of Isaiah) to the ninth century (*Life of Adam and Eve*, 4
Ezra) are known.

The situation in eastern Christian circles other than Greek is more difficult to assess because so little pertinent scholarly work has been done therein. There are a great many relevant early Coptic materials, from the fourth century onward, which seems to indicate that the canon-centered orientation of Shenouti and his monastically inclined followers was by no means universal among literate Coptic Egyptian Christians.[39] There is also a significant amount of relatively early material in Syriac,[40] notably *2 Baruch* and 4 Ezra from a sixth-century manuscript, and the *Psalms* and *Odes of Solomon* from the tenth century. If it is assumed that most of the pseudepigrapha now preserved in Arabic were translated from Syriac, the impression that Syriac Christianity suffered little from the anti-pseudepigrapha attitudes of the orthodox Greek Christians is fortified. When we turn to the national churches in which the Armenian (from the fifth century), Ethiopic (from the fourth/fifth? century), and Old Slavic (from the eighth? century) languages were central, we are flooded with copies of a great variety of pseudepigraphical texts, dating mostly from the twelfth century onward. These riches lie mostly untapped, and almost no precise information is available about the conditions under which the pseudepigrapha were introduced among those Christians. I have little idea of the extent to which other relatively early Christian literatures and traditions such as those in Gothic, Georgian, Old Irish,[41] Nubian, Sogdian, or Anglo-Saxon[42] can contribute additional materials of relevance to this discussion.

In a nutshell, the situation seems to have been approximately as follows: from about the fourth century onward, *classical* Greek and Latin Christianity tended to oppose the (public) use of non-canonical religious literature and to identify it closely with heterodoxy. But as the threat of "the old heresies" waned, and as hagiographical traditions became more and more important to orthodoxy, the Greek churches came to accept and rework certain types of pseudepigraphical literature in great quantity. It is possible, as J. Lebreton once suggested,[43] that orthodox editors actually purified some apocrypha of their heretical connections and sought "beneath gnostic accretions some harmless primitive tradition." It is not clear where the Greeks *obtained* the pseudepigraphical writings and traditions. My hunch is that many were preserved in Greek by monastics whose concern for personal piety and whose passive disdain for what was felt to be the tainted herd-mentality of urban organized Christianity led them to ignore prohibitions of such material. Chronographic and related "scholarly" interests doubtless played a role as well (see above, n.32). Apparently many pseudepigrapha were available in such languages as Coptic or Syriac even from the fourth to the ninth centuries, and it is not likely that they would have disappeared extensively in Greek. Nor is it impossible that some traditions that had disappeared in *written* Greek form could be reintroduced from *oral* sources or from non-Greek literature. Our knowledge of eremetic outlooks, literary practices, and contacts with other monastics of various language groupings is extremely poor, especially for the period from the fifth through the ninth centuries. And our knowledge of general developments in non-Latin Christianity in that period is not much better.

What influence did the rise and spread of Islam during the seventh through the ninth centuries have on this situation? We know that there were concerted efforts by Muslim leaders and scholars to translate all sorts of Greek and Syriac materials into Arabic, especially in the late eighth and early ninth centuries.[44] This doubtless brought many literate Christians and Jews who knew at least Syriac and perhaps also Greek into closer contact with each other. And Muslims were interested in Jewish and Christian traditions of various sorts, including apocalyptic, as is evident from Islamic literature.

Furthermore, reports of the discovery of non-canonical ancient Jewish writings come from this period -- including the report of a Nestorian Christian leader (Timotheos, ca. 800) whose informants seem to be in fairly close contact with the Jewish discoverers.[45] The Jewish Karaite movement[46] develops in the late eighth century, with adherents who look with favor on Jesus as a Jewish righteous teacher, and who present an elaborate angelology to mediate between God and his creation. Karaite tradition also knows of an influential Jewish messianic movement in this period, and there are a spate of Jewish would-be messiahs in succeeding centuries. Whether apocalyptic pseudepigrapha had any role in these phenomena is unknown to me, but the possibility deserves mention. The probable connection between the Karaites, the Cairo Geniza materials, and the Dead Sea sectaries (or at least their cave-deposited literature) should not be overlooked in this connection.

Whether any significant "millenarian movements" developed in eastern Christianity in the same period, and how they related to Jewish movements, would also be worth knowing for our purposes. The period around the year 1000 seems to have witnessed a rise in apocalyptic expectations in Christian circles,[47] but the detailed story remains to be written. Similarly, the history of contacts between Jews and Christians in this period, and especially with Christians who spoke Syriac, Arabic, Armenian, Ethiopic, and perhaps even Old Slavic, also has yet to be written. I suspect it would be extremely enlightening for pseudepigrapha studies. Indeed, it probably cannot be written without careful attention to the topic of "the pseudepigrapha in Christianity."

Working Backwards Towards the Origins

Methodological rigor requires us to work from what is more or less securely known towards what is unknown or only suspected. In the study of ostensibly Jewish pseudepigrapha, the area of what is unknown dominates. Nevertheless, some controls are available to help chart a path for further investigation. We do possess copies of certifiably Jewish writings that have been transmitted over long periods of time by Christian transcribers.[48] The most obvious examples are the canonical writings. There is extremely little evidence that Christian copyists tampered in a tendentious manner with those works. A couple of problematic passages appear in some manuscripts and/or versions of Psalms and even more rarely elsewhere. The mysterious "sexta" version of Hab 3:13 is reported to have rendered the Hebrew לישע ("to save") as διὰ Ιησοῦν ("through Joshua/Jesus"), which has been taken as evidence that the translator was Christian.[49] Allegedly Christian abbreviations of key terms (e.g., man, heaven, salvation) and key names (especially Jesus) appear throughout the manuscripts, but do not affect the meaning.[50] Occasionally prefixed superscriptions or affixed subscriptions to particular scriptural writings contain *clearly* Christian comments, but these are just as clearly differentiated by the annotator from the sacred text itself. Various claims have been made to the effect that Christian transcribers have sometimes changed an Old Testament text to harmonize with a variant New Testament quotation of that text, but such allegations are extremely difficult to substantiate. On the whole, the evidence is *strong* that Christian transcribers were very careful and faithful to the text when they copied Jewish writings that they considered canonical.[51] To what extent Christian transcribers may consciously have eliminated "Christian" sorts of variants they found in the Old Testament manuscripts in order to foster scriptural harmony and sanctity can no longer be determined.[52] It is certainly not at all impossible that at a very early period in Christian history, before the issue of scriptural canonization had become such an obsession, characteristically Christian changes were introduced into some Jewish scriptural texts, only to prove an embarrassment at a later date, when the Jewish origin and orientation of the Christian "Old Testament" text became a cornerstone of the emerging orthodox faith. But that is uncontrolled conjecture on my part, given the present state of the evidence.

On the other hand, there is strong evidence that some Christian transcribers sometimes did insert tendentious changes into the (non-canonical) Jewish texts they transmitted. The Josephus tradition is perhaps the best known example with its extremely laudatory testimony about Jesus and the various additions of possibly Christian significance in the Old Slavic version.[53] I am not aware of any similar problems with Philo texts[54] or with the most widely accepted "deutero-canonical" writings. Text-critical problems do exist in all these works, but there is nothing characteristically Christian about the preserved variants. Perhaps more detailed study of the entire textual tradition (including versional evidence) would modify this impression, since modern editors are usually more concerned with establishing the supposedly original form of the text than with identifying late and tendentious variants. But for the moment, the available evidence does *not* suggest that Christian transcribers regularly tended to insert characteristically Christian passages into the Jewish texts they copied. Occasionally a relatively clear instance appears, either as a variant in the textual stream or, as with the Josephus passage about Jesus, as material that seems highly incompatible with its supposed Jewish origins. Although the apocalypse dubbed "4 Ezra" cannot be classified as "certifiably Jewish" on the basis of external criteria alone, its textual transmission offers a good example of what appears to be Christian interpolation in some witnesses. At 4 Ezra 7:28, where the other extant versions refer to "messiah" or to "my son the messiah," Latin manuscripts have "my son *Jesus*." While it is possible that an original "Jesus" or "Jesus Christ/Messiah" reference has been removed by copyists because of its incongruity with the rest of the document, it is more likely that Christian interest caused the insertion of the specific name "Jesus."[55]

The evidence is also clear that Christians sometimes radically revised and reedited texts they transmitted. This can be seen most clearly with certifiably Christian texts, where no question arises as to whether the revisions had already taken place under Jewish auspices. It should be unnecessary to list examples -- if the synoptic problem or the western text of Acts do not seem to be immediately relevant, the three recensions of the letters of Ignatius[56] or the modification of *Didache* for incorporation into the *Apostolic Constitutions*[57] should suffice to illustrate the point. In fact we need not even go that far afield. The *Ascension of Isaiah* is a patently Christian composition in its preserved form, whatever one thinks about its opening sections which many scholars treat as a separate Jewish document and call the *Martyrdom of Isaiah*. Virtually the same material that is present in the *Ascension of Isaiah* appears in a reshuffled and equally Christian form in a twelfth-century Greek text entitled "Prophecy, Apocalypse and Martyrdom of ... Isaiah."[58]

Similar types of editorial activity are also demonstrable on the part of Jewish transmitters of Jewish literature. We have received two rather different forms of the biblical book of Jeremiah.[59] Ben Sira is preserved in variant Hebrew forms.[60] My point is that the presence of two or more versions of the same basic material in Christian hands does not necessarily mean that the variation originated with the Christians. There are numerous problems of this sort among the pseudepigrapha. Two radically different forms of the *Testament of Abraham* have been preserved.[61] The *Adam and Eve* literature is found in a seemingly endless variety.[62] Various recensions of the *Lives of the Prophets* exist.[63] There are shorter and longer forms of *Paraleipomena Jeremiou*.[64] *5 Ezra* appears in two significantly different Latin forms.[65] How do we know who has made the changes and for what reasons? With regard to writings that have been preserved in a relatively less complicated state, how do we know we are not simply victims of circumstance who have inherited only one stage (the latest?) of a rather lengthy development? By and large, the desired control evidence is inconclusive. Other lines of approach, such as careful linguistic analysis in relation to a wide selection of literature from approximately the same period, need to be carefully explored.

There is another type of control that would be very helpful, but strict methodological considerations make it difficult to isolate. I *expect* that there were self-consciously Christian authors who wrote new works that focused on Jewish persons or traditions and contained no uniquely Christian passages.[66] Motives for producing this sort of quasi-Jewish literature would vary from the rather innocent homily on the heroic life of a Job or a Joseph to what we might call premeditated forgery for apocalyptic or hagiographical or some other purposes. But unless we have the testimony of some informed and reliable witness to what is taking place, we have only the evidence contained in the writing itself. And if, by definition, the writing contains no uniquely Christian elements, we will be at a loss to identify it as of Christian origin!

Of course, we do have witnesses from Christian antiquity who claim to know that some Christians were forging Jewish pseudepigrapha. It is a polemical claim made and repeated from the late second century onward.[67] But as with most polemically conditioned claims, we do well to take it with a large lump of salt. The claim is probably accurate to the extent that heterodox groups made use of Jewish, or apparently Jewish, pseudepigrapha. But the accusation that the heterodox were actually writing or compiling such works in an original manner can hardly be accepted at face value from witnesses like Irenaeus, Athanasius, and Epiphanius. We only reach a methodological impasse along this avenue of inquiry, although I suspect that the polemicists are at least partly correct!

From my perspective, "the *Christianity* of the Pseudepigrapha" is not the hidden ingredient that needs to be hunted out and exposed in contrast to a supposed native *Jewish* pre-Christian setting. On the contrary, when the evidence is clear that only Christians preserved the material, the Christianity of it is the given, it is the setting, it is the starting point for delving more deeply into this literature to determine what, if anything, may be safely identified as originally Jewish. And even when the label "originally Jewish" can be attached to some material in the pseudepigrapha, that does not automatically mean pre-Christian Jewish, or even pre-rabbinic Jewish. It might mean post-Yavneh Jewish -- rabbinic Jewish or Karaite Jewish, for example; unless one assumes that neither the rabbis nor the Karaites ever reshaped traditions to be more useful for their immediate purposes, it could mean originally Jewish from Islamic times!

Furthermore, in a Christian setting that is almost obsessed with multiplying examples of God's righteous athletes who struggled and conquered their demonic opponents in life and even in death, the characteristically Christian elements in a sermon or a narration may be entirely coextensive with possible Jewish interest. In a Christian setting that is self-conscious of its Jewish heritage and thrives on visions and revelations, how can one tell whether the predictions and prescriptions found in the mouth of Adam or Seth were put there by a Jewish or a Christian author? We need to examine the literature as it has been preserved for us, attempt to recreate the conditions under which it was preserved and transmitted, and then perhaps we will be in a position to identify the sort of "Jewishness" it might represent. For the most part, and with significant exceptions (e.g., at least part of *1 Enoch*[68]), this has not been the normal approach to the pseudepigrapha in recent decades. I believe that our knowledge of Christian pluralism has suffered from this fact, and although our awareness of early Jewish pluralism has profited, this has been at the expense of methodological rigor and may be paying us an inflated dividend.

---

[1] This essay has rested uneasily in my files for more than fifteen years, waiting for me to find or take time to annotate it! As the years passed, I considered simply rewriting and updating it. But now that it has been "dusted off" at long last, I have decided to leave the text basically as it was delivered in 1976, and to do all the significant updating in the notes. Otherwise, its original flavor and (at least to me) excitement will have been diluted and sometimes simply lost. Much relevant research has appeared in the intervening years, of which the footnotes attempt to give some notice (I am indebted to John C. Reeves for his assistance with the annotation). In various particulars, the essay does need to be rewritten today. But in its general thrust, its challenge to responsible scholarship still stands. In the footnotes, *EJMI* refers to *Early Judaism and its Modern Interpreters* (ed. R.A. Kraft and G.W.E. Nickelsburg; Atlanta: Scholars Press, 1986).

[2] I am not the first to make such observations or to think them of foundational importance. Note, for example, Marinus de Jonge, *The Testaments of the Twelve Patriarchs: A Study of Their Text, Composition and Origin* (Assen: Van Gorcum, 1953), and the prize essay contest sponsored with his encouragement by the Teyler Foundation at Haarlem (The Netherlands) in 1985 on the subject "An investigation concerning the use and transmission of originally Jewish writings (and/or writings incorporating much Jewish traditional material) in early Christianity." See also J. Jervell, "Ein Interpolator interpretiert: Zu der christlichen Bearbeitung der Testamente der Zwölf Patriarchen," *Studien zu den Testamenten der Zwölf Patriarchen* (BZNW 36; ed. W. Eltester; Berlin: A. Topelmann, 1969) 30-61; or H.W. Hollander and M. de Jonge, *The Testaments of the Twelve Patriarchs: A Commentary* (Leiden: Brill, 1985) Introduction ##8-9.

[3] It has come to be expected that scholars worry about whether the *original* language of any given writing was Hebrew or Aramaic or Greek or whatever, but few have concerned themselves with the language in which the text has survived *as a piece of valuable historical information in its own right*. Some earlier authors comment on this type of problem, but do not exploit it: for example, M.R. James describes the language of the *Apocalypse of Sedrach* as "neo-Greek" since it "degenerates not seldom into modern Greek" (*Apocrypha Anecdota: A Collection of Thirteen Apocryphal Books and Fragments* [ed. M.R. James; Cambridge: Cambridge University Press, 1893] 127-28), but he is mostly concerned about parallels in language and ideas to earlier materials. S. Agourides (*OTP* 1.606) also simply notes in passing the "late" linguistic features of that text. For the early Greek translations of Jewish scriptures, H. St. J. Thackeray attempted to establish some linguistic-geographical correlations in his 1920 Schweich Lectures published as *The Septuagint and Jewish Worship: A*

Study in Origins (London: H. Milford, 1921), but not many have pursued that sort of approach further. In more recent times, see David Satran, "Daniel: Seer, Philosopher, Holy Man," *Ideal Figures in Ancient Judaism: Profiles and Paradigms* (ed. J.J. Collins and G.W.E. Nickelsburg; Chico, CA: Scholars Press, 1980) 33-48; idem, *Early Jewish and Christian Interpretation of the Fourth Chapter of the Book of Daniel* (Ph.D. dissertation, Hebrew University, 1985).

4   *A Patristic Greek Lexicon* (ed. G.W.H. Lampe; Oxford: Clarendon, 1961).

5   F.T. Gignac, *A Grammar of the Greek Papyri of the Roman and Byzantine Periods* (2 vols.; Milano: Istituto editoriale cisalpino-La goliardica, 1976-).

6   Efforts and products along these lines have multiplied in recent times, especially with the advent of computer-based texts and tools. The ability to search and analyze the data interactively is rapidly coming to replace the static concordances and linguistic aids of the past, and such "hardcopy" tools can in any event be produced more easily now with computer assistance, as for example, A.-M. Denis, *Concordance grecque des pseudépigraphes d'Ancien Testament* (Louvain-la-Neuve: Université catholique de Louvain, Institut orientaliste, 1987); also the various publications in "The Computer Bible" series edited by J. Arthur Baird, et al. (published by Biblical Research Associates, College of Wooster, Ohio). Now that the magnificent TLG data bank of Greek literature is almost complete (TLG updated CD-ROM "D" appeared in 1993), along with pioneering efforts in more detailed analysis (such as the Computer Assisted Tools for Septuagint Studies [= CATSS] Project, co-directed by Emanuel Tov and myself; see the Packard Humanities Institute [PHI] CD-ROM 1, 1987, and PHI CD-ROM 5.3, 1992), major advances in comparative linguistic research can be expected. For some first fruits from the CATSS Project, see *A Greek-English Lexicon of the Septuagint, Part 1: A-I* (ed. J. Lust, E. Eynikel, and K. Hauspie; Stuttgart: Deutsche Bibelgesellschaft, 1992). Josephus and Philo are both available in the TLG data bank, and can be searched for concording and other purposes quite easily. Peder Borgen (Trondheim, Norway) also has created an electronic Philo data bank for the production of concordances and other tools. On Josephus, see also the more traditional tool edited by K.H. Rengstorf, *A Complete Concordance to Flavius Josephus* (4 vols.; Leiden: Brill, 1973-83). I am not sure where the related Josephus lexicon project now stands, after the death of Horst Moehring (Brown University). A team of Australian scholars, including John A.L. Lee and Gregory Horsley, is engaged in the creation of a new Moulton-Milligan lexicon to the New Testament, with computer assistance. For some other examples of computer projects and tools, see John Hughes, *Bits, Bytes, & Biblical Studies* (Grand Rapids, MI: Zondervan, 1987), and more recently *The Humanities Computing Yearbook: 1989-90* (ed. Ian Lancashire; Oxford: Clarendon, 1991).

7   Raymond A. Martin, *Syntactical Evidence of Semitic Sources in Greek Documents* (SCS 3; Missoula: Scholars Press, 1974); idem, "Syntax Criticism of the Testament of Abraham," *Studies on the Testament of Abraham* (SCS 6; ed. G.W.E. Nickelsburg; Missoula: Scholars Press, 1976) 95-120. See also Benjamin G. Wright, "A Note on the Statistical Analysis of Septuagintal Syntax," *JBL* 104 (1985) 111-114.

8   See Marcel Simon, *Verus Israel: étude sur les relations entre chrétiens et*

juifs dans l'empire romain (135-425) (2d ed.; Paris: E. de Boccard, 1964); English translation, *Verus Israel: A Study of the Relations Between Christians and Jews in the Roman Empire (135-425)* (trans. H. McKeating; New York: Oxford University Press, 1986); John G. Gager, *The Origins of Anti-Semitism: Attitudes Toward Judaism in Pagan and Christian Antiquity* (Oxford: Oxford University Press, 1985) 113-191. Regarding specific Church Fathers, see A.L. Williams, *Justin Martyr: The Dialogue with Trypho* (London: SPCK, 1930), esp. the Introduction; Melito of Sardis, *On Pascha and Fragments* (ed. S.G. Hall; Oxford: Clarendon, 1979); I. Angerstorfer, *Melito und das Judentum* (Regensburg: Universität Regensburg, 1986); David P. Efroymson, *Tertullian's Anti-Judaism and its Role in His Theology* (Ph.D. dissertation, Temple University, 1976); idem, "The Patristic Connection," *Anti-Semitism and the Foundations of Christianity* (ed. Alan Davies; New York: Paulist Press, 1979) 98-117; N.R.M. de Lange, *Origen and the Jews* (Cambridge: Cambridge University Press, 1976); Robert L. Wilken, *Judaism and the Early Christian Mind: A Study of Cyril of Alexandria's Exegesis and Theology* (New Haven: Yale University Press, 1971); idem, *John Chrysostom and the Jews: Rhetoric and Reality in the Late 4th Century* (Berkeley: University of California Press, 1983). Similar studies with their focus on Epiphanius and Jerome would also be illuminating.

9   For further details, see my article "Reassessing the 'Recensional Problem' in the Testament of Abraham," *Studies on the Testament of Abraham* (see n.7 above) 121-37 (also available as an electronic resource from ccat.sas.upenn.edu or on the listserv of the IOUDAIOS Electronic Discussion Group).

10   In addition to various efforts at cataloguing existing manuscripts (e.g., the project of Marcel Richard at Paris), note the development of the Ancient Biblical Manuscript Center at Claremont and the Hill Monastic Library Project in Minnesota. But in general, the interest in microform seems to have waned somewhat, or at least is being challenged by the development of computer technologies capable, among other things, of capturing (e.g. on CD-ROM) and even transmitting (on the international electronic networks) digitized images (equivalent to color photographs), enhancing and otherwise manipulating the images, and linking images and transcribed text along with other pertinent items in a "hypertext" electronic environment. A growing number of older and newer editions and translations of ancient texts are finding their way into electronic collections and archives in this new technological world. On electronic resources and developments in general, see Lancashire, *Yearbook* (above n.6).

11   There have been a number of recent works relating to the multiplicity of forms of Judaism in the Greco-Roman world. See, e.g., E. Schürer, *The History of the Jewish People in the Age of Jesus Christ* (4 vols. in 3; ed. G. Vermes, F. Millar, and M. Goodman; Edinburgh: T. & T. Clark, 1973-87); John J. Collins, *Between Athens and Jerusalem: Jewish Identity in the Hellenistic Diaspora* (New York: Crossroad, 1983); S.J.D. Cohen, *From the Maccabees to the Mishnah* (Philadelphia: Westminster, 1987); E.J. Bickerman, *The Jews in the Greek Age* (Cambridge, MA: Harvard University Press, 1988); Gabrielle Boccaccini, *Middle Judaism: Jewish Thought, 300 B.C.E. to 200 C.E.* (Minneapolis: Fortress, 1991); L.L. Grabbe, *Judaism from Cyrus to Hadrian* (2

vols.; Minneapolis: Fortress, 1992). For a more traditional synthesis of the same evidence, see L.H. Feldman, *Jew and Gentile in the Ancient World* (Princeton: Princeton University Press, 1993). A survey and analysis of mid-twentieth century scholarship on Judaism to about 1980 can be found in *EJMI*. For some recent studies on varieties of early Christianity, see the following note.

12 For an application of such insights to early Christianity, see John G. Gager, *Kingdom and Community: The Social World of Early Christianity* (Englewood Cliffs, NJ: Prentice-Hall, 1975), and the literature cited there; idem, *RelSRev* 5/3 (1979) 174-80; W.D. Davies, "From Schweitzer to Scholem: Reflections on Sabbatai Svi," *JBL* 95 (1976) 529-58; G. Theissen, *The Sociology of Early Palestinian Christianity* (Philadelphia: Fortress, 1978); idem, *The Social Setting of Pauline Christianity* (Philadelphia: Fortress, 1982); D.J. Harrington, "Sociological Concepts and the Early Church: A Decade of Research," *TS* 41 (1980) 181-90; W.A. Meeks, *The First Urban Christians: The Social World of the Apostle Paul* (New Haven: Yale University Press, 1983); R.A. Horsley, *Jesus and the Spiral of Violence* (San Francisco: Harper & Row, 1987); idem, *Sociology and the Jesus Movement* (New York: Crossroad, 1989).

13 The editions and monographs cited in this paragraph are well known in the field. Recent literature that provides a larger context for this discussion includes *EJMI* (cf. n.1 above), with standard abbreviations and an appendix on editions; G.W.E. Nickelsburg, *Jewish Literature Between the Bible and the Mishnah: A Historical and Literary Introduction* (Philadelphia: Fortress, 1981); *Jewish Writings of the Second Temple Period* (CRINT; ed. M.E. Stone; Assen and Philadelphia: Van Gorcum and Fortress, 1984); and the recent anthologies such as *La Bible: écrits intertestamentaires* (ed. A. Dupont-Sommer and M. Philonenko; Paris: Gallimard, 1987), Charlesworth's *OTP*, and *The Apocryphal Old Testament* (ed. H.F.D. Sparks; Oxford: Clarendon, 1984). For a review article on the latter two works, see M.E. Stone and R.A. Kraft, *RelSRev* 14/2 (1988) 111-117.

14 After all, the etymological sense of "falsely attributed authorship" applies equally to some writings included in the traditional Old and New Testament canons, and some of the writings usually discussed under the wider heading of "pseudepigrapha" do not have the same sort of authorship ascription problem -- e.g., *Lives of the Prophets*, 3-4 Maccabees. Furthermore, the newly discovered materials from the Judean Desert ("Dead Sea Scrolls") need to be worked into the broader classification scheme somehow. For a discussion of some of these issues, see Stone and Kraft, *RelSRev* 14/2 (1988) 111-117; see also Kraft's review in *JBL* 106 (1987) 736-39. Note that Sparks preferred to use the term "apocryphal" in its general sense in his edition (above, n.13).

15 Examples may be found in the relevant articles by these scholars in the *Jewish Encyclopedia* (13 vols.; ed. I. Singer; New York and London: Funk and Wagnalls, 1901-7). E.g., see L. Ginzberg, "Abraham, Apocalypse of," 1.91-92; idem, "Abraham, Testament of," 1.93-96; idem, "Adam, Book of," 1.179-80; idem, "Baruch, Apocalypse of (Greek)," 2.549-51; idem, "Baruch, Apocalypse of (Syriac)," 2.551-56; K. Kohler, "Job, Testament of," 7.200-202; idem, "Testaments of the Twelve Patriarchs," 12.113-118. See also Ginzberg, *The Legends of the Jews* (7 vols.; Philadelphia; Jewish Publication Society, 1909-38).

16 Samuel Sandmel, "Parallelomania," *JBL* 81 (1962) 1-13.

17 The journal *Revue de Qumran* is devoted to the study of these materials. For a general update and bibliography, see J. Murphy-O'Connor, "The Judean Desert," *EJMI* 119-56; J.A. Fitzmyer, *The Dead Sea Scrolls: Major Publications and Tools for Study* (rev. ed.; Atlanta: Scholars Press, 1990).

18 See, for example, Walter Bauer, *Rechtgläubigkeit und Ketzerei im ältesten Christentum* (Tübingen: Mohr/Siebeck, 1934); 2d ed., reprinted and supplemented by Georg Strecker (Tübingen: Mohr, 1964); English translation, *Orthodoxy and Heresy in Early Christianity* (ed. R.A. Kraft and G. Krodel; Philadelphia: Fortress Press, 1971).

19 Adolf Harnack, *Geschichte der altchristlichen Literatur bis Eusebius* (2 vols. in 4; Leipzig, 1893; 2d ed.; reprinted, Leipzig: J.C. Hinrichs, 1958) 1/2.845-65: "Übersicht über die von den Christen angeeignete und zum Theil bearbeitete jüdische Litteratur."

20 Ibid. 1/2.861.

21 *APOT* 2.126-27.

22 F.C. Burkitt, *Jewish and Christian Apocalypses* (London: H. Milford, 1914) 76.

23 See H.B. Swete, *An Introduction to the Old Testament in Greek* (2d ed., supplemented by R.R. Ottley; Cambridge: Cambridge University Press, 1914; reprinted, New York: Ktav, 1968) part 2 chap. 1; Schürer, *History* 3/2.797-98.

24 See further R.A. Kraft, "Christian Transmission of Greek Jewish Scriptures: A Methodological Probe," *Paganisme, judaisme, christianisme: Influences et affrontements dans le monde antique: Mélanges offerts à Marcel Simon* (ed. A. Benoit et al.; Paris: Boccard, 1978) 207-26.

25 See the index of scriptural citations supplied in the four-volume GCS edition of Clement of Alexandria (GCS 12, 15, 17, 39) begun by Otto Stählin in 1905, subsequently revised by Ludwig Früchtel and Ursula Treu, and still in process (the 4th ed. of volume 2 appeared in 1985). Unfortunately, the Strasbourg project does not include nonbiblical citations in its *Biblia Patristica: Index des citations et allusions bibliques dans la littérature patristique* (5 vols.; ed. J. Allenbach; Paris: Editions du CNRS, 1975-).

26 See Jean Doresse, *The Secret Books of the Egyptian Gnostics* (London, 1960; reprinted, Rochester, VT: Inner Traditions, 1986) 20.

27 See in general de Lange, *Origen and the Jews* (n.8 *supra*); R.P.C. Hanson, *Allegory and Event: A Study of the Sources and Significance of Origen's Interpretation of Scripture* (London: SCM Press, 1959). Studies that focus upon specific correspondences between the teachings of Origen and the Sages include E.E. Urbach, "Homiletical Interpretations of the Sages and the Expositions of Origen on Canticles, and the Jewish-Christian Disputation," *ScrHier* 22 (1971) 247-75; R. Kimelman, "Rabbi Yohanan and Origen on the Song of Songs: A Third-Century Jewish-Christian Disputation," *HTR* 73 (1980) 567-95; and D.J. Halperin, "Origen, Ezekiel's Merkabah, and the Ascension of Moses," *CH* 50 (1981) 261-75.

28 There is revived interest in the Elkesaites, partly due to the recent discovery and publication of the *Cologne Mani Codex* (see below, n.32). Consult Origen *apud* Eusebius, *Hist. eccl.* 6.38; Hippolytus, *Ref.* 9.13-17; 10.29; Epiphanius, *Pan.*

19.1-6; 53.1; W. Brandt, *Elchasai: Ein Religionsstifter und sein Werk* (Leipzig: J.C. Hinrichs, 1912); A.F.J. Klijn and G.J. Reinink, *Patristic Evidence for Jewish-Christian Sects* (Leiden: Brill, 1973) 54-67; idem, "Elchasai and Mani," *VC* 28 (1974) 277-89; G.P. Luttikhuizen, *The Revelation of Elchasai* (Tübingen: Mohr, 1985); A. Henrichs and L. Koenen, "Ein griechischer Mani-Codex (P. Colon. inv. nr. 4780)," *Zeitschrift für Papyrologie und Epigraphik* (= *ZPE*) 5 (1970) 97-217, esp. pp. 133-60. For a recent attempt to link the Elkesaites to Jewish literature and institutions, see J.C. Reeves, "The Elchasaite Sanhedrin of the Cologne Mani Codex in Light of Second Temple Jewish Sectarian Sources," *JJS* 42 (1991) 68-91.

[29] For references and discussion, see Bauer, *Orthodoxy and Heresy* 170 n.42.

[30] Epiphanius, *Panarion* 55. Interest in this sect has been spurred by the discovery and publication of Melchizedek texts from both Nag Hammadi (NHC IX 1) and Qumran (11QMelch). See A.S. van der Woude, "Melchisedek als himmlische Erlösergestalt in den neugefundenen eschatologischen Midraschim aus Qumran Höhle XI," *OTS* 14 (1965) 354-73; J.T. Milik, "*Milki-sedeq* et *Milki-reša'* dans les anciens écrits juifs et chrétiens," *JJS* 23 (1972) 95-144; F.L. Horton, *The Melchizedek Tradition: A Critical Examination of the Sources to the Fifth Century A.D. and in the Epistle to the Hebrews* (Cambridge: Cambridge University Press, 1976); P.J. Kobelski, *Melchizedek and Melchireša'* (Washington: Catholic Biblical Association of America, 1981); E. Puech, "Notes sur le manuscrit de XIQ Melkisedeq," *RevQ* 12 (1987) 483-513; B.A. Pearson, "The Figure of Melchizedek in the First Tractate of the Unpublished Coptic-Gnostic Codex IX from Nag Hammadi," *Proceedings of the XIIth International Congress of the International Association for the History of Religion* (Leiden: Brill, 1975) 200-208; *Nag Hammadi Codices IX and X* (NHS 15; ed. B.A. Pearson; Leiden: Brill, 1981).

[31] On a possible connection between Bardaisan and the *Odes of Solomon*, see W.R. Newbold, "Bardaisan and the Odes of Solomon," *JBL* 30 (1911) 161-204; J. Daniélou, *The Theology of Jewish Christianity* (French original, Paris: Desclee, 1958; trans. John A. Baker; Chicago: Regnery, 1964) 30-33; H.J.W. Drijvers, *Bardaisan of Edessa* (Assen: Van Gorcum, 1966) 209-12.

[32] The quotation is taken from *Kephalaia* 154; see C. Schmidt and H.J. Polotsky, "Ein Mani-Fund in Ägypten," *SPAW* (1933) 41 (text p. 85). Our knowledge about the milieu from which Manichaeism sprang has been augmented by the discovery and publication of the *Cologne Mani Codex*. See A. Henrichs and L. Koenen, "Ein griechischer Mani-Codex (P. Colon. inv. nr. 4780)," *ZPE* 5 (1970) 97-217; idem, "... Edition der Seiten 1-72," *ZPE* 19 (1975) 1-85; idem, "... Edition der Seiten 72,8-99,9," *ZPE* 32 (1978) 87-199; idem, "... Edition der Seiten 99,10-120," *ZPE* 44 (1981) 201-318; idem, "... Edition der Seiten 121-192," *ZPE* 48 (1982) 1-59; L. Koenen and C. Römer, *Der Kölner Mani-Kodex: Abbildungen und diplomatischer Text* (Bonn: Habelt, 1985); idem, *Der Kölner Mani-Kodex: Kritische Edition* (Opladen: Westdeutscher Verlag, 1988). For an English translation of the initial portion of the Codex, see Ron Cameron and Arthur J. Dewey, *The Cologne Mani Codex (P. Colon. inv. nr. 4780) "Concerning the Origin of his Body"* (SBLTT 15; Missoula: Scholars Press, 1979). A recent comprehensive study that incorporates the new information

about Mani is S.N.C. Lieu, *Manichaeism in the Later Roman Empire and Medieval China* (2d ed.; Tübingen: J.C.B. Mohr, 1992).

[33] ·The *Cologne Mani Codex* contains five citations from otherwise unknown pseudepigraphic works attributed to Adam, Seth, Enosh, Enoch, and Shem. Albert Henrichs has suggested that *CMC* 7.2-14 reflects dependence upon the *Testament of Abraham*; see Henrichs, "'Thou Shalt Not Kill a Tree': Greek, Manichaean and Indian Tales," *BASP* 16 (1979) 105-106; idem, "Literary Criticism of the Cologne Mani Codex," *The Rediscovery of Gnosticism: Proceedings of the International Conference on Gnosticism at Yale, New Haven, Connecticut, March 28-31, 1978* (2 vols.; ed. B. Layton; Leiden: Brill, 1980-81) 2.729 n.20. A reliance upon Jewish Enochic literature has been vigorously advocated by J.C. Reeves, "An Enochic Motif in Manichaean Tradition," *Manichaica Selecta: Studies Presented to Professor Julien Ries on the Occasion of his Seventieth Birthday* (ed. A van Tongerloo and S. Giversen; Louvain: International Association of Manichaean Studies, 1991) 295-98; idem, *Jewish Lore in Manichaean Cosmogony: Studies in the Book of Giants Traditions* (Cincinnati: Hebrew Union College Press, 1992).

[34] See H. Chadwick, *Priscillian of Avila: The Occult and the Charismatic in the Early Church* (Oxford: Clarendon, 1976).

[35] For the evidence, see A.-M. Denis, *Introduction aux pseudépigraphes grecs d'Ancien Testament* (Leiden: Brill, 1970); S.P. Brock, "Other Manuscript Discoveries," *EJMI* 157-73.

[36] See especially the materials collected by F. Halkin, *Bibliotheca Hagiographica Graeca* (3 vols.; 3d ed.; Bruxelles: Société Bollandistes, 1957).

[37] For the development of such materials, see Martha Himmelfarb, *Tours of Hell: An Apocalyptic Form in Jewish and Christian Literature* (Philadelphia: University of Pennsylvania Press, 1983), and now her *Ascent to Heaven in Jewish and Christian Apocalypses* (Oxford: Oxford University Press, 1993).

[38] An interest that I have largely overlooked, but that may have served as a preserver of traditions and "pseudepigrapha awareness" at a more "scientific-historical" level, is in world chronography, recently more clearly identified and documented by William Adler, *Time Immemorial: Archaic History and its Sources in Christian Chronography from Julius Africanus to George Syncellus* (Washington: Dumbarton Oaks, 1989), esp. pp. 80-97. In various ways, pseudepigraphic literatures seem to have been able to serve a wide range of interests in the "middle ages," including science (especially astronomological and calendric issues), history, popular piety (especially with folkloristic tales), and ordinary worship (e.g., with models of prayer/hymn language). The interrelationship of such motives among Christian transmitters deserves closer study.

[39] See, e.g., Janet Timbie, *Dualism and the Concept of Orthodoxy in the Thought of the Monks of Upper Egypt* (Ph.D. dissertation, University of Pennsylvania, 1979). For general background on the development of Christian communities in Egypt, see Bauer, *Orthodoxy and Heresy* 44-60, and more recently *The Roots of Egyptian Christianity* (ed. Birger A. Pearson and James E. Goehring; Philadelphia: Fortress, 1986).

[40] See David Bundy, "Pseudepigrapha in Syriac Literature," *SBL 1991 Seminar*

Papers (Atlanta: Scholars Press, 1991) 745-65.

[41] M. McNamara, *The Apocrypha in the Irish Church* (Dublin: Dublin Institute for Advanced Studies, 1975); see also *Irish Biblical Apocrypha: Selected Texts in Translation* (ed. M. McNamara and M. Herbert; Edinburgh: T. & T. Clark, 1989).

[42] See Frederick M. Biggs, et al., "Apocrypha," in *Sources of Anglo-Saxon Literary Culture: A Trial Version* (ed. Frederick M. Biggs, T.D. Hill, and P.E. Szarmach; Binghamton, NY: Center for Medieval and Early Renaissance Studies, State University of New York at Binghamton, 1990). A good example of the cross-fertilization of some of these developments can be seen in E. Ann Matter, "The 'Revelatio Esdrae' in Latin and English Traditions," *RBén* 92 (1982) 376-92. Other examples may be found in the electronic logs of the network discussion groups ANSAX-L and MEDTEXTL.

[43] Jules Lebreton and Jacques Zeiller, *The History of the Early Church* (trans. Ernest C. Messenger; 4 vols.; New York: Collier, 1962) 4.90.

[44] The individual pre-eminently associated with this effort was the Christian physician Ḥunayn b. Isḥāq (809-874 CE), regarding whom see G. Strohmaier, "Ḥunayn b. Isḥāk al-'Ibādī," *EI*[2] 3.578-81. For a general discussion, see M. Plessner, "Science: The Natural Sciences and Medicine," *The Legacy of Islam* (2d ed.; ed. J. Schacht and C.E. Bosworth; Oxford: Clarendon, 1974) 425-60, esp. pp. 430ff.

[45] O. Braun, "Ein Brief des Katholikos Timotheos I über biblische Studien des 9. Jahrhunderts," *OrChr* 1 (1901) 299-313. In his letter, Timotheos recounts a report (received from some Jewish converts to Christianity) of the recent discovery of a number of biblical and non-biblical manuscripts in a cave near Jericho. These manuscripts were removed to Jerusalem for further study. For further discussion of this find and its possible significance for Qumran, see O. Eissfeldt, "Der gegenwärtige Stand der Erforschung der in Palästina neu gefundenen hebräischen Handschriften," *TLZ* 74 (1949) 597-600; R. de Vaux, "A propos des manuscrits de la mer Morte," *RB* 57 (1950) 417-29; A. Paul, *Ecrits de Qumran et sectes juives aux premiers siècles de l'islam* (Paris: Letouzey et Ané, 1969) 94-96.

[46] For the origin and history of the Karaite schism, see S.W. Baron, *A Social and Religious History of the Jews* (18 vols.; 2d ed.; New York and Philadelphia: Columbia University Press and the Jewish Publication Society, 1952-83) 5.209-85; L. Nemoy, et al., "Karaites," *EncJud* 10.761-85. Regarding the possible reliance of the Karaites upon non-canonical sources, see H.H. Rowley, *The Zadokite Fragments and the Dead Sea Scrolls* (Oxford: Blackwell, 1952) 22-29, and Y. Erder and H. Ben-Shammai, "The Connection of Karaism with the Dead Sea Scrolls and Related Apocryphal Literature," *Cathedra* 42 (1987) 53-86 (Hebrew). Some have also assessed the complicated problem of whether traces of the "pseudepigrapha" have survived in the literature of classical Judaism. In addition to the references cited in n.15 above, see H. Albeck, "Agadot im Lichte der Pseudepigraphen," *MGWJ* 83 (1939) 162-69; Y. Dan, "Apocrypha and Pseudepigrapha in Medieval Hebrew Literature," *EncJud* 3.186-87; idem, *Ha-sippur ha-'ivri beyemey ha-baynayyim* (Jerusalem: Keter, 1974) 133-41 (Hebrew); M. Himmelfarb, "R. Moses the Preacher and the Testaments of the

Twelve Patriarchs," *AJS Review* 9 (1984) 55-78.

47 H. Focillon, *The Year 1000* (New York: Harper & Row, 1971), but see Bernard McGinn, *Visions of the End: Apocalyptic Traditions in the Middle Ages* (New York: Columbia University Press, 1979) 88, 306 n.1. For general discussions of medieval millenarianism, see Norman Cohn, *The Pursuit of the Millennium* (3d ed.; New York: Oxford University Press, 1970); P.J. Alexander, *Religious and Political History and Thought in the Byzantine Empire* (London: Variorum, 1978); idem, *The Byzantine Apocalyptic Tradition* (Berkeley: University of California Press, 1985).

48 See Kraft, "Transmission" (above, n.24). Some recent studies of the Christian transmission of Jewish materials include David T. Runia, *Philo in Early Christian Literature: A Survey* (CRINT; Assen and Philadelphia: Van Gorcum and Fortress, 1993); James C. VanderKam, "1 Enoch in Early Christianity," (CRINT forthcoming).

49 E.g., Swete, *Introduction* 56.

50 On the treatment of such "nomina sacra" in the manuscript traditions, see Ludwig Traube, *Nomina Sacra: Versuch einer Geschichte der christlichen Kürzung* (Quellen und Untersuchungen zur lateinischen Philologie des Mittelalters 2; Munich: C.H. Beck, 1907), and A.H.R. Paap, *Nomina Sacra in the Greek Papyri of the First Five Centuries AD: The Sources and Some Deductions* (Papyrologica Lugduno-Batava 8; Leiden: Brill, 1959).

51 See Kraft, "Transmission" (above, n.24).

52 As claimed by M.R. James for one Latin recension of *5 Ezra*; see now also T. Bergren on *5 Ezra* (below n.64), and my own article "Towards Assessing the Latin Text of '5 Ezra', *Christians Among Jews and Gentiles: Essays in Honor of Krister Stendhal on his Sixty-fifth Birthday* (ed. G.W.E. Nickelsburg and G.W. MacRae; Philadelphia: Fortress, 1986) 158-69.

53 For literature discussing the *Testimonium Flavianum* (*Ant.* 18.63-64), see Josephus, *Jewish Antiquities, Books XVIII-XIX* (LCL; ed. L.H. Feldman; reprinted, Cambridge, MA: Harvard University Press, 1981) 419-21; Schürer, *History* 1.428-41; L.H. Feldman, *Josephus and Modern Scholarship 1937-1980* (Berlin: W. de Gruyter, 1984) 679-703; J.P. Meier, *A Marginal Jew: Rethinking the Historical Jesus* (2 vols.; New York: Doubleday, 1991-) 1.56-88; S. Pines, *An Arabic Version of the Testimonium Flavianum and its Implications* (Jerusalem: Israel Academy of Science and Humanities, 1971). Regarding Slavonic Josephus, see the references in Schürer, *History* 1.60-61; Meier, *Marginal Jew* 71-72 n.5.

54 See now the careful study by Runia, *Philo* (above n.48). There is an interesting phenomenon in the Philonic textual tradition in which one family of MSS contains a different text type for the Jewish scriptural quotations, but there is nothing overtly or identifiably "Christian" about the results (despite the conjecture of Katz to this effect) -- indeed, Barthélemy argues for a "Jewish" reviser; see Runia, *Philo* 24ff. for a succinct survey of the relevant literature and arguments, starting with Peter Katz, *Philo's Bible: The Aberrant Text of Bible Quotations in Some Philonic Writings and its Place in the Textual History of the Greek Bible* (Cambridge: Cambridge University Press, 1950).

55 Compare the Armenian version at *Paraleipomena Jeremiou* 9:14, and see

n.63 below.

56 See M.P. Brown, *The Authentic Writings of St. Ignatius* (Durham, NC: Duke University Press, 1963); W.R. Schoedel, *Ignatius of Antioch: A Commentary on the Letters of Ignatius of Antioch* (Philadelphia: Fortress, 1985) 3-7.

57 See R.A. Kraft, *Barnabas and The Didache* = volume 3 of *The Apostolic Fathers: A New Translation and Commentary* (ed. R.M. Grant; New York: Nelson, 1965) 58-59.

58 O. von Gebhardt, "Die Ascensio Isaiae als Heiligenlegende," *ZWT* 21 (1878) 330-53; see the updated description by M.A. Knibb, *OTP* 2.146.

59 A long form (represented by MT) and a shorter form (at Qumran and in OG). For discussion, see E. Tov, "The Literary History of the Book of Jeremiah in the Light of Its Textual History," *Empirical Models for Biblical Criticism* (ed. J.H. Tigay; Philadelphia: University of Pennsylvania Press, 1985) 211-37; and more recently idem, *Textual Criticism of the Hebrew Bible* (Minneapolis: Fortress, 1992) 319-27.

60 See A.A. Di Lella, *The Hebrew Text of Sirach: A Text-Critical and Historical Study* (The Hague: Mouton, 1966); P.W. Skehan and A.A. Di Lella, *The Wisdom of Ben Sira: A New Translation with Notes* (AB 39; New York: Doubleday, 1987) 51-62; Benjamin G. Wright, *No Small Difference: Sirach's Relationship to its Hebrew Parent Text* (SCS 26; Atlanta: Scholars Press, 1989), esp. 1.1.

61 See Kraft article noted above, n.9, and more recently E.P. Sanders, *OTP* 1.871-73.

62 See M.D. Johnson, *OTP* 2.249-51, with reference also to J.L. Sharpe, *Prolegomena to the Establishment of the Critical Text of the Greek Apocalypse of Moses* (Ph.D. dissertation, Duke University, 1969). Among related texts mentioned by Johnson are *Apocalypse of Moses, Life of Adam and Eve, Cave of Treasures, Combat of Adam and Eve, Testament of Adam,* and *Apocalypse of Adam* (p. 250). See also D.A. Bertrand, *La vie grecque d'Adam et Eve* (Paris: A. Maisonneuve, 1987); W. Lowndes Lipscomb, *The Armenian Apocryphal Adam Literature* (University of Pennsylvania Armenian Texts and Studies 8; Atlanta: Scholars Press, 1990); M.E. Stone, *A History of the Literature of Adam and Eve* (Atlanta: Scholars Press, 1993).

63 See E. Nestle, *Marginalien und Materialien* (Tübingen: J.J. Heckenhauer, 1893) 1-83; T. Schermann, *Prophetarum vitae fabulosae indices apostolorum discipulorumque Domini Dorotheo, Epiphanio, Hippolyto aliisque vindicate* (Leipzig: Teubner, 1907); idem, *Propheten- und Apostellegenden nebst Jüngerkatalogen des Dorotheus und verwandter Texte* (TU 31.3; Leipzig: J.C. Hinrichs, 1907); C.C. Torrey, *The Lives of the Prophets: Greek Text and Translation* (JBL Monograph Series 1; Philadelphia: Society of Biblical Literature, 1946); D.R.A. Hare, *OTP* 2.379-84.

64 The situation is summarized by S.E. Robinson, *OTP* 2.413-14, under the title "4 Baruch"(!) See also R.A. Kraft and A.-E. Purintun, *Paraleipomena Jeremiou* (Missoula: Society of Biblical Literature, 1972).

65 See now Theodore A. Bergren, *Fifth Ezra: The Text, Origin and Early History* (SCS 25; Atlanta: Scholars Press, 1990).

66 See also Sparks, *Apocryphal Old Testament* xiv-xv.

67 Irenaeus, *Adv. haer.* 1.20.1 (Marcosians); Eusebius, *Hist. eccl.* 3.25; Athanasius, *Festal Letter 39*; Epiphanius, *Panarion* 39.5.1 (Sethians); 40.2.1 (Archontics).
68 D.W. Suter, *Tradition and Composition in the Parables of Enoch* (Missoula: Scholars Press, 1979) 11-33; see also M. de Jonge on *T. 12 Patr.* (above n.2). Note M.R. James' suggestion (above n.52) that the more "Jewish" sounding text of *5 Ezra* might be due to Christian editorial excision of overtly "Christian" elements!

JEWISH PSEUDEPIGRAPHA
IN MUSLIM LITERATURE:
A BIBLIOGRAPHICAL AND
METHODOLOGICAL SKETCH

Steven M. Wasserstrom
Reed College

Introductory Observations[1]

> The fifth to the ninth centuries, far from being, as is often
> alleged, an era of intellectual sterility, were the heyday of
> midrashic literature. The same unruly but creative forces
> of the people which found an outlet in the sectarian
> religious quests also produced constant reformulation of
> the traditional teachings within the framework of orthodox
> Judaism.

Salo Baron thus dates "the heyday of midrashic literature" to a period
straddling the emergence of Islam as the dominant religious force
across the Nile-Oxus region.[2] *Pirke Rebbe Eliezer*, generally dated to
the eighth century, perhaps marks the immediate post-Islamic
culmination of this sustained period of aggadic redaction.[3] In addition
to midrashic collection, apocalypses also continued to be disseminated
during this period. The apocalyptic *Secrets of Shimon bar Yochai* was
written in response to the apparently terrifying ascent of the 'Abbāsid
Caliphate in the mid-eighth century.[4] More generally, the esoteric
traditions of the Gaonic period, especially *Sefer Hekhalot* (*3 Enoch*),

reflect an ongoing interpenetration of Jewish esoteric, apocalyptic, and midrashic traditions at that time.[5] Significantly, the aforementioned works are themselves pseudepigraphic compositions, respectively being attributed to Rebbe Eliezer, Shimon bar Yochai, and Enoch. The first observation to be made, then, is that the high period of midrash activity was one which overlapped the initial Islamic centuries, and which manifested a sustained interest in the pseudepigraphic conceit.

Recognizing that, like medieval *aggadah*, Islamic traditions also preserved motifs from ancient pseudepigrapha, the pioneer comparativists Grünbaum, Heller, and Ginzberg traced numerous motifs from Jewish pseudepigrapha in Muslim literatures.[6] Such a procedure was warranted by early Muslim sources themselves, which explicitly mentioned scriptures, scrolls (*ṣuḥuf*), and non-scriptual texts circulating widely in the first years of Islam, and which left traces in those sources.[7] More generally, the enormous collections of *ḥadīth*, *qiṣaṣ al-anbiyāʾ*, and related traditional anthologies, also contain such materials. Moreover, later literatures, such as *adab* collections, cosmological treatises, hermetic and alchemical texts, Sufi literature, and so-called "folktale" collections, like the *1001 Nights* (*Alf Laylah wa Laylah*), continued to draw from a narrative pool which was distributed throughout Islamicate lands, and which conserved ancient traditions wholesale.[8] Unfortunately, it is a truism to observe that these vast resources remain under-utilized for the purposes of *Religionsgeschichte*. But, fortunately, researchers on this subject do possess at least three modest advantages (not to speak of obvious disadvantages) over earlier students of Jewish and Muslim narrative. First, Jewish pseudepigrapha now have been collected, edited, translated, and -- still, to a much lesser extent -- analyzed.[9] Second, the manuscript discoveries of Qumran, Nag Hammadi, and the Cairo Geniza have provided new texts with which to help secure our comparisons.[10] And, third, work on *qiṣaṣ* and *Isrāʾīliyyāt* has progressed to the point where we can begin to speak about these Muslim narrative genres with more control that has been possible heretofore, especially for the researcher who does not control Arabic.[11]

Sectarian Survivals and Textual Transmission

Islamicate heresiographies, the so-called *Milal wa Niḥal* ("Religions and Sects") collections preeminently, described sects, Jewish, quasi-Jewish and otherwise, who had, by definition, interests in purveying their stories.[12] Despite the existence of this considerable body of evidence, and of other kinds of evidence, the study of Jewish sectarianism under Islam nevertheless largely has been neglected in recent years, with the notable exception of Karaite studies.[13] No consensus has been reached concerning the conjectured historical continuity of ancient Jewish sects flowing into early Islam. While for many years it was suggested that the community who authored the Dead Sea Scrolls may have (or their traditions may have) survived into early Islamic times, leaving traces in Qur'ān and other early Islamic texts, this survival has yet to be proven.[14] Likewise, the repeated suggestions and arguments made by Shlomo Pines and those following him have asserted an ongoing presence of "Jewish-Christians" known to Muslim authors till the tenth century, but this argument similarly awaits substantiation.[15]

On the other hand, a consensus holds firm concerning ancient sectarian manuscripts discovered during the early Islamic period. A remarkable story, retold many times, recounts the recovery of ancient Jewish manuscripts from a cave near Jericho around the year 800 CE.[16] It would seem that some found their way into Christian-Syriac collections, and others turned up in the Cairo Geniza. The medieval rediscovery of these texts moreover is said to have stimulated the development of early Karaism, and perhaps as well that of a sect known as the "Cave People" (Maghāriyya).[17] Furthermore, provocative arguments concerning the survival of these texts into Muslim traditions has been ventured, though usually without follow-up or development.[18]

It lies beyond the scope of the present inquiry to survey comprehensively the sectarian question. But it should be noted that arguments which assert the survival of Jewish pseudepigrapha conveyed by means of specified Jewish sectarians remain, for the moment, only answers to an obscurity by means of a deeper obscurity. This difficulty, of course, should not be taken as an impasse. Still, inasmuch as the manifold Jewish texts which come into Muslim letters cannot be attributed definitively to an identifiable group, it would constitute a fundamental if not fatal methodological error to assume that a given tradition originated in a particular group, unless internal evidence warrants such an identification.

Jewish Pseudepigrapha in Muslim Texts

A. *Isrā'īliyyāt*

Isrā'īliyyāt ("Israelite traditions") were the manifold and miscellaneous traditions which the early Muslim community received, through uncertain channels, from the *Banū Isrā'īl*, the Children of Israel. These largely aggadic, sometimes halakhic, and less frequently pseudepigraphic materials, could be branded as suspect and sometimes were proscribed outright.[19] But the prevalent form of canonical tradition in this regard was the frequently reported statement of the Prophet Muḥammad: "narrate [traditions] from the Children of Israel and there is nothing objectionable in that."[20] With this Prophetic permission, tradents who dealt with *Isrā'īliyyāt* could explicitly declare that such stories derived from foreign sources. Jewish and Christian scriptures thus were commonly cited as such, though almost always on an oral and not textual basis.[21] In fact, the two most popular tradents of *Isrā'īliyyāt* were Jewish converts, an identity that remained famous throughout later tradition.[22]

One could go farther, however, and note that the collection of extrabiblical traditions, if not explicitly, at least implicitly was encouraged by the very structural relation of the Islamic revelation to the Torah. That is, while the Qur'ān proclaimed its continuity with biblical prophecy, it rejected the extant text of the Torah in the possession of contemporaneous Jews. This conflict was resolved by the Qur'ānic accusation of the wilful corruption of ancient Holy Books (Qur'ān 2:75, 4:46, 5:13, 5:41). A fundamental principle for Muslim scholars dealing with biblical materials, this doctrine of corruption (*taḥrīf*) resolved every interreligious discrepancy in favor of the Muslim reading.[23] But proscribing the biblical text whose revelational status it affirmed problematically asserted an identity even as it negated its particularity. In a kind of compensation for such a double-bind, Muslim scholars were permitted to collect and recount extrabiblical tales of the ancient prophets. The result was that Abrahamic narratives, appropriated and properly Islamicized, eventually underwrote Islamicate world-history as such. The pre-Islamic (*jāhiliyya*) component of Ṭabarī's great history, for example, or the *Tales of the Prophets* (*qiṣaṣ al-anbiyā'*) collections, made edifying reading (or listening) for all levels of culture, but were much more. They presented a view of history which was almost unanimously accepted as the historical worldview of Islamicate civilization. This was a real history of the world.[24]

Muslims, in effect, piously altered previously Jewish traditions, just as they claimed that Jews impiously had done to the Torah. The fascinating irony of this intertextuality, finally, is that Jewish traditions thereby came to testify historically to the revelation of Islam, but only through the filter of what might be called Muslim *taḥrīf*, their pious fraud applied to *Isrā'īliyyāt*. By this means much Jewish pseudepigrapha could find its way into the imagination of Muslims.

B. Shī'ī Evidence: Wise Child's Alphabet

> Rabbi: Now little Jesus, the carpenter's son,
>   Let us see how Thy task is done;
>   Canst thou thy letters say?
> Jesus: *Aleph.*
> Rabbi: What next? Do not stop yet!
>   Go on with all the alphabet.
>   Come, *Aleph, Beth*; dost thou forget?
>   Cock's soul! Thou'dst rather play!
> Jesus: What *Aleph* means I fain would know
>   Before I any farther go!
>
> Longfellow, *The Golden Legend*

A prophet, as a young child, attends school for the first time. The teacher prompts him, *Say 'A'!* to which the child-prophet responds '*A*.'

The teacher then proceeds, *Say 'B'!* to which the wise child answers,
Tell me the meaning of A and I will tell you B! The dumbfounded
teacher faints. The child then recites the meaning of the entire
alphabet, with a mystical meaning attached to each letter. This story is
told of the Buddha,[25] of Jesus,[26] of the Shi'ite Fifth Imam,[27] of the
Jewish Ben Sira,[28] of the Sikh Guru Nanak,[29] and of the Bāb of the
Bahā'ī.[30] It is told of each of them in a form which is structurally
almost identical in each tradition. According to this discrete mytheme,
"The Wise Child's Alphabet," the prophet-child's knowledge exists *a
priori* to education.

     In the case of the Islamic use of the "Wise Child's Alphabet," it is
told in two distinct forms. The first version, very widely repeated, is
told of the child Jesus at school. This version is found in all *Isrā'īliyyāt*
collections, even the oldest known such collections.[31] It is frequently
repeated in Sunni and Shī'ī sources as well.[32] The second, unique,
instance is told about Muḥammad al-Bāqir, the Fifth Imam. In this
version, which comprises the frame-story for the extreme-Shī'ī (*ghulāt*)
gnostic apocalypse known as the *Umm al-Kitāb*, Muḥammad al-Bāqir
is the child at school: his wise child's response to the unsuspecting
teacher comprises a comprehensive review not only of the mystical
meaning of the alphabet, but of all things, which are revealed
subsequently and comprise the body of the book itself.[33]

     This proto-Shī'ī version of the Wise Child's Alphabet mytheme
may be traced with some accuracy, for we know that Jewish and
Christian legendary traditions were especially welcomed through proto-
Shī'ī channels, particularly in Iraq and specifically in Kūfa, in the
second and third Islamic centuries.[34] Rubin appears to be correct in his
observation that the "Shī'ī preoccupation with traditions which deal
with the prophets of *Banū Isrā'īl* as pre-figuring its own heroes dates
back to the earliest stages of its development. In fact, the Shī'a seems
to be responsible for the main flow of Judaeo-Christian motifs into the
Muslim literature already since the first century A.H."[35]

C. Apocalyptic

Perhaps the most richly represented genre of pseudepigrapha which survives in Muslim letters is that which falls under the rubric of *apocalyptic*. "Apocalyptic" comprises a revelational genre, primarily though not universally eschatological in orientation, which purports to reveal the secret workings of the cosmos in the form of a panoramic overview.[36] Jewish apocalyptic itself enjoyed a certain resurgence during the rise of Islam. Apocalypses were written which reacted (fairly explicitly and directly) to the perceived crisis posed by Islamization.[37] These apocalypses were sometimes expressed in the regnant Merkavah rhetoric, in the case of so-called "esoteric texts," but sometimes took a more exoteric, midrashic form.[38] Evidence continues to accumulate with respect to the transmission of these Jewish and other ancient apocalyptic traditions into early Islamic eschatological narratives.[39] For example, while the direct relation between both kinds of Jewish apocalypses and Muslim eschatological narratives (*malāḥim* and *fitan*) has not been determined with precision, a number of secondary filiations are possible to trace.[40]

Almost by definition, apocalyptic obviated designation of human authorship, instead claiming pseudepigraphic authorship (if any at all). In this sense, as well as in matters of content, it is akin to folklore, though this latter category must be used with care.[41] Research in this area thus must cautiously consider the overlapping apocalyptic contents of pseudepigrapha, folktales, and the *qiṣaṣ* literature. While it remains to account for this overlap in theoretical terms, in practical terms it suggests that attention must be paid to groupings of themes in the process of transmission.

One apocalyptic grouping of texts may be cited as an example of this internally coherent pluralism and complexity. The pseudo-Clementine writings, as epitomized in the *Apocalypse of Peter,* and the *Schatzhöhle* bear close textual filiations, and share some demonstrable survivals into early Islamic traditions.[42] For example, the *Kitāb al-Majāll* (*Book of Rolls*) treats the twin sisters of Adam and Eve, reflecting similar Mandaean, and ultimately Jewish, precursors. Those then find their way into early Shīʿī traditions.[43]

Examples of Jewish Pseudepigraphic Works in Muslim Sources

One of the earliest and most lastingly influential of the Jewish pseudepigrapha, the *Book of Jubilees*, has enjoyed considerable prestige in recent years due in part to its recognized importance among the Qumran scrolls.[44] But its effect may have extended after antiquity. Its apparent influence on early Shīʿī narratives has been argued by Rubin.[45] Certainly, its impact on the antediluvian traditions of al-Ṭabarī seems beyond dispute.[46]

A suggestive conjecture emerges from a recent study of the Jewish *Apocalypse of Baruch* undertaken by Fred Leemhuis. He argues that the Arabic version, whose Mt. Sinai version was published in 1986, was composed not by Christians but by a Muslim author.[47] But Adriana Drint has now refined this hypothesis.[48] Drint's work demonstrates the filiation between this work and so-called *Berlin Sprenger 30*, an anonymous, supposedly Nestorian chronicle which preserved ancient Jewish materials, and which independently sustained an impact on the development of chronography under Islam.[49]

Drint further argues that *Berlin Sprenger 30* was of Muslim and not Christian provenance, and demonstrates that it strikingly preserves a citation from 4 Ezra: "This fragment of IV Ezra [XIV 37-50] figures in the anonymous chronicle of Muslim origin in an enumeration of canonical and non-canonical biblical books of which a quotation is given!".[50] Importantly, 4 Ezra has been studied in its subsequent Muslim transformation by Hava Lazarus-Yafeh. She has shown that al-Thaʿlabī, among others, knew some version of this work. As she puts it, "Although there is no explicit evidence in Arabic literature prior to Ibn Ḥazm, we may assume that al-Thaʿlabī was familiar with such arguments, either directly from the Jewish-Christian material he studied in composing his book, or from other sectarian sources of information."[51]

Elsewhere I have dealt with the apparent Islamization of the *Apocalypse of Abraham* in the popular eleventh-century *Qiṣaṣ al-*

Anbiyā' of al-Thaʻlabī. I argue there that an interactive reading of narrative-cycles found in *Isrā'īliyyāt* and the Judeo-Arabic tales recovered from the Geniza illuminates the relationship between Jewish pseudepigrapha and such *Qiṣaṣ al-Anbiyā'* as that of Bulūqiyyā.[52]

Methodological Reflections

A. Field-theory Strategies

No amount of motif-gathering can prove conclusively that any particular Muslim collector knew any particular version of a pseudepigraph. The extent of atomization, on the one hand, and the paucity of critical editions, on the other, renders such a goal impossible to attain at the present state of scholarship. It would be unrealistic, in any case, to expect to find ancient texts transposed wholesale into Muslim guise.[53] The ancient pseudepigrapha were themselves eclectically composed, internally differentiated, being comprised of heterogeneous narrative elements. We therefore can not expect coherent narratives to turn up within a Muslim anthology: complete and unadulterated Jewish pseudepigrapha in the same form in which they survived in Christian hands will not be found in Muslim *Tales of the Prophets* (*Qiṣaṣ al-Anbiyā'*). A more realistic goal would be to search *Tales of the Prophets* for comparatively coherent tales -- subunits or mythemes -- deriving from Jewish pseudepigrapha.[54] To do so could help to avoid the notorious talleying of atomized "parallels." A properly reasonable research agenda, in particular, would be to identify patterns of transposition. If one is to succeed in such an endeavor, attention accordingly must be paid to psychological and sociological as well as literary constraints on narrative transformation.[55]

B. Myths, themes, and mythemes

In order to secure constants amid what seems a sea of textual variables, it is preferable, then, to trace narrative units, motifs, mythemes, and the like, as opposed to isolated names, discrete phrases, single images, or individual ideas. One example may suffice here. The so-called "combat myth" was widely distributed and deeply rooted in the ancient cultures absorbed by Islam.[56] The tales of the fallen angels, the origins of evil, and the eternal enmity to God was not only generally known, however. Indeed, many specific features familiar from pseudepigrapha survived. One particularly significant example of such survival is that of the "angel" Azāziel.[57]

C. Fields of texts

Traditional criticism of the *Isnād* (chain of transmitters), and especially the expansive biographical dictionaries which grew out of that traditional science, provide basic information concerning individual transmitters, and can thus help establish benchmarks in chronology.[58] But only formal analysis can confirm dates of transmission on the basis of internal criteria. The precise mention of a given "text" by name may tell us when that name was used, but it cannot guarantee the content of that text.

Accordingly, a complementary approach may be considered. Form criticism has been applied successfully to the study of the Hebrew Bible, rabbinic literature, and the New Testament. However, it has not been applied broadly or rigorously to the sources of early Islam as a religion. In particular, the form-critical techniques developed by Peter Schäfer for the study of Merkavah, Geniza, and magical texts would almost certainly provide helpful models for the Islamicate instance.[59] One finding of value from his work is that Jewish manuscripts

> do not recognize the existence of ... a 'corpus' or 'literature' any more than they recognize the existence of finished, finally redacted individual Hekhalot treatises. *Ma'aseh Merkavah* material shades off imperceptibly into *Ma'aseh Bere'shit*, into straightforward magic, into *Qabbalah* and into works of uncertain genre and diverse content such as Midrash *Ella Ezkerah* and the Alphabet of Aqiva.[60]

Keeping in mind this significant *caveat*, an example may be taken up which exemplifies this issue. For some time it has been noticed that comparable patterns are observable in the so-called "heavenly ascent" literatures, for example, between the Jewish Merkavah tradition and the *mir'āj* ascent literature.[61] Michael Sells has demonstrated that *Sefer Hekhalot* (*3 Enoch*) bears unmistakable affinity with early *mir'āj* texts, particularly that of Abū Yazīd al-Bisṭāmī.[62] Other evidence shows that early Muslim writers knew Jewish apocalyptic, esoteric, and Hekhalot texts. This is confirmed by the surprisingly widespread awareness of the Jewish angel Metatron, the superstar of *3 Enoch*, in an surprising variety of Muslim sources.[63] Finally, with regard to these esoteric traditions, David J. Halperin has demonstrated a number of powerfully argued Jewish-Muslim textual relations in a lengthy appendix to his magisterial study of the Hekhalot traditions, *Faces of the Chariot*.[64]

D. Tracing names: Melkizedek

One of the most difficult but nevertheless important areas of research concerns tracing "ideal figures": angels, prophets, divine potencies, and the like.[65]

Melkizedek, the ancient king mentioned in Genesis, gains a certain pride of place by virtue of his association with the figure of the Christ in the New Testament Epistle to the Hebrews.[66] Friedlaender showed how the pseudepigraphic traditions concerning Melkizedek eventuated in the legend of Khaḍir, the mysterious savior-figure mentioned in the Qur'ān.[67] Eventually, Melkizedek came into early Ismā'īlī traditions, but as three personages, Malik al-Salām, Malik Yazdāq, and Malik Shūlīm. Vajda has shown how Christian and Jewish pseudepigrapha provided the material support for this elaboration.[68]

E. Tracing figures: Norea, "Our Lady of the Light"

The fascinating transformations undergone by the "Near Eastern Maiden of Light" (*Lichtjungfrau*) may be traced briefly here.[69] Complex though well-grounded suggestions have been made which ultimately link the Gnostic savior-figure Norea with the ancient Near Eastern goddess Inanna/Ishtar/Venus.[70] Without reviewing the equally elaborate but similarly persuasive arguments for an additional Jewish background for this goddess, suffice it to say she was known in

Gnostic texts under many (closely related) names; was seen variously as the daughter of Adam and Eve, the wife-sister of Seth, and the wife of Noah or Shem; and played a role of indisputable importance in the myth itself.[71] Exemplified by her role in the combat myth of the fallen angels, the *Lichtjungfrau* operated at the interstices between gnosticism and the Abrahamic traditions. In addition to her complex and exalted role in Gnostic myth, Norea somehow entered Muslim traditions as well, as Doresse recognized.[72] Study of early Shī'ī traditions, which are especially rich in motifs form the pseudepigrapha, has clarified this reception.[73]

As was typical with many of the materials under discussion here, it seems that Norea moved full-circle back into Jewish traditions. Joseph Dan has observed that the "Daughter of Light" (בת האור) in the *Sefer ha-Bahir* may be related to the figure of Norea.[74] While Scholem had long argued for the specifically Gnostic antecedents to this figure, Dan's additional insight constitutes a helpful advance. Again, it may be that the Islamic materials, little utilized by Scholem or Dan, now further may fill in some remaining gaps in the picture. The close association of the *Sefer ha-Bahir* with the Persian-language gnostic-Muslim *Umm al-Kitāb* provides these additional connections.[75] The first of these is that the "daughter of light" figure in *Sefer ha-Bahir* has been shown to be closely related to the Maiden of Light in the apocryphal *Acts of Thomas*.[76] Independently, Albright noticed that what he called the "Goddess of life and wisdom" evenuated in the "daughter of light" in the *Acts of Thomas*.[77] Moreover, this figure, and other material from the apocrypha, seems to be reflected in the apotheosis of Fatima so vividly depicted in the *Umm al-Kitāb*.[78] Fatima eventually became known as *al-Zahra*, the Radiant One, a title which associated her explicitly with light as well as with the planet Venus.[79]

One of the most suggestive clues concerning the survival of this goddess was offered by Segelberg, who points to a extant shrine in Beirut dedicated to "Our Lady of the Light."[80] In short, when one considers present interest in "goddess spirituality," and when one considers the apparently sustained survival of the "Lady of Light" goddess complex within the Abrahamic traditions, it seems warranted to suggest that a full study of this figure, from Ishtar to the present shrine in Beirut, surely is a scholarly (not to speak of popular) desideratum. For purposes at hand, it is enough to note that the intermediary role played by Jewish pseudepigrapha in Muslim traditions provided an important link in this survival.

Conclusions: On Conceptualization

It is unlikely that Jewish pseudepigrapha deriving from the Second Temple period were directly reclothed in Muslim garb. What we do know without question is that Christian Arabic and Syriac versions of most of the Jewish pseudepigrapha were transmitted throughout this period.[81] One implication of this fact, obviously, is that the question of Christian intermediation must always be kept in mind. Rarely if ever will it be certain that an ancient Jewish pseudepigraph was taken over into Muslim narrative without such Christian intermediation. The intermediation of Christian Arabic texts therefore should be reviewed systematically.[82] Similarly, the geographical intermediation of Arabic texts on the road to Eastern and Western Europe must also be studied more closely.[83]

Locating traditions in time and space is an intellectual operation mandatorily undertaken by the historian of religions. But pressing the prestige of the *a priori* distorts this inquiry -- and such Orientalist preoccupation with the Abrahamic antecedents of Islamic tradition unsurprisingly has offended many Muslims. The procedure of "tracing," after all, implies a desired trajectory backward to some presumptive origin. But this preference for the prior obviates the adequacy of reception, the lived response, the critical novelty of intentional reappropriation. Islam is neither a "borrowing" nor the product of "influence." Rather, the manifold Muslim uses of Judaism comprised languages stating at least one thing in common: *There is no god but God and Muhammad is the Messenger of God. Isrā'īliyyāt* represents a significantly self-conscious and self-referential expression of this unanimous intent. In the case of *Isrā'īliyyāt*, a new religion overcomes its "anxiety of influence" by recreating its own sacred histories. This rewritten salvation-history, without question, draws from Jewish pseudepigrapha, as well as countless other literatures. But it is nonetheless created by a distinctively new personality, and therefore cannot usefully be reduced to "the derivative." And so it follows that we must treat a new religion as a new adult and not reductively as a product of its parents. The history of religions can no longer be content to merely point to the family background of a new religion as "sufficient explanation" of that new religion. But, rather, through detailed historical analysis, we should elucidate the dynamics by which religions incorporate, idealize, repress, deny, and otherwise remake their inheritance, as that inheritance is recreated into the adult personality of the new religion.

Finally, it makes no sense to talk about new representation of older materials without simultaneously showing that that new re-reading is reciprocally returned to the chronologically prior tradition. I have tried to make this point in tracing the dialectic of *Isrā'īliyyāt*. It is necessary to critique the quest for priority, the incessant "tracing" of motifs to earlier "sources," without a countervailing recognition of the interactive character of such inter-hermeneutic encounters. Reception-Criticism provides some tools for understanding the means by which subsequent readers receive earlier traditions.[84] One is encouraged by recent arguments to the effect that active reading of "biblical" or "extrabiblical" narratives by Muslims was an exercise which reflexively illuminates those "original" sources.[85] David J. Halperin, most directly, has argued that Muslim tradents tended to make manifest what had been typically left latent in the Jewish version which they received.[86]

As Goitein and others have shown, there was no unidirectional flow of influences into formative Islam. There was, rather, a synergy, a two-way-street: certainly in the case of Judaism, we know that it was altered, root and branch, in its growth in the soil of Islamicate civilisations. In one of his last published statements, Goitein began his remarks with these unequivocal observations: "Every aspect of what we regard today as Judaism -- the synagogue service and prayer book, law and ritual, theology and ethics, the text of the Bible, the grammar and vocabulary of the Hebrew language -- was consolidated, formulated and canonized in [the first centuries of Islamicate civilization]."[87] At the least, this common development of Judaism and Islam in the first centuries of Islamicate civilization provides historians of religions with another instance of the positive synergy between religious traditions. With W.C. Smith I would ask, "Shall we not say that once again the history of one tradition is in part a function of the history of another?"[88]

Appendix: Azazel/Azāziel

The literature of Azazel and the fallen angels in Judaism is too vast to treat adequately here. Still useful is Bernard J. Bamberger, *Fallen Angels* (Philadelphia: Jewish Publication Society, 1952); J.T. Milik, *The Books of Enoch: Aramaic Fragments from Qumrân Cave 4* (Oxford: Clarendon, 1976) 330 n.3; and especially Gedaliahu G. Stroumsa, *Another Seed: Studies in Gnostic Mythology* (Leiden: Brill, 1984). For the sectarian antiquity of the transformation of Azazel into a chief antagonist, see Sidney Hoenig, "The New Qumran Pesher on Azazel" *JQR* 56 (1966) 248-53 (his conclusions may be ignored safely), and now Devorah Dimant, "The Pesher on the Periods" (4Q180 and 4Q181)," *IOS* 9 (1979) 77-103.

The Mandaean tradition may be important, as with so much of the present discussion. This point was already noted in 1904 in the article on "Azazel" in the *Jewish Encyclopedia*. In the Mandaean tradition, Azazael and Azaziel were two of the four angels of the West: H. Halm, "Buch der Schatten II," *Der Islam* 98 (1981) 52. Halm and Tijdens observe a similarity between the Mandaean Joshamin and the Azāziel of *Umm al-Kitāb*. Joshamin was a Mandaean demiurge; like Abatur, a fallen Being of Light: see K. Rudolph, *Die Mandäer* (2 vols.; Göttingen: Vandenhoeck & Ruprecht, 1960-61) 1.81 n.4; idem, *Theogonie, Kosmogonie und Anthropogonie in den mandäischen Schriften* (Göttingen: Vandenhoeck & Ruprecht, 1965) 103ff., esp. 119ff. (I owe these last references to Jarl E. Fossum, *The Name of God and the Angel of the Lord* [Tübingen: Mohr, 1985] 318 n.162). Finally,

Azāziel is found in the incantation bowls, some of which were written by or for Mandaeans: C.D. Isbell, *Corpus of the Aramaic Incantation Bowls* (Missoula, MT: Scholars Press, 1975) 68; E.A.W. Budge, *Amulets and Superstitions* (London, 1930; reprinted, New York: Dover, 1978) 278. An Aramaic incantation bowl links "Aza'el" with Metatron: C.H. Gordon, *AfO* 6 (1934) 328-30 (glossed in Milik, *Books of Enoch* 129). For other Mandaean usages, see W. Fauth, "Ṭaṭrosjah-Ṭoṭrosjah und Meṭaṭron in der jüdischen Merkabah-Mystik," *JSJ* 22 (1991) 40-87, at p. 52 (citing *Ginza*).

Fundamental to the early medieval transformations, especially as they come into Islamic garb, is the *Midrash Abkir*. See B. Heller, "La chute des anges: Schemhazai, Ouzza et Azaël," *REJ* 60 (1910) 202-12. The modes by which the *aggadah* of Azazel was taken up by Muslim *quṣṣāṣ* is not yet adequately explicated. Azāzīl is found quite early as the transformation of Iblīs. See Jonas Ansbacher, *Die Abschnitte über die Geister und wunderbaren Geschöpfe aus Qazwinī's Kosmographie* (Kirchhaim N.-L.: Buchdruckerei von M. Schmersow, 1905) 8; Sibṭ ibn al-Jauzī, *Mirāt al-Zamān fī Ta'rīkh al-Imān* (ed. Iḥsān 'Abbās; Beirut, Cairo, London, 1985/1405) 130; the *Rasā'il Ikhwān al-Ṣafā'*, most recently treated in *Mensch und Tier vor dem König der Dschinnen* (trans. Alma Giese; Hamburg: F. Meiner, 1990) 32-39; M. Grünbaum, *Neue Beiträge zur semitischen Sagenkunde* (Leiden: Brill, 1893) 261, from Ṭabarī; and Toufy Fahd, *Génies, anges et démons* (Paris: Sevil, 1971) 204 n.69, from Dāmirī.

The role of Azāzīl in early cosmological *tafsīr* has also been reviewed recently by M.J. Kister, "Legends in *tafsīr* and *ḥadīth* Literature: The Creation of Adam and Related Stories," *Approaches to the History of the Interpretation of the Qur'ān* (ed. A. Rippin; Oxford: Oxford University Press, 1988) 82-114, esp. pp. 90-91. He was eventually a figure of some importance in the Sufi tradition: Jalāl al-Dīn Rūmī, *The Mathnawī* (trans. R.A. Nicholson; 8 vols.; London: Luzac, 1925-40) s.v. "Azazil"; Hujwiri, *Kashf al-Mahjūb* (trans. R.A. Nicholson; Leiden: Brill, 1911) 412: "I myself was once 'Azāzil and am now Iblīs ..."; Louis Massignon, *The Passion of Al-Hallāj* (4 vols.; Princeton: Princeton University Press, 1982) 3.308-15, esp. pp. 313-14, on Azāzīl's states of consciousness according to al-Hallāj; Abū Bakr al-Razī (following Ṭabarī and Anṣārī), cited in L. Bogdanov, "The Idea of Man and Knowledge in the Conception of Persian Mystics," *BSO(A)S* 6 (1930) 151-77, at pp. 164-71 (who mistakenly has "Azrael"). These states of consciousness became a central feature of the Sufi theodicy: see Peter Awn, *Satan's Tragedy and Redemption: Iblis in Sufi Psychology* (Leiden: Brill, 1983). See also Henry Corbin, "From the Gnosis of Antiquity to Ismaili Gnosis," in his *Cyclical Time and Ismaili Gnosis* (London: Kegan Paul, 1983) 151-93, at pp. 170-73.

Eventually, some Jews of the East reappropriated the figure of Azāzīl as found in Muslim sources. See now Amnon Netzer, "The Story of Adam in the *Bereshit-Namah* of Shahin," *Proceedings of the First European Conference of Iranian Studies, Part 2: Middle and New Iranian Studies* (ed. G. Gnoli and A. Panaino; Rome: Istituto italiano per il medio ed estremo oriente, 1990) 497-509, at pp. 499-502.

---

[1] Inasmuch as the intended audience for the present volume is not restricted to Islamicists and Judeo-Arabists, in the following I shall concentrate on translations available in English and European languages whenever possible. Also, the foregoing study is subtitled "a sketch" on the basis of a sanguine conviction that we are not yet equipped *systematically* to survey this research area.

[2] *A Social and Religious History of the Jews* (18 vols.; 2d ed.; New York, London, and Philadelphia: Columbia University Press and Jewish Publication Society, 1952-83) 6.154-55.

[3] Gerald Friedlander, the translator of *Pirqe Rabbi Eliezer* (*Pirke de Rabbi Eliezer* [London, 1916; reprinted, New York: Sepher-Hermon, 1981]), provides an extensive cross-referencing of pseudepigrapha with his "P.R.E. and the Pseudepigrapha and Apocrypha," pp. xxi-liii. For an up-to-date and annotated bibliography on this important resource, see now H.L. Strack and G. Stemberger, *Introduction to the Talmud and Midrash* (trans. Markus Bockmuehl; Minneapolis: Fortress, 1992) 356-58.

[4] Studied by Bernard Lewis, "An Apocalyptic Vision of Islamic History," *BSOAS* 13 (1950) 308-38, and again by Michael Cook and Patricia Crone, *Hagarism: The Making of the Islamic World* (Cambridge: Cambridge University Press, 1977) 4-5, 35-37.

[5] P.S. Alexander has translated it with an extensive apparatus in *OTP* 1.223-317.

[6] Max Grünbaum, *Neue Beiträge zur semitischen Sagenkunde* (Leiden: Brill, 1893) and *Gesammelte Aufsätze zur Sprach- und Sagenkunde* (Berlin: S.

Calvary & Co., 1901); Louis Ginzberg, *The Legends of the Jews* (7 vols.; Philadelphia: Jewish Publication Society, 1909-38); and Bernhard Heller, "Ginzberg's *Legends of the Jews*," *JQR* 24 (1933-34) 51-66, 165-90, 281-307, 393-418; 25 (1934-35) 29-52; idem, "La légende biblique dans l'Islam," *REJ* 98 (1934) 1-18; idem, "Récits et personnages bibliques dans la légend mahometane," *REJ* 85 (1927) 113-36.

[7] Joseph Sadan, "Some Literary Problems Concerning Judaism and Jewry in Medieval Arabic Sources," *Studies in Islamic History and Civilization in Honour of Professor David Ayalon* (Leiden and Jerusalem: E.J. Brill, 1986) 353-98; R.G. Khoury, "Quelques réflexions sur la première ou les premières bibles arabes," *L'arabie préislamique et son environment historique et culturel* (ed. T. Fahd; Leiden: E.J. Brill, 1989) 549-61. On the question of the orality versus textuality of transmission, see A. L. de Premare, "Comme il est écrit, l'histoire d'un texte," *Studia Islamica* 70 (1989) 27-56.

[8] Haim Schwarzbaum, *Biblical and Extra-Biblical Legends in Islamic Folk Literature* (Waldorf-Hessen: Verlag für Orientkunde Dr. H. Vorndran, 1982), esp. pp. 50-75 ["Islamic Legends of the Prophets (i.e. the so-called 'Qiṣaṣ al-Anbiyā')"].

[9] *OTP* is the landmark effort in this regard. The editor of *OTP*, J.H. Charlesworth (assisted by P. Dykers and M.J.H. Charlesworth), has also produced a helpful companion, *The Pseudepigrapha and Modern Research: With a Supplement* (Chico, CA: Scholars Press, 1981).

[10] To cite just one example: the study of Merkavah mysticism, the most mysterious "Major Trend" in Jewish Mysticism (in the terms established by Scholem in his classic *Major Trends in Jewish Mysticism*), has been fundamentally re-evaluated by reference to materials discovered in all three locations. For Qumran, see C. Newsom, "Merkabah Exegesis in the Qumran Sabbath Shirot," *JJS* 38 (1987) 11-30; J. Strugnell and D. Dimant, "The Merkabah Vision in *Second Ezekiel* (4Q385 4)," *RevQ* 44 (1990) 331-47; and Joseph M. Baumgarten, "The Qumran Sabbath Shirot and Rabbinic Merkabah Traditions," *RevQ* 49-52 (1988) 199-213. For Nag Hammadi, see P.S. Alexander, "Comparing Merkavah Mysticism and Gnosticism: An Essay in Method," *JJS* 35 (1984) 1-18. And for the Geniza, see now Peter Schäfer's *Synopse zur Hekhalot-Literatur* (Tübingen: Mohr, 1981), based on Geniza texts. A major classic of this literature, *3 Enoch/Sefer Hekhalot*, is included in *OTP* (1.223-317).

[11] Since the earlier work done by I. Goldziher, "Isrā'īliyyāt," *REJ* 44 (1902) 63-66, and S.D. Goitein, "Isrā'īliyyāt," *Tarbiz* 6 (1935) 89-101, 510-22 (Hebrew), more recent overviews have been written by M.J. Kister, "*Haddithū 'an banī isrā'īla wa-lā haraja*," *IOS* 2 (1972) 215-39, and Gordon D. Newby, "Tafsīr Isrā'īliyyāt," *JAAR* [Thematic Issue S] (1980) 685-97. As for *qiṣaṣ*, English language versions have become available through the following: Wheeler Thackston, *Tales of the Prophets of al-Kisā'ī* (Boston: Twayne Publishers, 1978), and the first four volumes of the monumental SUNY translation of al-Ṭabarī's history. See *The History of al-Ṭabarī: Volume I. General Introduction and From the Creation to the Flood* (trans. Franz Rosenthal; Albany: State University of New York Press, 1989); *Volume II. Prophets and Patriarchs*

(trans. William M. Brinner; Albany: SUNY Press, 1987); *Volume III. The Children of Israel* (trans. William M. Brinner; Albany: SUNY Press, 1991); and *Volume IV. The Ancient Kingdoms* (trans. Moshe Perlmann; Albany: SUNY Press, 1987). Perhaps the richest resource yet will be the forthcoming translation of the *Qiṣaṣ al-anbiyā'* of al-Thaʻlabī by William M. Brinner.

12 Shahrastānī, Ibn Ḥazm, and Bīrūnī are by far the most valuable sources, but many others exist. The erudite collections of Maqdisī (*Kitāb al-Bad' wal-Ta'rīkh*) and Ibn al-Nadīm (*Fihrist*), for example, provide additional information. See I. Goldziher's review of Baghdādī's *Farq* in *ZDMG* 65 (1911) 349-63; H. Laoust, "La classification des sectes dans l'hérésiographie ash'arite," *Arabic and Islamic Studies in Honor of H.A.R. Gibb* (ed. G. Makdisi; Cambridge, MA: Harvard University Press, 1965) 377-86; idem, "L'hérésiographie musulmane sous les Abbassides," *Cahiers de civilisation médiévale* 10 (1967) 157-78; F.E. Peters, *Aristotle and the Arabs* (New York: New York University Press, 1968), esp. pp. 244-46; H. Ritter, "Muhammadanische Häresiographien," *Der Islam* 18 (1929) 34-59; R. Strothmann, "On the History of Islamic Heresiography," *Islamic Culture* 12 (1938) 5-16; J. Waardenburg, "Jugements musulmans sur les religions non-islamiques à l'époque médiévale," *La signification du Bas Moyen Age dans l'histoire et la culture du monde musulman: Actes du 8me congrès de l'Union Européenne des arabisants et islamisants* (Aix-en-Provence: Edisud, 1978) 323-41.

13 The question of the origins of Karaism and sectarianism has also been recently reviewed in Haggai Ben-Shammai, "Between Ananites and Karaites: Observations on Early Medieval Jewish Sectarianism," *Studies in Muslim-Jewish Relations* 1 (1993) 19-31. The long-standing theory that the Qumran sectaries (or their literary remains) somehow survived to influence nascent Karaism was most fully argued by N. Wieder, *The Judaean Scrolls and Karaism* (London: East and West Library, 1962). The question was reconsidered in B. Dupuy, "Les karaïtes sont-ils descendents des esséniens?" *Istina* 29 (1984) 139-51.

14 For a recent return to this once popular theory, see Yoram Erder, "The Origin of the Name Idrīs in the Qur'ān: A Study of the Influence of Qumran Literature on Early Islam," *JNES* 49 (1990) 339-51. I have reviewed the question of Jewish sectarianism more generally in "Who Were the Jewish Sectarians under Early Islam?" *Jewish Sects, Religious Movements and Political Parties* (ed. Menahem Mor; Omaha: Creighton University Press, 1992) 101-113.

15 Steven M. Wasserstrom, "Jewish Pluralism in the Geonic Period: The Case of the 'Jewish-Christians,' *Journal of the American Society of Rabbis in Academia* 1 (1991) 75-81.

16 The letter of Bishop Timotheos which describes the find was published and translated by O. Braun, "Ein Brief des Katholikos Timotheos I über biblische Studien des 9 Jahrhunderts," *OrChr* 1 (1901) 299-313. The relevant passage was translated into English by A.A. Di Lella, "Qumran and the Geniza Fragments of Sirach," *CBQ* 24 (1962) 245-67, at pp. 247-48.

17 For ostensible influence on Karaism, see n.13 above. This theory was popularized by Paul Kahle, *The Cairo Geniza* (2d ed.; Oxford: Basil Blackwell, 1959), esp. pp. 17-28. For a comprehensive review of the "Cave People," see Jarl Fossum, "The Magharians: A Pre-Christian Jewish Sect and its Significance for

the Study of Gnosticism and Christianity," *Henoch* 9 (1987) 303-44. In addition to the Hebrew Book of Ben Sira, it is generally believed that, among others, the following texts relevant to the present discussion were recovered at that time: The *Damascus Document*; The Aramaic *Testament of Levi*; and the apocryphal Syriac Psalms, most notably Psalm 151. The literature on the survivals of these ancient texts in the Cairo Geniza is reviewed in Johann Maier, "Bedeutung und Erforschung der kairoer 'Geniza'," *JAC* 13 (1970) 48-61, at pp. 53-54 ["Frühjüdische ausserbiblische Literatur"]. Di Lella compared the Qumran and Geniza fragments of Sirach, and explained their filiation on the basis of the eighth-century discovery.

[18] Perhaps the most fully developed such theory is that which concerns the apocryphal Psalms discovered in Cave 11. It is widely accepted that the five apocryphal Psalms were rediscovered at that time: John Strugnell, "Notes on the Text and Transmission of the Apocryphal Ps. 151, 154 (= SYR II) and 155 (= SYR III)," *HTR* 59 (1966) 257-81, at p. 258; M.M. Goshen-Gottstein, "The Psalms Scroll (11QPs^a)," *Textus* 5 (1966) 22-33, at p. 32 n.45; Sebastian Brock, "Jewish Traditions in Syriac Sources," *JJS* 30 (1979) 223-24: "These were almost certainly translated in the late eighth century, as the result of a discovery ...." Specifically relevant to the purposes at hand, these Psalms are also said to have influenced Muslim traditions, starting with the Qur'ān. Special attention in this regard has been paid to the allegedly "Orphic" image of King David which has been traced through this channel of transmission: M. Philonenko, "Une tradition essénienne dans le Coran," *RHR* 170 (1966) 143-57; A. Dupont-Sommer, *Le mythe d'Orphée aux animaux et ses prolongements dan le judaisme, le christianisme et l'islam* (Problemi attuali di scienza e di cultura quaderno n. 214; Roma: Accademia nazionale dei Lincei, 1975); R. Stehly, "David dans la tradition islamique à la lumière des manuscrits de Qumran," *RHPR* 59 (1979) [= *Mélanges Edmond Jacob*] 357-67. More generally, influences from Qumran have been argued on other aspects of Muslim tradition. See for example H. Nibley, "Qumran and the 'Companions of the Cave'," *RevQ* 5 (1965) 177-98; E.F.F. Bishop, "The Qumran Scrolls and the Qur'ān," *The Muslim World* 48 (1958) 223-36; idem, "Qumran and the Preserved Tablet(s)," *RevQ* 5 (1965) 253-56; and Chaim Rabin, *Qumran Studies* (Oxford: Oxford University Press, 1957) 112-30.

[19] See above n.3. See also S.D. Goitein, "Isrā'īliyyāt," *EI*^{2}. Muḥammad ibn Muḥammad Abū Shuḥbah, *al-Isrā'īliyyāt wa al-mawḍū'āt fi kutub al-tafsīr* (Cairo, 1393/1973) provides an extensive treatment of these materials in the *tafsīr* literature.

[20] See Kister (cited in n.11 above).

[21] R.G. Khoury, "Quelques réflexions sur les citations de la Bible dans les premières générations islamicques du premier et du deuxième siècles de l'Hégire," *Bulletin d'études orientales* 29 (1977) 269-78 [= *Mélanges H. Laoust*]. And see Hava Lazarus-Yafeh, *Intertwined Worlds: Medieval Islam and Bible Criticism* (Princeton: Princeton University Press, 1992): "... exact literal Biblical quotations are extremely rare [and so one makes] the assumption of oral tradition ..." (pp. 112, 114).

[22] For Wahb ibn Munnabih, see Nabia Abbott, "Wahb b. Munabbih: A Review

Article," *JNES* 36 (1977) 103-112, and "The Beginnings of Historical Folklore: Wahb ibn Munabbih," in A.A. Duri, *The Rise of Historical Writing Among the Arabs* (trans. Lawrence I. Conrad; Princeton: Princeton University Press, 1983) 122-36. For Kaʿb al-Aḥbār, see Jacob Mann, "An Early Theological-Polemical Work," *HUCA* 12 (1937) 411-59 (reprinted in *The Collected Articles of Jacob Mann* [3 vols.; Jerusalem: Gedera, 1971] 3.1-49); Bernard Chapira, "Légendes bibliques attribués à Kaʿb el-Aḥbār," *REJ* 69 (1919) 86-108; Moshe Perlmann, "A Legendary Story of Kaʿb al-Aḥbār's Conversion to Islam," *Joshua Starr Memorial Volume* (New York: Conference on Jewish Relations, 1953) 85-99; idem, "Another Kaʿb al-Aḥbār Story," *JQR* 14 (1954) 48-58.

23 Moshe Perlmann, "Medieval Polemics Between Islam and Judaism," *Religion in a Religious Age* (ed. S.D. Goitein; Cambridge, MA: Association for Jewish Studies, 1974) 103-139. For more see now Lazarus-Yafeh, *Intertwined Worlds*, esp. pp. 26-29, 58-72.

24 See Duri, cited in n.22 above.

25 For the Buddha's *Schulanekdote* and its relation to the apocryphal Infancy Gospels, see Arthur Lillie, *The Popular Life of the Buddha* (London: K. Paul, Trench & Co., 1883) 30; Archibald Scott, *Buddhism and Christianity* (Edinburgh: David Douglas, 1890) 162-64, on the *Lalita Vistara* and Christianity; E. Kuhn, "Buddhistisches in den apokryphen Evangelien," in *Gurupujakaumudi: Festgabe ... Albrecht Weber* (Leipzig: Harrassowitz, 1895) 116-19; G. Buhler, *On the Origin of the Indian Brahma Alphabet* (Strassburg: K.J. Trübner, 1898) 29; Louis Gray, "Some Indian Parallels to the Apocryphal New Testament," *JAOS* 22 (1901) 398-440; Albert J. Edmunds, *Buddhist and Christian Gospels, Now First Compared from the Originals* (2 vols.; Philadelphia: Innes and Sons, 1908-09) 2.243-44; Walter Bauer, *Das Leben Jesu* (Tübingen: J.C.B. Mohr, 1909) 96-97; Richard Garbe, *Indien und das Christentum* (Tübingen: Mohr, 1914) 70-80; J. Kennedy, "The Gospels of the Infancy, the Lalita Vistara and the Vishnu Purana: On the Transmission of Religious Legends Between India and the West," *JRAS* (1917) 209-43, 469-540, esp. pp. 520-23. For the carved depictions of the Buddhist *Schulanekdote*, see N.J. Krom, *The Life of Buddha on the Stupa of Barabudur according to the Lalitavistara Text* (The Hague: M. Nijhoff, 1926) 44; A. Foucher, *The Life of the Buddha* (trans. S.B. Boas; Middletown, CT: Wesleyan University Press, 1963) 55-56. S. Radhakrishnan provides yet more literature on this once "hot" topic in his *Eastern Religions and Western Thought* (Oxford, 1939; reprinted, New York: Oxford University Press, 1959) 185 n.1. One scholar who actively continues to pursue these parallels is J. Duncan M. Derrett. See his "A Moses-Buddha Parallel and its Meaning," *ArOr* 58 (1990) 310-17. The textual question is reviewed in Norbert Klatt, *Literarische Beiträge zum Problem christlich-buddhistischer Parallelen* (Köln: Brill, 1982), and in Zacharias Thundy, *Buddha and Christ* (Leiden: Brill, 1993). For a thoroughgoing critique of the theory and method involved in seeking such "parallels," see Jonathan Z. Smith, *Drudgery Divine: On the Comparisons of Early Christianities and the Religions of Late Antiquity* (Chicago: University of Chicago Press, 1990).

26 Henry Sike is credited with the first edition and translation of the apocryphal Infancy Gospels, that of Cambridge, 1697. For other early texts and translations,

see J.C. Thilo, *Codex Apocryphus Novi Testamenti* (Leipzig: F.C.G. Vogel, 1832), esp. pp. 122-23, and *The Apocryphal New Testament* (trans. William Hone; London: W. Hone, 1820) 38, for more on the early literature. Most recently, a range of versions of the "Alpha-Beta Logion" were compared by Stephen Gero in his work on the "Infancy Gospel of Thomas," *NT* 13 (1971) 46-80, at pp. 71-73. See esp. p. 72: "One is immediately struck by the fact that the core of the saying itself has been transmitted in a remarkably constant form ...." The range of texts is translated and thoroughly annotated in Paul Peeters, *Evangiles apocryphes* (2 vols.; Paris: A. Picard, 1911-14) 2.58-62, 208-13, 302-305. The Muslim Arabic (as distinct from Christian Arabic sources, such as the Arabic Infancy Gospel) sources on this mytheme are likewise vast. For a few of these, which do not vary substantially in form (e.g. the teacher in some is called *mu'addib*, and in other *mu'allim*), see Kulaini, *Al-Kāfī*, vol. VI p. 192; Majlisī, *Bihār al-Anwār*, vol. 14 p. 286; Abū Nu'aim, *Hilyāt al-Awliyā' wa Tabaqāt al-Asfiyā'* vol. VII pp. 251-52; *Les légendes prophetiques dans l'Islam depuis le Ier jusqu'au IIIe siècle de l'hégire* (ed. R.G. Khoury; Wiesbaden: Harrassowitz, 1978) 324-25 (text); Tha'labī, *Qisas al-Anbiyā'* (Cairo, A.H. 1347) 270; and the important translation and richly annotated text of *Futūh al-Bahnasa* by Emile Galtier (*Memoires publiés par les membres de l'Institut Francaise d'Archeologie orientale du Caire* 22 [1909] 17-19). The only major difference in these versions is the contents of the meaning of each letter of the mystical alphabet revealed by the child Jesus.

27 As found in the *Umm al-Kitāb*: First annotated by Ivanow in "Notes sur l'«Ummu'l-Kitāb» des Ismaëliens de l'Asie centrale," *Revue des études islamiques* 6 (1932) 419-81, esp. p. 438; idem, "[Text of *Umm al-Kitāb*]," *Der Islam* 23 (1936) 1-132; see also the annotated Italian translation by Pio Filippani-Ronconi, *Ummu'l-Kitâb, Introduzione, traduzione e note* (Naples: Istituto universitario orientale di Napoli, 1966) and the abridged German translation by Heinz Halm, *Die islamische Gnosis* (Zürich and München: Artemis Verlag, 1982) 113-99, esp. 128-32, "Baqir deutet das Alphabet"; the fullest commentary is that of E.F. Tijdens, *Der mythologisch-gnostische Hintergrund des Umm al-Kitāb* (Acta Iranica VII; Leiden: Brill, 1977), esp. pp. 276-99.

28 See now the exhaustive *The Tales of Ben Sira in the Middle Ages* by Eli Yassif (Jerusalem: Magnes, 1984) [Hebrew], which surveys all the primary and secondary literature. In English, his "Pseudo Ben Sira and the 'Wisdom Questions' Tradition in the Middle Ages," *Journal of Folklore Studies* 23 (1982) 48-63 is relevant to the present discussion. On the relation of *The Alphabet of Ben Sira* to the Infancy Gospels, see M. Steinschneider, *JQR* o.s. 7 (1900) 482-83. On its relation to the Indian Arabic fable literature, see Bernhard Heller, *JQR* 24 (1933-34) 413. On its influence on the Latin-French "L'Enfant Sage," see Steinschneider, *Il Buonarroti* 7 (1872) 235-47. See further, on its quotation by Peter the Venerable, Saul Lieberman, *Shkiin* (2d ed.; Jerusalem: Wahrmann, 1970) 32-42 (Hebrew). Compare the pioneering investigation of Israel Lévi, "La nativité de Ben Sira," *REJ* 29 (1894) 197-205. For the text and discussion, see Samuel T. Lachs, "The Alphabet of Ben Sira: A Study in Folk-Literature," *Gratz College Annual of Jewish Studies* (1973) 9-28, at p. 18. Norman Bronznick, David Stern, and Mark Jay Mirsky translated the work in *Rabbinic Fantasies:*

Imaginative Narratives from Classical Hebrew Literature (ed. D. Stern and M.J. Mirsky; Philadelphia and New York: Jewish Publication Society, 1990) 167-203. For a subsequent version see *Mimekor Yisrael* 1.193-96.

[29] Max A. Macauliffe, *The Sikh Religion* (6 vols.; Delhi: S. Chand, 1963) 1.3-15. And see W. Owen Cole, *Sikhism and its Indian Context, 1469-1708* (London: Darton, Longman and Todd, 1984) 172-73.

[30] Nabil-i-A'zam, *The Dawn-Breakers* (trans. Shoghi Effendi; Wilmette, Ill.: Bahai Pub. Committee, 1962) 72; J.E. Esslemont, *Baha'u'llah and the New Era* (Wilmette, Ill.: Bahai Pub. Committee, 1976) 27 n.1.

[31] For example, the early text of Wathīma b. 'Umāra in Khoury, *Les legendes prophetiques* 324-25.

[32] For Shī'ī versions, see, for example, al-Kulainī, *Al-Kāfī* VI 192, and al-Majlisī, *Bihār al-Anwār* XIV 286. For Sunni versions see Abū Nu'aim, *Hilyāt la-Awliyā' wa-Tabaqāt al-Asfiyā'* VII 251-52; Tha'labī, *Qisas al-Anbiyā'* 230; and Galtier (see n.26 above).

[33] The most recent and most reliable work done on *Umm al-Kitāb* has been done by Heinz Halm (see n.27 above). Sections of *Umm al-Kitāb* are translated there, and the section under discussion can be found on pp. 128-32. See also my discussion of this work in *Between Muslim and Jew: The Problem of Symbiosis* (Princeton: Princeton University Press, forthcoming).

[34] Etan Kohlberg, "Some Shī'ī Views of the Antediluvian World," *Studia Islamica* 52 (1980) 41-66, at p. 65; and Josef Van Ess, "The Youthful God: Anthropomorphism in Early Islam," *The University Lecture in Religion at Arizona State University* (Tempe, AZ: Arizona State University, 1988), at pp. 12-13 on Jewish gnostics in Kufa.

[35] Uri Rubin, "Prophets and Progenitors in the Early Shī'a Tradition," *Jerusalem Studies in Arabic and Islam* 1 (1979) 41-65, at p. 55.

[36] See *Apocalypticism in the Mediterranean World and the Near East* (ed. David Hellholm; Tübingen: J.C.B. Mohr, 1983).

[37] See n.12 above.

[38] Philip S. Alexander, "Late Hebrew Apocalyptic: A Preliminary Survey," *La fable apocryphe* (ed. P. Geoltrain, J.-C. Picard, and A. Desreumaux; Brussels: Brepols, 1990) 197-217.

[39] Michael Cook has recently illuminated the likely transmission of a Christian apocalyptic text into Muslim eschatological traditions ("An Early Islamic Apocalyptic Chronicle," *JNES* 52 [1993] 25-29). For Persian traditions see Hans G. Kippenberg, "Die Geschichte der mittelpersischen apokalyptischen Traditionen," *Studia Iranica* 7 (1978) 49-80. Particularly important are the (tragically posthumous) studies of Suliman Bashear, "Apocalyptic and Other Materials on Early Muslim-Byzantine Wars: A Review of Arabic Sources," *JRAS* (1991) 173-207; idem, "Riding Beasts on Divine Missions: An Examination of the Ass and Camel Traditions," *JSS* 37 (1991) 37-75.

[40] See the respective entries in the new *Encyclopedia of Islam*.

[41] See James H. Charlesworth, "Folk Traditions in Jewish Apocalyptic Literature," *Mysteries and Revelations: Apocalyptic Literature Since the Uppsala Colloquium* (ed. J.J. Collins and J.H. Charlesworth; Sheffield: Sheffield University Press, 1991) 91-113.

42 *Kitāb al-Majāll/Apocalypse of Peter* derives from a Pseudo-Clementine milieu, as A. Mingana showed in his edition and translation: "The Apocalypse of Peter," *Woodbrooke Studies* 3 (1931) 93-450 (also edited by M.D. Gibson, *Apocrypha arabica* [Studia Sinaitica 8; London: C.J. Clay, 1901] as *Kitāb al-Majāll, The Book of Rolls*). Mingana emphasized the Clementine; i.e. anti-Pauline, tendency of the *Apocalypse of Peter* to be "the most extraordinary thing I ever saw in any Christian document" (p. 349). This book continued to be known, for example to the early Ismāʿīlī missionary Ḥamīd al-Dīn al-Kirmānī (996-1021), as a "Book of Clement" (*Kitāb Iklīmas*): see A. Baumstark, "Zu den Schriftzitaten al-Kirmani's," *Der Islam* 20 (1932) 308-13, at 312-13. See also G. Graf, *Geschichte der christlichen arabischen Literatur* (5 vols.; Rome: Biblioteca Apostolica Vaticana, 1944-53) 1.283-92 ["Ps.-Klementine Rollenbuch"]. W. Bousset long ago demonstrated the relation between this text, the apocalypse of Pseudo-Methodius, and the Syriac Apocalypse of Ezra (*Der Antichrist in der Überlieferung des Judentums, des Neuen Testaments und der alten Kirche* [Göttingen: Vandenhoeck und Ruprecht, 1895] 72ff.). See also *La caverna dei tesori: testo arabo con traduzione italiana e commento* (ed. A. Battista and B. Bagatti; Jerusalem: Franciscan Printing Press, 1979); Kohlberg, "Some Shīʿī Views" 58-59. On the popularity of the *Schatzhöhle* in Muslim letters see also I. Goldziher, *Abhandlungen zur arabischen Philologie* (2 vols.; Leiden: Brill, 1896-99) 2.1; and Alexander Fodor, "The Metamorphosis of Imhotep -- A Study in Islamic Syncretism," *Akten des VII Kongresses für Arabistik und Islamwissenschaft* (Abh. der Akad. der Wiss. Göttingen, Phil./Hist. Kl. 98; ed. A. Dietrich; Göttingen: Akademie der Wissenschaften, 1976) 155-81, at p. 169.

43 Eric Segelberg, "Old and New Testament Figures in Mandaean Version," *Syncretism* (ed. Sven S. Hartman; Stockholm: Almqvist and Wiksell, 1969) 228-39, at p. 232; Kohlberg, "Some Shīʿī Views" 41-66; Brock, "Jewish Traditions" 228, on these sisters in *Midrash ha-Gadol, Schatzhöhle*, and Pseudo-Methodius.

44 This work continues to be understood as "among the most important books at Qumran" (James C. VanderKam, "The Jubilees Fragments from Qumran Cave 4," *The Madrid Qumran Congress: Proceedings of the International Congress on the Dead Sea Scrolls, Madrid 18-21 March, 1991* [2 vols.; ed. J. Trebolle Barrera and L. Vegas Montaner; Leiden: Brill, 1992] 2.635-48, at p. 648).

45 Uri Rubin, "Prophets" (cited in n.35 above) 56-58; and idem, "Ḥanīfiyya and Kaʿba: An Inquiry into the Arabian Pre-Islamic Background of *dīn Ibrāhīm*," *Jerusalem Studies in Arabic and Islam* 13 (1990) 84-112.

46 See for example *The History of al-Ṭabarī: Volume I. General Introduction and From the Creation to the Flood* (trans. Franz Rosenthal; Albany: State University of New York Press, 1989) s.v. "Jubilees." J.T. Milik's suggestion that medieval Jews possessed Jubilees was based on a citation concerning Sar Mastema made by Yefet ibn ʿAlī: "For certainly medieval Jews did not know 'Prince Mastema' from any other source ..." (*The Books of Enoch: Aramaic Fragments from Qumran Cave 4* [Oxford: Clarendon, 1976] 331).

47 Fred Leemhuis, "The Arabic Version of the Apocalypse of Baruch: A Christian Text?" *JSP* 4 (1989) 19-26.

48 Adriana Drint, "The Mount Sinai Arabic Version of IV Ezra," *Oriens Christiana Periodica* 58 (1992) 401-22.

49 *De chronographo arabe anonymo qui codice Berolinensi sprengeriano tricesimo continetur commentationem* (ed. J.G. Rothstein; Bonn: C. Georgi, 1877), analyzed in G. Rothstein, "Der Kanon der biblischen Bücher bei den babylonischen Nestorianern im 9-/10 Jhdt.," *ZDMG* 58 (1904) 634-63; S.M. Stern, "Abū 'Īsā ibn al-Munajjim's Chronography," *Islamic Philosophy and the Classical Tradition: Essays Presented by his Friends and Pupils to Richard Walzer on his 70th Birthday* (ed. S.M. Stern, A.H. Hourani, and V. Brown; Oxford: Bruno Cassirer, 1972) 437-66 (reprinted in S.M. Stern, *Medieval Arabic and Hebrew Thought* [ed. F.W. Zimmermann; London: Variorum Reprints, 1983]). The text-history of *MS. Sprenger 30* is clarified by Mario Grignaschi, "La *Nihāyatu-L-'Arab fi Ahbāri-l-Furs wa-l-'Arab* et les *Siyaru Mulūki-l-'Ağam* du Ps. Ibn al-Muqaffa'," *Bulletin d'études orientales* 26 (1973) 83-184.

50 Drint, "Mount Sinai" 418.

51 Lazarus-Yafeh, *Intertwined Worlds* 58.

52 Steven M. Wasserstrom, "Jewish Pseudepigrapha and the *Qiṣaṣ al-Anbiyā'*," a paper presented at the international and interdisciplinary conference in honor of William Brinner, University of California at Berkeley, March 30, 1993 (publication forthcoming). See also the contribution of Stephanie Dalley to the present volume. I thank Dr. Dalley for her correspondence with me on this subject.

53 An exception, in fact, may be the *Apocalypse of Abraham*. See my study cited in the preceding note.

54 To take an example for which we have a translation and an analysis, see the account of the creation of the sun and the moon (transmitted from Ka'b al-Aḥbār) given by al-Ṭabarī (*Volume I. From the Creation to the Flood* 232-35). The Jewish antecedents of this tradition were studied by David J. Halperin and Gordon D. Newby, "Two Castrated Bulls: A Study in the Haggadah of Ka'b al-Aḥbār," *JAOS* 102 (1982) 631-38.

55 Compare the study by Eli Yassif, "Traces of Folk Traditions of the Second Temple Period in Rabbinic Literature," *JJS* 39 (1988) 212-33; and, more generally, his *Jewish Folklore: An Annotated Bibliography* (New York and London: Garland, 1986).

56 Neil Forsyth, *The Old Enemy: Satan and the Combat Myth* (Princeton: Princeton University Press, 1987). Note that this fine work, like the extensive studies of apocalypticism found in Hellholm (see n.36 *supra*), lamentably does not engage Islamicate materials, even when unrestricted from doing so by chronological or geographical parameters.

57 See the Appendix below.

58 Schwarzbaum correctly notes that folklorists are concerned with the *matn*, the content, at the expense of attention paid to the *isnād*, the chain of tradents. For the study of biographical dictionaries, see B. Scarcia Amoretti, "'Ilm al-Ridjāl," *EI*² 4.1150-52; J. Sublet, "La Prosopographie arabe," *Annales* 25 (1970) 1236-39; *Cahiers d'onomastique arabe* (ed. J. Sublet; Paris: CNRS, 1979); and Marcia K. Hermansen, "Interdisciplinary Approaches to Islamic Biographical Materials," *Religion* 18 (1988) 163-82.

59 Schäfer, *Synopse*.

60 Philip S. Alexander, review of Schäfer's *Synopse* in *JJS* 34 (1983) 102-106,

at p. 106.

[61] Various Islamicists have noted this phenomenon, but it has not been studied systematically. Annemarie Schimmel emphasized this point from the perspective of Islamic mysticism, and drew up four features in common; see her *And Muhammad was his Messenger: The Veneration of the Prophet in Islamic Piety* (Chapel Hill: University of North Carolina Press, 1985) 298 n.8. Toufy Fahd glosses the image of *haykal* in Ṭabarī (in the English translation of Rosenthal cited above in n.11, pp. 207-208) to the effect that this "... tradition, plus curieuse encore, inspirée sans doute des spéculations gnostiques de la mystique juive des Hekhaloth ..." ("Naissance du monde" 248). A.S. Tritton recognized that an anti-Merkavah polemic may lie behind the injunction "Speak of what is below the throne, not of what is above it" see his "Discords and Differences in Islam," *Essays in Honour of Griffithes Wheeler Thatcher 1863-1950* (ed. E.C.B. MacLaurin; Sydney: Sydney University Press, 1967) 85-102, at p. 93 n.17 (from al-Harāwī, *dhamm al-kalām*). Some further notes on reflections of the Merkavah in Muslim sources have been made by Moshe Idel, "The Concept of Torah in Heikhalot Literature and Kabbalah," *Jerusalem Studies in Jewish Thought* 1 (1981) 23-84, at pp. 36-37 n.39, and pp. 46-47 nn.68-70 (Hebrew). The historian of religions Ioan Culianu [Couliano] addressed this question in several general works, each of which repeats the same material in slightly different forms: *Psychanodia I: A Survey of the Evidence Concerning the Ascension of the Soul and its Relevance* (Leiden: Brill, 1983); *Expériences de l'extase: Extase, ascension et récit visionnaire de l'hellénisme au Moyen Age* (Paris: Payot, 1984); *Out of This World: Otherworldly Journeys from Gilgamesh to Albert Einstein* (Boston and London: Shambhala, 1991).

[62] Michael Sells, "*3 Enoch (Sefer Hekhalot)* and the *Mi'rāj* of Abū Yazīd al-Bisṭāmī," paper presented at the Annual Meeting of the American Academy of Religion, 1989 [unpublished]. I thank Professor Sells for sharing a typescript with me. Another (forthcoming) study of relevance here is Daniel C. Peterson and Stephen D. Ricks, "The Throne Theophany/Prophetic Call of Muhammad." I thank Professor Ricks for sharing a typescript with me.

[63] See my discussion of the sources in *Between Muslim and Jew* (forthcoming). I have addressed this question more briefly in my "The Magical Texts in the Cairo Genizah," *Genizah Research After Ninety Years: The Case of Judaeo-Arabic* (ed. Joshua Blau and Stefan C. Reif; Cambridge: Cambridge University Press, 1992) 160-67, esp. pp. 164-65.

[64] David J. Halperin, *The Faces of the Chariot: Early Jewish Responses to Ezekiel's Vision* (Tübingen: J.C.B. Mohr, 1988) 467-91.

[65] *Ideal Figures in Ancient Judaism* (ed. J.J. Collins and G.W.E. Nickelsburg; Chico, CA: Scholar's Press, 1980) has no comparable partner in Islamic studies. See the dissertation presently underway at University of California, Santa Barbara by James Lindsay on the Prophet David in the *Ta'rīkh Dimashq* of al-Suyūṭī, or the recent study of Abraham-traditions by Reuven Firestone, *Journeys in Holy Lands: The Evolution of the Abraham-Ishmael Legends in Islamic Exegesis* (Albany: SUNY Press, 1990). Neither of these works explicitly deal with pseudepigrapha. On the other hand, H. Schützinger, *Ursprung und Entwicklung der arabischen Abraham-Nimrod-Legende* (Bonn: Selbstverlag des

Orientalischen Seminars der Universität Bonn, 1961) remains an exemplary model for the tracing of a figure from pre-Islamic into Islamic literature.

[66] Georges Vajda, "Melchisédech dans la mythologie ismaélienne," *JA* 234 (1943-45) 173-83; V. Ivanow, "Noms bibliques dans la mythologie ismaélienne," *JA* 237 (1949) 249.

[67] Israel Friedlaender, "Zur Geschichte der Chadirlegende," *ARW* 13 (1910) 92-110.

[68] See n.66 above. For the Ismā'īlī versions, see Marshall G.S. Hodgson, *The Order of Assassins* ('s-Gravenhage: Mouton, 1955) 171, 292.

[69] Miroslav Marcovich employs this appellation in his "The Wedding Hymn in *Acta Thomae*," *Studies in Graeco-Roman Religions and Gnosticism* (Leiden: Brill, 1988) 156-73. Brilliant connections concerning Jewish background were made by G.G. Stroumsa, *Another Seed: Studies in Gnostic Mythology* (Leiden: Brill, 1984) 56-58.

[70] Stroumsa establishes this connection (*Another Seed* 53-61). Some years ago, a similar association was made by W.F. Albright in his ingenious discussion of the "Goddess of Life and Wisdom," *AJSL* 36 (1920) 258-94, esp. pp. 289-90.

[71] The Gnostic Norea was thoroughly reviewed by Birger A. Pearson in his "Revisiting Norea," a paper delivered at the Annual Meeting of the American Academy of Religion, Anaheim, 1985, which refers to the literature known at that date.

[72] In connection with Seth, sometimes known as "*uriyya*" (master), see Jean Doresse, *The Secret Books of the Egyptian Gnostics* (New York: Viking, 1960) 317. Doresse relied for some Islamicate materials on the article by C. Huart on Seth in the first edition of the *Encyclopedia of Islam* s.v. "Shith."

[73] Kohlberg (see n.33 above); M.J. Kister, "Legends in *tafsīr* and *ḥadīth* Literature: The Creation of Adam and Related Stories," *Approaches to the History of the Interpretation of the Qur'ān* (ed. A. Rippin; Oxford: Oxford University Press, 1988) 114.

[74] J. Dan, *Gershom Scholem and the Mystical Dimension of Jewish History* (New York and London: New York University Press, 1987) 138.

[75] I explore this affiliation at length in my forthcoming study *Between Muslim and Jew.*

[76] Michael Lafargue, *Language and Gnosis: The Opening Scenes of the Acts of Thomas* (Philadelphia: Fortress, 1985). Scholem sketched this point in his *Origins of the Kabbalah* (Princeton: Princeton University Press, 1987), for example at pp. 94-95.

[77] Cited above, n.70. See p. 294 of Albright's study.

[78] See nn.25-33 above.

[79] Wilhelm Eilers gathered much relevant material concerning the mythic prehistory of Fāṭima in his "Schiitische Wasserheilige," *Die islamische Welt zwischen Mittelalter und Neuzeit* (ed. U. Haarman and P. Bachman; Wiesbaden and Beirut: Franz Steiner Verlag, 1979) 94-124.

[80] Segelberg (cited in n.43 above), esp. pp. 234-35 on Norea. His discussion of "Our Lady of the Light" is found on p. 235.

[81] For Arabic versions of the Pseudepigrapha, one may now conveniently consult the bibliographies appended to the entries in *OTP*. For Syriac texts, see

David Bundy, "Pseudepigrapha in Syriac Literature," *Society of Biblical Literature 1991 Seminar Papers* (ed. Eugene H. Lovering, Jr.; Atlanta: Scholars Press, 1991) 745-66.

[82] Michel Van Esbroeck, "Incidence des versions arabes chrétiennes pour la restitution des textes perdus," *Traduction et traducteurs au Moyen Age* (Paris: CNRS, 1989) 133-43.

[83] N.A. Meščerskij, "Les Apocryphes de l'Ancien Testament dans la littérature slave ancienne," *Bulletin d'études karaites* 2 (1989) 47-64.

[84] For two current overviews of Reception-Criticism, see Hans Robert Jauss, "Historia Calamitatum et Fortunarum Mearum or: A Paradigm Shift in Literary Study," *The Future of Literary Theory* (ed. Ralph Cohen; New York and London: Routledge, 1989) 112-29, and "The Theory of Reception: A Retrospective of its Unrecognized Prehistory," *Literary Theory Today* (ed. P. Collier and H. Geyer-Ryan; Ithaca, NY: Cornell University Press, 1990) 53-74.

[85] For intrahermeneutical readings of shared narratives, see Marilyn Robinson Waldman, "New Approaches to 'Biblical' Material in the Qur'an," *The Muslim World* 75 (1985) 1-16; Reuven Firestone, "On Scripture and its Exegesis: The Abraham-Ishmael Stories in the Torah and the Qur'an," *Muslims and Christians, Muslims and Jews: A Common Past, A Hopeful Future* (ed. Marilyn Robinson Waldman; Columbus, OH: The Islamic Foundation of Central Ohio, The Catholic Diocese of Columbus, and Congregation Tifereth Israel, 1992) 7-19; idem, "A Fresh Look at the *Akedah* (Gen. 22) in Light of Islamic Exegesis," paper delivered at the international and interdisciplinary conference in honor of William M. Brinner, Berkeley, March 28-31, 1993 (publication forthcoming).

[86] The most explicit and theoretically developed treatments of this question, composed from a psychoanalytic perspective, are those of David J. Halperin, "The Hidden Made Manifest: Muslim Traditions and the 'Latent Content' of Biblical and Rabbinic Stories", paper delivered at the Annual Meeting of the American Academy of Religion, Anaheim, 1985, and "Can Muslim Narrative be Used as Commentary on Jewish Tradition?", paper delivered at the Annual Meeting of the American Academy of Religion, Boston, 1987. I thank Professor Halperin for sharing these unpublished typescripts with me, and for our illuminating discussions and correspondence concerning this work.

[87] "Political Conflict and the Use of Power in the World of the Geniza," *Kinship and Consent: The Jewish Political Tradition and its Contemporary Uses* (ed. Daniel J. Elazar; Washington: University Press of America, 1983) 169-81, at p. 169.

[88] "Traditions in Contact and Change: Toward a History of Religion in the Singular," *Traditions in Contact and Change* (ed. Peter Slater and Donald Wiebe; Waterloo, Ontario: Wilfred Laurier University Press, 1983) 1-25, at p. 22.

SOME ECHOES OF *JUBILEES*
IN MEDIEVAL HEBREW LITERATURE

Martha Himmelfarb
Princeton University

The book of *Jubilees* has come down to us in Ethiopic, preserved by Ethiopian Christians. The original language of *Jubilees* was Hebrew, but like most of the literature of the Second Temple period, it was not transmitted by Jews into the Middle Ages. Nor was it read for long by Christians in Europe. A single manuscript of the Latin version survives; it dates from the fifth or sixth century.[1] There is no manuscript evidence at all for the Greek version that was the basis for the translations into Latin and Ethiopic, although numerous allusions and citations are preserved in the chronographic tradition.[2]

Yet there are a number of passages in medieval Hebrew works that reflect knowledge of the book of *Jubilees*. H. Albeck noted three in *Midrash Aggadah*, a work drawn from the commentary on the Torah of R. Moses the Preacher of Narbonne, who lived in the eleventh century.[3] A. Epstein pointed to three more in *Midrash Tadshe*, an unusual work consisting to a large extent of lists.[4] Two of the parallels to *Jubilees* in *Midrash Tadshe* are lists. Another list connected to *Jubilees* appears in three unrelated medieval Hebrew works.

R. Moses could not have borrowed *Jubilees* back from his Christian neighbors in Provence because the Latin version was long out of circulation by this time. I have argued elsewhere that R. Moses derived his knowledge of the passages of the *Testaments of the Twelve Patriarchs* that appear in his *Bereshit Rabbati* from the Jews of Byzantine Italy.[5] The *Testaments* is a Christian work, composed in Greek. But it undoubtedly drew on Jewish sources like the Aramaic Levi document known from the Geniza and Qumran. In theory it is possible that the passages cited in *Bereshit Rabbati* derive from such ancient sources.[6] But a close examination of the passages persuaded me that the differences between them and the Greek *Testaments* are best explained as the result of revision by a medieval Jew, often in order to strengthen the connections between the narrative source and the biblical verses to which he wishes to attach it in his commentary. In other words, R. Moses appears to have borrowed passages from the *Testaments* "back" from Christians, although unbeknownst to him, what he borrowed had never been Jewish to begin with.

These findings ran up against a historical problem: the *Testaments* was not available in western Europe until the middle of the thirteenth century.[7] Thus R. Moses could not have found the work in the hands of his neighbors in Provence. But the *Testaments* was undoubtedly available in the Byzantine empire. We know that there was contact between the Jews of Provence and the Jews of Lucca and Rome,[8] and I suggested that these northern Italian communities served as a conduit between Provence and the Jewish communities in the Byzantine-ruled southeastern portion of the Italian peninsula.[9] We have confirmation that such contact was possible in the person of Nathan b. Yehiel of Rome, the compiler of the *Arukh*, who was a student of R. Moses and seems also to have studied with Moses Kalfo of Bari, a town of Byzantine Italy that was both a center of Jewish learning and the seat of an archbishop.[10]

The passages from the *Testaments* probably came to R. Moses in Hebrew. It is highly unlikely that a Provençal rabbi would have known Greek. And even if R. Moses had been able to read Greek, it is hard to imagine that he would have introduced passages from a Greek text with "Our rabbis of blessed memory said ...," as he introduced some of the passages from the *Testaments* in *Bereshit Rabbati*.[11] But a Jew somewhere in Byzantine Italy who came upon the *Testaments of the Twelve Patriarchs* might have read it and been filled with the desire to take back what seemed to him good Jewish traditions despite their current suspect location.[12] Such a reader might have decided to translate parts of this very interesting document "back," as he would have understood it, into Hebrew. By the time his translations reached R. Moses, their dubious origins would have been successfully forgotten.

Jubilees *and the Byzantine Chronographers*

Since there is no evidence that the Greek version of *Jubilees* was still in circulation in R. Moses' time, the solution to the problem of R. Moses' knowledge of *Jubilees* must be somewhat different from the one I proposed for his knowledge of the *Testaments*. An inventory of the passages dependent on *Jubilees* in medieval Hebrew texts suggests a direction for exploration: with the exception of some of the lists, all draw on passages in *Jubilees* that were used by the Byzantine chronographers.

It is clear that the passages in the medieval Hebrew texts are not drawn directly from the chronographers. At a number of points the medieval Hebrew versions are closer to *Jubilees* than the excerpts in the chronographers, which often paraphrase *Jubilees* rather than quote it. But W. Adler has recently suggested a theory about the chronographers' use of Jewish pseudepigrapha and other ancient sources that may help to explain this phenomenon. H. Gelzer saw the Byzantine chronographers as dependent on earlier chronicles, now lost, for their knowledge of the ancient works they cite, including *Jubilees*. Against Gelzer, Adler argues that the Byzantine chronicles drew not on the earlier chronicles, but on collections of excerpts from ancient sources on various subjects of interest to the chronographers. There is evidence for such collections of differing opinions in the works of both Syriac and Byzantine chronographers, who sometimes cite a variety of opinions on a particular subject. Even the collections did not draw directly on the ancient Jewish works, but rather on early chronicles such as those of Julius Africanus and Panodorus.[13] Nonetheless, the passages in these collections are likely to have been closer to the ancient Jewish works from which they were excerpted than their presentation in the chronographers, who stand at several removes from them. In light of R. Moses' knowledge of passages from the *Testaments of the Twelve Patriarchs*, it is not too difficult to imagine a Jewish reader somewhere in Byzantium, perhaps in Byzantine Italy, coming upon such collections and translating into Hebrew materials that he found particularly interesting. I hope that the following discussion of individual passages will make this case seem plausible.

A. Midrash Aggadah *and* Jubilees *on Jared and the Watchers*

On Gen 5:18, "And Jared lived," *Midrash Aggadah* comments: "Why was he called Jared (ירד)? Because in his days the angels descended (ירדו) from heaven and taught humanity to serve the Holy One, blessed be he."[14] *Jub.* 4:15 reads "... He named him Jared because during his lifetime the angels of the Lord who were called Watchers descended to earth to teach mankind and to do what is just and upright upon the earth."[15] The same etymology is presupposed also in *1 Enoch* 6:6: "And they were two hundred who descended in the days of Jared ...."[16] But while the name Jared has the potential to suggest a play on the root ירד to any reader, there is nothing in the name or in its context in the biblical genealogy to connect the descent with angels. For example, the Oxford manuscript published by Salomon Buber in his edition of *'Aggadat Berešit* asks, "Why was his named called Jared? Because in his lifetime his generation descended (ירדו) to the lowest level."[17] But of all the literature of the Second Temple period, only *Jubilees* holds the view that the angels descended for pious purposes.[18] *Midrash Aggadah*'s picture of the descent of the Watchers argues for knowledge of *Jubilees* rather than some other work containing the etymology of Jared.

The correlation of the lifetime of Jared with the descent of the Watchers based on etymology has an important place in Christian chronology.[19] As far as I know, none of the chronographers shares *Jubilees'* view of the motives of the Watchers, but a collection of materials of the kind Adler suggests might have contained the relevant information from *Jubilees*. The positive view of the Watchers' motives would not have appealed to the chronographers because by Byzantine times the dominant view held that the sons of God of Genesis 6 were the Sethites, while readings of Genesis 6 that understood the sons of God as angels shared the low opinion of the Watchers found in the Enochic *Book of the Watchers*.[20] Thus a chronographer might well have discarded *Jubilees'* view of the Watchers while using its etymology of Jared.

B. On Enoch's Astronomical Knowledge

Immediately following the play on Jared, *Midrash Aggadah* comments on Gen 5:24: "'And Enoch walked with God.' He walked with the angels for three hundred years. He was with them in the Garden of Eden, and he learned intercalation, seasons, constellations, and much wisdom from them." The *Book of the Watchers* describes the time Enoch spent with the angels on his tour to the ends of the earth and the cosmological secrets revealed to him in the course of the tour (*1 Enoch* 17-36). But the specifics of *Midrash Aggadah* recall *Jubilees*, although the list of what Enoch learns while with the angels in *Midrash Aggadah* is by no means identical to *Jub.* 4:17:

> He was the first of mankind who were born on the earth who learned (the art of) writing, instruction, and wisdom and who wrote down in a book the signs of the sky in accord with the fixed pattern of their months so that mankind would know the seasons of the years according to the fixed patterns of each of their months .... He was, moreover, with God's angels for six jubilees of years. They showed him everything on earth and in the heavens -- the dominion of the sun -- and he wrote down everything .... He was taken from human society, and we led him into the Garden of Eden for (his) greatness and honor .... (4:17, 21, 23)

Enoch is not associated with astronomical knowledge in rabbinic literature.[21] But he is closely associated with astronomical knowledge in the Christian chronographic tradition, although I do not know of any quotations of the passage from *Jubilees*.[22]

The basis for the claim that Enoch spent three hundred years with the angels, a number *Jubilees* expresses according to its ideology of jubilees, can be found in Gen 5:22: "Enoch walked with God after he begat Methuselah for three hundred years ...." J.C. VanderKam has suggested that the routine plural form of האלהים ("God") in this verse provided an opening for an understanding of the word as divinities or angels.[23] Thus walking with האלהים meant not that Enoch was God's intimate for three hundred years, but rather that Enoch spent those years in the company of the angels. This interpretation was of course widespread in the literature of the Second Temple period.

In its interpretation of the conclusion of Gen 5:24 ("And he was not, for God took him"), *Midrash Aggadah* identifies Enoch with Metatron: "Because he was righteous, the Holy One, blessed be he, took him from men and turned him into the angel Metatron." The transformation of Enoch into Metatron, God's heavenly vicegerent, in the *Hekhalot* text *3 Enoch* (*Sepher Hekhalot*) can be traced back through *2 Enoch*, where Enoch is transformed into an angel who learns secrets never before revealed, to the *Book of the Watchers*, where Enoch remains human, but enjoys the fellowship of the angels, the view reflected also in *Jubilees*.[24] R. Moses, of course, would not have been aware of this line of development, but his knowledge of the identification of Enoch with Metatron may account for his receptivity to *Jubilees*' picture of Enoch's time with the angels despite the rather negative view of Enoch from *Gen. Rab.* 25.1, which he also quotes, in abbreviated form, in *Midrash Aggadah* to Gen 5:24.[25] According to this view, Enoch vacillated between good and evil and his early removal from the world was intended to preserve him in his good behavior.

C. On Canaan's Transgression of the Oath

The final passage from *Midrash Aggadah* related to *Jubilees* is an account of the division of the earth among Noah's sons. On Gen

12:6 ("The Canaanite was then in the land") *Midrash Aggadah* comments,

> For the land of Israel had fallen to the portion of Shem, as it says, 'Melchizedek, king of Salem' (Gen 14:8). When the Holy One, blessed be he, divided the world among them, Noah made his three sons swear (החרים) that none of them would enter the territory of another. But the seven nations passed through (עברו) the land of Israel and transgressed (עברו) the oath (החרם). Therefore the Holy One, blessed be he, commanded, 'You shall utterly destroy (החרם תחרימו) them.' At the time that Abraham passed through (עבר) they had not yet entered there except for the Canaanites. Thus the land of the seven nations fell to Israel, for all the lands of the seven nations had fallen to the portion of Shem. Thus it says, 'He set up boundaries for the nations according to the number of the children of Israel' (Deut 32:8).

From ancient times Jews felt compelled to defend themselves against the accusation that they had stolen their land since the Bible makes it perfectly clear that the Canaanites were there before Israel arrived.[26] The comment in *Midrash Aggadah* contains three separable attempts at defense. The first, which relies on Gen 14:8 as a prooftext, is a good indication of the difficulty of proving Israel's prior ownership from Scripture. It assumes the identification made by some rabbinic sources, including *Midrash Aggadah* to Gen 9:27, of the mysterious king of Salem with Shem, the son of Noah.[27] The point of the prooftext, then, is that Shem, Israel's ancestor, was already established in the land at the time of Abraham.

In its cryptic final sentence *Midrash Aggadah* draws on a defense of Israel's right to the land expressed more fully in *Midrash ha-Gadol* to Gen 10:1.[28] According to this view, when the world was divided up, God gave Israel twelve lands to correspond to the twelve sons of Jacob ("according to the number of the children of Israel"). The twelve lands were then occupied by the Canaanites, who can be considered twelve nations if Canaan himself is added to his eleven descendants listed in Gen 10:15-18. The twelve Canaanite nations served as caretakers of the land until Israel arrived on the scene. The passage from *Midrash ha-Gadol* concludes with the verse from Deuteronomy that constitutes the entirety of *Midrash Aggadah*'s version of this argument.

The central portion of the passage from *Midrash Aggadah* is very close to *Jubilees*. *Jubilees* reports that Noah divided the world among his three sons by lot and that each son in turn divided his portion among his sons (8:8-9:15). To Noah's delight, the holy land fell to Shem and his descendants (8:12-21). Then Noah had his sons take an oath to respect these boundaries: "He made (them) swear by oath to curse each and every one who wanted to occupy the share which did not emerge by his lot" (9:14). Later, however, Canaan found the land from Lebanon to the river of Egypt, which had fallen to Shem, so beautiful that he occupied it despite the warning of his father and his brothers: "You are cursed and will be cursed more than all of Noah's children through the curse by which we obligated ourselves with an oath before the holy judge and before our father Noah" (10:32).

R.H. Charles claims that the view that the Canaanites were trespassing in occupying Canaan is restricted to *Jubilees* and authors dependent on it, including George Syncellus (47.14-29).[29] The version of the story in *Midrash Aggadah* is more elaborate than that of Syncellus and has more in common with *Jubilees*, suggesting again that *Midrash Aggadah*'s debt is to the collections on which the chronographers drew rather than to the chronographers themselves.

Finally *Midrash Aggadah* places *Jubilees*' story in a different exegetical context. Gen 12:6 does not figure in *Jubilees*' narrative of Canaan's usurpation of the land at all. *Midrash Aggadah*'s view that of the seven nations only the Canaanites were there at the time of Abraham derives directly from this verse: if the other nations had been there, surely Genesis would have mentioned them. The punning on עבר, absent in *Jubilees*, seems also to derive from this verse. The root חרם, on the other hand, might well reflect the oaths and curses of *Jubilees*, which in the Hebrew original could have been expressed through a single root. But the culmination of this punning -- החרם תחרימו "you shall utterly destroy (them)" -- is not found in *Jubilees*.

Albeck shows that R. Moses often paraphrases, combines sources, and expands the passages from rabbinic texts on which he draws for his own purposes.[30] Unlike rabbinic texts, which are largely exegetical to begin with, *Jubilees* is a narrative. In *Bereshit Rabbati*, R. Moses has adapted the passages from the *Testaments of the Twelve Patriarchs* to make them fit their exegetical context.[31] The play on the verb עבר in the exegesis of Gen 12:6 in *Midrash Aggadah* may represent a similar kind of adaptation.

D. On Adam and Eve's Entrance into Paradise and the Laws of Leviticus on Purification After Childbirth

Midrash Tadshe (chap. 15) explains the laws of Leviticus 12 that set the length of the two periods of impurity after childbirth according to the sex of the child by reference to the chronology of the creation of Adam and Eve and their entrance into paradise. The same correlation is found in *Jubilees*, the first instance of its tendency to connect later laws to the patriarchs. According to *Jubilees*, Eve was separated from Adam, and thus in a sense created, in the second week, a view that seems to derive from the placement of the second creation account of Genesis after the conclusion of the first week according to the first creation account. The timing of the creation of the first man and first woman accounts for the differing periods of impurity for the mother after the birth of male and female decreed in Lev 12:1-5 -- a week for a boy, two weeks for a girl (*Jub.* 3:8). Adam, who was created outside Eden, entered it on the fortieth day, while Eve waited until the eightieth day to enter. This accounts for the forty days a woman must wait after the birth of a boy before entering the sanctuary and the eighty days after the birth of a girl, according to Lev 12:4-5 (*Jub.* 3:9-14).

Rabbinic sources do not make the connection between the laws of Leviticus 12 and the lives of Adam and Eve. But it does appear in Syncellus' chronicle in the discussion of the chronology of the lives of the ancestors of humanity (5.12-25).[32] Since this connection is by no means obvious, it is likely that Syncellus is here again dependent on *Jubilees*, although he does not mention *Jubilees* by name. The interest of this information about the chronology of the lives of Adam and Eve for the chronographers is clear, and once again it is plausible that a medieval Hebrew work owes its knowledge of *Jubilees* to the sort of collection Adler envisions.

E. On the Twenty-Two Works of Creation

The passages remaining for discussion are all lists. Two of them require a different type of explanation, but *Midrash Tadshe's* list of the twenty-two things created during the six days of creation (end of chap. 6), like the materials discussed to this point, could have been drawn from a collection of excerpts from ancient works on chronological questions. The list goes back to *Jub.* 2:1-23; lists based on this passage are also preserved in Epiphanius' *Weights and Measures* (chap. 22), Syncellus (3.6-18), other chronographic works,[33] and the Hebrew commentary on the Ten Commandments of the eleventh-century Karaite Nissi b. Noah.[34] The lists differ considerably in style. Epiphanius' list is the closest to *Jubilees*. Syncellus' version is very terse, although not as terse as *Midrash Tadshe's*, which preserves only the works without any account of the process of creation. Nissi's list is more expansive than *Midrash Tadshe's*, with the addition of prooftexts and, for the first day especially, other materials. Unlike the other lists, Nissi's never mentions the number twenty-two as the total of the works of creation.

Epiphanius follows *Jubilees* by including an elaborate list of angels among the creations of the first day. But this dating of the creation of angels was problematic for later users of the list. *Midrash Tadshe* omits angels and adds wind, a change Charles attributed to rabbinic anxiety about the threat to God's sovereignty entailed in placing the creation of angels on the first day.[35] Although we shall see in a moment that *Midrash Tadshe* was willing to correct its source to conform to rabbinic ideas, the Karaite Nissi and the Christian Syncellus make the same change. Syncellus here reflects the view of the Greek hexaemera, which understood the creation of angels to have been accomplished before the creation of the world.[36] It is thus likely that

Midrash Tadshe reflects not rabbinic tradition but a change already introduced into the list in its source.

Jubilees' list concludes by comparing the twenty-two works of creation to the twenty-two leaders of humanity from Adam to Jacob. As I have noted, Nissi's list does not mention the number twenty-two at all. *Midrash Tadshe* shares with Epiphanius and Syncellus a further comparison to the twenty-two letters of the Hebrew alphabet. Epiphanius and Syncellus contain a third comparison to the twenty-two books of the Hebrew Bible.[37] Charles argued that the additional comparisons were original.[38] But VanderKam rejects Charles' argument, since the wording of the verse in *Jubilees* assumes only a single comparison: "The latter is blessed and holy and the former, too, is blessed and holy. The one with the other served (the purposes of) holiness and blessing" (*Jub.* 2:23).[39] This suggests that the additional comparisons were added at some point in the transmission of the passage between *Jubilees* and Epiphanius; Epiphanius himself might have been responsible. The presence of the comparisons in later works fits well with the later authors' indirect knowledge of *Jubilees*. The absence of the comparison to the books of the Bible in *Midrash Tadshe* could represent a correction of the passage in light of the normal rabbinic reckoning of biblical books as thirty-nine rather than twenty-two.[40]

F. On the Birth-Dates of the Sons of Jacob

The two lists remaining for discussion stand in a different relationship to *Jubilees*. Both of these lists draw at least part of their content from *Jubilees*, but neither appears as a list in *Jubilees* itself.

Midrash Tadshe (chap. 8) gives the number of years that each of the patriarchs, matriarchs, and sons of Jacob lived, and also the day of the month on which Jacob's sons were born. The dates of birth correspond quite closely to those given in *Jubilees* 28, where they are not in list form, but appear in the course of the narrative; *Jubilees* provides the year of birth as well as the day of the month. Like

Jubilees, Midrash Tadshe identifies the months of birth by number rather than, as is usual in rabbinic literature, by name.[41]

The picture of *Jubilees* contains some internal contradictions.[42] The order of the narrative agrees with Genesis in making Judah the fourth son, and Dan the fifth, but according to the dates given in *Jubilees*, Dan must have been born before Judah. *Midrash Tadshe* lists Dan as the fourth son and Judah as the fifth. The narrative of *Jubilees* follows Genesis in placing Asher before Issachar, but the dates contradict this, and again *Midrash Tadshe* sides with *Jubilees*' dates against the Bible itself. Since Benjamin's birth occurred after the departure from Aram Naharaim, Benjamin is not mentioned in *Jubilees* 28. Neither Benjamin nor Zebulun appears in the list in *Midrash Tadshe*.[43]

Like Genesis, *Jubilees* provides the number of years of the lives of the three patriarchs, the four matriarchs, and Joseph, but not of the other sons of Jacob. The lengths of the lives of the sons of Jacob in *Midrash Tadshe*'s list correspond, with some exceptions, to the lengths given in the *Testaments of the Twelve Patriarchs*.[44] It seems more reasonable to suppose that the author of *Midrash Tadshe* found these elements already combined than to suppose that he knew both *Jubilees* and a complete text of the *Testaments*. Syncellus includes a list of the years in which the sons of Jacob were born (120.22-28) and then cites a number of early authorities on questions of the chronology of the lives of the patriarchs (121-24), a subject obviously of considerable interest to him. This suggests a context in which such a list might have been put together. Whatever its source, it is surprising that *Midrash Tadshe* did not correct the list to conform to the text of Genesis.

G. Jubilees *and the Names of the Wives of the Patriarchs*

The last list appears not in *Midrash Tadshe*, but in variant form in three other medieval Hebrew texts: Samuel Algazi's *Toledot Adam* (published in 1585); a manuscript in Damascus, which is no more closely identified in the excerpts published a century ago; and a fourteenth-century manuscript now in Munich.[45] This list contains the names of the wives of biblical heroes, especially the antediluvian patriarchs, based on *Jubilees*. Related lists appear in Greek, Syriac, and Armenian. According to W.L. Lipscomb, the Hebrew lists show a number of peculiarities that suggest that they go back to the Hebrew of *Jubilees* rather than to any of the translations or to other versions of the list; the source of the Christian lists is the Greek version of *Jubilees*.[46] This list, then, constitutes an exception to the pattern that has emerged so far. While there is no reason to believe that knowledge of the list implies knowledge of *Jubilees* as a whole, in this case there is reason to believe that the source for the Jewish works was not Greek and Christian, but rather Hebrew. For the other passages discussed here the collections of excerpts from ancient works used by the chronographers seem to be an adequate explanation, but the list of wives of the patriarchs at least appears to have reached medieval Jews through different channels.

The Noah Book and the Book of Asaph

Finally I would like to turn to a rather different kind of medieval Hebrew work that seems to know not *Jubilees* itself, but one of its sources. Over a century ago R.H. Charles pointed out that the introduction to a Hebrew medical work, the *Book of Asaph*, contained a passage that stood very close to *Jubilees*' account of the revelation to Noah of remedies to heal his offspring from the results of demonic attacks (10:1-14).[47] At first Charles understood the passage from the *Book of Asaph* as "based partly on the Book of Jubilees."[48] Later, however, he suggested that the *Book of Asaph* preserved the Hebrew form of a Noah book taken over also by *Jubilees*.[49]

Charles deduced the existence of this Noah book from passages in *Jubilees* and the Enochic corpus.[50] It does not survive intact in any language, and no Book of Noah is mentioned in the canon lists, which suggests that the work was not widely circulated among Christians. Since Charles' time the Dead Sea Scrolls have provided new evidence for the circulation of traditions about Noah.[51] The subject matter of the extant Noah material is quite diverse, and it is possible that it reflects more than one Noachic work.[52]

Before going any further, I must note that the passage from *Jubilees* about Noah's medical revelation was known to Syncellus, who alludes to the story as an example of the untrustworthiness of the apocrypha (27.33-28.9).[53] But even if the passage from *Jubilees* was available in the Byzantine world, I believe that Charles was correct in his later view that the *Book of Asaph* drew not on *Jubilees* but on the Noah book *Jubilees* used.

This somewhat surprising situation in which a medieval Jewish work shows knowledge of a lost ancient text is not unique. Chapters 2 and 3 of *Midrash Vayissa'u* draw on the source that stands behind the accounts of the battles fought by Jacob and his sons against the Amorites and Esau and his sons in the *Testament of Judah* and *Jubilees*.[54] The *Testament of Judah* gives a more elaborate account of the war against the Amorites than *Jubilees*, while *Jubilees* describes the war against Esau and his sons in greater detail. The accounts in *Midrash Vayissa'u* are more extensive than either the *Testament of Judah* or *Jubilees*, and they include details found in both ancient works.

The Hebrew *Testament of Naphtali* may constitute another instance of this phenomenon. T. Korteweg sees the longer and clearer visions of the Hebrew as a more accurate reflection of the source on which the *Testament of Naphtali* in the Greek *Testaments of the Twelve Patriarchs* drew for its less coherent visions. The clearly negative picture of Joseph in the Hebrew also reflects the ancient source. Traces of the negative picture remain in the depiction of Joseph in the Greek *Testament of Naphtali*, where the less than entirely positive view is notably different from the attitude toward Joseph of the *Testaments* elsewhere.[55]

The introduction to the *Book of Asaph* describes its purported author as one of the restorers of the medical knowledge originally revealed to the patriarch Noah after the flood. But this knowledge was lost when its heirs, Asclepius (here identified as a Greek sage) and his companions, attempted to pluck boughs from the Tree of Life and were consumed by lightning from the fiery sword that guards the Garden of Eden from invasion (Gen 3:24). Only 630 years later was this knowledge restored by Hippocrates, with assistance from Asaph, Dioscorides, and Galen, as well as other unnamed wise men.

Below I translate the relevant portion of the introduction. My translation is quite literal; I have provided versification for ease of reference. As far as I know this is the first time the passage has been translated into English.[56]

1. This is the book of remedies that the ancient sages copied from the book of Shem, the son of Noah. It was handed down to Noah on Mt. Lubar, one of the mountains of Ararat, after the flood. 2. For in those days the spirits of the bastards began to attack Noah's children, to lead them astray and to cause them to err, to injure them and to strike them with illness and pains and with all kinds of disease that kill and destroy human beings. 3. Then all Noah's children went, together with their children, and related their afflictions to Noah their father and told him about their children's pains. 4. Noah was troubled, for he realized that it was because of human transgression and their sinful ways that they were afflicted with all kinds of sickness and disease.

5. So Noah sanctified his children together with the members of his household and his house. He approached the altar and offered sacrifices, praying to God and beseeching him. 6. He (God) sent one of the angels of the presence, whose name was Raphael, from among the holy ones, to imprison the spirits of the bastards from under the heavens so they would do no more harm to mankind. 7. The angel did so, imprisoning them in the place of judgment. 8. But he left one in ten to go about on earth before the prince of enmity (המשטמה) to oppress evil-doers, to afflict and torture them with all kinds of disease and illness and to afflict them with pain.

9. Then the angel told him the remedies for the afflictions of mankind and all kinds of remedies for healing with trees of the earth and plants of the soil and their roots. 10. And he sent the princes of the remaining spirits to show Noah the medicinal trees with all their shoots, greenery, grasses, roots and seed, to explain to him why they were created, and to teach him all their medicinal properties for healing and for life. 11. Noah wrote all these things in a book and gave it to Shem, his

oldest son, and the ancient wise men copied from this book
and wrote many books, each one in his own language.

The Hebrew of *Jub.* 10:1-14 is lost to us; it has not been found
among the fragments from Qumran. A comparison of the Hebrew of
the two passages would surely be illuminating, although allowance
would have to be made for the influence of the language of the author
of the *Book of Asaph* on the early Hebrew of his source. The stories
are broadly similar and share a number of details. But there are also
some important differences. Often the differences can be explained by
the different goals of the two works.

The passage from the *Book of Asaph* emphasizes the medical
aspects of the story. It lavishes attention on the ills inflicted by the
wicked spirits, which are identified throughout as diseases, and on the
herbal remedies revealed to Noah. According to *Jubilees*, the impure
demons "mislead" the children of Noah's sons, "make them act
foolishly," and "destroy" them. The sons complain to Noah that the
demons are "misleading, blinding, and killing" the grandchildren (10:1-
2). Compare these afflictions to "illness," "pains," and "disease" as the
scourges of the evil spirits in the *Book of Asaph* (2), terms echoed in
the description of Noah's reaction to the news (4) and of the
continuing liberty of one-tenth of the evil spirits (8). None of the ills
of *Jubilees* is unambiguously a physical ailment. Placed parallel to
"misleading," "blinding" suggests spiritual rather than physical blindness.
Until the remedies are introduced in *Jub.* 10:10, it is not clear that the
afflictions caused by the evil spirits involve illness at all. The remedies
are characterized as "medicines for their diseases with their deceptions"
(10:12), including the spiritual even as the physical nature of the
afflictions is acknowledged.

It is thus not surprising that the remedies revealed to Noah are
described in far greater detail in the *Book of Asaph* than in *Jubilees*.
Indeed the only details about the nature of the remedies in *Jubilees* is
in the conclusion to the phrase quoted above: "medicines for their
diseases with their deceptions, so that he could cure (them) by means
of the earth's plants" (10:12). In contrast the *Book of Asaph* offers a

long list of the various parts of trees to be employed for medicinal purposes.

A related difference can be seen in the identity of the angels to whom the imprisonment of the evil spirits and the revelation of medical knowledge is attributed. In *Jubilees* these deeds are accomplished by anonymous angels, of whom the angelic narrator speaks in the first person plural. The *Book of Asaph* attributes them to a single angel, Raphael, whose name associates him with healing.

It seems likely that the compiler of the *Book of Asaph* elaborated the medical aspects of the story in his source to make it a suitable introduction to his work. It is also possible that *Jubilees* plays down the medical aspects with its picture of the spiritual afflictions caused by the evil spirits. *Jubilees* has a tendency to eliminate elements of the biblical narrative that could suggest magical practices on the part of its heroes. For example, its account of Jacob's request to Laban that the spotted and speckled kids and lambs be his wages at parting makes no mention of Jacob's techniques for inducing such offspring (*Jub.* 28:25-30; cf. Gen 30:25-43). The many wonders Moses performed in Egypt to show up Pharaoh's magicians are summarized briefly: "You performed the signs and miracles *which* you were sent to perform in Egypt against the pharaoh, all his house, his servants and his nation" (*Jub.* 48:4). The next verse goes on to enumerate the plagues, which are attributed entirely to God; there is no mention of Moses' role in setting them in motion as in the biblical narrative. Healing has strong connections with magic in the ancient Mediterranean world, as the Gospels or the magical papyri demonstrate. If the Noah book's account of the revelation contained even part of the medical emphasis of the *Book of Asaph*'s version, *Jubilees* might have felt it necessary to tone down its potentially magical implications.

For the compiler of the *Book of Asaph*, the story of the revelation to Noah promises both honorable antiquity and angelic origin for medical knowledge. But the angelic origin is not unclouded, as a close look at the story shows. The angel Raphael begins the process of revelation in the *Book of Asaph* (9). But to complete the revelation, he calls on the princes of the spirits who have not been imprisoned, that is, on demons (10). *Jubilees* has done a better job of covering up the tension in the picture of the origins of medical knowledge, but it can be discerned there too. "He told one of us that we should teach Noah all *their* medicines ..." (emphasis mine) (10:10). It is worth noting that the kinds of remedies given to Noah to ward off the evil spirits are included in the *Book of the Watchers* among the damaging secrets the fallen Watchers reveal: "And they taught them sorcery and spells and showed them the cutting of roots and herbs" (*1 Enoch* 7:1, cf. 8:3). Note the association of magic and medicine: the negative evaluation of medicine is part of the larger rejection of the arts of civilization in the *Book of the Watchers*.

The theory of the cause of disease put forward in the passage from the *Book of Asaph* is rather problematic for a medical practitioner: humanity is vulnerable to the onslaught of the evil spirits only because of sinfulness (4). If sin causes susceptibility to disease, one might think that pious behavior would constitute a sort of preventive medicine, more useful than anything the doctor could offer. But perhaps the compiler of the *Book of Asaph* took comfort in the same kind of pessimism about human nature that is attributed to Mastema in *Jubilees*: "The evil of mankind is great" (10:8). Sinlessness might work better, but given human nature, medicine would surely be necessary.

An important aspect of the Noah book that can be discerned through the passages discussed here is its understanding of Noah as priest. *Jubilees* emphasizes Noah's priestly role throughout its account of his life.[57] The idea that Noah offered a sacrifice on emerging from the ark is of course available to any reader of Genesis (8:20-22), but *Jubilees* expands on the biblical account of the sacrifice and associates it with the Feast of Weeks (chap. 6) and reports another sacrifice in honor of the festival of the first day of the first month (7:1-6). When Noah exhorts his grandchildren "to do what is right," (*Jub.* 7:39), the duties of avoiding the shedding of human blood and the eating of animal blood (7:27-33) figure prominently. *Jubilees'* juxtaposition of murder and the consumption of blood shares the priestly outlook of its source, Gen 9:4-5, which is particularly apparent in Noah's warning that the earth will become polluted by improper use of blood (*Jub.* 7:33).

The interest in blood in Noah's exhortation recalls the title of the one book of Noah referred to in ancient Jewish literature outside of *Jubilees*.[58] After giving his grandson Levi elaborate instructions about the performance of sacrifices in the addition to the *Testament of Levi* following *T. Levi* 18:2 in MS e of the *Testaments of the Twelve Patriarchs*, Isaac provides the authority for the instructions: "For thus my father Abraham commanded me for thus he found in the writing of the book of Noah concerning the blood."[59]

Jubilees shows considerable interest in the priestly activities of the other major pre-Levitical patriarchs (Enoch, Abraham, Isaac, and Jacob) as well.[60] As with Noah, much of this material involves elaboration of brief accounts of sacrifice in Genesis, which the author of *Jubilees* expands in keeping with his picture of the patriarchs' observance of the laws of the Torah and of the institution of the festivals before the giving of the Torah. But the fact that Noah offers a sacrifice after hearing of his grandchildren's afflictions in the passage from the *Book of Asaph* suggests that Noah's priestly role was not invented by the author of *Jubilees*, but rather goes back to their common source. In *Jubilees* Noah does not sacrifice, but rather prays a long prayer (10:3-6). I do not know how to explain *Jubilees'* omission of this sacrifice.

J.C. VanderKam has suggested that the revelation of remedies to Noah in *Jubilees* should be seen in the context of *Jubilees'* understanding of Noah as priest.[61] It is true that elsewhere in the ancient Near East priests performed rituals of healing, but judging the purity status of skin ailments and participating in the rituals necessary for purification from these ailments (Leviticus 13-14) is as close as the Torah allows priests to come to healing.[62] Thus this aspect of Noah's priestly behavior does not reflect the values of the priestly document of the Torah.

Without parallel material in other works to compare, any delineation of the material in *Jubilees* drawn from sources is speculative. But I hope it does not seem too speculative to suggest that

the Noah work that stands behind the passage from the *Book of Asaph*
and *Jub.* 10:1-14 included some of the material on which other parts of
Jubilees' treatment of Noah is based. The priestly portion of the
exhortation in *Jubilees* 7 is a prime candidate,[63] and if some further
speculation can be indulged, such a work might well have been called
"the book of Noah about blood."

   To this point I have referred to the *Book of Asaph* as a medieval
work. Now I shall try to be more specific about its date and
provenance. The *Book of Asaph* is a compilation. The medical
historian E. Lieber calls it "a Hebrew encyclopedia of Greek and
Jewish medicine."[64] Earlier scholars claimed that the absence of the
terminology and developments of Arab medicine pointed to a date in
the seventh century or even earlier and preferred an eastern location,
such as Palestine, Persia, or Mesopotamia, but Lieber has recently
argued for a date in the ninth or early tenth century and a location in
Byzantine-ruled southern Italy. The *Book of Asaph* seems to have
been known to Shabbetai Donnolo, the Jewish physician who lived
there in the tenth century.[65]

   The dominant influence on the *Book of Asaph*, as on other
medieval Jewish medical works, is the Greek medical tradition. But
Lieber considers the *Book of Asaph* unique for its systematic
employment of Jewish ideas as well.[66] She offers a number of
examples of the influence of biblical ideas and Jewish practice,
especially kosher slaughter, on the work. The most striking is the
Book of Asaph's understanding of the cardiovascular system, which
Lieber views as the earliest glimmer in medical writing of the
circulation of the blood, although without crucial elements of the
process. This remarkable insight derives from the *Book of Asaph's*
understanding of blood as "soul" in accordance with the biblical laws in
Gen 9:4-5 and Lev 17:10-14.[67] I suggested above that the Noah book
on which the *Book of Asaph* drew contained material like the
exhortation about the shedding and consumption of blood in *Jub.* 7:27-
33. It seems possible that the author of the *Book of Asaph* was
attracted to the book by this shared interest; for him, the exhortation

may have reinforced the picture of Noah as a source of great medical insight.

The author of the *Book of Asaph* was not the only Jewish doctor in medieval Italy with an interest in exotic ancient sources. The *Book of Yosippon* is a Hebrew history for which the main source, from which the work derives its name, is an abridged Latin translation of Josephus, the ancient Jewish historian who wrote in Greek for a Roman audience and whose work was transmitted by Christians. D. Flusser, the work's most recent editor, believes that its author was a physician writing in the middle of the tenth century in Naples, a southern Italian location where Byzantine influence was felt, but where Latin language and culture were dominant.[68] His training as a physician would account for the author's excellent knowledge of this language and culture as well as for his lesser rabbinic learning and his "secular" outlook.[69] Like my imagined translator of the passages from the *Testaments*, the author of the *Yosippon* was not reluctant to extract attractive, apparently Jewish traditions even when they were embedded in a work that belonged to Christians. In addition to his version of Josephus, he draws on books of what would later be called the Apocrypha, which were readily available to any European Jew who read Latin or Greek since they formed part of the Christian Bible. Like Nahmanides,[70] he accepts the Wisdom of Solomon as the words of King Solomon himself.[71]

The *Yosippon* is important for Lieber because it shows the power of Josephus' reputation among Jews in Byzantine Italy.[72] Abandoned by Jews as a traitor, Josephus became a wise man, astrologer, and healer in Christian legend. Lieber suggests that the otherwise unknown ancient physician to whom the *Book of Asaph* is attributed is actually Josephus, who had a medical reputation among the Christian contemporaries of the book's author; the name Asaph is to be understood as a variant of Yoseph, the Hebrew of Josephus.[73] If she is right, the attribution of the *Book of Asaph* would be another instance of the willingness of Jews in Byzantine Italy to borrow from Christians in order to reclaim what they took to be theirs.

If Flusser's identification of the profession of the anonymous author of the *Yosippon* is speculative, the medical career of Shabbetai Donnolo is well attested. Donnolo was born in Oria in 913 and practiced medicine in Byzantine Italy until at least 982. He wrote on astrology as well as medicine, and the culmination of his life's work was a commentary, known as *Sepher Hakhmoni*, to the mystical work *Sepher Yeṣirah*. In his introduction to *Sepher Hakhmoni*, Donnolo describes his eagerness to acquire wisdom from all possible sources, including gentiles.[74] The Noah book presented fewer problems to a Jew interested in ancient knowledge than the sources used by the author of the *Yosippon* or the translators into Hebrew of passages from the *Testaments of the Twelve Patriarchs* and *Jubilees*: it was preserved in Hebrew, and it was not found in Christian hands. In the world of the author of the *Yosippon* and Shabbetai Donnolo, it is not surprising that another physician author gave it a prominent place in his work.

---

[1] J.C. VanderKam, *The Book of Jubilees: A Critical Text* (CSCO, Scriptores Aethiopici 87; Louvain: E. Peeters, 1989) xiv.

[2] Ibid. xi-xii.

[3] *Midrash Aggadah* was published by Salomon Buber (2 vols.; Vienna: Abraham Fanto, 1894). On the relation of *Midrash Aggadah* to R. Moses' work, see *Midrash Bereshit Rabbati* (ed. H. Albeck; Jerusalem: Mekize Nirdamim, 1940) 5-15. The three passages from *Jubilees* discussed here are identified in Albeck's list of passages that he views as reflecting knowledge of texts of the Second Temple period in the introduction to *Bereshit Rabbati* (17-18). Most of the suggested parallels are not as persuasive as these.

[4] Epstein ("Le livre des Jubilés, Philon et le Midrasch Tadsché," *REJ* 21 [1890] 80-97; 22 [1891] 1-25) attributed *Midrash Tadshe* to R. Moses (p. 83), but Albeck rejects this claim and suggests that the common material in *Midrash Tadshe* and works of R. Moses derive from R. Moses' use of *Midrash Tadshe* (*Bereshit Rabbati* 16-17). Epstein developed the fanciful theory that *Midrash Tadshe* drew on an expanded version of *Jubilees* influenced by the ideas of Philo. Despite the problems with his theory, the parallels he points to (pp. 83-87) are impressive.

[5] "R. Moses the Preacher and the Testaments of the Twelve Patriarchs," *AJS Review* 9 (1984) 55-78.

[6] One of the longer passages in *Bereshit Rabbati* is a reworking of a passage from the Greek *Testament of Naphtali*. But the passage in question does not appear in any form in the Hebrew *Testament of Naphtali*. See Himmelfarb, "R.

Moses the Preacher" 60-64, 71-73.

7 H.J. de Jonge, "La bibliothèque de Michel Choniatès et la tradition occidentale des Testaments des XII Patriarches," *Studies on the Testaments of the Twelve Patriarchs* (SVTP 3; ed. Marinus de Jonge; Leiden: Brill, 1975), esp. 100-101.

8 B.Z. Benedict, "On the History of the Torah Center in Provence," *Tarbiz* 22 (1951) 91, 94-95 (Hebrew).

9 "R. Moses the Preacher" 73-74.

10 On R. Nathan, see S.W. Baron, *A Social and Religious History of the Jews* (18 vols.; New York: Columbia University Press, 1952-83) 7.29-31. On Bari, see A. Sharf, *Byzantine Jewry* (London: Routledge & Kegan Paul, 1971) 122-23, 164-68.

11 The passages so introduced are drawn from the *Testament of Judah.* They appear in *Bereshit Rabbati* 179 lines 7-10, and 180 lines 8-13.

12 I do not think it is too much to assume the existence of Byzantine Jews literate in Greek even if on the whole the Jews of the Byzantine empire spoke Greek but did not read or write it. Rather like many other Jews, they wrote in Hebrew or put their vernacular into Hebrew characters (A. Sharf, *The Universe of Shabbetai Donnolo* [Warminster: Aris and Phillips, 1976] 97-98).

13 Gelzer's work is *Sextus Julius Africanus und die byzantinische Chronographie* (2 vols.; Leipzig: Teubner, 1880-85). Gelzer claimed that Syncellus was dependent on the works of two early chronographers, Panodorus and Annianus, for his knowledge of ancient Jewish sources, while chronographers of the "Logothete" tradition relied on the chronicle of Julius Africanus. For Adler's critique of Gelzer and his development of his own view, see *Time Immemorial: Archaic History and Its Sources in Christian Chronography from Julius Africanus to George Syncellus* (Dumbarton Oaks Studies 26; Washington: Dumbarton Oaks, 1989) 158-231, with a convenient summation in the conclusion (pp. 229-31). Adler points to the evidence for collections containing a variety of opinions on a single subject on p. 167.

14 Translations from *Midrash Aggadah* are mine.

15 Throughout this study I use the translation of *Jubilees* by J.C. VanderKam, *The Book of Jubilees* (CSCO, Scriptores Aethiopici 88; Louvain: E. Peeters, 1989).

16 All translations of *1 Enoch* are taken from M. Black in consultation with J.C. VanderKam, *The Book of Enoch or 1 Enoch* (Leiden: Brill, 1985).

17 (Vilna: Romm, 1925). This manuscript contains a version of *'Aggadat Berešit* that, unlike the previously printed versions, includes the first *parashah* of Genesis (1:1-6:4; pp. xxii-xxiii). The passage about Jared appears on p. xxx.

18 On the use of the story of the Watchers in *Jubilees*, see J.C. VanderKam, "Enoch Traditions in Jubilees and Other Second-Century Sources," SBLSP 13 (2 vols; ed. P.J. Achtemeier; Missoula, MT: Scholars Press, 1978) 1.242-45.

19 Adler, *Time Immemorial* 180.

20 Ibid. 114-16 (Sethites); 210-11 (Watchers).

21 M. Himmelfarb, "A Report on Enoch in Rabbinic Literature," SBLSP 13 (see n.18 *supra*) 1.262-63.

22 Adler, *Time Immemorial* 86-97; see also R.H. Charles, *The Book of Jubilees*

or the Little Genesis (London: Adam and Charles Black, 1902) to *Jub.* 4:17.

23 J.C. VanderKam, *Enoch and the Growth of an Apocalyptic Tradition* (CBQMS 16; Washington: Catholic Biblical Association of America, 1984) 31-32, 130-31.

24 The Hebrew text of *3 Enoch* is available in P. Schäfer in collaboration with M. Schlüter and H. G. von Mutius, *Synopse zur Hekhalot-Literatur* (Texte und Studien zum antiken Judentum 2; Tübingen: Mohr [Siebeck], 1981) §§1-80 and parallels. For an English translation, see P. Alexander, "3 (Hebrew Apocalypse of) Enoch," *OTP* 1.223-315. On Enoch in rabbinic literature, the targumim, and the *Hekhalot* texts, see Himmelfarb, "Enoch in Rabbinic Literature" (cited in n.21).

25 References to *Genesis Rabbah* are to chapter and section in the edition of J. Theodor and H. Albeck, *Midrash Bereshit Rabba: Critical Edition with Notes and Commentary* (3 vols.; Jerusalem: Wahrmann, 1965).

26 For the rabbinic defense, see *Gen. Rab.* 1.2 and the parallels listed there in Theodor-Albeck. Rashi quotes this midrash in the introduction to his commentary on the Torah.

27 See L. Ginzberg, *The Legends of the Jews* (7 vols.; Philadelphia: Jewish Publication Society, 1909-38) 5.225 n.102 for an emendation of the obviously corrupt text of *Midrash Aggadah* there and for other instances of this identification in rabbinic literature. His reference to *Genesis Rabbah* should be to 26.3, and I am not persuaded that it actually presupposes the identification.

28 *Midrash Haggadol on the Pentateuch: Genesis* (ed. M. Margulies; reprinted, Jerusalem: Mossad Harav Kook, 1967) 193 lines 10-15. *Midrash ha-Gadol* is a Yemenite compilation of the thirteenth century. The source of this passage is unknown. See Margulies' note to 193 line 11, and Ginzberg, *Legends* 5.195-96 n.73.

29 Charles, *Jubilees,* commentary to 10:29. All references to Syncellus are to page and line in *Georgii Syncelli Ecloga Chronographica* (Bibliotheca Scriptorum Graecorum et Romanorum Teubneriana; ed. A.A. Mosshammer; Leipzig: Teubner, 1984).

30 *Bereshit Rabbati* 22-24.

31 Himmelfarb, "R. Moses the Preacher" 62, 67, 70-71.

32 Other Christian sources make this connection as well. See Charles, *Jubilees,* commentary to 3:8-14.

33 See the apparatus in *Ecloga Chronographica* (ed. Mosshammer) to 3.6-18.

34 The commentary was published by S. Pinsker in *Lickute Kadmoniot zur Geschichte des Karaismus* (2 vols.; Vienna: Adalbert della Torre, 1860) [Hebrew]; the passage in question appears in 2.7.

35 Charles, *Jubilees,* commentary to 2:2-3.

36 Adler (*Time Immemorial* 183) notes that while he rejects it, Syncellus explicitly mentions *Jubilees'* view on the subject, as do several other chronographers who do not include the list.

37 The three comparisons appear also in Theodosius Melitenus. See Adler, *Time Immemorial* 204.

38 Charles, *Jubilees,* commentary to 2:23.

39 VanderKam, *Jubilees* (CSCO 88), commentary to 2:23.

40 Charles, *Jubilees* xxxix-xl.

41 Epstein, "Livre des Jubilés" 87.

42 For tables and discussion of the dates in *Jubilees* and their relationship to Genesis, with some attention to the list in *Midrash Tadshe*, see Charles, *Jubilees*, commentary to 28:11-24.

43 A. Jellinek ("Midrasch Tadsche," *Bet ha-Midrasch* [6 vols.; reprinted, Jerusalem: Wahrmann, 1967] 3.171 n.2) notes that Benjamin and Zebulun do appear in the list as it is cited in Rabbenu Baḥya's commentary to the first portion of Exodus; the list is identified as drawn from *Midrash Tadshe* (Baḥya b. Asher, *Be'ur 'al ha-Torah* [3 vols.; ed. C. Chavel; Jerusalem: Mossad Harav Kook, 1967] 2.9). Chavel brackets the passage, noting that it does not appear in all editions of the commentary (n.57).

44 Charles, *Jubilees*, commentary to 28:11-24, provides the data in a convenient form.

45 W.L. Lipscomb, "A Tradition from the Book of Jubilees in Armenian," *JJS* 29 (1978) 149-63; for the brief description of the Hebrew texts, see p. 161.

46 Ibid. 151-56. Moreover, Lipscomb ("The Wives of the Patriarchs in the Ekloge Historian," *JJS* 30 (1979) 91) notes the existence of another Greek list, also derived from the Greek version of *Jubilees*.

47 Charles, *The Ethiopic Version of the Hebrew Book of Jubilees* (Oxford: Clarendon, 1895) 179.

48 Ibid. 179.

49 Charles, *Jubilees* xliv. This is also the position of more recent scholarship. See D. Flusser, "Mastema," *EncJud* 11.1119-20; M.E. Stone, "Noah, Books of," *EncJud* 12.1198. Both touch on the question only in passing.

50 Charles, *Jubilees* xliv, lxxi-lxxii; idem, *The Book of Enoch or 1 Enoch* (2d ed.; Oxford: Clarendon, 1912) xlvi-xlvii. Charles variously referred to the work as the Book or Apocalypse of Noah (book: *Jubilees* xliv; apocalypse: ibid., commentary to 10:1.)

51 See the discussion in J.T. Milik in collaboration with M. Black, *The Books of Enoch: Aramaic Fragments of Qumrân Cave 4* (Oxford: Clarendon, 1976) 55-60.

52 See Stone, "Noah, Books of" for a listing and characterization of this material.

53 Adler, *Time Immemorial* 153-54, 178.

54 Critical editions of *Midrash Vayissa'u* can be found in J.B. Lauterbach, "*Midrash Va-yissa'u*; or, The Book of the Wars of the Sons of Jacob," *Abhandlungen zur Erinnerung an Hirsch Perez Chajes* (Vienna: Alexander Kohut Memorial Foundation, 1933) 205-22 (Hebrew), and Y. Dan and T. Alexander, "The Complete *Midrash Va-yissa'u*," *Folklore Research Center Studies* 3 (1972) 67-76 (Hebrew). Each edition contains MSS unknown to the other. The war against the Amorites, chap. 2 of *Midrash Vayissa'u*, is described in *Jubilees* 34 and the *Testament of Judah* 3-7; the war against Esau and his sons, chap. 3 of *Midrash Vayissa'u*, appears in *Jubilees* 37-38 and the *Testament of Judah* 9.

55 "The Meaning of Naphtali's Visions," *Studies in the Testaments of the Twelve Patriarchs* (see n.7 *supra*) 260-90.

56 The *Book of Asaph* has never been published, much less translated, in its

entirety. There are eighteen known manuscripts of part or all of the work, and it seems to exist in editions of different lengths. See E. Lieber, "Asaf's *Book of Medicines*: A Hebrew Encyclopedia of Greek and Jewish Medicine, Possibly Compiled in Byzantium on an Indian Model," *Dumbarton Oaks Papers 38: Symposium on Byzantine Medicine* (ed. John Scarborough; Washington: Dumbarton Oaks, 1984) 238. For a list of publications and translations of sections of the book, see ibid., p. 237 n.33. For my translation, I rely on the text published by Jellinek, *Bet ha-Midrasch* 3.155-56; he used the Munich manuscript (3.xxx n.2). Süssman Munter (*Mavo l'Sepher Asaph haRophe* [Jerusalem: Geniza, 1957]) includes this passage as one of his samples of the work (pp. 147-54). He uses the Oxford and Munich MSS as the basis for his edition and compares them to other MSS. But since he does not indicate clearly which reading he is following at any given point, I preferred to use Jellinek's text. The differences between Munter's and Jellinek's texts are quite small.

57 See J.C. VanderKam, "The Righteousness of Noah," *Ideal Figures in Ancient Judaism* (SCS 12; ed. G.W.E. Nickelsburg and J.J. Collins; Chico, CA: Scholars Press, 1980) 19-23.

58 *Jubilees* itself refers twice to writings of Noah. Before his death, at the end of the passage about the medical revelation (10:14), Noah hands on the books he has written to Shem. Later, like Isaac in the addition to the *Testament of Levi*, Abraham attributes the instructions about sacrificial practice that he gives to Isaac to a book of his ancestors and to the words of Enoch and Noah (21:10). But since these writings are part of *Jubilees'* theory of the transmission of the content of the revelation at Sinai in the period before Sinai, these mentions cannot serve as evidence for the existence of actual works.

59 Translation is that of J.C. Greenfield and M.E. Stone, "The Aramaic and Greek Fragments of a Levi Document," in H.W. Hollander and M. de Jonge, *The Testaments of the Twelve Patriarchs: A Commentary* (SVTP 8; Leiden: Brill, 1985) 465, v. 57. The version of the *Testament of Levi* in this manuscript contains two passages of some length and one expansion of a single verse that do not appear in any other manuscript of the *Testaments*. The material found in these passages in Greek is paralleled by Aramaic Levi material from both Qumran and the Geniza. The text of the additional material of MS e appears in the apparatus of M. de Jonge in collaboration with H.W. Hollander, H.J. de Jonge, and T. Korteweg, *The Testaments of the Twelve Patriarchs: A Critical Edition of the Greek Text* (PVTG 1:2; Leiden: Brill, 1978). For a brief discussion of the relations among the various Aramaic Levi fragments and the material from MS e, see Hollander and de Jonge, *Commentary* 17-20.

60 Enoch: 4:25; Abraham: 13:4, 13:9, 13:25-27, 14:11, 15:2, 16:20-25, 21:6-19 (instructions to Isaac about sacrifice and the shedding of blood); Isaac: 22:3-6; Jacob: 31:1-3, 32:2-9, 32:27-29.

61 VanderKam, "Righteousness of Noah" 22-23.

62 On the attitude toward healing in the priestly document, see J. Milgrom, *Leviticus 1-16* (AB 3; New York: Doubleday, 1991) 258-61; 887-89.

63 This is part of the second passage (in addition to our passage) that Charles believed *Jubilees* took for a Noah book (*Jubilees* xliv).

64 See n.56 *supra*.

65 Lieber, "Asaf's *Book of Medicines*" 236-37, 246-47.

66 Ibid. 237-38.

67 Lieber suggests that William Harvey was also influenced by the biblical understanding in his discovery of the circulatory system (ibid. 240-43).

68 *Sepher Yosippon* (2 vols.; ed. D. Flusser; Jerusalem: Bialik Institute, 1978-80) 2.117-20. In addition to more general considerations, Flusser adduces geographical details of the work in favor of the identification of the location.

69 Ibid. 2.117-19.

70 "Sermon on the Words of Qohelet," *Kitvei Rabbenu Mosheh b. Nahman* (2 vols.; ed. C. Chavel; Jerusalem: Mossad Harav Kook, 1963) 1.182.

71 Flusser, *Sepher Yosippon* 2.132-33.

72 Flusser points out that the *Yosippon* is not a pseudepigraphon: the author refers to himself and his use of sources several times in the work. The attribution of the work to Yoseph b. Gorion is the work of others who were persuaded by its frequent references to Yoseph b. Gorion that he was in fact the author. In the meantime the name of the author was lost, if it was ever affixed to the work (ibid. 2.74-79).

73 Lieber, "Asaf's *Book of Medicines*" 247-49. Lieber's theory is even more complicated than this. She understands the Yoḥanan who appears as the author of portions of the *Book of Asaph* to be Yoḥanan b. Zakkai, the great first-century rabbi to whom the Talmud attributes not only the prophecy to Vespasian that Josephus claims for himself, but also the cure of Vespasian's foot, a deed attributed to Josephus in a southern Italian Christian chronicle of ca. 1000 (p. 248).

74 On Shabbetai Donnolo, see Sharf, *Universe*. Sharf translates the passage from *Sepher Ḥakhmoni* there (pp. 9-10).

JACOB OF EDESSA AND THE JEWISH
PSEUDEPIGRAPHA IN SYRIAC CHRONOGRAPHY

William Adler
North Carolina State University

While not as numerous as the excerpts in the Byzantine chronicles, the citations from Jewish pseudepigrapha in the Syriac universal chronicles pose textual problems rivalling their Greek counterparts in complexity.[1] Although there are grounds for suspecting an earlier Greek stage in the transmission of much of this literature in Syriac, the content of these citations does not always require the postulation of an intermediate Greek stage.[2] Reclaiming the textual history of these sources is also obstructed by the loss of vital links in the transmission of Jewish sources in Greek and Syriac. Julius Africanus (160-240 CE) and the Alexandrian monk Annianus (early fifth century) presumably played a role in mediating pseudepigraphic excerpts to their Byzantine and Syriac successors.[3] However, because these sources do not survive independently, they can now only be fragmentarily reconstructed from scattered citations in later chronicles. Important earlier stages in Syriac chronography are also lost. One obvious place from which to undertake an analysis of the pseudepigraphic citations in Syriac would be the influential chronicle of Jacob of Edessa (seventh century). Regrettably, however, only a fraction of his chronicle has survived.[4]

What does survive from this same author is correspondence with a colleague, John of Litarba. Intended to assist him with some of the more vexing conundra in Scripture, these wide-ranging letters offer a revealing insight into Syriac exegesis in the seventh century.[5] In one letter, Jacob appeals extensively to legends from extra-canonical Jewish literature, among them a work that he identifies only as "Jewish histories." What work did Jacob have in mind? In every instance in which Jacob cites a tradition from "Jewish histories," it is possible to find a reasonably close parallel in the book of *Jubilees*. At the same time, however, Jacob's source has variants from the preserved version of *Jubilees* which in some cases create a more fluid sequence of events than the corresponding version in *Jubilees*. Indeed, it was this feature of Jacob's source that led Sebastian Brock to the conclusion that Jacob's "Jewish histories" were not *Jubilees* at all, but rather a work independent of and older than it.[6]

The question of Jacob's "Jewish histories" and its affinities to *Jubilees* bears directly on the subject of the present volume. In Christian chronography, no other work of Jewish pseudepigrapha enjoyed a longevity comparable to *Jubilees*. On the other hand, citations similar but not identical to material from that work turn up under different names and in variant forms. How can we know whether these variants are traceable to differing sources or reflect instead continuous adaptation of a single work in the course of Christian transmission? The answer to this question can only be arrived at through examination of specific cases. But Jacob's "Jewish histories" offer one instance in which the technical demands of Christian chronography have reshaped the *Jubilees* narrative into a form quite distinct from the original.

Jacob's Views on the Legitimacy of Jewish Pseudepigrapha

Insofar as Byzantine and Syriac chroniclers depended on some of the same intermediaries for their knowledge of Jewish pseudepigrapha, it is not surprising to find considerable overlap in the material that they cite. Their respective attitudes to this literature, however, differ markedly. Although Byzantine historians quote freely from *Jubilees* and *Enoch*, they often hedge their citations with warnings about their dangers and corruptions "by Jews and heretics."[7] In later Byzantine chronicles, these warnings have hardened into positive hostility. A "joke ... and a diversion (γέλως ... καὶ παιγνία)" is the way Michael Glycas characterizes *Jubilees*, certainly clear testimony to the declining status of this literature in later Greek chronicles.[8]

What Jacob and the Syriac chroniclers who succeeded him say about this literature tells a different story. Rarely do Syriac chroniclers feel compelled to issue disclaimers about its reliability. In his correspondence with John, Jacob's own attitude toward these sources is anything but deprecating. No one should doubt, he says, that writing and books existed well before Moses. Evidence of this comes from *Enoch*, a work whose reputation, he insists, had been unjustly tarnished by Athanasius' anathema against it. Because heretics flourishing in his time had incorporated *Enoch* into their library of secret books, Athanasius mistakenly interdicted a genuine work of antediluvian origins.[9]

Fairly conventional arguments form part of Jacob's defense of *Enoch*'s authenticity. How likely is Athanasius' claim that for the entire duration of time before the flood, humanity would not have discovered something as useful as writing? Does not the Epistle of Jude's quotation from the book lend it credibility? But the unstated motive behind Jacob's endorsement of *Enoch* is that well after Athanasius' proscriptions against it, the work continued to find a favorable reception in both Greek and Syriac chronography.

A criterion that governs Jacob's assessment of disputed books is that preservation and use endow a work with a respectability sufficient to void objections even from the most respected authorities. On the one hand, he cautions John and his colleagues against dissipating their energies thinking about lost books attributed to Solomon, Ezra, and Moses. These works have not survived because "there would be no advantage for the spirit if they had come down to us."[10] The corollary to this, however, is that since God himself had provided for the survival of "useful" literature like *Enoch*, judicious consultation of such a work might assist inquiries into the meaning of Scripture. Jacob's counsel to John about the virtues of *Enoch* seems to have achieved the desired result. In their chronicles, either John or Jacob himself translated a Greek excerpt from the Enochic *Book of Watchers* (*1 Enoch* 6-36) into Syriac, thereby making Enochic literature available to a later generation of Syriac chronographers.[11]

It is not only *Enoch* that establishes for Jacob the pre-Mosaic origins of writing. "Written histories (ܟܬܒܐ ܕܬܫܥܝܬܐ) cited by the Jews," he says, credit Moses' father Amram with having instructed his son in Hebrew letters "when he was still a young man in the house of Pharaoh .... We can therefore conclude from this that there was in truth a system of writing and books before Moses."[12] Now the earliest attestation of this tradition about Amram's education of Moses in Hebrew is *Jub.* 47:9. Linguistic features of Jacob's citation suggest that this tradition about Amram was transmitted to him from a Greek authority.[13] Jacob himself expresses high regard for the source's reliability. "They are not untruthful" is the way he characterizes it.

Jacob's high estimation of his "Jewish histories" and its mediation from a Greek source thus create a strong presumption that the work, like *Enoch*, was already well-known in Christian chronographic circles. The question that follows, then, is what relationship does Jacob's "Jewish histories" have with *Jubilees*, the latter also a work well-known in Byzantine chronography?

Jubilees *and* Jacob's *"Jewish Histories" in the Resolution of* ἀπορίαι

Christian chronographers rarely referred to *Jubilees* by that name. In Syriac, unattributed excerpts from *Jubilees* are typically interwoven with source material from other histories and pseudo-histories. "Little Genesis (ἡ λεπτὴ Γένεσις)" or the "Apocalypse of Moses" were common alternative appellations in Greek sources. Elsewhere, *Jubilees* material is either unattributed, assigned to Moses, or even "Scripture." Too much significance should not be read into this labile nomenclature. None of the chronicles that preserve these excerpts knew Jewish pseudepigrapha firsthand. Several of them are chronological epitomes. In this genre, one expects to find unidentified traditions, or shorthand language like "Moses," "a tradition," or "Scripture."

Jubilees material also circulated under the name of multiple sources, for example, the *Testament of the Protoplasts*, and the *Life of Adam*.[14] A significant number of *Jubilees* citations are found under the name of Josephus.[15] Since chronographers often cited Josephus and *Jubilees* in tandem, the confusion of the two works may have been partly due to simple carelessness. But insofar as these false attributions always lead in one direction (that is, there are no cases in which material from Josephus is attributed to *Jubilees*), (ps-)Josephus cannot be dismissed entirely as an inadvertent invention of negligent copyists. At some stage in the transmission of *Jubilees*, chronographers must have found it expedient to transform the estimable Josephus into a corroborating witness to *Jubilees*. Greek chronographers also know of interpolations of *Jubilees* into the text of Eusebius.[16] In Syriac chronicles as well, one finds material from *Jubilees* attributed to a Jewish historian named Asaph.[17] The blurring of source material from *Jubilees* with other histories and pseudo-histories convinced the Byzantine chronographer George Syncellus that Jewish and Christian historians were directly influenced by that work.[18] Multiple attributions may also help to explain why Jacob in the seventh century knew his source only as "Jewish histories."

Interest in *Jubilees* was largely dictated by one concern: What data could be extracted from that work to help adjudicate familiar ἀπορίαι in biblical chronology? The same interest lies behind Jacob's own appeal to his "Jewish histories." John had set before him a familiar problem in Christian chronography. Why, after promising the land of Canaan to Abraham, had God delayed his realization of this promise for four hundred years and subjected his offspring to captivity in Egypt? A satisfactory solution to this query, Jacob insists, requires that the question be framed in a broader context. Of all the descendants of Shem, why had God chosen Abraham as the instrument for restoring to its rightful ownership the land that Canaan had seized? Why did God choose Abraham among all the peoples of the earth at

that time? Why had he chosen Ur of the Chaldees to issue his call to
Abraham? Why did Abraham leave the city with Terah and his
brother Nachor and come to Harran?[19]

Jacob's resolution of these questions consists mainly of an
abridgement of *Jubilees'* account of Canaan's transgression and a
narrative cycle of Abraham's early life and flight from Ur. But his
retelling of the story has been decisively shaped by prior adaptation of
this material in Christian chronography. As will be seen below, the
constituent parts of Jacob's narrative and their several variants from
the preserved text of *Jubilees* reflect the result.

Canaan's Transgression and the Problem of 400 Years of Captivity

A legend preserved in *Jubilees* 8-10 recounts how, in the days
of Peleg (פלג = "division"; cf. Gen 10:25), Noah's sons secretly divided
the known world among themselves. After further subdividing their
inheritance among their offspring, they bound themselves by an oath
in the presence of their father not to transgress the boundaries of their
estate. Envious of the prosperity of the region allocated to the
descendants of Shem, Canaan unlawfully seized a portion of that land
and brought upon himself the curse against anyone found in violation
of the oath (*Jub.* 10:29-34).

As is consistent with the tone of much of this work, the purpose
of this episode was to absolve the Israelites of any blame for the
conquest of Canaan. Christian writers who appropriated the legend
appealed to it for somewhat different reasons, however. In his
Panarion, Epiphanius found in the legend a rejoinder to the
Manichaean indictment against the God of the Hebrews for having
acted dishonorably in giving the Israelites someone else's property. For
Canaan and his progeny never lawfully possessed the land in the first
place:

> When the parcels of land were divided ..., Noah called upon
> his three sons and swore them by an oath, lest anyone of
> them trespass upon the inheritance of his brother and take
> advantage of his brother. But Canaan, the son of Ham,

being a greedy person, entered into the land of Palestine
and seized it.

Although God, as a token of his forebearance, allowed the Canaanites
four hundred years to make restitution for the transgression of their
father, he was finally compelled to "utterly destroy the sons of Canaan
in accordance with their oath and restore the land of Palestine to the
descendants of Shem."[20]

Since the witnesses to this tradition in Greek chronography
include the Byzantine epitomes of Julius Africanus, it is reasonable to
assume that the story of Canaan's transgression has roots in the
Christian universal chronicle dating back to the third century.[21]
Although the Byzantine witnesses to the story are too copious to
catalogue here, one typical version appears in the ninth-century
chronicle of George the Monk. "When the lands had been divided up
in this way," he writes,

> Canaan ... saw that the land towards Lebanon was fertile,
> and completely different from his own; and he seized it by
> force and drove out the children of Shem who were the
> heirs to it. In this way, the whole land of promise received
> the name Canaan. As a result, the righteous Judge
> returned this land to the sons of Israel, descendants of
> Shem, just as he had promised also to Abraham. For the
> Lord is righteous, and he is a lover of righteousness.[22]

Jacob himself invokes the story for precisely the same reason.
The answer to John's question about the four hundred years, he says, is
rooted in the oath that the three sons of Noah had sworn to their
father to uphold, and which they reaffirmed at the time of Peleg.
Already in his lifetime, Noah foresaw that Canaan was destined to
violate the oath by which he had bound his three sons; for that reason,
he used the issue of his nudity as a pretext for invoking a curse against
him. After the destruction of the tower of Babel and the ensuing
migrations, Canaan fulfilled Noah's prediction. Dwelling in the hot and
inhospitable territory of Egypt and Ethiopia, the descendants of Canaan
envied the more temperate regions of Phoenicia, Syria and Palestine to
the north. Because the inhabitants of Palestine were rather few in

number, the offspring of Canaan chose to violate the injunctions that had been twice ratified. Herein lay the answer to John's query. Although the restitution of the land to Abraham was entirely justified, God's foreordained postponement of the promise for four hundred years was meant in part to allow the Amorites sufficient time both for repentance and for the increase of sin. The other reason for the delay was to reaffirm the faith of the Israelites. For if the Israelites had been spared a harsh servitude in Egypt, they would have failed to appreciate the role that God had played in their restoration.

A comparison of some narrative details with the other versions of the story enables us to further refine the provenance of Jacob's "Jewish histories":

a) *The two divisions of the earth.* According to *Jubilees,* there were two divisions of the habitable earth, the first by Noah among his sons (8:10-30), the second a further subdivision among his grandsons (9:1-15). Both allocations occurred in the presence of Noah in the time of Peleg. By contrast, Jacob's source dates only the first partition during the life of Noah. The ensuing subdivision occurred after Noah's death, around the time of the birth of Peleg.

This variant reflects the influence of a Greek intermediary. The chronology of *Jub.* 8:8-10 had no difficulty synchronizing Noah's division of the earth with the life of Peleg. It dates Peleg's birth in *anno mundi* 1567, and Noah's division of the earth two years later. Greek chronographers who adapted *Jubilees* recognized the incompatibility of this chronology with the Septuagint. According to the more extended chronology of pre-Abrahamic history found in the Greek text of Genesis, Noah was already dead when Peleg was born. In order, therefore, to preserve the deeply embedded Jewish/Christian tradition that the division of the earth occurred during the time of Peleg, a Greek redactor of Jacob's "Jewish histories" was obliged to date the second allocation well after Noah's death.[23]

Emendation of *Jubilees*' pre-Abrahamic chronology to accommodate the Greek chronology of Genesis is well-attested in Byzantine chronicles.[24] Elsewhere, Jacob himself claims that "accurate Hebrew histories" confirmed the archaic chronology of the Greek text of Genesis and proved that the Jews had deliberately abbreviated the chronology of the Hebrew Bible in order to show that "Christ had not yet arrived."[25] Of course, his open-ended reference to "Hebrew histories" makes identification of his source uncertain. But Jacob's praise of the accuracy of these "Hebrew histories" is very similar to his laudatory characterization of his "Jewish histories" in his letter to John. All of this creates a strong presumption that Jacob's "Jewish histories" were a version of *Jubilees* emended by a Greek editor in order to validate the chronology of the Greek version of Genesis.

b) *The blessing of Japhet.* Like many other Jewish interpreters of the blessing of Noah (Gen 9:27), *Jubilees* understood the words "he will dwell in the tent of Shem" to refer to God, not Japhet.[26] It construes the verse in the following way: "God shall enlarge Japhet and God shall dwell in the dwelling of Shem" (7:12). After the allocation of the territory to Shem, *Jub.* 8:18 has Noah again recalling his blessing upon Shem: "Blessed be the Lord God of Shem, and may the Lord dwell in the dwelling of Shem." By contrast, the Byzantine chronographers who report the *Jubilees* story of Noah's blessing refer the antecedent to Japhet. The understanding that they typically assign the passage is that Noah's blessing foreshadowed both Japhet's inheritance of a portion of Shem's allocation in Asia and the ultimate inclusion of Japhet's portion (Europe) into the church.[27]

Jacob adheres to the older Jewish interpretation. After his account of Noah's first division of the earth, Jacob glosses Gen 9:27 with the following explanation: "This land that God promised to the race of Abraham was given by Noah to Shem, that is why he blessed it and said, 'He will dwell in the tent of Shem.'"[28] The context of the citation thus makes it clear that Jacob assumes that it is God himself who will dwell in Shem's tent. Although the significance of Jacob's adherence to the older Jewish exegetical tradition is unclear, it would seem to indicate that the Greek source of Jacob's "Jewish histories" represents an earlier stage in transmission than the parallel material cited in the Byzantine chronicles.

Why Was Abraham Called Out Of Ur?

After his narration of the division of the earth, Jacob takes up some correlative issues associated with Abraham's call. The first question that he feels obliged to answer is why, of all the descendants of Shem dispersed over the earth, did God choose Abraham in Ur of the Chaldeans as the instrument to recover the land taken by Canaan? The reason why God placed Abraham, the most righteous man of his time, in Ur was that only the Hebrews, the descendants of Eber, were permitted to remain in Babylon after the dispersion of the races. This region, then, was the only place on earth where Hebrew, the language of Adam, continued to be spoken. A marked departure from the conventional Syriac position on the primacy of Syriac, Jacob's assertions about the originality of Hebrew reflect an ongoing discussion about the subject in Christian chronography and the Jewish sources on which they drew.

A tradition widely disseminated in Jewish sources held that after the destruction of the tower and the dispersion of the races, only Eber and his offspring continued to use the language of Hebrew.[29] According to *Jubilees*, Hebrew, the "language of creation," ceased "from the mouths of all the children of men from the day of the overthrow." When Abraham revived the language after learning from God in Harran how to read and write in Hebrew, he "took the books of his fathers, and these were written in Hebrew, and he began from thenceforth to study them" (12:25-27). The actual origin of the word "Hebrew" was also the subject of speculation. Josephus offered one explanation, deriving the word "Hebrew" from the patriarch Eber.[30] But an opposing derivation, already attested in Philo, traced it to the Hebrew word עבר ("pass over"). The word Ἑβραῖος, he says, is best translated in Greek as περατής ("crosser"), referring to those who "quit the objects of sense perception and go after those of the mind."[31]

Christian chroniclers faithfully reported both etymologies. In his chronicle, Julius Africanus, a writer with an impressive and competent knowledge of Jewish sources, acknowledges that "some think (οἴονται τινες)" that the name of the Hebrews originated from Eber. The truth is, however, that "Hebrews means 'crossers' ('Εβραῖοι ... οἱ Περαταί ἑρμηνεύονται)" and originated when Abraham crossed the river Euphrates.[32] Although several Greek commentators of the fourth century continued to favor Africanus' etymology, in other quarters the derivation of the word Hebrew from עבר fell into disfavor, replaced by the earlier Jewish tradition tracing the origin of the word Hebrew to Eber. Already known to Diodore (fourth century), this etymology is widely attested in Byzantine chronography.[33] At the same time, Byzantine chroniclers revived the older Jewish view about the primordial origins of Hebrew and its subsequent revival by Abraham. Thus, on the authority of "Little Genesis," Syncellus reports that "the angel speaking to Moses said to him, 'I have taught Abraham the Hebrew language according to the language of the ancestral traditions spoken from the beginning of creation.'"[34]

It is a measure of the influence of this older Jewish tradition on the later chronographers that even the Byzantine epitomes of Africanus embraced the etymology that Africanus himself had spurned. One of these epitomes is the chronicle of Leo Grammaticus. This chronicle, whose account of pre-Abrahamic history contains copious allusions to *Jubilees*, has the following narrative of the aftermath of the destruction of the tower:

> It is said that only Eber preserved the ancient tongue. And his descendants who received this language called themselves 'Hebrews' after the name of their forefather (πατρωνυμικῶς) and called the language Hebrew. Proof that this was the language in existence before the confusion of tongues is provided by the names of the men of old. It is possible to explain what their names signify in no other language ... For example, while the meaning of the name Adam can be discovered in no other language, in this language it will be discovered to mean "man." And although the name of Noah has no meaning in any other tongue, in this language it means "righteousness," and Cush means "Ethiopian," and Mestraeim "Aegyptus" and Phalek "division."[35]

Now there is every reason to suppose that Jacob's own arguments on behalf of the originality of Hebrew and the derivation of the name Hebrew from Eber form part of the same complex of Jewish/Christian traditions. Indeed, Michael Syrus later claims that Jacob established his case from "ancient chronographers."[36] In response to John's inquiries about the primacy of the Hebrew language, Jacob concedes that many "illustrious and remarkable" authorities identified the language of Adam as either Syriac or Aramaic. Despite their claims, however, Jacob vigorously presses the case for the originality of Hebrew. Pitting himself against an "inept man" who proposed that the name Hebrew arose when Abraham crossed the Euphrates, Jacob insists that the word is derived from the name of the patriarch Eber. As we have seen, the etymology of this "inept man" is the same as the one favored by Africanus. Most telling are the similarities of Jacob's arguments to Leo's. Like Leo, Jacob makes his case for the primacy of the Hebrew language largely on onomastic arguments. Thus, on the basis of information he attributes to Eusebius of Emesa, Jacob holds that in the context of the Genesis narrative the names Adam and Eve are meaningful only in Hebrew.[37]

Jacob's maverick views about the primacy of Hebrew must have ignited a small controversy in Syriac chronography. His arguments apparently prevailed over his colleague John, for Michael Syrus later credits both men with having endorsed the derivation of Hebrew from Eber. Later Syriac chroniclers, under the pressure of national loyalty, demurred. While respectfully acknowledging the opinions of Jacob and John, Michael invokes the authority of Ephrem and Basil and reverts to the more traditional Syriac position.[38]

Abraham's Call and the Migration From Ur

The nucleus of Jacob's narrative is the story of Abraham's call and migration. Although Brock has noted several elements of his account that deviate from the comparable version in *Jubilees*, there are strong reasons for not ascribing the story to an independent version. The variants are rather a by-product of the use of *Jubilees* to untangle a thicket of problems having to do with the sequence of events leading up to Abraham's flight from Ur and his subsequent migration from Harran.

a) *Was there a first call in Ur?* One problem involved an apparent discrepancy between Gen 12:1 and Stephen's speech in the New Testament book of Acts. In his speech to the Jews, Stephen reminded them how, before God settled Abraham in Harran, he had told him to "go forth from thy country and from thy kindred and come into that land that I will show you" (7:2). But this was difficult to square with Genesis' notice that the call to Abraham occurred only after he and the other members of his family had already migrated to Harran. A typical harmonizing reading of Acts and Genesis postulated two calls, the first to Abraham in Ur *pace* Acts, the second *pace* Genesis after he was already residing in Harran. But what were the actual circumstances of this first call? And if the call had been to Abraham only, why had Terah and the other members of his family accompanied him as far as Harran? This is where chronographers enlisted the aid of *Jubilees*.

There is no explicit reference in *Jubilees* to a divine call to Abraham when he was still in Ur. It does, however, record a chain of fateful events bringing Abraham into escalating conflict with his father's practice of idolatry. What seemed to inaugurate all of these incidents was Abraham's experience of the evils of idolatry and his prayer to God at age fourteen to be spared from such impiety (11:17). For in that same year, Abraham turned away the ravens sent by Mastema to devour the seed. Fourteen years later, Abraham launched his campaign against his father's craft, culminating in his burning of the temple of idols and the migration to Harran (11:14-12:14). In *Jubilees*, these events do not bear a tight causal connection to one other. But the chronographers, seeking a context for Abraham's first call, assumed that Abraham's prayer to God portended something quite momentous, namely his first encounter with the true God. Thus, in a list of references that he attributes to "Little Genesis" and (ps-)Josephus, Syncellus states that in his fourteenth year "Abraham discovered the

God of the universe and worshipped him."[39] It was this enlightenment that triggered Abraham's first migration to Harran:

> ... before the death of Terah God told Abraham to go out from his land; this is also shown from what was said by the first martyr (i.e. Stephen), namely that before he settled him in Harran, God appeared to him in Mesopotamia, that is in the land of the Chaldeans. *Therefore, the correct inference will be that it was not after Terah's death that God divinely spoke with Abraham; rather this occurred while he was still in his native land, dedicating himself to God and turning away from the idols of his father, as is reported in many places.* He set fire to these idols at night, so it is said, and his brother Haran was consumed with them, in attempting to extinguish the fire before his father Terah.[40]

In Syncellus' narrative of events, Abraham's experience of God at age fourteen serves the purpose of resolving the discrepancy between Acts and Genesis. The story establishes that God had first spoken with Abraham while still a young man in Ur, as a result of which Abraham began his campaign against idols. Insofar as Syncellus ascribes the legend to many sources, including (ps-)Josephus, we may also conclude that by the early ninth century the legend was popularly known (ὡς πολλαχοῦ ἱστορεῖται).

Jacob's narrative of events draws the same inference from *Jubilees'* story of Abraham's encounter with God as a young man. In the original version of *Jubilees*, Mastema, not God, sends the ravens yearly to ravage the fields. Abraham's prayer -- which is for deliverance from idolatry, not ravens -- actually precedes his first encounter with these birds. Moreover, Abraham manages to chase the ravens off by his own efforts. As Brock has observed, Jacob's "Jewish histories" presents a different and more causally linked narrative.[41] It describes how at age fifteen Abraham, in his desperation to rid the field of the ravens, called upon God for assistance. After chasing the ravens from the field, God then reveals to Abraham that "I am the God who has made heaven and earth ... It is I who have sent these ravens against you, and because you have called me and known my name, I have heard you and chased the ravens from your field." Now the purpose of this rewritten narrative is transparent: it is to transform the whole episode of the ravens into Abraham's first fateful encounter with the true God of the universe, that is, his first divine call. Indeed, in three places Jacob makes a point of saying that Abraham's ordeal with the ravens and his prayer to God marked his "first call (ܪܚܒܝܐ ܪܚܒܘܪܐ)." At that time, he says, Abraham "was called by God and was confirmed in truth in the belief in God." In Jacob's "Jewish histories," the *Jubilees* story has been tailored in such as a way as to complement more directly Stephen's report of the "first call" to Abraham in Ur.[42]

b) *Why did Terah and Nachor accompany Abraham from Ur?* If, as Acts maintained, there had been a first call to Abraham in Ur, commentators wondered why Terah took the initiative in leading his family out of Ur (Gen 11:31). This act seemed to imply that Terah also participated somehow in the first call in Ur. What else would have motivated him and his family to leave Ur? "God appeared to our father Abraham before he settled him in Harran," writes Diodore; "from this it is clear that because the vision occurred to Abraham when he was in Babylon, Terah went forth with his family to settle Palestine."[43] John Chrysostom conjectures that perhaps Terah chose to leave Ur "out of love for and loyalty" to his son.[44] There was also speculation that a preceding verse in Genesis might bear in some way on the circumstances of Terah's migration from Ur. This verse referred mysteriously to Haran's death "before Terah his father in the land of his birth in Ur of the Chaldeans" (Gen 11:28). But without additional documentation from corroborating sources, there was no way to fill in the gaps.

Jewish sources had already succeeded in supplying some of the missing details. Based on the connection between Ur and the Hebrew word for fire, Jewish legend traced Haran's premature demise to a conflagration somehow connected with his devotion to idols.[45] In *Jubilees'* version of the legend, the fire was ignited by Abraham himself. After failing to wean Terah away from idolatry, Abraham resolved to burn the house of idols. "Haran hurried to save them, but the fire flamed over him, and he was burnt in the fire" (12:14). This, therefore, was what Moses was alluding to when he had spoken darkly about Haran's death "before Terah his father in Ur of the Chaldees." *Jubilees* then records how, following Haran's abortive attempt to rescue the idols, Terah escorted his family from Ur.

From this story Christian chronographers pieced together a coherent chain of cause and effect, linking together the burning of the temple, Haran's death, and Terah's subsequent flight to Harran. According to one reconstruction, the purpose of Moses' remark about Haran's death "before his father" was to draw attention to the uniqueness of a son's death chronologically preceding his father's. Haran's premature death in the temple conflagration, says George the Monk, was God's punishment against Terah for his trafficking in idols.[46] For other interpreters, however, Genesis' reference to Haran's death "before Terah (ἐνώπιον τοῦ Θάρα)" implied that Haran perished in the physical presence of Terah when both attempted to rescue the idols. Syncellus, for example, reports that Abraham's brother Haran was consumed in the temple conflagration "before his father" when he tried to extinguish the flames. For Syncellus, this event bore directly on Terah's decision to lead his family out of Ur. "As Terah also went forth," he says, "the rest of his family, recipients with Abraham of the promise (ἐπαγγελομένους), journeyed together with him to the land of Canaan, just as Scripture states, especially if we suppose that the patriarch Abraham was encouraging them." It will be noted here that Syncellus makes a point of explaining the circumstances of Terah's migration with Abraham. With the help of *Jubilees*, Syncellus thus succeeded in connecting what seemed otherwise to be a disjointed and inexplicable sequence of events.[47]

Now where does Jacob's narrative of Haran's death stand in relationship to this chronographic tradition? As Brock notes, a clue to the Greek provenance of Jacob's narrative is suggested by his variant text of Gen 11:28. In contrast to the Peshitta's orthography of the name Haran, Jacob spells the name of Haran with *'ālaphs*. Like his spelling of the name Amram, this reflects the Greek orthography (ﬡﬧﬡﬤ = Ἀῤῤάν). And whereas the Syriac text states that Haran died "during the life of" Terah, Jacob's citation reveals clear affinities with the Old Greek text of Gen 11:28: "Haran died before his father Terah (ܕܐܒܘܗܝ ܐܪܐ ܡܢ ܗܪܢ ܡܝܬܗ), in the land in which he was born in Ur of the Chaldeans."[48]

Jacob's preference for a Greek rendering of Gen 11:28 is not fortuitous. His own reconstruction of events preceding the migration from Ur presupposes it. In a scholium to Gen 11:28, Jacob acknowledges that since sons often predecease their father "doubt and contention exist among readers" as to why "Scripture has made mention of the death of Haran being before that of his father." According to one of his two explanations, the specific incidents to which Moses was referring were Abraham's destruction of the temple and Haran's death when he ran to extinguish the flames. Jacob's rendition of Haran's death "before his father" and the subsequent course of events thus has the same objective as that of the Greek chronographers. His death, Jacob writes, "marks secretly and mysteriously and indicates the cause of the exodus of Terah and his sons from the land of the Chaldees."[49]

In his letter to John, Jacob's "Jewish histories" pursues the same objective of conforming the *Jubilees* narrative of the burning of the temple to the exegetical problems posed by Genesis 12. *Jub.* 12:14-15 is entirely silent about the motives behind Terah's decision to leave Ur. Indeed, by interposing a two-year hiatus between Haran's death and the migration from Ur, it effectively uncouples the two events causally. But as in the other versions of the story given by the Greek chronographers, Jacob adapted the story to address the exegetical problem. According to Jacob's "Jewish histories," Abraham, fired by zeal for God after his first enlightenment, undertook the religious reformation of his family. Failing at this, he then took the extreme measure of burning the temple of idols, resulting in Haran's death. The citizens of Ur were so incensed by Abraham's act of arson that they threatened to kill Terah and burn his house if he did not surrender Abraham to be killed. Under pressure from the other members of his community, Terah had no choice but to leave. This latter narrative embellishment, entirely missing from the original *Jubilees* story, has its origin in the same exegetical problem that the Greek chronographers faced. In Jacob's own words, it provides "the reason for the departure of Terah and Abraham from Ur of the Chaldeans." By establishing a causal connection between the burning of the temple, Haran's death, and the exodus from Ur, Jacob's "Jewish histories" solved the ἀπορία of why Terah decided to accompany Abraham from Ur.[50]

One final expansion of the *Jubilees* story of the burning of the temple deserves a note. This is Jacob's report that the "celebrated" temple burned by Abraham was dedicated to Kainan, "the god of the Chaldeans."[51] Brock is certainly correct in identifying this god as the second, postdiluvian Kainan (cf. LXX Gen 10:25). It is less likely, however, that the source of this embellishment is independent of *Jubilees* and represents a rival tradition tracing the origins of idolatry to Kainan and not Serug.[52] Christian chronographers actively endorsed the "euhemeristic" theory of the origin of religion; that is, the gods of the gentiles were only human beings divinized because of their discoveries and achievements. Now according to *Jubilees*, Kainan discovered stelae left by the fallen Watchers on which were inscribed "the omens of the sun and the moon and stars in all the signs of heaven" (8:3-4). Since Kainan was one of the forefathers of the Chaldeans, the polemical point of this legend in *Jubilees* was to link Chaldaism to the betrayal of heavenly secrets by a class of fallen angels.[53] Recognizing this, chronographers concluded that the wicked arts of the Chaldeans must have originated with him. To honor his contributions to their civilization, Kainan's successors began the practice of idolatry. "According to what is said," writes Bar Hebraeus, "it was he (Kainan) who invented Chaldaism; his sons worshipped him as a god, and set up an image of him; thence began the worship of idols."[54] And so, as if to round out the story, Abraham put an end to this practice by his daring exploit in the temple dedicated to him.

c) *Why did Abraham leave Terah behind in Harran?* A discrepancy in Genesis' account of Terah's age at the time of Abraham's migration from Harran furnished Christian chronographers and commentators the occasion for probing into Terah and Abraham's character and their mutual relationship. The problem here was chronological. If Terah was 70 years of age when he fathered

Abraham (Gen 11:26), and Abraham was 75 years of age when he left Harran (Gen 12:4), then Terah could only have been 145 years of age when Abraham left Harran. Since Terah lived to be 205 (Gen 11:32), Abraham by this reckoning must have left Harran when Terah was still alive. But this chronology raised seemingly insuperable problems. If Terah had been involved in the first call, why would he have remained behind in Harran when Abraham received his second call to "go forth into the land of Canaan"? It also raised doubts about Abraham's filial loyalty: to suppose that Terah was still alive at the time of Abraham's migration imputed to him the character flaw of having irresponsibly abandoned his father. Moreover, the verse immediately preceding God's call to Abraham in Harran recorded Terah's death at age 205, thus implying that Terah was already dead when Abraham migrated. This inference was further confirmed by Stephen's unequivocal assertion in Acts 7:4 that "*after his father died,* God removed him (Abraham) from there into the land in which you are now living."

By the fourth century the debate was already waxing vigorous. Arguing against those who leave the matter of years "unresolved" by dating Abraham's migration after Terah's death, Diodore insists that the only viable solution to the problem is to assume that Abraham received a second call in Harran "when his father was still alive." Far from an act of filial infidelity, however, his decision to leave his father was a response required of "the father of the Church," acting in accordance with the verse "He who loves his father or mother more than me is not worthy of me" (cf. Matt 10:37). Besides, it had been the will of God all along to allot only Abraham and his offspring the land of promise.[55] Later interpreters proposed a variety of equally inventive solutions, all aimed at resolving the chronological and moral implications of Abraham's migration from Harran at age seventy-five.[56]

Jewish sources were no less attentive to the problem. An allegorical solution offered by *Genesis Rabbah* postulated that although Terah was physically alive at the time of Abraham's migration from Harran, he was already spiritually dead in the sense that he continued to practice idolatry there. Thus, in order to relieve Abraham of any responsibility for having abandoned his father, God recorded Terah's "death" before the migration.⁵⁷ Another explanation, which Jerome attributes to Jewish sources, held that Abraham's 75 years of age was calculated from the time of his conversion at age 60. In this way, Abraham was actually 135 years old at the time of his migration from Harran, thereby ensuring that Terah was already deceased.⁵⁸

Although *Jubilees* does not resolve the problem as elegantly as either of these previously mentioned Jewish sources, the author of that work was certainly cognizant of the issues. The fact that *Jubilees* dates Abraham as 60 years of age when he set fire to the temple suggests a common tradition with Jerome's Jewish informants. But, as we have seen, *Jubilees* inexplicably delays the migration from Ur for two years, and oddly assigns Abraham the age of 77, not 75, at the time of his migration from Harran. Nor does *Jubilees* attempt to justify Abraham's abandonment of his father by suggesting that Terah was already dead at the time of Abraham's migration from Harran. To relieve Abraham of the onus of having abandoned his father, it reports how Terah issued a blessing on his son as he left Harran, asking only that Abraham return for him when he finds "a land pleasant to the eyes" (12:29-31).

Brock may be right in supposing that the author of *Jubilees* drew on an older tradition that he only imperfectly grasped.⁵⁹ But it is far less likely that Jacob's "Jewish histories" reflects this older tradition. From as early as Julius Africanus, the *Jubilees* story of Abraham's call in Harran was widely known to Greek chronographers. But in every case, they have smoothed out the narrative, in part to solve the chronological inconsistencies of Terah's death. Syncellus' reconstruction of events is typical. On the authority of "Little Genesis," he reports how Abraham, at age 61(!), burned the idols in Ur. Thereupon Terah "went out with Abraham in order to go to the land of Canaan." Fourteen years later Abraham, at age 75, migrated to Harran "by a divine oracle."⁶⁰ But although Terah had originally participated in the divine call, he reverted to idolatry in Harran and remained there until his death. It is clear that Syncellus has completely reworked the *Jubilees* narrative in the interests of solving the chronological and exegetical problems posed by Abraham's apparent abandonment of Terah in Harran. Although Terah was physically still alive when Abraham left Harran, it was entirely appropriate, Syncellus says, for Genesis to imply and for Stephen to say outright that he had died. For insofar as he had elected to remain in Harran to continue plying his craft as an idol-maker, Terah was "spiritually" dead.[61] This latter symbolic explanation of Terah's death, entirely at odds with the *Jubilees* account, is actually quite close to the one found in *Genesis Rabbah*.[62] It reveals the extent to which *Jubilees'* narrative has been rewritten to address the chronological and exegetical problems associated with Abraham's migration from Harran.

Compare now the version of events supplied by Jacob's "Jewish histories" with the parallel account in *Jubilees*. After recording Abraham's burning of the temple at age sixty, it has the following:

> Terah ... fled by night from Ur, secretly taking his son Abraham with him, as well as Lot, Haran's son and his grandson, and Sarah his daughter-in-law. And he came to Harran to the land of Mesopotamia, and lived there. And afterward, Nahor, Abraham's brother, also came to him. And after fourteen years, Terah died. This is the reason why Terah and Abraham left Ur of the Chaldeans.[63]

Like the Greek versions of the story, Jacob's source eliminates *Jubilees'* two-year hiatus before the actual migration from Ur takes place. As Brock notes, this is to establish a causal link between the burning of the temple and the migration from Ur.[64] The parenthetical notice about Nachor's later arrival in Harran is inserted to explain why Genesis did not include Nachor among those who accompanied Terah from Ur, even though, as Jacob states, it was "well-known that he was with them in Harran."[65] Most notable, however, is Jacob's flat assertion, against *Jubilees*, that Terah died after residing in Harran for fourteen years. Unlike Syncellus' version of events, Jacob's source was apparently not troubled by the chronological inconsistency posed by this sequence of events. But by having Terah's death precede

Abraham's migration, Jacob's version conveniently managed both to avoid traducing Abraham's honor and to incorporate Stephen's version of events in Acts 7:4.[66]

Jacob's "Jewish Histories" and His Legacy to Syriac Chronography

Jacob's correspondence with John represents only one context in which these reworked *Jubilees* citations appear. Portions from the same narrative cycle about Abraham in Ur are also found in Syriac chronicles, catenae, scholia, and commentaries.[67] Material based on *Jubilees* thus functioned in Syriac literature both as an adjunct to biblical exegesis, and as narrative raw material for universal chronography. Indeed, this seems to be broadly true of much of the transmission history of *Jubilees*. The highly redacted contents of Jacob's "Jewish histories" reflect the result. Very little survives in this source that cannot be linked to a prominent chronological, historical, or exegetical problem in Genesis.

While there is no way to know the precise date or provenance of the Greek source for Jacob's "Jewish histories," a case might be made for the fourth or early fifth century CE. A productive period in the development of Christian chronography, the late fourth century witnessed the formulation of most of the problems treated by Jacob's "Jewish histories." Gelzer has shown that Syriac chroniclers received at least a portion of their pseudepigraphic citations from Annianus, an Alexandrian chronographer of the early fifth century.[68] And in his letters to John, the Christian writers with whom Jacob enters into dialogue are mainly luminaries of the fourth century: Eusebius of Emesa, Epiphanius, Athanasius, and Gregory Nazianzen.

Although an examination of the later transmission of *Jubilees* and other Jewish sources in Syriac chronography would take us far afield from our original topic, it is worth commenting briefly on this neglected area of research. The same cycle of stories found in Jacob's "Jewish histories" resurfaces later in the chronicles of Michael Syrus and Bar Hebraeus. Since both of these writers acknowledge the chronicles of Jacob and John as authorities, it is reasonable to assume that Jacob subsequently incorporated his "Jewish histories" into the more developed narrative format of a universal chronicle. Michael's chronicle also includes a few other citations from *Jubilees*, as well as *Enoch*. Like Jacob's "Jewish histories," much of this material probably originated in a Greek source. Michael's citation from *Enoch* and his interpretation of that book are based on the Greek chronicle of Annianus, and the other expansions of *Jubilees* reveal the unmistakable imprint of a Greek intermediary.[69]

We cannot assume, however, that Michael depended entirely on Greek authorities for their knowledge of Jewish sources. Interwoven into Michael's narrative of events from the flood up the time of Abraham are several fabulous tales about ancient Chaldea, the purpose of which seems to be to promote Syrian national identity. Among the several (probably fictitious) Oriental historians cited is a figure whom Michael knows as "Asaph the Jew."[70] The citations from this Asaph credit him with having analyzed the genealogy of Job, and with recording events in Chaldea on the eve of Abraham's attempted reforms. A portion of his narrative parallels material found in *Jubilees* and the derivative "Jewish histories," for example, the tradition tracing idolatry and Chaldaism to Serug, the legend about the idol temple in Ur destroyed by Abraham, and Cainan's discovery of Chaldean sciences.[71]

Asaph the Jew was a figure celebrated as a physician and historian among Arabic and Syriac historians.[72] Jewish tradition also refers to a medical book written by Asaph the Jew and based on a "Book of Remedies," the earliest attestation of which is *Jubilees*. The book purportedly came into being when Noah gave his son Shem a divinely inspired collection of remedies meant to ward off the depredations of demons.[73] While it cannot be shown with certainty that Asaph the Jewish physician and Asaph the Jewish historian were one and the same person, Michael's citations from Asaph the Jew represents a body of pseudepigraphic lore in Syriac that is unattested in Greek chronography. The character and origin of the "Asaph" source and its relationship to other Jewish pseudepigrapha are subjects worth exploring in further detail.[74]

The rather extensive citations from *Jubilees* preserved in the chronicle *ad annum 1234* pose an entirely different set of problems. There is little doubt that the author of this chronicle, who cites Jacob and Annianus as his authorities, knew some of his pseudepigraphic sources through Greek intermediaries. His interpretation of the legend of *Enoch*'s story of the fallen Watchers is clearly derived from Alexandrian chronography, and some of the citations from *Jubilees* contain the same embellishments of that work found in the Byzantine chronographers and Jacob's "Jewish histories." At the same time, however, Tisserant has shown that the bulk of this material is much more extensive and faithful to the preserved text of *Jubilees* than the heavily redacted and condensed citations found in Greek and other Syriac chronicles.[75] The *sui generis* character of the *Jubilees* citations in this chronicle amply testifies to the many unresolved questions surrounding the transmission of Jewish pseudepigrapha in Syriac.

---

[1]   Among the previous studies of this subject, see Heinrich Gelzer, *Sextus Julius Africanus und die byzantinische Chronographie* (2 vols.; Leipzig, 1880-85; reprinted, New York: Burt Franklin, 1967) 2.396-97, 403-404, 440-47; Albrecht Wirth, *Aus orientalischen Chroniken* (Frankfurt: Moritz, 1894) 66-68, 217-27; Eugène Tisserant, "Fragments syriaques du Livre des Jubilés," *Recueil Cardinal Eugène Tisserant* (2 vols.; Louvain: Centre international de dialectologie générale, 1955) 1.25-87 (originally published in *RB* 30 [1921] 55-86; 206-32); Sebastian Brock, "A Fragment of Enoch in Syriac," *JTS* 19 (1968) 626-31; idem, "Abraham and the Ravens: A Syriac Counterpart to *Jubilees* 11-12 and its Implications," *JSJ* 9 (1978) 135-52.

[2]   See below, pp. 24-26.

[3]   For discussion, see Gelzer, *Sextus Julius Africanus* 1.57-85; 2.249-97; 402-92, esp. 440-44; William Adler, *Time Immemorial: Archaic History and its Sources in Christian Chronography from Julius Africanus to George Syncellus* (Dumbarton Oaks Studies 26; Washington: Dumbarton Oaks Center for Byzantine Studies, 1989) 159-231.

[4]   The surviving fragments of the chronicle of Jacob of Edessa are published in *Chronica Minora* (CSCO Scriptores Syri 4-6; ed. I. Guidi, E.W. Brooks, and J.-B. Chabot; Paris, 1903-05; reprinted, Louvain: Durbecq, 1955) 261-327.

[5]   W. Wright, "Two Epistles of Mar Jacob, Bishop of Edessa," *Journal of Sacred Literature and Biblical Record* n.s. 10 (1867) 430ff. F. Nau later published an annotated French translation of these two epistles: "Traduction des lettres XII et XIII de Jacques d'Édessa," *Revue de l'orient chrétien* 10 (1905) 198-208; 258-82. This work is henceforth cited as *Ep.* Brock ("Abraham and

the Ravens" 137-39) gives an English translation of a portion of *Ep.* 13.

6   Brock, "Abraham and the Ravens" 151.

7   See George Syncellus, *Ecloga Chronographica* (ed. A.A. Mosshammer; Leipzig: Teubner, 1984) 4.21-23; 27.11.

8   Michael Glycas, *Annales* 1.156.12-17 (CSHB; ed. I. Bekker; Bonn: Weber, 1836).

9   *Ep.* 13.2 (Nau 206; 114^v).

10   *Ep.* 13.15 (Nau 274-76; 120^v). Here Jacob acknowledges that Solomon was the author of works on "trees, roots, animals, birds, reptiles, fish, knowledge that belongs to the art of bodily medicine and which we find in the books of the Greeks and the Egyptians." But since "none of the commentators or the Hebrews have told us" about the titles or contents of Solomon's writings, "we are not able to speak of that which has not come to us and has not been transmitted to us." The same is true of the lost writings of Moses and the prophets. God allowed Ezra to preserve and arrange only those fragments of their works that contributed to "knowledge of useful things." Ezra himself, Jacob says, was a prolific writer, but "the books of Ezra have not completely come to us." For divine providence had seen to it that the useful things of the book would survive. Of the 90 books credited to Ezra, Jacob says, "there only remain the books read in the Church." Here Jacob appears to be drawing on Jewish tradition (cf. 4 Ezra 14:44-46) which states that Ezra composed 94 books in 40 days, of which only 24 books were published.

11   See Brock, "A Fragment of Enoch in Syriac" 629. On admittedly little evidence, Brock argues that John of Litarba, not Jacob, was the mediary of the Enoch fragment.

12   *Ep.* 13.2 (Nau 207; 115^r).

13   As opposed to the rendering of Amram's name in the Syriac text of Genesis (ܥܡܪܡ; cf. MT עמרם), Jacob spells the name of Amram with *'ālaph*s. The variant almost certainly reflects the use of a Greek source, with *'ālaph*s representing here Greek *alpha*s: ܐܡܪܡ = 'Αμραμ. The same orthographic variant appears elsewhere in Jacob's citations from his "Jewish histories" (see below). Jacob's reference to *Enoch* in his letter to John reveals the influence of a Greek source, since he follows Septuagintal chronology in assigning more than 2000 years to antediluvian chronology (Nau 207; 115^r).

14   Cf. Sync. 3.19-22; Michael Glycas 1.156.12-156.4.

15   See Gelzer, *Sextus Julius Africanus* 2.278-80.

16   John Malalas 56.1-9 (CSHB; ed. L. Dindorf; Bonn: Weber, 1831) attributes to Eusebius a tradition resembling *Jub.* 12:1-15; see William Adler, "The Origins of the Proto-heresies: Fragments from a Chronicle in the First Book of Epiphanius' *Panarion*," *JTS* 41 (1990) 484-88.

17   See below, pp. 24-25.

18   Sync. 4.19-22; see also 124.1-14, where, after giving a series of extracts from *Jubilees* under the heading "'Ιωσήπου," Syncellus adds the following tag: " ταῦτα ἐν λεπτῇ Γενέσει φέρεται."

19   *Ep.* 13.1 (Nau 200; 112^r).

20   Epiphanius, *Panarion* 66.83-84 (GCS 25; ed. K. Holl; Leipzig: J.C. Hinrichs, 1915).

21 See Adler, "The Origins of the Proto-heresies" 491-92.

22 George the Monk, *Chronicon* 1.57.1-9 (ed. C. de Boor; Leipzig: Teubner, 1904); see also Cedrenus, *Compendium Historiarum* 1.24.11-25.7 (CSHB; 2 vols.; ed. I. Bekker; Bonn: Weber, 1838-39).

23 The reason for this is that the chronology of the Greek text of Genesis expands the postdiluvian period by adding a second Kainan and an additional 100 years to the age at which the patriarchs father offspring. Greek and Syriac chronographers comment extensively on the problem.

24 See Hermann Rönsch, *Das Buch der Jubiläen* (Leipzig: Fues, 1874) 284-86.

25 In G.S. Assemani, *Bibliotheca Orientalis Clementino-Vaticana* (3 vols. in 4; Rome: Sacrae Congregationis de Propaganda Fide, 1719-28) 1.85, quoted by Rönsch, *Jubiläen* 284.

26 See also *Tg. Onq.* Gen 9:27, which eliminates all ambiguity about the antecedent with its rendering, "And he shall make his Shekinah to dwell in the tabernacles of Shem."

27 Sync. 55.22-56.5; Ced. 1.26.1-8; see also Jerome, *Quaestiones hebraicae* on Gen 9:27 (CChr Series Latina 72; Turnholt: Brepolis, 1959): the passage is a prophecy about the gentiles. Already Philo (*Sob.* 61-68) wavers between the two explanations, one making Japhet the subject, the other God.

28 *Ep.* 13.1 (Nau 200; 112^V).

29 Thus the Hebrew *Testament of Naphtali* reports that after the division of tongues at the time of Peleg "the holy language, the Hebrew language, remained only in the house of Shem and Eber, and in the house of Abraham our father, who is one of their descendants" (8.4-6); see also *Gen. Rab.* 18.4. For discussion, see Louis Ginzberg, *The Legends of the Jews* (7 vols.; Philadelphia: Jewish Publication Society, 1909-38) 5.205 n. 91.

30 *Ant.* 1.146: "Heber, after whom the Jews were originally called Hebrews."

31 Philo, *Mig.* 20. *Gen. Rab.* 42.8 knows the same conflicting etymologies: "R. Nehemiah said, 'It was because he (Abraham) came from Eber.' Rabbis say, 'It is because he came from across the river, that he spoke the language of Hebrew'" (trans. Jacob Neusner, *Genesis Rabbah, The Judaic Commentary to the Book of Genesis: A New American Translation* [3 vols.; Brown Judaic Studies 104-106; Atlanta: Scholars Press, 1985] 2.112).

32 Quoted in Sync. 112.17-21.

33 Diodore, cited in *Catena of Nicephorus* (Breitkopf, 1772) 1.178; see also Ced. 1.49.12 (who reports both etymologies without judgment). For survival of the competing view linking Hebrew to "crosser," see Theodoret, *Quaest. in Gen.* 9.10 (*PG* 80.165); John Chrysostom, *In Genesim Sermo IX* (*PG* 54.624-25; see also *PG* 53.326, 364).

34 Sync. 112.4-6.

35 Leo Grammaticus, *Chronographia* 13.4-16 (CSHB; ed. I. Bekker; Bonn: Weber, 1842). For this chronicle as an epitome of Africanus, see Gelzer, *Sextus Julius Africanus* 1.57ff.

36 Michael Syrus 2.3; Syriac text and translation of Michael's chronicle by J.-B. Chabot, *Chronique de Michel le Syrien, patriarche jacobite d'Antioche, 1126-1199* (4 vols.; Paris, 1899-1924; reprinted, Brussels: Culture et Civilisation, 1963).

37 *Ep.* 13.14 (Nau 274; 120^V).

38 Michael Syrus 2.3; see also Bar Hebraeus: "But the pious Jacob and John of Yathreb think that Hebrew was the first (oldest) language -- the Hebrew which was preserved with Eber, for he was a righteous man and did not agree to the building of the Tower. Others think that the word 'Hebrew' is so called from Abraham, who crossed the rivers and crossed the divided pieces and passed from the paganism of his father to the Faith which is in God" (E.A.W. Budge, *The Chronography of Gregory Abu'l Faraj* [London: Humphrey Milford, 1932] 8). Unless otherwise specified, citations from Bar Hebraeus are from Budge's translation.

39 Sync. 111.13-15.

40 Sync. 107.16-24.

41 Brock, "Abraham and the Ravens" 140-41.

42 *Ep.* 13.1 (Nau 202-3; 112^V-113^r).

43 Cited in *Catena of Nicephorus* 1.181.

44 Cited in *Catena of Nicephorus* 1.180: When Terah learned of Abraham's call, "even though he was an unbeliever, nevertheless out of love for his son, he agreed to join him on his journey abroad."

45 See Ginzberg, *Legends* 5.214-15 n.40.

46 Before Haran's death, says George the Monk (1.92.17-94.21), "fathers always died before their sons, leaving them as successors to their affairs .... At that time, Terah acted in rivalry with God, through his own making of statues ... Haran died in the fire in which Abraham burned the idols of his father when Haran went in to rescue them. Therefore, divine scripture, wondering at this says, 'Haran died before Terah his father.'" Epiphanius, *Panarion* 1.3.6 has an abbreviated version of the same explanation.

47 Sync. 107.27-29. Notice here the distinction that Syncellus makes between Terah and the rest of his household. After the idols in Ur were destroyed by Abraham, Terah "went out (ἐξελθεῖν)" from Ur for the purpose of seeking gain from idolatry. The rest of his family, however, as recipients with Abraham of God's promise, were Abraham's companions (συμπορευθῆναι) in his journey to Canaan.

48 Brock conjectures that Jacob's text was mediated to him from "an independent Jewish Greek translation of the Hebrew" ("Abraham and the Ravens" 146). The Old Greek text of Gen 11:27-28 has the following: καὶ ἀπέθανεν Ἀρρὰν ἐνώπιον Θάρρα τοῦ πατρὸς αὐτοῦ ἐν τῇ γῇ ῇ ἐγεννήθη.

49 *Scholia on Passages of the Old Testament by Mar Jacob, Bishop of Edessa* (ed. and trans. George Phillips; London, Edinburgh: Williams and Norgate, 1864) 3-5 (scholium 2, on Gen 11:27-32). See also *Catena of Severus* (ninth century): "after Abraham's brother Haran entered to put out the fire and save the carved idol, he fell down there and died. For this reason, it was necessary to indicate his death before Terah his father" (trans. Brock, "Abraham and the Ravens" 138-39).

50 *Ep.* 13.1 (Nau 204; 113^V); cf. Brock, "Abraham and the Ravens" 141.

51 *Ep.* 13.2 (Nau 203; 113^V); see also Michael Syrus 2.5-6; Bar Hebraeus 9.

52 See Brock, "Abraham and the Ravens" 150. According to *Jub.* 11:7, idolatry began in the time of Serug.

53 See Martin Hengel, *Judaism and Hellenism* (2 vols.; Philadelphia: Fortress Press, 1974) 1.242.

[54]   Bar Hebraeus 7. For Kainan as discoverer of astrology and related sciences, see the anonymous scholion to Gen 5:21 tracing the origins of astronomy and auguries to the time of Kainan (cited in the *Catena of Nicephorus* 1.172); also John of Nikiu, *Chronicle* 4.1-2 (trans. R.H. Charles; London: Williams and Norgate, 1916). On Kainan's discovery of stelae, see Sync. 90.11-12 (= Ced. 1.27.11), who reports the *Jubilees* legend with the curious variant that the stelae were left by the Giants, not the Watchers. It is conceivable that the original version of *Jubilees*, following the Hebrew text of Genesis, did not include the second Kainan in its narrative. In this respect, it is striking that although the preserved text of *Jubilees* ascribes the discovery of the stelae to Kainan, the Greek epitomes of Africanus report that it was Shelah, not Kainan, who made the discovery. This would suggest that at some later date in the Greek transmission of *Jubilees* the tradition was transferred to Kainan; for discussion, see Gelzer, *Sextus Julius Africanus* 2.275. In Bar Hebraeus' notice about Kainan, he acknowledges that neither the Syriac nor the Hebrew version of Genesis knew of a postdiluvian Kainan. This again would point to dependence on a Greek source.

[55]   Cited in *Catena of Nicephorus* 1.182.

[56]   Syncellus refers to some chroniclers who had proposed that the expression "Terah begat Abraham, Nachor, and Haran" did not mean that Terah fathered all three children at once. After all, they were not triplets. Although Moses named Abraham first, he was actually born sometime later (106.16-22; see also Augustine, *Quaestiones in Heptateuchum* 25.2 [CChr Series Latina 33; Turnholt: Brepolis, 1958]). For discussion of this question, see William Adler, "Abraham and the Burning of the Temple of Idols: *Jubilees*' Traditions in Christian Chronography," *JQR* 77 (1986-87) 104-117.

[57]   *Gen. Rab.* 39.7, on the authority of R. Isaac.

[58]   Jerome, *Quaestiones hebraicae* on Gen 12:4 (see n.27 above).

[59]   Brock, "Abraham and the Ravens" 144-146.

[60]   Sync. 112.7-12.

[61]   Sync. 107.30-108.5. On Terah's reversion to idolatry in Harran, see also Eusebius of Emesa, who quotes Josh 24:2 to support this interpretation: "your fathers sojourned beyond the river, even Terah, the father of Abraham and the father of Nachor; and they served other Gods" (in *L'héritage littéraire d'Eusèbe d'Émèse* [ed. E.M. Buytaert; Louvain: Bureaux du Muséon, 1949] 106 [on Gen 11:31-12:5]).

[62]   See Ginzberg, *Legends* 5.219 n.53.

[63]   *Ep.* 13.2 (Nau 204; 113^V).

[64]   Brock, "Abraham and the Ravens" 141.

[65]   Phillips, *Scholia on Passages of the Old Testament* 5 (on Gen 11:27-32).

[66]   *Ep.* 13.1 (Nau 204; 113^V). Later Syriac chroniclers continued to comment on the problem. Bar Hebraeus maintains that Abraham had actually made two trips from Harran, of which Genesis only recorded the first; see *Barhebraeus' Scholia on the Old Testament* (OIP 13; eds. Martin Sprengling and William Creighton Graham; Chicago: University of Chicago Press, 1931) 49 (on Gen 12:4). In his chronicle, however, he reports only that after residing in Harran for fourteen years Abraham departed from his father (p. 10).

[67] In addition to the works already cited, see also Jacob bar Salibi's *Commentary on Genesis* (MS syr. 66, fol. 21, cited by Nau 204 n.2).

[68] Gelzer, *Sextus Julius Africanus* 2.440ff.

[69] Cf. Michael Syrus 1.1,3-4; for discussion, see Gelzer, *Sextus Julius Africanus* 2.440-41. When Michael (2.2), followed by Bar Hebraeus (p. 7), describes the division of the earth among Noah's sons, he departs from the geographical boundaries of *Jubilees* 8 and substitutes it with a scheme attested as early as the chronicle of Hippolytus. The Syriac version of the division of the earth bears the closest affinities to that found in Syncellus; see A. von Gutschmid, "Untersuchungen über den Διαμερισμὸς τῆς γῆς und andere Bearbeitungen der Mosaischen Völkertafel," *Kleine Schriften* (5 vols.; ed. Franz Rühl; Leipzig: Teubner, 1894) 5.692-96.

[70] Michael Syrus 2.4. The others include the Canaanite Aroud, the magians Menander and Zamardos, and the Assyrian Qomabaros.

[71] See Michael Syrus 2.4, where he states on the authority of Asaph that Serug instructed his son Nachor in the Chaldean religion, magic, and astrology (cf. *Jub.* 11:6-9). Later he quotes Asaph to the effect that "from the time of Terah, the Egyptians acquired the doctrines of the Chaldeans and established a statue of gold to the idol Ninus" (2.6). At 2.7, he states that it is written that "Cainan ... discovered magic, auguries, and sorcery, and that he was venerated as a god." As Chabot notes (p. 30, n.1), this latter citation appears to be a continuation of Asaph's chronicle.

[72] For discussion, see Chabot's introduction to his translation of Michael Syrus (1.xxvii); Wirth, *Aus orientalischen Chroniken* 217; Ludwig Venetianer, *Asaf Judaeus* (3 vols.; Jahresbericht der Landes-Rabbinerschule in Budapest 38-40; Budapest: Országos Rabbiképzë Intézet, 1915) 1.18≟39; Assemani, *Bibliotheca Orientalis* 2.313.

[73] See Adolph Jellinek, *Bet ha-Midrasch* (3d ed.; 6 vols. in 2; Jerusalem: Wahrmann Books, 1967) 3.155-156; for Noah's medical book, see *Jub.* 10:10-13.

[74] A. Geiger first suggested that the two Asaphs referred to the same figure (in *ZDMG* 14 [1860] 277-78). It is possible that the Asaph whom the Syriac writers cite is a pseudonym. Bar Hebraeus and Jacob bar Salibi (quoted by Nau, "Traduction" 261 n.1) identify him as a "Hebrew priest, brother of Ezra and an author of books"; see Venetianer, *Asaf Judaeus* 34.

[75] Tisserant, "Fragments syriaques" 30ff. Edition and Latin translation of this chronicle by J.-B. Chabot, *Anonymi auctoris Chronicon ad annum Christi 1234 pertinens* (CSCO Scriptores Syri 36, 37, 56; reprinted, Louvain: Durbecq, 1952-53). Like Jacob's "Jewish histories," this chronicle seems to imply that Abraham's first call began with the crisis with the ravens: "from that time Abraham knew God and promised to serve him" (Chabot trans. 38.25-27 [p. 51]). It also reports the legend about the "god" Kainan (34.4-7 [p. 46]; 39.3 [p. 52]). On the other hand, it says nothing about Terah's death in Harran before Abraham's departure; instead it simply reprises Terah's farewell address in *Jub.* 12:29-31 (39.23-25 [p. 52]). The fact that the author weaves into the *Jubilees* narrative material from the *Cave of Treasures*, a pseudepigraphic work of native Syriac provenance, strengthens the possibility that the author's text of *Jubilees* did not come to him entirely via Greek intermediaries.

JEWISH PSEUDEPIGRAPHA IN MANICHAEAN LITERATURE: THE INFLUENCE OF THE ENOCHIC LIBRARY

John C. Reeves
Winthrop University

Manichaean writings are not logical candidates for the preservation and transmission of patently Jewish literary motifs. The critical attitude of Mani and his religion toward the Hebrew Bible and Judaism is well exemplified by the testimony of Titus of Bostra, who opens the fourth book of his refutation of Manichaeism by stating "he (i.e., Mani) attributes the Old Testament fully and completely to the archons of Hyle."[1] This denigrating stance is not of course a unique one in the appraisal of ancestral religions during late antiquity. It is shared by (some would say borrowed from) representatives of the classical Gnostic and Mandaean religious communities. Ironically though, in spite of their anti-Jewish bias, the aforementioned religious currents display clear indications that they were heavily dependent upon both Jewish literature and Jewish exegetical traditions, at least during their formative periods.[2]

Recent research is making it increasingly apparent that Manichaeism is ultimately indebted to Second Temple era Jewish thought and literature.[3] While it is true that Manichaean texts rarely cite the Hebrew Bible, it nevertheless seems certain that important characters and events featured in the Hebrew Bible, particularly those within the primeval history of Genesis 1-11, assume a major significance in the ideological development of Mani's thought. The accounts of creation, the experiences of the protoplasts and their progeny, the generational succession of the primal patriarchs, the angelic corruption and enslavement of humankind, the roles of Enoch and Noah, the cataclysmic Flood, the prominence of Shem, and possibly even Abraham, in the preservation of antediluvian wisdom -- all of these biblically based actors and episodes receive varying amounts of attention in the Manichaean corpus of writings. Yet, as previously mentioned, the Manichaean texts do not recount these stories in their biblical guise. They instead rely upon, transmit, and further develop the expanded and embellished forms of these stories that we find earlier in Jewish pseudepigraphic works and rabbinic haggadic traditions.[4]

The reason for this peculiar (at least to us) reliance has been clarified by the great manuscript discoveries of the present century that have revolutionized Manichaean studies.[5] Manichaean texts attest that Mani viewed himself as the final link of a chain of incarnations of the heavenly Apostle of Light, periodically dispatched to humankind to proclaim the Manichaean message of redemption. Manichaeism assigned certain biblical figures important roles in this conception of the historical progress of religious revelation. According to the literature, the prophetic succession envisioned by Manichaeism consisted initially of certain biblical patriarchs from the antediluvian and immediately postdiluvian periods: Adam, Seth, Enosh, Enoch, Noah, Shem, and possibly Abraham.[6] The series of authentic prophets continued with Zoroaster, Jesus, and the Buddha, and perhaps inserted the names of Elchasai, Marcion, and/or Bardaisan[7] before culminating with the "seal of the prophets," Mani himself.[8] While these earlier prophets experienced some personal success in the promulgation of the teachings among their generations, their message was inevitably corrupted and distorted by its subsequent faulty (and in some cases deliberately falsified) transmission.[9] The disciples and followers of each preceding apostle were overwhelmingly incompetent (and in some cases deceitful) custodians of the divine message. The results of their literary labors, whether well- or ill-intentioned, were the canonical scriptures of the ancestral religions; i.e., Judaism, Christianity, Zoroastrianism, and Buddhism. These were accordingly of limited value for the transmission of the pristine Gospel of Light. In order to recover the *original* message of these divine emissaries, it was necessary to consult literary testimonia that allegedly stem from the apostles themselves. Herein lies the significance of what modern scholars term "pseudepigrapha" attributed to the apostolic line, and the basic reason for the Manichaean disparagement of earlier canonical scriptures.

Affirmation of the fundamental importance of writings authored by these precursors of Mani has lately been supplied by the *Cologne Mani Codex*, a Greek manuscript purporting to provide a Mani *vita* that was apparently prepared by early leaders of the Manichaean community not long after the founder's demise.[10] The role of these writings, not only as testimonies to the proto-Manichaean flavor of the instructions of the forebears, but also as apologia for the religious experience and teachings of Mani himself, is well expressed in this redactional seam of the *Codex*:

> Furthermore, let him who is willing hearken and pay attention to how each one of the primeval patriarchs communicated his own revelation to a select (group) whom he chose and gathered together from that generation during which he appeared, and after writing (it down), he left it for future generations. Each (patriarch) revealed (information) about his heavenly journey, and they (i.e., the chosen group) promulgated beyond ... to record and display afterwards, and to laud and extol their teachers and the truth and the hope that was revealed to them. Thus each one spoke and wrote down a memoir recounting what he saw, including (an account) about his heavenly journey, during the period and cycle of his apostleship.[11]

This explanation introduces quotations from the "recorded memoirs" of these "primeval patriarchs": five "apocalypses" attributed to Adam, Seth, Enosh, Shem, and Enoch.[12] These testimonies are then followed by two citations from the epistles of the Christian apostle Paul,[13] and the whole series of textual references culminates with several quotations from two of Mani's own writings.[14]

The citations from works allegedly authored by Adam, Seth, Enosh, Shem, and Enoch are of particular interest for our present purpose, since they clearly fall into the category of "Jewish pseudepigrapha."[15] Interestingly, they do not textually correspond to any great extent with any previously known works attributed to these same authors. They all display a general similarity in formal structure. Each citation is introduced as an "apocalypse" (ἀποκάλυψις) of the named author, and each concludes with a notice about other "writings" (γράφαι) supposedly authored by these seers which supplement the excerpted vision. Each visionary experiences an angelophany, a vision of one or more angelic beings that in two of the instances are identified by name: Balsamos[16] (Adam) and Michael (Enoch). Each seer is transported to heaven and views certain sights or is made privy to certain secrets. In one case, that of Shem, the very throne-room of God is seen (and heard). Each apocalypse contains some expression of the tension between the corporeal status of the visionary and the ecstatic privilege which each is granted. Enoch and Enosh quake and shudder involuntarily, Shem falls prostrate[17] until a voice from the throne-room "raised me (and) blew a breath of life into my nostrils, increasing my power and glory," and Seth and Adam are explicitly transformed into divine beings. Finally, two of the fragments stress the careful preservation and transmission of the revealed mysteries by exhorting the seers (Adam and Enosh) to take special pains in the preparation of their testimonia.

Perhaps the most significant point to note about these fragments is their close affinity to that genre of Jewish literature termed *Hekhalot* texts. As some have observed, these citations are replete with the *termini technici* of the *Hekhalot* tradition.[18] Yet they also display clear connections with ancient Jewish apocalyptic traditions, particularly those wherein the seer is shown various heavenly mysteries, or is conducted about the heavens to view the inhabitants or contents of each supernal level. These fragments would seem to supply some important textual evidence for an unbroken chain of tradition connecting Second Temple Jewish apocalyptic texts to the earliest *Hekhalot* literature, a linkage which was forcefully argued by the late G. Scholem in spite of a dearth of textual witnesses.[19] Scholem postulated a continuous transmission and development of what has been termed "Merkavah mysticism" from the esoterically inclined learned circles of scribes considered responsible for the production of apocalyptic literature during the Second Temple era to the Amoraic and Geonic sages of Palestine and Babylonia, laying particular stress upon the presumed role of certain Tannaitic *ḥakhamim* in this process.[20] Significantly, however, Scholem also recognized that certain "subterranean" currents of transmission might explain the transit of these motifs, currents whose flow was "independent of, and often in isolation from, the schools and academies of the Talmudic teachers."[21]

Are *these* heretofore unattested fragments representative of one (or more) of Scholem's "subterranean connections"? Their arresting blend of elements from both the "older" apocalyptic tradition and the "later" *Hekhalot* corpus would seem to point in this direction. The utilization of these fragments in a Manichaean apologetic text presumably directed toward individuals or groups who would respect such testimonia indicates that there were audiences who would be affected by this sort of argument. Moreover, there is also further evidence that bolsters the probability that amalgams of apocalyptic and mystical strands of thought were produced and cherished by Jewish groups who stood outside of the traditional Tannaitic circles.

A particularly appropriate example of this sort of speculation is Elchasai, the reputed founder of the baptist sect among whom Mani was reared. To judge from the limited evidence concerning his teachings, Elchasai was a Jewish visionary who apparently lived during the early part of the second century CE and who claimed to be in possession of a "heavenly book."[22] Short excerpts from this book survive in the hostile surveys of Elchasaite doctrine provided by Hippolytus and Epiphanius.[23] Despite its fragmentary state, the eschatological flavor of the book's message is clearly manifest. One prophecy contained therein predicted a final battle "among the wicked angels of the north," an event apparently dependent upon the Gog and Magog tradition of Ezekiel 38-39.[24] Another passage of the work featured an encoded Aramaic testimonium to be recited during daily prayer that reads (when deciphered) "I (who? Elchasai? some heavenly advocate?) will bear witness on your behalf on the day of the great judgment."[25] As J.M. Baumgarten has perceptively pointed out, the expression "day of the great judgment" is a *leit-motif* of the Enochic apocalyptic library.[26]

Yet in addition to this apocalyptic slant, there seems to be evidence that Elchasai and/or those responsible for producing his book were conversant with certain strands of Merkavah mysticism. Both Hippolytus and Epiphanius refer to Elchasai's report of a vision in which he beheld two divine beings of gargantuan proportions, boasting heights of 24 *schoinoi* (96 miles) and breadths of 6 *schoinoi* (24 miles). Long ago G. Alon suggested that the immense dimensions of the divine beings revealed to Elchasai were reminiscent of *Shi'ur Qomah* speculation.[27] More recently Baumgarten has resolved several problematic *cruces* in the Elchasaite material by demonstrating that they are most plausibly explained within the context of the practice of "heavenly ascent." For example, a cryptic reference in Elchasai's book to the illusory appearance of fire contrasted with the dependable sound of water alludes not, as previously thought, to a sectarian rejection of sacrificial cultus, but rather to "perils of the kind associated with the heavenly ascent" that are familiar from the *Hekhalot* tradition.[28] If Alon and Baumgarten are correct, it would appear that Elchasai (and presumably his sect) could be classed among the early representatives of the *yordey merkavah.*

The fact that Mani spent approximately twenty-one years among an Elchasaite group in southern Babylonia[29] suggests that apocalyptic and Merkavah traditions, presumably revered and transmitted within the sect,[30] could have been studied, expounded, and even practiced by this third-century religious founder. Is there any evidence that Mani engaged in such activities either during his Elchasaite sojourn or after his break with this baptist sect?

Mani's devotion to and promulgation of apocalyptic traditions has never been seriously doubted.[31] Most of the prominent heresiological sources for the principles of Manichaeism devote some space to the description and refutation of its eschatological teachings. Authentic Manichaean writings prove that there was a considerable eschatological component to the religion's doctrines. The *Shābuhragān*, a work purportedly authored by Mani for the instruction of Shapur I, contained a lengthy recountal of apocalyptic prophecies presumably derived from Matthew 24-25.[32] Mani apparently had some interest in the so-called *Oracles of Hystaspes*, a Parthian apocalypse which enjoyed wide popularity during the early centuries of the Common Era.[33] Even the skeletal structure of Mani's religion, often encapsuled as the teaching concerning "the Two Principles" (i.e., Light and Darkness) and "the Three Times" (i.e., past, present, and future),[34] underscores this eschatological orientation. In the words of A. Henrichs,

> ... he (Mani) had been sent to bring final salvation to every country and every person on earth. Once his mission was completed, the world would soon come to an end, the Last Judgment would divide the righteous from the sinners, and the original separation of Light and Darkness would be restored for all eternity.[35]

Moreover, there is also evidence that Mani was an adept in the techniques of "heavenly ascent." While the angelophanies experienced by the young Mani are ambiguous with regard to their stimulation and setting,[36] it does seem possible that some of these visions and auditions involved transport to the Realm of Light. The sights and sounds need not necessarily be confined to an earthly locale. However, there are two clear instances in Manichaean tradition where Mani's practice of "heavenly ascent" is attested.[37]

One excellent demonstration of Mani's mystical prowess occurs in a prose text that recounts a missionary journey to the region of Mesene.[38] This province was governed by Mihrshah, a brother of the Sasanian monarch Shapur I, and the text informs us that Mihrshah was exceedingly hostile to the new doctrine promulgated by Mani. This same Mihrshah possessed a garden of extraordinary beauty in which he took especial delight, and Mani, perceiving an opportunity, resolved to seek an audience with the ruler. In the course of their conversation, Mihrshah scornfully asked Mani whether the "paradise" which the apostle preached contained any garden that could rival his own treasured park, and in response Mani conducted the astonished governor on a tour of the

> miraculous wonders of the Paradise of Light with all (its) deities, divinities, and the immortal breath of life, and gardens of every type, and also the other magnificent sights which were there. He lay unconscious for three hours ... until the Apostle laid his hand on his head.[39]

The text unfortunately breaks off shortly after this point. Since Manichaean historiography attributes Mani's subsequent friendly reception at the court of Shapur I to the sponsorship of a brother of the king,[40] we should probably conclude that Mihrshah was converted to the new faith.

Another piece of testimony concerning Mani's typical behavior among his disciples appears in the valuable description of Manichaeism that is provided by the eleventh-century polymath al-Bīrūnī. This passage reads as follows:

> ... that the king Shapur came to believe in him when he had ascended with him towards heaven, and they had been standing in the air between heaven and earth. Mani, thereby, made him witness a miracle. Besides, they relate that he sometimes used to rise to heaven from among his companions, to stay there for some days, and then to redescend to them.[41]

This passage attests not only another guided tour of the heavens, this time for the *shahanshah* himself, but also that "heavenly ascent" was habitually practiced by Mani, presumably for the purpose of instructing his disciples. "Ascension" thus seems to be an important motif shared by certain pre-Mosaic biblical forefathers, Elchasai, and Mani himself. The apocalyptic fragments quoted in the *CMC* are valued for precisely that component of their contents.[42] The ascension of each "author" provides the guarantee for the verity of their experiences, and of course concomitantly the writings that recount such experiences, and demonstrates furthermore that Mani should be numbered among these illustrious worthies.

But from whence do these apocalyptic fragments stem? Biblical tradition does feature occasional prophetic excursions to heaven -- one thinks of Isaiah 6, Zechariah 3, and 1 Kings 22:19-22 -- and speaks of two "permanent" ascensions, those of Enoch and Elijah.[43] Medieval rabbinic sources expand the list of those privileged "not to taste death,"[44] but earlier literature exhibits a general suspicion of such traditions, probably in reaction to the prominent role these play in apocryphal and pseudepigraphic texts.[45] Indeed, R. Abbahu disapprovingly chides certain "sectarians" (*minim*) who occupy themselves with the ascensions of Enoch and Elijah.[46] It is perhaps such groups of *minim* (among whom we might plausibly number the Elchasaites) who should be held responsible for the preservation and promulgation of works like those quoted in the *CMC*, as well as many of the other pseudepigraphic texts which have come down to us from the Second Temple period.

The "Apocalypse of Enoch" in the Cologne Mani Codex

As previously mentioned, the apocalyptic fragments cited in the *CMC* exhibit no great degree of textual correspondence with previously known works ascribed to Adam, Seth, Enosh, Enoch, or Shem.[47] This does not mean however that they are totally divorced from the extant literary traditions associated with each forefather.[48] While space does not permit a thorough analysis of each citation, some specific observations can be made about one of these fragments, the so-called "Apocalypse of Enoch."[49] The fragment reads as follows:

> Moreover Enoch also speaks in a similar manner in his "Apocalypse": 'I am Enoch the righteous. My sorrow was great, and a torrent of tears (streamed) from my eyes because I heard the insult which the wicked uttered.' He says: 'While the tears were still in my eyes and the prayer

was yet on my lips, I beheld approaching me s[even] angels
descending from heaven. [Upon seeing] them I was so
moved by fear that my knees began knocking.' He says
moreover: 'One of the angels, whose name was Michael,
said to me: I was sent to you for this purpose -- in order
that I might show you all the deeds and reveal to you the
place (appointed) for the pious, and to show you the place
(appointed) for the impious and what sort of place of
punishment the lawless are experiencing.' He says also:
'They seated me upon a chariot of wind and brought me to
the ends of the heavens. We traversed worlds -- the world
of [dea]th, the world of [dar]kness, and the world of fire.
And after these (worlds) they brought me into a world of
extraordinary richness which was resplendently luminous,
even more beautiful than the heavenly luminaries which I
(also) beheld.' All these things he saw, and he questioned
the angels, and that which they told him he recorded in his
writings.[50]

While it is true that this fragment finds no verbatim
correspondence within the previously known Enochic works, the
passage is nevertheless rife with allusions to motifs and events that
figure in the extant narratives of *1* and *2 Enoch*. The actual text of the
fragment begins with the statement "I am Enoch the righteous
(δίκαιος)." This epithet accorded Enoch is a stock feature of the extant
Enochic literature, and in itself legitimates this fragment's status within
the Enochic corpus.[51] The singling out of Michael for special
recognition recalls the similarly specified role that this archangel plays
in the heavenly ascension of Enoch that is described in *1 Enoch* 71.[52]
The specific reference to a "chariot of wind" (ἅρματος ἀνέμου) as
Enoch's mode of conveyance in the *CMC* fragment in fact possesses a
direct parallel in *1 Enoch* 70:2, where Enoch is also raised to heaven
through the agency of "chariots of wind."[53] The topography of the
supernal regions traversed by Enoch -- a world of death, a world of
darkness, a world of fire, and a world of bright richness -- would seem
to reflect the divisions of Sheol viewed by Enoch in *1 Enoch* 22, which
constructs a schema of three dark and tortuous places for sinners
alongside another for the righteous which contains a "bright spring."[54]
Credulity would be stretched to its extreme limit were one to ascribe

all of these correspondences, as well as the others identified above, to mere chance.

It had of course been long suspected that Mani was an avid student of Enochic lore. Ever since the ground-breaking study of I. de Beausobre, scholars have speculated that Mani may have relied upon one or more "books of Enoch" as a source for some of his distinctive ideas.[55] The important recovery and publication of Coptic and Middle Iranian Manichaean texts during the first half of the present century has dramatically confirmed the earlier suspicions. In a series of significant studies, W.B. Henning conclusively established that Mani had utilized Aramaic Enochic texts in the composition of several of his "scriptural" works.[56] Mani's prowess in Aramaic was hardly surprising, given his nativity and the explicit traditions regarding the production of his books.[57] Further proof for Mani's dependence upon Jewish Enochic literature was supplied in 1971 by J.T. Milik. Milik successfully demonstrated that an Aramaic Enochic text discovered at Qumran was actually the *Vorlage* for one of Mani's canonical scriptures entitled the "Book of Giants."[58] In fact, it seems extremely likely that in addition to this "Book of Giants" other portions of what comprise the contemporary versions of what is now called *1 Enoch* were also studied and adapted by Mani. These include those sections conventionally designated "Astronomical Enoch" (*1 Enoch* 72-82),[59] the "Book of Watchers" (*1 Enoch* 1-36),[60] and the "Similitudes" (*1 Enoch* 37-71).[61] In light of the above investigation, it would appear now that additional Enochic texts also exerted influence upon nascent Manichaeism.

One must conclude that the early Manichaean community, like its sectarian predecessors, had access to a larger corpus of Jewish pseudepigraphic, and particularly Enochic, literature than do modern scholars today. The broad dimensions of what, for instance, might be termed the "Enochic library" are already remarked in ancient literature: the Muslim scholar al-Ṭabarī speaks of "thirty scrolls" published by Enoch,[62] whereas the text of Slavonic Enoch itself reports the production of an assuredly fantastic 360 works by the antediluvian sage.[63] A cursory survey of the many citations and allusions to "books," "apocalypses," and "prophecies" of Enoch in Jewish, Christian, and even Muslim texts suggests that the relatively sober enumeration of al-Ṭabarī is by no means exaggerated.[64] Of course not all of these Enochic works need necessarily be traced back to Second Temple scribal circles. Christians and Muslims were perfectly capable of fabricating "new" Enochic books, as the aforementioned instance preserved in the chronicle of Michael the Syrian demonstrates.[65] However, the "Apocalypse of Enoch" quoted in the *CMC* does not seem to fall into this latter category of forgeries. Neither does it, nor for that matter, the remaining *CMC* citations from Jewish "apocalypses" betray any sign of Christian origin. Their affinities lie rather with the earlier Jewish pseudepigraphic and presumably contemporaneous mystical traditions.

2 Enoch and Manichaean Traditions

The Jewish pseudepigraphon popularly designated "Slavonic" or *2 Enoch* is notable for its intense interest in cosmogonical and cosmological subjects, and foreshadows and/or parallels in several important respects the contents and concerns of *Hekhalot* and classical Gnostic cosmogonies. G. Scholem has called attention to several intriguing correspondences that link certain features of *2 Enoch* with material found in later midrashic and early kabbalistic literature.[66] Recently M. Scopello has presented a compelling case for the textual dependence of the *Apocalypse of Zostrianos* upon *2 Enoch*, the former work figuring among the non-Christian Gnostic documents found at Nag Hammadi.[67] It seems to the present writer that a plausible argument can also be made for Mani's possible reliance upon portions of this same Enochic composition.

The first of these possible connections involves the existence of a group of "heavenly prisoners." A very curious passage in *2 Enoch* 4 reads as follows:

> And those two men took me up into the second heaven ...
> and showed me the prisoners, under guard, of the
> immeasurable judgement; and there I saw angels that had

been condemned, weeping. And I said to the men who were with me, Why are these in torment? The men answered me, These are apostates from the Lord, who were not obedient to the Lord's commands, but took counsel with their own will ... And the angels bowed low to me and said, Man of God, we ask you that you would pray to the Lord for us.[68]

This particular text obviously refers to the angelic insurrection that took place in the days of Yared, the father of Enoch.[69] The prisoners in this "second heaven" are in fact those Watchers who violated the divinely decreed barriers separating heaven and earth by taking human wives and fathering bastard offspring, the infamous Giants. Their identity as rebellious Watchers is further underscored by the petition they press upon Enoch: "Man of God, we ask you that you would pray to the Lord for us." This request is reminiscent of the language of *1 Enoch* 13:4: "And they [i.e., the Watchers] asked me to write out for them the record of a petition that they might receive forgiveness, and to take the record of their petition up to the Lord in heaven."[70] It seems clear that the narrative focus of both Enochic texts is identical.

However, the *2 Enoch* passage is peculiar in that it places the prison for the incarcerated Watchers in heaven itself. This transcendent location contradicts the explicit testimonies of other works about where these rebellious Watchers are held; viz., beneath the earth.[71] Moreover, a later passage in *2 Enoch* is simultaneously cognizant of this latter tradition: "And I said to the Watchers, I have seen your brothers, and I have heard what they did; ... and I prayed for them. And behold, the Lord has condemned them below the earth until the heavens and the earth pass away ..."[72] The reference in this text is surely to the imprisoned Watchers that Enoch had previously encountered in the second heaven. But here, while touring the "fifth heaven," the imprisoned Watchers are spoken of as being "beneath the earth"! As many have observed, there would seem to be some confusion in the recountal of this particular tradition.[73]

The puzzling reference to angels incarcerated as "heavenly prisoners" in *2 Enoch* 4 is quite intriguing. Interestingly, a similar group of heavenly captives also figures in the cosmogonical and exegetical literature of Manichaeism.[74] According to Manichaean tradition, the divine evocation termed the "Great King of Honor" guards an unspecified number of captive archons from the Realm of Darkness.[75] These archons escaped the fate suffered by many of their brethren during the initial response of the Realm of Light to the assault of Darkness; that is to say, they were not slain or skinned during the creation of the physical cosmos.[76] Instead, they are held as prisoners in the heavens. Various terms are employed to describe the type of incarceration they endure, but most witnesses agree that they are somehow "fastened upon" or "suspended from" the firmament.[77] In addition to the prominent role these archons play in the creation of organic life upon earth, there exist some intriguing traditions about the role they play in human history.

Our most reliable accounts of Manichaean cosmogony relate that ten heavens[78] and eight earths were fabricated by those entities responsible for demiurgic activity. The five "sons" of the Living Spirit were assigned "watchposts" at various strategic points within this created cosmos.[79] Enthroned in the seventh heaven is the Great King of Honor,[80] wherein he keeps guard over the entire celestial structure, including the aforementioned bound archons, who are apparently affixed to the zodiacal firmament. At some point in history two hundred of these archons escaped their supernal prison and fled to earth.[81] These fugitive archons proceeded to engender progeny termed "giants," to engage in assorted forms of lawless behavior, and to instruct humans in various types of esoteric knowledge. As a result of their activities, "rebellion and ruin came about on the earth ...."[82] In order to repair the damage produced by this revolt, four archangels were dispatched to sequester the rebellious archons "beneath the mountains" and to destroy their monstrous children.[83]

It seems abundantly clear that the archonic rebellion described in Manichaean tradition is identical with the fall of the Watchers recounted in Enochic sources, particularly that version provided by *1 Enoch* 6-16. Yet Mani did not simply incorporate this tale verbatim. Certain adjustments were required in order to bring the story in line with emergent Manichaean doctrine. The earlier form of the tale presumes that evil spontaneously erupts in heaven -- divine beings originally good metamorphose into lust-crazed demons -- and then spreads to earth.[84] Such a metaphysic was foreign to Mani's understanding of the fundamental ontological distinction between Good and Evil. Good cannot possibly produce evil, nor can evil possess a rightful locale in heaven.[85] If, as the Enochic tale alleges, evil came to earth from heaven (and bearing in mind Enoch's status as an Apostle of Light in Manichaean teaching), then a neat solution for this apparent enigma is to identify the wicked Watchers of Enoch with captive archons from the Realm of Darkness who were imprisoned in heaven by agents of the Realm of Light.[86] Such an interpretive step receives textual warrant only through *2 Enoch* 4. It thus seems highly likely that Mani was cognizant of at least this peculiar tradition, and moreover utilized its testimony in adapting the Enochic tale of the "descent of the Watchers" to its new Manichaean setting. Furthermore, Mani could simultaneously incorporate the traditional motif of the Watchers' incarceration "beneath the earth" by referring it to a later point in the "historical" narrative; viz., the archangelic cleansing of the despoiled earth immediately prior to the Flood. Enochic integrity is thereby cleverly preserved.

Another intriguing correlation between material found in Slavonic Enoch and Manichaean traditions involves the motif of a "heavenly paradise" that features a supernal Tree of Life. In *2 Enoch* 5 we read the following account:

> And the men took me from there and led me up to the third heaven, and set me in the midst of Paradise. And that place is more beautiful than anything there is to see -- all trees in full bloom, all fruit ripe, every kind of food always in abundance, every breeze fragrant ... the whole garden is good, producing what is good to eat. And the tree of life is in that place, where the Lord rests, when he goes to Paradise; and that tree is indescribable for the quality of its fragrance ... And every tree is laden with good fruit: there is no tree there without fruit; and the whole place is blessed.[87]

Furthermore, note well the additional qualifiers supplied in *2 Enoch* 13:27: "And from there I went up into the Paradise of the righteous; and I saw there a blessed place, and every creature is blessed, and all live in joy and gladness, and in measureless light, and in eternal life."

These remarkable passages merit comparison with some valuable fragments of Manichaean cosmology preserved within a sixth-century homily of the Monophysite patriarch Severus of Antioch.[88] Severus informs us that he is quoting from Manichaean scripture -- unfortunately we do not know which specific work he has used, despite some ingenious attempts to deduce its identity. In these citations, the expression "Tree of Life" functions as an alternate designation for the *summum bonum* of Manichaean cosmology: the Realm of Light. A symmetrical parallel to this usage is the expression "Tree of Death," which Mani or one of his disciples employed to designate the evil Realm of Darkness.[89] Therein we read:

> They say: That which is Good, also named Light and the Tree of Life, possesses those regions which lie to the east, west, and north; for those (regions) which lie to the south and to the meridian belong to the Tree of Death ...[90]
> Likewise does the Tree of Life exist, which is there adorned with every sort of pleasing and lovely, beautiful thing. It is filled and covered with all sorts of good things ... its fruits cover it, and majesty belongs to it.[91]
> In the Realm of Light there is no burning fire which could be discharged against that which is evil. There is neither an iron (weapon) for cutting, nor overwhelming waters, nor any other evil substance like those. Instead, all is Light and (every) place is noble.[92]
> The Tree of Death is divided into many (parts); war and bitterness characterize them ... good fruits are never upon them ... all of them form rottenness for the corruption of their place.[93]
> [The members of the Realm of Darkness] provoked and stirred each other up until they came unto the boundaries of the glorious land of Light. When they beheld that marvelous and surpassingly beautiful sight, they gathered together ... and plotted against the Light regarding how they could mix themselves with it. Due to (their) frenzy, they were unaware that the powerful and mighty God dwelt in it (the region of Light).[94]

One cannot fail to note a host of interesting overlaps between these two distinct textual traditions. Of fundamental significance is the fact that *2 Enoch* and Manichaean tradition share the concept of a heavenly Tree of Life. R.H. Charles states that the fourth-century Christian heresiologist Epiphanius denounced the idea of a heavenly Tree of Life as a specifically Manichaean heresy,[95] although it is unclear (at least to this writer) which specific passage of Epiphanius is being referenced. Perhaps Charles is thinking of those several sections wherein the gospel parable of the "good" and "worthless" trees and their respective fruit-producing capacities are given a Manichaean interpretation. To judge from our extant textual evidence, it is this parabolic imagery (i.e., good/worthless) that eventually generates the Tree of Life/Tree of Death symmetry.[96] Nevertheless, notwithstanding Charles, allusions to or even elaborate descriptions of a celestial *gan 'eden* appear in a variety of sources,[97] and some of them incorporate the motif of a heavenly Tree of Life.

Other intriguing correspondences between the Enochic and Manichaean texts can also be observed. One notes, for example, that both the Enochic Paradise and its Manichaean counterpart feature the quality of luminosity. This is not an attribute that emerges naturally from a cursory study of the Eden narrative of Genesis 2-3, but it is certainly intelligible given the supernal locale of this Paradise in both traditions.[98] Both realms are explicitly described as "beautiful" and filled with "delectable fruits." The Enochic Tree possesses an indescribably pleasant fragrance that permeates the garden.[99] While an allusion to the aroma of the Tree of Life is lacking in the Severan Manichaean fragments, we might infer its pleasing odor from the negative evidence pertaining to the Tree of Death, where "rottenness" and "corruption" rule. *2 Enoch* also explicitly states that "the whole garden is good," a theme which positively invites textual comparison with that Manichaean fragment that reads "that which is good, also named Light and the Tree of Life ...."

But perhaps the most interesting overlap of all concerns the close connection between God himself and the Tree of Life. Note again the language of our sources. *2 Enoch* 5:4 says: "And the tree of

life is in that place, where the Lord rests, when he goes to Paradise ...."
Manichaean tradition *apud* Severus states: "they (the denizens of the
Realm of Darkness) were unaware that the powerful and mighty God
dwelt in it (the realm of the Tree of Life)." In other words, there is a
conception common to both traditions that the Tree of Life serves as
either a temporary or permanent domicile for God. Parallels for this
idea are not difficult to find in Jewish tradition.

The point of origin is apparently *1 Enoch* 25:2-5:

> Then I, Enoch, answered him (i.e., Michael), saying, I wish
> to learn about everything, but especially about this tree.
> And he answered me, saying, This high mountain which
> you saw, whose summit is like the throne of the Lord, is
> the throne where the Holy and Great One, the Lord of
> Glory, the Eternal King, will sit when he comes down to
> visit the earth for good. And this beautiful fragrant tree ...
> will be given to the righteous and humble. Its fruit will be
> to the chosen as food that grants life ....[100]

A linkage is thus established between the location of the Tree of Life
and eschatological judgment. The motif is developed further in the so-
called *Apocalypse of Moses*:

> And in that same hour, we [Adam and Eve] heard the
> archangel Michael blowing with his trumpet and calling to
> the angels and saying: Thus saith the Lord, Come with me
> to paradise and hear the judgement with which I shall
> judge Adam. And when God appeared in paradise,
> mounted on the chariot of his cherubim with the angels
> proceeding before him and singing hymns of praise, all the
> plants of paradise ... broke out into flowers. And the
> throne of God was fixed where the Tree of Life was.[101]

The intriguing nexus of the Tree of Life and divine judgment
may even serve to illuminate a curious aggadic tradition found in
Sefer ha-Bahir which places the Tree of Life by the waters of Marah
during the Israelites' wilderness journey (Ex 15:23-25).[102] At this
location, according to this tradition, Satan sought to demoralize the
Israelites by providing a graphic description of the hardships awaiting
them in the desert -- the bitter waters of Marah were but a foretaste of

worse to come. Moses however successfully intervenes: he renders the bitter waters potable by tossing a branch from the Tree of Life into them, and God proceeds to pronounce "a decree and judgment" upon Satan.[103] Here again we discover a textual juxtaposition of the Tree of Life and divine judgment, suggested perhaps by traditions analogous to those just outlined.[104]

Therefore it seems possible that Slavonic Enoch, or at least an earlier version thereof, may have been available to Mani and/or his early disciples and exploited as source material for the development of certain Manichaean teachings. The overlaps identified above point in this direction, and this hypothesis gains strength from the aforementioned studies of Scholem and Scopello which demonstrate the influence of *2 Enoch* upon later Jewish and Gnostic literary texts. That Mani was an avid student of Enochic lore is hardly surprising, given Enoch's status as an authentic representative of the heavenly Apostle of Light and the frequent quotations from and allusions to Enochic traditions in extant Manichaean literature. It thus seems plausible to conclude that *2 Enoch* has indeed influenced certain traditions found in Manichaeism.

---

[1] Titus Bostrensis, *Titi Bostreni contra manichaeos libri quatuor syriace* (ed. P.A. de Lagarde; Berlin: C. Schultze, 1859) 129: ܡܠܐܘܢ,ܗܢ ܪ݁ܚܠܘܘ݁ܗܘ ܪܨܘܘ݁ܗ ܪܠܗܢ,ܗܢ ܪ݁ܠ݁ܩܐܘ݁ܝܪ ܚܘ ܡܣܘܘ ܚܘ݁ܪܠܣܘ ; Syriac text also cited by K. Kessler, *Mani: Forschungen über die manichäische Religion* (Berlin: G. Reimer, 1889) 302. Note also the testimony of Ephrem: ܝܗ݁ܝ ܐܘ݁ܘ݁ܝ݁ܝ ܝ݁ܗܘ݁ܪ ܝܠ݁ܗ ܪ݁ܚܘܘ݁ܚܘ ܝܠ݁ܗ_ ܐܘ݁ܗ ܐܘ݁ܘ݁ܝ݁ܝ ܪ݁ܚ݁ܝ݁ܘ ܪ݁ܚܘ݁ܚܘ݁ܗ ܝܠ݁ܗ ܪ݁ܚܘ݁ܗܘ݁ܝ݁ܗ "for just as the Jews revile the New Testament, they (the Manichaeans) revile our Old Testament." Text cited from *S. Ephraim's Prose Refutations of Mani, Marcion, and Bardaisan* (2 vols.; ed. C.W. Mitchell; London: Williams and Norgate, 1912-21) 1.43 lines 40-44. See also Epiphanius, *Panarion* 66.31.2 (GCS 37; ed. K. Holl; Leipzig: J.C. Hinrichs, 1933) 69.

[2] The Jewish background of classical Gnostic thought (as represented for example in the Nag Hammadi corpus) hardly requires detailed demonstration. A comprehensive overview of this issue is provided by B.A. Pearson, "Jewish Sources in Gnostic Literature," *Jewish Writings of the Second Temple Period* (ed. M.E. Stone; Philadelphia: Fortress Press, 1984) 443-81. For Mandaeism, see especially I. Scheftelowitz, "Die mandäische Religion und das Judenthum," *MGWJ* 73 (1929) 211-32; K. Rudolph, "A History of the Development of the Mandaean Religion," *HR* 8 (1969) 210-35.

3   G.A.G. Stroumsa, *Another Seed: Studies in Gnostic Mythology* (Leiden: Brill, 1984) 145-67; J. Tubach, "Spuren des astronomischen Henochbuches bei den Manichäern Mittelasiens," *Nubia et Oriens Christianus: Festschrift für C. Detlef G. Müller zum 60. Geburtstag* (ed. P.O. Scholz and R. Stempel; Köln: J. Dinter, 1988) 73-95; J.C. Reeves, "An Enochic Motif in Manichaean Tradition," *Manichaica Selecta: Studies Presented to Professor Julien Ries on the Occasion of his Seventieth Birthday* (ed. A. van Tongerloo and S. Giversen; Louvain: International Association of Manichaean Studies, 1991) 295-98; idem, *Jewish Lore in Manichaean Cosmogony: Studies in the Book of Giants Traditions* (Cincinnati: Hebrew Union College Press, 1992).   Note the unintentional support given this perception by I.P. Couliano: " ... 'mitigated' gnostics saw in the biblical Genesis a Manichaean text (*avant la lettre*, of course), and they would have condemned Manichaeism, as strange as this might sound, as a Judaic heresy." Quote cited from Couliano, *The Tree of Gnosis: Gnostic Mythology from Early Christianity to Modern Nihilism* (New York: HarperCollins, 1992) 94.

4   For example, see the Manichaean rendition of Adam and Eve's sojourn and adventures in the Garden related by ibn al-Nadīm in his *Fihrist*. The Arabic text is provided by G. Flügel, *Mani: seine Lehre und seine Schriften* (reprinted, Osnabrück: Biblio Verlag, 1969) 58-61; translations in ibid., 90-93; B. Dodge, *The Fihrist of al-Nadīm* (2 vols.; New York: Columbia University Press, 1970) 2.783-86.   B.A. Pearson discusses this pericope in his "The Figure of Seth in Manichaean Literature," *Manichaean Studies: Proceedings of the First International Conference on Manichaeism* (ed. P. Bryder; Lund: Plus Ultra, 1988) 148-50; see also Stroumsa, *Another Seed* 149-52.

5   C. Schmidt and H.J. Polotsky, "Ein Mani-Fund in Ägypten," *SPAW* (1933) 4-90; M. Boyce, *A Catalogue of the Iranian Manuscripts in Manichaean Script in the German Turfan Collection* (Berlin: Akademie-Verlag, 1960) ix-xxi; W. Sundermann, "Recent Work on Iranian Turfan Texts," *Iran: From Monarchy to Republic* (ed. G. Barthel; Berlin: Akademie-Verlag, 1983) 136-44; idem, "Studien zur kirchengeschichtlichen Literatur der iranischen Manichäer I," *Altorientalische Forschungen* 13 (1986) 42-45; A. Henrichs and L. Koenen, "Ein griechischer Mani-Codex (P. Colon. inv. nr. 4780)," *Zeitschrift für Papyrologie und Epigraphik* (= *ZPE*) 5 (1970) 97-217.

6   An exhaustive accounting of the evidence can be found in H.-C. Puech, *Le manichéisme: son fondateur - sa doctrine* (Paris: Civilisations du Sud, 1949) 61-62 and esp. p. 144 n.241. See also M. Tardieu, *Le manichéisme* (Paris: Presses Universitaires de France, 1981) 20-24. Since the name of Abraham appears only once in these rosters (that provided by al-Shahrastānī), his status as an authentic link in the succession of prophets has been questioned. See W.B. Henning, "Ein manichäisches Henochbuch," *SPAW* (1934) 27 n.4; Tardieu, *Le manichéisme* 24.

7   Cf. *Kephalaia* 13.30-32: "Zu dieser selben Zeit wiederum in der letzten Kirche ein Gerechter (und) Wahrhaftiger, der zum "Reich" gehörte, erschien; er traf zusammen mit ... sie operierten (?) die Kirche unseres Herrn gemäss ...". Candidates for these apostles are Marcion, Bardaisan, and Elchasai. See A. Henrichs, "Mani and the Babylonian Baptists: A Historical Confrontation," *Harvard Studies in Classical Philology* 77 (1973) 53 n.111; A. Henrichs and L.

Koenen, *ZPE* 32 (1978) 189.

8 See Reeves, *Jewish Lore* 4 n.4.

9 M 5794: *dwdyg kw dyn 'y pyšyn 'ndwm d'š s'r'r'n p'q'n 'ndr bwd hynd ... 'wd c'wn s'r'r'n 'hr'ft hynd 'ygyš'n dyn whwryd 'wd pd 'ndrz 'wd qyrdg"n swst bwd hynd* "Second, as long as there were pure leaders in the earlier religion(s) (they adhered to the teachings), but when such leaders had ascended (i.e., to the Realm of Light), then their religion(s) became confused, and they (i.e., the founded communities) became lax (with regard to) commandments and actions." Text cited from M. Boyce, *A Reader in Manichaean Middle Persian and Parthian* (Leiden: Brill, 1975) 29-30; see also F.C. Andreas and W.B. Henning, "Mitteliranische Manichaica aus Chinesisch-Turkestan II," *SPAW* (1933) 295. Compare also *Kephalaia* 6.18-9.10; Epiphanius, *Panarion* 66.30.1 (quoting from *Acta Archelai*): περὶ δὲ τῶν παρ' ὑμῖν προφητῶν οὕτως λέγει· πνεύματα εἶναι ἀσεβείας ἤτοι ἀνομίας τοῦ σκότους τοῦ ἀπ' ἀρχῆς ἀνελθόντος, καὶ διὰ τούτων πλανηθέντες <ἐν ἀληθείᾳ> οὐκ ἐλάλησαν. ἐτύφλωσεν γὰρ αὐτῶν ὁ ἄρχων <ἐκεῖνος> τὴν διάνοιαν.

10 Henrichs-Koenen, *ZPE* 5 (1970) 97-217; idem, "... Edition der Seiten 1-72," *ZPE* 19 (1975) 1-85; idem, "... Edition der Seiten 72,8-99,9," *ZPE* 32 (1978) 87-199; idem, "... Edition der Seiten 99,10-120," *ZPE* 44 (1981) 201-318; idem, "... Edition der Seiten 121-192," *ZPE* 48 (1982) 1-59; L. Koenen and C. Römer, *Der Kölner Mani-Kodex: Abbildungen und diplomatischer Text* (Bonn: Habelt, 1985); idem, *Der Kölner Mani-Kodex: Kritische Edition* (Opladen: Westdeutscher Verlag, 1988).

11 *CMC* 47.1-48.15: ὁ γάρ τοι βουλόμενος ἀκουέτω καὶ προσεχέτω ὡς εἷς ἕκαστος τῶν προγενεστέρων πατέρων τὴν ἰδίαν ἀποκάλυψιν ἔδειξεν τῇ ἑαυτοῦ ἐκλογῇ, ἥν ἐξελέξατο καὶ συνήγαγεν κατ' ἐκείνην τὴν γενεὰν καθ' ἥν ἐφάνη, καὶ γράψας κατέλειψεν τοῖς μεταγενεστέροις. καὶ ὁ μὲν περὶ ἁρπαγῆς αὐτοῦ ἐδήλω[σ]εν, οἱ δὲ ἔξω ὡμίλ[η]σαν ... γράψαι καὶ ἀποδεῖξαι μετέπειτα καὶ ἐγκωμιάσαι καὶ μεγαλῦναι τοὺς διδασκάλους ἑαυτῶν καὶ τὴν ἀλήθειαν καὶ τὴν ἐλπίδα τὴν ἀποκαλυφθεῖσαν αὐτοῖς. οὕτω τοίνυν εἷς ἕκαστος κατὰ τὴν περίοδον καὶ περιφορὰν τῆς ἀποστολῆς αὐτοῦ ὡς ἐθεώρησεν εἶπεν καὶ γέγραφεν πρὸς ὑπομνηματισμὸν ἔτι δὲ καὶ περὶ τῆς ἁρπαγῆς αὐτοῦ. For the importance of this passage, see especially M. Himmelfarb, "Revelation and Rapture: The Transformation of the Visionary in the Ascent Apocalypses," in *Mysteries and Revelations: Apocalyptic Studies since the Uppsala Colloquium* (ed. J.J. Collins and J.H. Charlesworth; Sheffield: Sheffield Academic Press, 1991) 79-80.

12 Adam (48.16-50.7), Sethel (50.8-52.7), Enosh (52.8-55.9), Shem (55.10-58.5), and Enoch (58.6-60.7).

13 Gal 1:1 (60.18-23), 2 Cor 12:1-5 (61.2-14), Gal 1:11-12 (61.16-22).

14 Mani's "Epistle to Edessa" (64.8-65.22), Mani's "Gospel" (66.4-68.5; 68.6-69.8; 69.9-70.10).

15 *Contra* J. Maier, "Zum Problem der jüdischen Gemeinden Mesopotamiens im 2. und 3. Jh. n. Chr. im Blick auf den CMC," *Codex Manichaicus Coloniensis: Atti del Simposio Internazionale (Rende-Amantea 3-7 settembre 1984)* (ed. L. Cirillo and A. Roselli; Cosenza: Marra Editore, 1986) 54.

16 "I am Balsamos (Βάλσαμος), the greatest angel of Light" (*CMC* 49.3-5). On

the interpretation of this name, see especially B.A. Pearson, "The Problem of 'Jewish Gnostic' Literature," *Nag Hammadi, Gnosticism, and Early Christianity* (ed. C.W. Hedrick and R. Hodgson, Jr.; Peabody, MA: Hendrickson, 1986) 28 n.77, wherein Balsamos is equated with the Phoenician deity Baal Shamem "lord of Heaven". Support for Pearson's identification appears in *PGM* IV.1020 (perhaps also XII.495): ἐγώ εἰμι ὁ πεφυκὼς ἐκ τοῦ οὐρανοῦ, ὄνομά μοι Βαλσάμης, and see Preisendanz's note *ad loc.* A. Christensen (*L'Iran sous les Sassanides* [Copenhagen: Levin & Munksgaard, 1936] 186) refers to a "Syrian angel" named Bar-Simus; compare the Manichaean angel-list M 20: *xwd'y br symws* "the lord Bar Simus" (text *apud* Boyce, *Reader* 192) and W. Sundermann, *Mitteliranische manichäische Texte kirchengeschichtlichen Inhalts* (Berlin: Akademie-Verlag, 1981) 148-49 s.v. *'bwrs'm*. Henceforth this work will be cited as Sundermann, *KG*. The most intriguing explanation has been offered by B. Visotzky. He suggests that Balsamos may correspond to Hebrew בעל שם "possessor of the Name," making Balsamos thus equivalent to the so-called "lesser Yahweh" (Syriac ܐܝܚܘܬܐ ܙܥܘܪܐ ; cf. J. Bidez and F. Cumont, *Les mages hellénisés* [Paris: Société d'éditions "Les belles lettres", 1938] 2.115) or Metatron. See Visotzky, "Rabbinic Randglossen to the Cologne Mani Codex," *ZPE* 52 (1983) 298.

17   Or dead? Shem collapses upon beholding the throne-room (καθεστήριον) and its occupants. Then "a voice (בת קול ?) called to me from the throne-room. Coming to me, it grasped my right hand and raised me (μοι ... ἀνέστησεν!). It blew the breath of life into my nostrils, adding to my power and glory" (*CMC* 57.12-19). There is a clear echo here of Gen 2:7, wherein God animates the carcass of Adam via the "breath of life."

18   Henrichs-Koenen, *ZPE* 19 (1975) 57 n.97; I. Gruenwald, "Manichaeism and Judaism in Light of the Cologne Mani Codex," *ZPE* 50 (1983) 29-45; Visotzky, *ZPE* 52 (1983) 295-300.

19   G. Scholem, *Major Trends in Jewish Mysticism* (reprinted, New York: Schocken, 1961) 40-79; idem, *Kabbalah* (Jerusalem: Keter, 1974) 10-22; idem, *Origins of the Kabbalah* (Princeton: Princeton University Press, 1987) 18-35.

20   See I. Gruenwald, *Apocalyptic and Merkavah Mysticism* (Leiden: Brill, 1980) 73-97; C. Rowland, *The Open Heaven: A Study of Apocalyptic in Judaism and Early Christianity* (New York: Crossroad, 1982) 269-348; P.S. Alexander, "Appendix: 3 Enoch," in E. Schürer, *The History of the Jewish People in the Age of Jesus Christ* (ed. G. Vermes, F. Millar, and M. Goodman; Edinburgh: T. & T. Clark, 1973-87) 3/1.273-74; idem, "Comparing Merkavah Mysticism and Gnosticism: An Essay in Method," *JJS* 35 (1984) 10-11; M. Himmelfarb, "Heavenly Ascent and the Relationship of the Apocalypses and the Hekhalot Literature," *HUCA* 59 (1988) 73-77. Scholem's evolutionary scheme has been forcefully challenged by D.J. Halperin. See especially his *The Faces of the Chariot: Early Jewish Responses to Ezekiel's Vision* (Tübingen: J.C.B. Mohr, 1988) 5-9, 63-114, and *passim*.

21   Scholem, *Major Trends* 42; Himmelfarb, *HUCA* 59 (1988) 76 n.14.

22   W. Brandt, *Elchasai: ein Religionsstifter und sein Werk* (Leipzig: J.C. Hinrichs, 1912); G. Strecker, "Elkesai," *RAC* 4.1171-86; K. Rudolph, *Antike Baptisten: zu den Überlieferungen über frühjüdische und -christliche*

Taufsekten (Berlin: Akademie-Verlag, 1981) 13-17; G.P. Luttikhuizen, *The Revelation of Elchasai* (Tübingen: J.C.B. Mohr, 1985).

[23] Hippolytus, *Refutatio* 9.13-17; 10.29; Epiphanius, *Panarion* 19 and 53. See A.F.J. Klijn and G.J. Reinink, *Patristic Evidence for Jewish-Christian Sects* (Leiden: Brill, 1973) 54-67, 114-23, 154-61, 194-97.

[24] Hippolytus, *Ref.* 9.16.4. Cf. Reeves, *Jewish Lore* 178 n.24.

[25] Epiphanius, *Pan.* 19.4.3. The solution to this puzzle was supplied by M.A. Levy, "Bemerkungen zu den arabischen Analekten des Herrn Prof. Hitzig," *ZDMG* 12 (1858) 712; cf. H. Gressmann, "Jüdisch-Aramäisches bei Epiphanius," *ZNW* 16 (1915) 191.

[26] J.M. Baumgarten, "The Book of Elkesai and Merkabah Mysticism," *JSJ* 17 (1986) 219-20.

[27] G. Alon, *The Jews in Their Land in the Talmudic Age* (reprinted, Cambridge: Harvard University Press, 1989) 301. I am grateful to Professor Baumgarten for bringing Alon's remarks to my attention.

[28] Baumgarten, *JSJ* 17 (1986) 212-23. The quotation comes from page 216.

[29] Henrichs-Koenen, *ZPE* 5 (1970) 119, based on the testimony of *CMC* 11.1-5; 12.6-11; 73.5-11.

[30] Cf. nn.24-25 *supra*. Note also the eschatological oracle preserved in *CMC* 86.17-87.6, regarding which see Henrichs-Koenen, *ZPE* 32 (1978) 152-61; J.C. Reeves, "The 'Elchasaite' Sanhedrin of the Cologne Mani Codex in Light of Second Temple Jewish Sectarian Sources," *JJS* 42 (1991) 88-91.

[31] See especially L. Koenen, "Manichaean Apocalypticism at the Crossroads of Iranian, Egyptian, Jewish and Christian Thought," *CMC: Atti* (cf. n.15 *supra*) 285-332.

[32] D.N. MacKenzie, "Mani's Šābuhragān," *BSOAS* 42 (1979) 500-34; 43 (1980) 288-310; Sundermann, *KG* 91-98. See now M. Hutter, *Manis kosmogonische Šābuhragān-Texte: Edition, Kommentar und literaturgeschichtliche Einordnung der manichäisch-mittelpersischen Handschriften M 98/99 I und M 7980-7984* (Wiesbaden: O. Harrassowitz, 1992).

[33] According to the *Fihrist* of ibn al-Nadīm, the second chapter of Mani's "Book of Mysteries" featured an exegesis of this apocalypse. See Flügel, *Mani* 72 line 12 (text), 102 (translation), and my study "An Enochic Citation in *Barnabas* 4:3 and the *Oracles of Hystaspes*," *Pursuing the Text: Studies in Honor of Ben Zion Wacholder on the Occasion of his Seventieth Birthday* (ed. J. Kampen and J.C. Reeves; Sheffield: Sheffield Academic Press, forthcoming).

[34] "Le déroulement du mythe se scandera donc selon trois phases: un moment antérieur ou passé, où il y avait disjonction, dualité parfaite des deux substances; un moment médian ou présent, où s'est produit et dure le mélange; un moment postérieur, futur ou final, où la division primordiale sera rétablie. Adhérer au Manichéisme n'est pas autre chose que professer cette double doctrine des Deux Principes et des Trois Temps ou des Trois Moments." (Puech, *Le manichéisme* 74). For references to those texts that describe "cette double doctrine", see ibid. 157-59 n.284.

[35] A. Henrichs, "The Timing of Supernatural Events in the Cologne Mani Codex," *CMC: Atti* (cf. n.15 *supra*) 187-88.

[36] *CMC* 3.7-12; 4.7-12; 12.1-6; 13.2-14; 17.8-16; 18.10-17; 20.7-17; 23.1-24.15;

26.7-15; 32.3-33.6; 34.1-9; 43.1-11; 64.8-65.22; 67.7-11; 104.10-105.21; 118.8-120.16; 124.1-15; 126.2-129.17; 133.4-134.10; 135.6-136.16; 153.1ff.; 156.5ff. See I. Gruenwald, "Prophecy, Jewish Apocalyptic Literature and the Problem of Uncanonical Books," in idem, *From Apocalypticism to Gnosticism* (Frankfurt am Main: Peter Lang, 1988) 19-20 n.10.

[37] One should also note the evidence of the premonitory dream of the mother of Mani as reported by ibn al-Nadīm in his *Fihrist* account of Manichaeism. According to this source, Mani's mother "while pregnant with Mani ... experienced a beautiful dream. She watched with rapt attention (as) a certain entity seized him and ascended with him into the air. There he arrived with him and ... remained one or two days, and then returned." The text of this *Fihrist* citation can be found in Flügel, *Mani* 50 lines 5-8.

[38] M 47. See Boyce, *Reader* 37-38; Sundermann, *KG* 102-103.

[39] *'dy'n pd wrc nm'd whyšt rwšn 'd hrwyn bg'n yzd'n 'wd w'd 'nwšg cy jywhr 'wd bwdyst'n wysp zng 'wd 'nyc gw'nyg dydn cy 'wwd hmpd 'by 'wš kft yd 'w hry jm'n ... 'dy'n fryštg dst pd sr 'wyst'd.* Text cited from Boyce, *Reader* 38.

[40] Identified as Peroz, brother of Shapur b. Ardashir. See al-Nadīm, *Fihrist* (*apud* Flügel, *Mani* 52 line 2 [text]); S.N.C. Lieu, *Manichaeism in the Later Roman Empire and Medieval China* (2d ed.; Tübingen: J.C.B. Mohr, 1992) 76.

[41] al-Bīrūnī, *al-Athār al-bāqiya 'ani'l-qurūn al-khāliya* (cf. *Chronologie orientalischer Völker von Albêrûnî* [ed. C.E. Sachau; Leipzig: F.A. Brockhaus, 1878] 209 lines 5-7). Translation is that of C.E. Sachau, *The Chronology of Ancient Nations* (London: William H. Allen & Co., 1879) 191.

[42] See Himmelfarb, "Revelation and Rapture" (n.11 *supra*) 81, although she underestimates the importance of the ascent-motif for Mani and nascent Manichaeism. Note especially *CMC* 71.6-72.4: τούτου δὲ χάριν ἐδευτερώσαμεν ἀπὸ τῶν προγόνων ἡμῶ[ν] πατέρων τήν τε ἁρπαγὴν αὐτῶν καὶ ἀποκάλυψιν ἑνὸς ἑκάστου .... ὁπηνίκα γὰρ ἕκα[στος αὐ]τῶν ἡρπάζετο, [ἅπερ ἐθεώ]ρει καὶ ἤκουε [ταῦτα πάντα ἔ]γραφεν καὶ ὑπεδεί[κ]νυεν καὶ αὐτὸς αὐτοῦ [τῆς ἀποκαλύψεως μάρτυς ἐγένετο "For this reason we (the compilers of *CMC*) have transmitted the ascension and the revelation of our forefathers ... for when each of them had ascended, [all those things which he sa]w and heard he recorded and revealed, and he himself bore witness to his revelation." Compare *Jub.* 4:19: "And what was and what will be he (Enoch) saw in a vision in his sleep ... and he wrote his testimony and left it as a testimony on earth for all the sons of men for every generation." Translation is that of R.H. Charles and C. Rabin, "Jubilees," *The Apocryphal Old Testament* (ed. H.F.D. Sparks; Oxford: Clarendon, 1984) 23. J.R. Russell perceptively recognizes the significance of "heavenly ascent" in Manichaean tradition, although he apparently presumes that this motif is wholly derived from Zoroastrian tradition such as that found in the *Ardā Vīrāz Nāmag*. See his "Kartīr and Mānī: A Shamanistic Model of Their Conflict," *Iranica Varia: Papers in Honor of Professor Ehsan Yarshater* (Leiden: Brill, 1990) 180-93.

[43] Gen 5:24; 2 Kgs 2:11. "Permanent" in the sense that they did not return to earth again, although such a possibility in the future is not precluded. See Mal 3:23-24; *m. 'Ed.* 8:7. The eventual return of such worthies to earth forms the conceptual background for doctrines like the *parousia* of Jesus, the "true

prophet" succession of the Ebionites, and the "apostle of Light" cycle of Manichaeism. Note too that according to Manichaean tradition, Mani did not "die." Rather, he was "removed" (*à la* Enoch) from earth to return to the Paradise of Light. The language used is identical to that employed in the traditions about Enoch. See Flügel, *Mani* 66 lines 9-10; Reeves, *Jewish Lore* 139 n.109.

[44] E.g., *Der. Er. Zut. pereq* 1 end: ט' נכנסו בחייהם בגן עדן ואלו הן חנוך בן ירד ואליהו ומשיח ואליעזר עבד אברהם וחירם מלך צור ועבד מלך הכושי ויעבץ בנו של רבי יהודה הנשיא ובתיה בת פרעה וסרח בת אשר ויש אומרים אף רבי יהושע בן לוי "Nine entered Paradise alive, and they are: Enoch b. Yared, Elijah, Messiah, Eliezer servant of Abraham, Hiram king of Tyre, Ebedmelek the Cushite, Yabez b. R. Judah ha-Nasi, Bityah daughter of Pharaoh, and Serah daughter of Asher. Some say also R. Joshua b. Levi." For additional references to such lists and a comprehensive discussion of the issue, see especially L. Ginzberg, *The Legends of the Jews* (Philadelphia: Jewish Publication Society, 1909-38) 5.95-96.

[45] *Tg. Onq.* Gen 5:24; *Gen. Rab.* 25 (cf. *Midrash Bereshit Rabba* [3 vols.; ed. J. Theodor and H. Albeck; reprinted, Jerusalem: Wahrmann, 1965] 1.238-39; *b. Sukk.* 5a (referring to Moses and Elijah); *Sifre* Deut §357 (ed. Finkelstein, 428) and *b. Soṭa* 13b (referring to Moses). Halperin (*Faces* 304-305) calls attention to the importance of Ps 68:18-19 and its later interpretations for traditions about the ascension of Moses. Wis 4:10-14 certainly refers to Enoch, but is hardly complimentary of his fortitude. On the negative attitude of the Sages to Enoch, see Ginzberg, *Legends* 5.156-57. An intriguing exception to this tendency occurs in *Pesiqta de Rab Kahana* within a passage that celebrates God's special favoritism for the number seven. We read therein: בדורות השביעי חביב אדם שת אנוש קונן מהללאל ירד חנוך ויתהלך חנוך את האלהים באבות השביעי חביב אברהם יצחק ויעקב לוי קהת עמרם משה ומשה עלה אל האלהים "Of the (antediluvian) forefathers the seventh was beloved: Adam, Seth, Enosh, Kenan, Mahalalel, Yared, *Enoch* 'and Enoch walked with God' (Gen 5:24). Of the patriarchs the seventh was beloved: Abraham, Isaac, Jacob, Levi, Qahat, Amram, *Moses* 'and *Moses ascended to God*' (Ex 19:3)". This juxtaposition of Enoch and Moses with its explicit reference to an "ascension" of Moses is quite suggestive. The passage is cited from S. Buber, *Pesiqta [de Rav Kahana]* (reprinted, n.p., n.d.) *pisqa* 23, 155a.

[46] *Gen. Rab.* 25.1: המינים שאלו את רבי אבהו אמרו לו אין אנו מוצאים מיתה לחנוך אמר להם למה אמרו לו נאמר כאן לקיחה ונאמר באליהו לקיחה אמר להם אם לקיחה אתם דורשים נאמר כאן לקיחה ונאמר ביחזקאל הנני לוקח את מחמד וגו' "(Once) the *minim* challenged R. Abbahu, saying to him: We do not find death ascribed to Enoch. He said: Why (do you conclude this)? They responded: Here (Gen 5:24) the expression "taken" is used, and the same expression "taken" is also used in (the story of) Elijah (2 Kgs 2:11). He answered: If your interpretation hinges on the expression "taken," (what about this?) Here (Gen 5:24) the expression "taken" is used, and in (the story of) Ezekiel it is used: 'I am taking away the delight of your eyes ... (Ezek 24:16)." The Ezekiel verse refers to the death of the wife of the prophet. Passage is cited from Theodor-Albeck 238-39. For a similar "heretical" (probably Manichaean) juxtaposition of the ascensions of Enoch and Elijah, compare Ephrem, *Hymnus XIX* 4 1-2 in *Des heiligen Ephraem des Syrers Hymnen contra Haereses* (2 vols.; ed. E. Beck; Louvain: L. Durbecq, 1957) 1.68.

47   A "book of Adam" was known to the Sages; cf. *b. 'Abod. Zar.* 5a; *b. B. Meṣ.*
85b-86a. A "book of Adam" (presumably a magical treatise) is condemned by
the ninth-century Karaite Daniel al-Qumisi; see J. Mann, *Texts and Studies in
Jewish History and Literature* (2 vols.; Philadelphia: Jewish Publication Society,
1931-35) 2.76 line 2, 79 line 5, 81 lines 1-2; 82 line 1; and Scholem, *Origins* (cf.
n.19 *supra*) 106-107. For a "book of Shem," see "Sefer Noah," *Bet ha-Midrasch*
(= *BHM*) (6 vols.; ed. A. Jellinek; reprinted, Jerusalem: Bamberger & Wahrmann,
1938) 3.155 lines 1-3. The ninth-century Karaite Salmon b. Jeroham also cites a
"book of Shem" (see *BHM* 2.xxx). Mani's disciples quote from a "Prayer of
Sethel" (*Kephalaia* 42.25-32). The fragments attributed to Adam, Seth, and
Shem in the *CMC* do not apparently belong to the similarly ascribed works
found in the Nag Hammadi corpus. Cf. K. Rudolph, "Mani und die Gnosis,"
Manichaean Studies (cf. n.4 *supra*) 194. M. Philonenko has proposed *1 Enoch*
90:41 as the locus for the Enochic fragment ("Une citation manichéenne du livre
d'Enoch," *RHPR* 52 [1972] 337-40), but the correspondence is, as Henrichs and
Koenen (*ZPE* 19 [1975] 58 n.105) have already recognized, remote.
48   B.A. Pearson has called attention to the similarity of *CMC* 50.1-4 ("and he
[i.e., Adam] became greater than all the powers and angels of the created order")
to *Apoc. Adam* (NHC V 5) 64.14-19: "and we resembled the great eternal angels,
for we were higher than the God who had created us and the powers with him
..."; see his "Jewish Sources" (n.2 *supra*) 451. The quotation from *Apoc. Adam* is
cited from *The Nag Hammadi Library in English* (ed. J.M. Robinson; reprinted,
San Francisco: Harper & Row, 1981) 257. For traditions about the ascension of
Seth, see Augustine, *Contra Faustum* 19.3; Syncellus, *Chronographia* (*Georgii
Syncelli Ecloge Chronographica* [ed. A.A. Mosshammer; Leipzig: Teubner,
1984] 9): "in Adam's 270th year Seth, snatched up by angels, was taught ...";
translation cited from Stroumsa, *Another Seed* 109. Pearson ("Seth in
Manichaean Literature" 153) notes also Epiphanius, *Pan.* 40.7.1-2, wherein the
Archontic Gnostics speak of an ascent of Seth-Allogenes. With regard to Enosh,
compare the tradition reported by Moses of Chorene in his *History of the
Armenians* (which is therein ascribed to Josephus) that two inscriptions
containing revealed knowledge were erected by either Seth or Enosh (cf. Moses
Khorenats‘i, *History of the Armenians* [ed. R.W. Thomson; Cambridge: Harvard
University Press, 1978] 71). While the Armenian text is ambiguous (note also
Josephus, *Ant.* 1.69-71), Thomson's introduction to his English edition assumes
that the reference is to Enosh (p. 26). The revelatory role of Shem is
presumably dependent upon the aggadic identification of Shem with
Melchizedek.
49   A reference to an "apocalypse of Enoch" (ܢ ܐܘܣܬ ܟܠܝܢ) appears in the
twelfth-century universal history of Michael the Syrian, wherein we read that
Cyriacus of Segestan and Bar Salta of Resh‘ayna "composed a book of lies and
named it 'revelation of Enoch' ...", but the work seems to be political propaganda
directed toward the last Umayyad caliph, Marwan II. See *Chronique de Michel
le Syrien, patriarche jacobite d'Antioche, 1166-1199* (4 vols.; ed. J.-B. Chabot;
reprinted, Bruxelles: Culture et civilisation, 1963) 4.465 (text). Note D. Bundy,
"Pseudepigrapha in Syriac Literature," *SBL 1991 Seminar Papers* (Atlanta:
Scholars Press, 1991) 751; see also J.T. Milik, *The Books of Enoch: Aramaic*

Fragments of Qumrân Cave 4 (Oxford: Clarendon, 1976) 116.

50 *CMC* 58.6-60.7: πάλιν καὶ ὁ Ἐνὼχ τοῦτον τὸν τρόπον ἔφη ἐν τῇ αὐτοῦ ἀποκαλύψει· ἐγώ εἰμι Ἐνὼχ ὁ δίκαιος. λύπη μοί ἐστιν μεγάλη καὶ χύσις δακρύων ἐκ τῶν ὀφθαλμῶν μου διὰ τὸ ἀκηκοέναι με τὸν ὀνειδισμὸν τὸν προελθόντα ἐκ στόματος τῶν ἀ[σ]εβῶν. ἔλεγεν δὲ [ὅ]τι τῶν δακρύων ἐν [τοῖ] ς ὀφθαλμοῖς μου ὄν[των] καὶ δεήσεως ἐν τῷ [στό]ματι ἐθεώρησα ἐπι[στάν] τας μοι ἀγγέλους ἑ[πτὰ ἐκ το]ῦ οὐρανοῦ κα[τερχομέ]νου[ς. ἰδὼν δὲ] αὐτοὺς ἐκινήθην ὑπὸ δέους ὥστε τὰ γόνατά μου ἀλλήλοις προσαράσσειν. καὶ πάλιν εἶπεν οὕτως· ἔφη μοι εἷς τῶν ἀγγέλων Μιχαὴλ τοὖνομα· τούτου χάριν πρὸς σὲ ἀπεστάλην ἵνα ὑποδείξωμέν σοι τὸν τῶν εὐσεβῶν χῶρον καὶ χῶρόν σοι δείξω τὸν τῶ[ν] δυσσεβῶν καὶ ὁποῖος τυγχάνει ὁ τῆς τιμωρίας τῶν ἀνόμων τόπος. φησὶ δὲ πάλιν ὅτι ἐκεῖνο[ι] ἐπεκάθισάν με ἐπὶ ἅ[ρ]ματος ἀνέμου καὶ ε [ἰς] τὰ πέρατα τῶν οὐρ[αν]ῶν ἀνήνεγκαν. καὶ το[ὺς κό]σμους διεπέρασαμ[εν] , τόν τε κόσμον [τοῦ θανά]του [καὶ κό]σμο[ν τοῦ σκό]τους καὶ τοῦ πυρὸς τὸν κόσμον. καὶ μετὰ ταῦτα εἰσῆξάν με εἰς κόσμον πλουσιώτατον ὅς εὐκλεέστατος μὲν τῷ φωτὶ ἐτύγχανεν, περικαλλέστερος δὲ ὧν εἶδον φωστήρων. πάντα δὲ ἐθεώρησεν καὶ ἐξήτασεν τοὺς ἀγγέλους, καὶ εἴ τι αὐτῷ εἶπον, ἐνεχάραξεν αὐτοῦ ταῖς γραφαῖς.

51 See *1 Enoch* 1:2 (Greek); *2 Enoch* prologue (short version); *T. Dan* 5:6; *T. Levi* 10:5; *T. Judah* 18:1; and in general, Henrichs-Koenen, *ZPE* 19 (1975) 58 n.105. Compare also *1 Enoch* 12:4. All references to or citations from the Greek versions of *1 Enoch* rely upon *Apocalypsis Henochi Graece* (ed. M. Black; Leiden: Brill, 1970).

52 *1 Enoch* 71:3-4: "And the angel Michael, one of the archangels, took hold of me by my right hand, and raised me, and led me out to all the secrets of mercy and the secrets of righteousness. And he showed me all the secrets of the ends of heavens ...." Translation cited from M.A. Knibb, "1 Enoch," *Apocryphal Old Testament* 255.

53 *Contra* J.C. Greenfield and M.E. Stone, "The Enochic Pentateuch and the Date of the Similitudes," *HTR* 70 (1977) 62, the expression "chariot of wind" is not absent from the text of *1 Enoch*. See especially *1 Enoch* 70:2: *wa-tala"ala ba-saragalāta manfas wa-wad'a sem ba-mā'kalomu*. Ethiopic text is cited from the edition of J. Flemming, *Das Buch Henoch: Äthiopischer Text* (Leipzig: J.C. Hinrichs, 1902) 86-87; see also Gruenwald, *Apocalyptic* 119. Note that in *1 Enoch* 71, Enoch receives a heavenly tour from Michael, thus displaying the same sequence of events found in the *CMC* fragment. Note also *1 Enoch* 14:8 "winds"; 39:3 and 52:1 "whirlwind." Compare the chapter "Life of Enoch" in the medieval *Sefer Hayashar* (excerpted in Jellinek, *BHM* 4.129-32): ‏וילך הסוס ברוח‎ ‏לארץ‎ "and the horse came *in a wind* to earth." See also *Adam and Eve* 25:3; *3 Enoch* 7 (= Schäfer §10). I owe the last reference to Gruenwald, *Apocalyptic* 202 n.35. *3 Enoch* passages are keyed to *Synopse zur Hekhalot-Literatur* (ed. P. Schäfer; Tübingen: J.C.B. Mohr, 1981).

54 The Greek text of *1 Enoch* 22 describes them as "four hollow places"; compare al-Nadîm, *Fihrist* (Flügel, *Mani* 73 line 4) with its reference to "three trenches" in a similar setting. Note also the "two chasms (ܩܘ̈ܦܐ) and one cave (ܡܥܪܬܐ)" in the 6th praxis of the *Acts of Thomas* (cf. W. Wright, *Apocryphal Acts of the Apostles* [reprinted, Amsterdam: Philo Press, 1968] 1.225-26 [text]);

the Greek version of the same adds an extra "chasm" (χάσματα). Greenfield-Stone (*HTR* 70 [1977] 62) note the possible relevance of *1 Enoch* 22, but conclude there is "no parallel."

55 I. de Beausobre, *Histoire critique de Manichée et du Manichéisme* (Amsterdam: J.F. Bernard, 1734-39) I 428-29; Kessler, *Mani* (cf. n.1 *supra*) 199-200. For the evidence provoking such suspicions, see Reeves, *Jewish Lore* 9-49.

56 W.B. Henning, "Ein manichäisches Henochbuch" (n.6 *supra*) 27-35; idem, "Neue Materialen zur Geschichte des Manichäismus," *ZDMG* 90 (1936) 1-18; idem, "The Book of the Giants," *BSOAS* 11 (1943-46) 52-74.

57 Reeves, *Jewish Lore* 33 n.1.

58 J.T. Milik, "Problèmes de la littérature hénochique à la lumière des fragments araméennes de Qumrân," *HTR* 64 (1971) 366-72; idem, "Turfan et Qumran, Livre des Géants juif et manichéen," *Tradition und Glaube: Das frühe Christentum in seiner Umwelt* (ed. G. Jeremias, H.-W. Kuhn, and H. Stegemann; Göttingen: Vandenhoeck & Ruprecht, 1971) 117-27; idem, *Books of Enoch* (cf. n.48 *supra*) 298-339. See also Reeves, *Jewish Lore* 51-164.

59 F.C. Andreas and W.B. Henning, "Mitteliranische Manichaica aus Chinesisch-Turkestan I," *SPAW* (1932) 188-91; Henning, "Ein manichäisches Henochbuch" 32-35; Tubach, "Spuren" (cf. n.3 *supra*) 73-95.

60 Stroumsa, *Another Seed* 145-67; Reeves, *Jewish Lore* 185-206.

61 Reeves, "An Enochic Motif" (cf. n.3 *supra*) 295-98.

62 al-Ṭabarī, *Ta'rīkh ar-rasul wa-l-mulūk* (cf. *Annales quos scripsit Abu Djafar Mohammed ibn Djarir at-Tabari* [15 vols.; ed. M.J. De Goeje; reprinted, Leiden: Brill, 1964-65] 1.173 line 3, 174 lines 6, 8-9). Ṭabarī actually says that these scrolls were revealed by God to Enoch, but we must presume that they circulated among subsequent generations under Enoch's name. See also the next note.

63 *2 Enoch* 10:2, 5-7 (short version; cited according to the chapter divisions of A. Vaillant, *Le livre des secrets d'Hénoch: texte slave et traduction française* [Paris: Institut d'études slaves, 1952]): "And the Lord said to Vreveil, Take the books from their storeplace, and give Enoch a pen and dictate the books to him ... And all that it was proper that I should learn Vreveil explained to me in thirty days and thirty nights: his lips were never silent, as he went on speaking; and I, for my part, had no rest for thirty days and thirty nights, as I made my notes. And when I had finished, Vreveil said to me, Sit down: write out everything I have explained to you. And I sat down a second time for thirty days and thirty nights; and I wrote out everything exactly. And I wrote three hundred and sixty books." Note the repeated occurrence of the phrase "thirty days and thirty nights," a numerical reckoning that may explain the form of the authorship tradition transmitted by al-Ṭabarī. This passage from *2 Enoch* is cited from the translation of A. Pennington, "2 Enoch," *Apocryphal Old Testament* 338; compare F.I. Andersen, "2 (Slavonic Book of) Enoch," *OTP* 1.141.

64 The present author is currently compiling and analyzing these traditions with the intention of producing a comprehensive study for eventual publication.

65 See n.48 *supra*.

66 G. Scholem, *Origins* 73-74; idem, *On the Mystical Shape of the Godhead* (New York: Schocken, 1991) 29-30; 98-101. One can supplement his

correspondences with an additional parallel. *2 Enoch* 11:1 states: "And the Lord called me, and he set me *on his left hand, nearer than Gabriel*; and I worshipped the Lord." (Pennington 339). Compare *Sefer ha-Bahir* §11 (ed. Margolioth): ... וגבריאל שר שמאלו של הקדוש ברוך הוא . Cf. Scholem, *Das Buch Bahir* (Leipzig: W. Drugulin, 1923) 11 n.1; idem, *Origins* 147-51. Note also *Pirqe R. El.* 4: ארבעה כתות של מלאכי השרת מקלסין לפני הקדוש ברוך הוא ... מחנה שניה של גבריאל על ... שמאלו . Unless otherwise noted, this latter text is cited from the edition of D. Luria (reprinted, Jerusalem: [s.n.], 1970).

67 M. Scopello, "The Apocalypse of Zostrianos (Nag Hammadi VIII.1) and the Book of the Secrets of Enoch," *VC* 34 (1980) 376-85.

68 Pennington 330-31.

69 4QEn^a I iii 4; *1 Enoch* 6:6 (Syncellus); *Jub.* 4:15, 5:1-6; 1QapGen 3:3.

70 Knibb 199.

71 *1 Enoch* 10:4-7, 12-14; 88:3; *Jub.* 5:6, 10; 2 Pet 2:4.

72 *2 Enoch* 7:7 (Pennington 335).

73 See especially A. Rubinstein, "Observations on the Slavonic Book of Enoch," *JJS* 13 (1962) 7-10.

74 This particular correspondence was also noticed by W. Bousset, *Hauptprobleme der Gnosis* (reprinted, Göttingen: Vandenhoeck & Ruprecht, 1973) 53.

75 The "Great King of Honor" (ܡܠܟܐ ܪܒܐ ܕܐܝܩܪܐ ; Latin rex honoris) is one of the five "sons" evoked by the "Living Spirit" (ܪܘܚܐ ܚܝܐ) to assist in the construction and governance of the physical universe. Theodore bar Konai, *Liber Scholiorum* (2 vols.; ed. A. Scher; Paris: Carolus Poussielgue, 1912) 2.315 lines 16-18: "After the heavens and earths were made, the Great King of Honor took a seat in the midst of the heavens and kept watch over the whole." See also Andreas-Henning, *SPAW* (1932) 178 lines 14-18; A.V.W. Jackson, *Researches in Manichaeism* (reprinted, New York: AMS Press, 1965) 296-313.

76 Theodore bar Konai 315 lines 7-12: "Then the Living Spirit commanded three of his sons, that each should kill and should skin the archons, the sons of Darkness, and bring (them) to the Mother of Life. The Mother of Life stretched out the heavens from their skins, and she made eleven (sic!) heavens. They threw down their bodies to the Land of Darkness, and they made eight earths." Note also Epiphanius, *Panarion* 66.32.3 (ed. Holl 72) and Ephrem's references to the "shed skins" (ܡܫܠܚܬܐ) of the archons in his *Prose Refutations* (ed. Mitchell; cf. n.1 *supra*) 1.13 lines 23, 25; 1.15 line 25; 2.228 line 44; 2.229 line 2. For yet further references and discussion, see F. Cumont and M.-A. Kugener, *Recherches sur le manichéisme* (Bruxelles: H. Lamertin, 1908-12) 26-28.

77 *Acta Archelai* 8 = Epiphanius, *Panarion* 66.25.8 (ed. Holl 56); the Greek text is also cited by Cumont-Kugener, *Recherches* 30 n.4. See also *Chronicon Maroniticum* (cf. *Chronica Minora* [ed. I. Guidi; Paris: Carolus Poussielgue, 1903] 60 lines 18-19); al-Nadīm, *Fihrist* (apud Flügel, *Mani* 56 lines 9-10); Andreas-Henning, *SPAW* (1932) 179 lines 6-8, 183 line 24, etc.; W. Sundermann, *Mittelpersische und parthische kosmogonische und Parabeltexte der Manichäer* (Berlin: Akademie-Verlag, 1973) 45 lines 835-38. This work is henceforth cited as Sundermann, *KT*. Further references and discussion in Cumont-Kugener, *Recherches* 54 n.4; Jackson, *Researches* 233-34 n.45.

[78] *Kephalaia* 88.6-7; 118.20; 170.4; Ephrem, *Prose Refutations* (ed. Mitchell) 2.204 lines 45-46; W.B. Henning, "A Sogdian Fragment of the Manichaean Cosmogony," *BSOAS* 12 (1947-48) 307 lines 78,81,etc.; W. Sundermann, *KT* 56 line 1054. Further references and discussion are provided by Puech, *Le manichéisme* 170-71 n.319. Interestingly the concept of "ten heavens" is also present in some manuscripts of the so-called "long recension" of *2 Enoch*: "And I saw the eighth Heaven, which is called in the Hebrew tongue Muzaloth ... And I saw the ninth Heaven, which is called in Hebrew Kuchavim ... On the tenth Heaven, Aravoth, I saw the appearance of the Lord's face ...." Text cited (with some omissions) from N. Forbes and R.H. Charles, "The Book of the Secrets of Enoch," *APOT* 2.442. Apart from later kabbalistic texts (note Ginzberg, *Legends* 5.10), this seems to be the sole reference to "ten heavens" in Jewish cosmological discussion.

[79] *Kephalaia* 86.5-6; 170.20-171.11.

[80] *Kephalaia* 87.34; 91.23-24; Henning, *BSOAS* 12 (1947-48) 313 n.6.

[81] The number "two hundred" indicates a clear linkage between Enochic and Manichaean literature. See *1 Enoch* 6:6; *2 Enoch* 7:4; Henning, *BSOAS* 11 (1943-46) 60, 69-71.

[82] *Kephalaia* 92.31.

[83] *Kephalaia* 93.23-28; 117.1-4; Sogdian superscription *iv fryštyt δn CC* "the four angels with the two hundred [demons]" (Henning, *BSOAS* 11 [1943-46] 68). Note that these Manichaean texts are also cognizant of the rival tradition that binds the defeated Watchers "beneath the earth." See below.

[84] See Reeves, *Jewish Lore* 185-88.

[85] *Kephalaia* 17.5-9 (quoting Lk 6:43-44); *Acta Archelai* 5 = Epiphanius, *Panarion* 66.6.7-8 (ed. Holl 27).

[86] Clearly signaled in the name these beings bear in both traditions; viz., ἐγρήγοροι.

[87] *2 Enoch* 5:1-6, with some omissions (Pennington 331).

[88] These fragments are presented and analyzed in Reeves, *Jewish Lore* 165-83.

[89] There may be some connection between the Manichaean Tree of Death and the Qur'ānic "accursed tree" *Zaqqūm* which grows in Hell and whose bitter fruits sinners shall eventually consume. See Qur'ān 17:60; 37:62-65; 44:43-46; 56:52. I am grateful to David J. Halperin for reminding me of these passages.

[90] M. Brière, "Les Homiliae Cathedrales de Sévère d'Antioche, traduction syriaque de Jacques d'Édesse CXX à CXXV," *PO* 29 (1960) 152 lines 14-16.

[91] Ibid., 154 lines 9-18, with some omission. Compare *Kephalaia* 20.32-33; *Psalm-Book* 219.23-30.

[92] Ibid., 166 lines 10-13.

[93] Ibid., 162 lines 6-10, with some omission. For discussion of the Manichaean imagery of the Tree of Life and Tree of Death, see especially V. Arnold-Döben, *Die Bildersprache des Manichäismus* (Köln: Brill, 1978) 8-17.

[94] Ibid., 164 lines 17-22.

[95] Cited by Forbes-Charles, *APOT* 2.434. I discern no specific references to the terminology "Tree of Life/Tree of Death" as evidenced by Severus, although Epiphanius is familiar with the "good tree/worthless tree" parabolic language exploited by Mani.

96 See especially Puech, *Le manichéisme* 159-61 n.285.

97 Allusions to a heavenly "paradise," with or without reference to the Tree of Life, appear in 2 Cor 12:4; Rev 2:7, 22:2; 4 Ezra 4:7-8, 8:52; *2 Apoc. Bar.* 4:2-7; *Adam and Eve* 25:3; *Apoc. Mos.* 40:2; *b. Ḥag.* 14b and parallels; *Tri. Trac.* 96.28-30; *Gos. Thom.* 19. Detailed descriptions of a celestial *gan 'eden* occur in *Midrash Konen* (*BHM* 2.28-30); *Seder Gan 'Eden* (ibid., 2.52-53, 3.131-40, 194-98); *Ma'aseh de R. Joshua b. Levi* (ibid., 2.48-51); *Gan 'Eden we-Gehinnom* (ibid., 5.42-51).

98 Note *Odes Sol.* 11:19, which associates "light" with Paradise, and Charlesworth's plausible reconstruction of the Syriac text of 11:16c (now extant only in Greek), which if accepted, posits "luminous fruits" in Paradise. See J.H. Charlesworth, *The Odes of Solomon: The Syriac Texts* (reprinted, Chico: Scholars Press, 1977) 57 n.33. Ephrem describes the Tree of Life as "the sun of Paradise"; cf. the citation from one of his "Hymns on Paradise" supplied by N. Séd, "Les Hymnes sur le Paradis de Saint Ephrem et les traditions juives," *Le Muséon* 81 (1968) 487; also 488 n.71. Note *Lev. Rab.* 11.7: אור סימון בר יהודה א״ר שברא הקב״ה ביום ראשון אדם צופה ומביט בו מסוף העולם ועד סופו כיון שראה הקב״ה מעשה דור אנוש ומעשה דור המבול שהן מקלקלין <u>עמד וגנזו מהן</u> הה״ד וימנע מרשעים אורם <איוב לח> <u>והיכן</u> <u>גנזו בגן עדן</u> שנא״ אור זרוע לצדיק ולישרי לב שמחה <תהלים צז>. Compare also *Gen. Rab.* 3.6 (Theodor-Albeck 21-22); *b. Ḥag.* 12a.

99 The association of perfume with Paradise is already found in *1 Enoch* 24:4; cf. also *Jub.* 4:25. See also Séd, *Muséon* 81 (1968) 495-500. Compare *Seder Gan 'Eden* (*BHM* 2.53 lines 4-5): "its (the Tree's) fragrance permeates the entire world." Ephrem's references to the Manichaean Realm of Light frequently remark its pleasant fragrance.

100 Knibb 214.

101 *Apoc. Mos.* 22:1-4, cited from L.S.A. Wells, "The Books of Adam and Eve," *APOT* 2.147.

102 *Sefer ha-Bahir* §161 (ed. Margolioth = Scholem §107). See Scholem, *Bahir* 115-16; idem, *Origins* 148-49.

103 שם שם לו חק ומשפט לשטן. Regarding the identification of the "wood" mentioned in Ex 15:23-25 with the Tree of Life, see already *Bib. Ant.* 11:15 and especially *Mek. de R. Y., Beshallaḥ* 1 (ed. Horovitz-Rabin 155-56): רבי שמעון בן יוחאי אומר דבר מן התורה הראהו שנאמר ויורו ה'עץ ויראהו ה'עץ' אינו אומר אלא וירהו כענין שנאמר ויורני ויאמר לי יתמוך דברי לבך <משלי ד ד> ... דורשי רשמות אמרו הראהו דברי תורה שנמשלו לעץ שנאמר עץ חיים היא למחזיקים בה וגו' <שם ג יח>. Note also Ginzberg, *Legends* 6.14-15.

104 Note also the so-called *3 Enoch* for the juxtaposition of the Tree of Life, the presence of God, and the judgment of Adam in Schäfer §7.

THE CONVERSATION OF PALM TREES

Burton L. Visotzky
The Jewish Theological Seminary

"Wirklich wurde Joseph ... eingesetzt zur Gartenpflege; und zwar war es der Baumgarten, wo er Arbeit erheilt, -- noch genauer der Palmengarten ... kurz gesagt, ist das ein göttlicher Baum."

Thomas Mann, *Joseph und seiner Brüder*

I

In late antique society the palm tree was recognized as the epitome of ecological economy. "Nothing goes to waste in the palm," say the rabbis.[1] "The dates are for eating, the fronds for reciting *Hallel*, dried branches for thatching, hemp for making rope, the panicles for architectural adornment, the sturdy trunks for beaming houses."[2] Typically, the rabbis of the midrash wax poetic and liken the trusty palm tree to God's people, Israel, made up of many useful parts: "masters of Scripture, masters of Mishnah, masters of Talmud, masters of Narrative Lore."[3] This analogy is suggested, of course, by the trope of Ps 92:13 ("The righteous flower like the date palm, thrive like a cedar in Lebanon"), upon which the rabbis remark, "just as the hearts of palm and cedar incline upward, so the hearts of the righteous incline toward the blessed Holy One."[4]

The tendency to doubly bind the palm through listing of virtues and through comparison to the righteous Jew finds an even clearer expression in rabbinic literature in an aretological passage extolling the legendary founder of post-destruction rabbinic Judaism, Yohanan ben Zakkai.[5]

> They said of Rabban Yohanan ben Zakkai that he did not leave [anything unstudied. He mastered] Scripture, Mishnah, Gemara, Law, and Narrative Lore, the grammar of Torah[6] and the grammar of Scribes, inferences from minor to major, inferences from common verbal stems, calendric seasons, numerology,[7] the conversation of ministering angels, the conversation of demons and *the conversation of palm trees*, fuller fables and fox fables,[8] matters large and small. Matters large refers to the workings of the celestial chariot;[9] matters small refers to the dialectics of [the future Babylonian Rabbis] Abaye and Rava. Thus did [Rabban Yohanan ben Zakkai] fulfill that which is written, 'I bequeath substance to those who love me, I fill full their treasuries' (Prov 8:21).[10]

Tempting though it is to offer exegesis and philological commentary to this florilegium of rabbinic arcana, I will focus only on the emphasized passage, which is the subject of this essay. Rashi, the famous eleventh-century Narbonnese commentator to the Talmud, puts the problem succinctly when he states, "The conversation of palm trees -- I don't know what it is."[11]

His gaonic predecessors were somewhat more prolix on the passage, although it is not clear that we know any more about it at the end of their responsum:

> As to your question about the conversation of palm trees: It is said that on a day when no wind is blowing and if you spread a sheet it will not flap; then the one who knows stands between two date palms which are close to one another and observes how the fronds sway. There are discernable signs by which many things may be recognized. They say that Mr. Abraham Kabasi Gaon (may he rest in peace) understood this conversation of palm trees and

would reveal great wonders which people recognized as
the truth.[12]

It may well be that Mr. Kabasi could read palms, but I am dubious that
his revelations have much to do with understanding our passage. It is
here that the topic of this volume, the vitality of pseudepigrapha,
serves us. By tracing the threads of various texts backward we may be
able to expose the woof and warp of a pattern running through
disparate fragments of ancient literature. The fabric one hopes to
restore might provide exegesis of a variety of passages in light of one
another and the possibility of a small contribution to the history of
religious thinking in late antiquity. What we shall learn is that Rabban
Yohanan ben Zakkai was not the only adept to whom the
conversation of palm trees was revealed.

The Talmudic passages that speak of Rabban Yohanan's studies
were redacted in Babylonia in the late fifth century. They speak of a
Palestinian sage who flourished four centuries earlier, but the accuracy
of such testimony is notoriously uncertain. Minimally we can learn
that the chatting of palm trees was an art to be valued in the Fertile
Crescent somewhat before the year 500 CE and was listed alongside
conversations of ministering angels and of demons as an item worth
attending to.

II

There exists another fifth-century text documenting life in
Babylonia that also knows the value of the conversation of palm trees.
I refer now to a little book called the *Cologne Mani Codex*
(henceforth *CMC*). This work is a papyrus codex of 192 pages, each
about one inch square with some two dozen lines of text per side --
very tiny Greek writing which purports to be a first-person account of
the founder of Manichaeism's upbringing, persecution, and founding of
his new religion.[13] Mani himself lived in the first half of the third
century and was raised in a Jewish-Christian sect in southern
Babylonia.[14] The *CMC*, most scholars agree, is a translation of an

earlier Syriac original. In other words, we have another Semitic
account of the conversation of palm trees.

The *CMC*'s text is far more exciting than the Talmud's mere
listing. In the *CMC* we are treated to the actual conversation which
takes place between the palm and, apparently, the human beings with
whom it speaks. The little *CMC* is chewed up around the edges, so
words are missing at key junctures. At best, a spotty reconstruction of
the tree's admonitions can be offered. As the exceedingly fragmentary
opening words of the *CMC* remind us about recovering the history of
religions, "[...] little by little [...] I have shown you [...] but you will be
able to behold that mystery magnificently and most lucidly."[15] The
limits of our lucidity are further tested by what appears to be a
misordering of pages in the bound codex. When juxtaposed below
they may make some sense:

> We went away to a certain date [palm] and he climbed up [.
> ...][16] <The palm tree spoke:> "If you keep the pain away
> from us you will [not] perish with the murderer."
> Then that Baptist, gripped by fear of me <Mani>, came
> down from it in confusion, and fell at my feet and said, "I
> did not know that this secret mystery is with you. Whence
> was revealed to you [...][17]
> Again he (Mani) points out that a date palm tree spoke
> with Aianos, the Baptist from Koche, and commanded him
> to say to <its> lord, "Don't cut me down because my fruit
> is stolen ..." But it also commanded him to say to that man
> who was stealing its fruit: "Do not come at this season to
> steal my fruit away. If you come, I shall hurl you down
> from my height and you will die."[18]

Apparently, the palms revealed important things to Mani and the
Baptists with whom he associated. The latter revelations are part of a
series of speeches by water, earth, bread, and vegetables. For all that
these revelations played an important part in the sect's severe dietary
restrictions, each revelation is limited to the narrow self-interest of the
hypostasized speaker. If this is mystical revelation, it is of a decidedly
practical nature.

The content of the revelations may be disappointing, but the fact
of them is illuminative. Palm trees speak with human beings. The

human beings who are privileged to hear the palms seem to have certain qualifications: they are the founders (Mani and Rabban Yohanan) or the associates of founders (Mani's Baptists) of a new Semitic religion.

Date palms, being as important as they are in the Near East, are naturals as the bearers of revelatory tidings. Albert Henrichs, one of the original editors of the *CMC*, suggests that the key to understanding this as a religious phenomenon is the dual belief in animism and metempsychosis. He posits that eastern, particularly Indian, metaphysics lies behind Mani's talking trees and bleeding plants. He may well be correct. This would surely account for the esoteric nature of the doctrine of the date palms, particularly when it is attributed to a rabbinic adept like Rabban Yohanan ben Zakkai. But I suspect that Henrichs may be equally correct when he writes, "to the Greeks of the second century A.D., it was hardly more than an amusing status symbol of exotic sages."[19]

III

There is, yet, a middle ground between the droll sage-tales of the Greek sophists and the animism of the Indian gymnosophists. This middle ground is occupied by fable and folklore. What can they teach us of the conversation of palm trees and its meaning?

Returning to the *Genesis Rabbah* text with which we opened, we find a folktale that surely underscores Henrichs' emphasis on animism. The fourth-century Palestinian sage, Rabbi Tanḥuma,

> tells a story of a certain female date palm in the town of Amto which would not bear any fruit. Once a specialist in fructifying date palms came by and looked it over. He suggested that the palm lusted for a certain male palm tree in Jericho. When he rode the tree [climbing it to implant pollen from that male into the female], it bore fruit.[20]

The animism is surely evident here, as are perhaps sufficient aspects of human psychology to suggest metempsychosis. What is lacking, however, is conversation. This folktale and others carry some aspects of the conversation of palms, but not the full motif. It is in fact quite rare to find date palms chatting, whether with the opposite sex of their species or with *homo sapiens*. Nevertheless, it is worth a brief survey to gain background to the phenomenon.

Folkloric literature from antiquity has abundant reports of other tree conversations, if not those of palm trees. R.J. Williams pointed out some decades ago that "The Fable in the Ancient Near East" includes a motif of "dispute" fables in which trees debate their superiority. He cites the Akkadian version of the dispute between the tamarisk and the date palm as a prime example.[21] Williams goes on to cite many other examples of talking trees, particularly in the Bible,[22] but only the Old Babylonian dispute transcribes the conversation of a palm tree. Just a few years later W.G. Lambert included the same dispute in his chapter on "Fables or Contest Literature" in his collection of *Babylonian Wisdom Literature*.[23] The dialogue between the tamarisk and the date palm is fragmentary, each tree apparently claiming its superiority due to its general usefulness and its particular place in the royal household. While these fragments are entertaining, they are far too early to be at the root of our textual crux. Nevertheless, it is an important precedent in the field: trees talk to one another.

In 1914, A. Marmorstein zeroed in on "Sprechende Bäume" in his "Legendmotive in der rabbinischen Literatur."[24] He cites many accounts of conversations of various species of trees with one another. Surveying the folk material it seems it was hard to get trees to ever be silent. This may be due to the proclivity of folk types to hear messages in the whispering of pines and susurrations of saplings. Whatever the causes, they are not specific to the date palm's conversations.

Nevertheless, Marmorstein and others point to another famous pseudepigraphic text which shares a conversation between a tree and a Semitic founder of a religion: Abraham. The Greek *Testament of Abraham*[25] reports the message and even refers to it as "a mystery."[26] Accordingly, the reported content of the tree's revelation is limited.[27] Though the "B" Recension of the *Testament of Abraham* attributes the revelation to a tamarisk, the "A" Recension can offer no more than a cypress -- again, no conversation of palm trees. With the one exception of the old Akkadian dispute between the tamarisk and palm, we are offered no true hearings of the conversation of palm trees in folklore and fable.

IV

Abraham has been the occasion for much conversation among trees. The cypress and tamarisk speak to him in the two recensions of the *Testament of Abraham*. The *Genesis Rabbah* texts cited thus far are located as commentary to Gen 12:17 even as they are coupled with the verse of Ps 92:13. One last part of that *Genesis Rabbah* text makes the link between those verses of Scripture explicit:

> ['The righteous flower like the date palm, thrive like a cedar in Lebanon' (Ps 92:13)]. In the case of the date palm and cedar, anyone who ascends the former and does not watch out for himself will fall and die. Thus it is with those who seek to unite with Israel; in the end they will get theirs by Israel's hand. So it was that Pharaoh drew Sarah to him but for one night and as a result he and his entire household were smitten, thus it is, 'God plagued Pharaoh and his household with a great plague on account of Sarai, the wife of Abram' (Gen 12:17).[28]

This midrash comments, of course, on that most unsavory of biblical narratives where Abraham actually instructs his wife, *Tell 'em your my sister so things will go well for me thanks to you* (Gen 12:13). Countless generations of pious Bible commentators have bent over backwards to try and rescue Abraham from this less than righteous posture. Linking the outcome of the passage with cedars and palms, *Genesis Rabbah* recalls an earlier attempt to protect Abraham's virtue (if not Sarah's) through the conversation of palm trees.

Centuries before *Genesis Rabbah*, midway between the palm groves of Jericho and Ein Gedi, the Dead Sea community read targum to this passage of the Bible. That unusual first-person account, called today the *Genesis Apocryphon*,[29] shifts the blame for Abraham's ruse from his shoulders. "I had a dream," we are told,

> And I saw in my dream a cedar and a very beautiful date
> palm. Humans came to chop down and uproot the cedar
> and leave the date palm by herself. The date palm cried
> out and said, 'Do not chop down the cedar, cursed[30] be he
> who throws down the cedar.' So they spared the cedar
> because of the date palm and it was not [chopped down].
> I woke from my slumber that night and said to Sarai, 'My
> wife, I had a dream, and I am frightened by that dream ....'

The *Genesis Apocryphon* goes on to recount how Abraham told his
dream to Sarah and interpreted it as referring to their own marriage;
he was the cedar and she was the palm. It is then, under the revelatory
influence of his dream,[31] that Abraham ventures to suggest the now
infamous wife-sister motif. Leaving aside the moral niceties, it must be
noted that Abraham, founder of a Semitic religion, about to encounter
the Pharaoh-king, is privileged with a dream-vision in which the
conversation of a palm tree not only saves his life, but brings him
much wealth and success.

V

The *Genesis Apocryphon* displays, in the Aramaic of first-
century Palestine,[32] many of the features we have surveyed in our
tracing backward the threads of the conversation of palm trees. Like
the *CMC*, it has the palm tree threaten a human who is intent on
harming a tree. Like in much of the folklore, trees in the *Genesis
Apocryphon* converse with one another. Finally, this Qumranic
targum shares with the other texts we have surveyed the belief that
the conversation of palm trees reveals special knowledge to the
founder of a Semitic religion, be he Abraham, Mani, or Rabban
Yohanan ben Zakkai.

For a period of close to five hundred years, stories from Semitic
religious communities preserved (in Palestinian Aramaic, *koine* Greek,
and rabbinic Hebrew) snatches of the conversation of palm trees. The
palms speak in dreams to one another and in broad daylight to those
who would transgress against them. What seems to bind the dialogues
together is that in every case, the ultimate hearer is a towering

religious figure. The date palm chooses human conversation partners as valuable to Middle Eastern culture as she is herself.[33]

---

1   Gen. Rab. 40(41).1 (ed. Theodor-Albeck 388; see the notes ad loc.). All translations are mine unless otherwise noted.
2   The term Hallel refers to the liturgical recitation of Psalms 113-118. The translation follows Theodor's notes and the definitions of J. Levy, Neuhebräisches und Chaldäisches Wörterbuch über die Talmudim und Midraschim (Leipzig: F.A. Brockhaus, 1883) s.v. סנס (p. 557), שפעה (p. 598).
3   Gen. Rab. 40(41).1.
4   Ibid. (Theodor-Albeck 389).
5   For more on this figure and the difficulties of writing his biography see J. Neusner, A Life of Yohanan ben Zakkai (2d ed.; Leiden: Brill, 1970), and idem, Development of a Legend: Studies in the Traditions Concerning Yohanan ben Zakkai (Leiden: Brill, 1970).
6   דקדוקי תורה, lit. "small details of Torah." Rashi explains it as legal derivations from niceties of grammar.
7   גמטריות . Perhaps "geometry," but more likely the numerology derived from assigning each letter a numerical value. See S. Lieberman, Hellenism in Jewish Palestine (2d ed.; New York: Jewish Theological Seminary of America, 1962) 47-82.
8   Two forms of folktale entertainment, the former somewhat like our travelling salesmen jokes, the latter known from Aesopica.
9   Mystical speculation based on Ezekiel 1. See G. Scholem, Major Trends in Jewish Mysticism (3d ed.; New York: Schocken, 1961) 40-78.
10   b. Sukk. 28a = b. B. Bat. 134a (with minor variations in order). See Tractate Soferim MS Adler 2237 (ed. Higger 290 line 47) where the conversation of palms is part of Hillel's curriculum. See also the Alphabet of Ben Sira (Eli Yassif, The Tales of Ben Sira in the Middle Ages [Jerusalem: Magnes, 1984] 213 [Hebrew], and in J.D. Eisenstein, Otzar Midrashim [New York, 1915; reprinted, 1969] 45) where Ben Sira is said to have studied the same. Each of the latter are dependent on the Babylonian Talmud passage. Cf. 'Abot R. Natan A 14 where the list (including our palm tree) has been truncated -- perhaps because the late redactor was stymied about the meaning of individual terms.
11   Rashi to b. Sukk. 28a.
12   Otzar ha-Gaonim (13 vols.; ed. B.M. Lewin; Haifa and Jerusalem: [s.n.], 1928-) 6.31 ad b. Sukk. 28a, with Lewin's comments ad loc. See also I. Gruenwald, "Manichaeism and Judaism in Light of the Cologne Mani Codex," Zeitschrift für Papyrologie und Epigraphik (= ZPE) 50 (1983) 29-45, who translates this passage (p. 45). Gruenwald was the first to connect this passage with the Cologne Mani Codex, which will be discussed in more detail below.
13   The Greek text with German translation and an exhaustive commentary was published by A. Henrichs and L. Koenen, "Der Kölner Mani-Kodex (P. Colon. inv. nr. 4780) ...," ZPE 19 (1975) 1-85; 32 (1978) 87-199; 44 (1981) 201-318; 48 (1982) 1-59. All citations here are from the first two of those volumes

(published in 1975 and 1978). This first half of the codex was published by the Society of Biblical Literature in an English translation by R. Cameron and A. Dewey (Missoula, Mont.: Scholars Press, 1979). For more on the relationship of the *Cologne Mani Codex* to rabbinic literature and for more general bibliography, see B. Visotzky, "Rabbinic Randglossen to the Cologne Mani Codex," *ZPE* 52 (1983) 295-300. The descriptions which follow depend on the bibliography cited ibid., p. 295 n.3.

[14] On the problems manifest in the study of Jewish-Christianities in this era, see B. Visotzky, "Prolegomenon to the Study of Jewish-Christianities in Rabbinic Literature," *AJS Review* 14 (1989) 47-70.

[15] Following Cameron and Dewey to p. 2.

[16] Ibid., p. 6 lines 12ff., checked against the facsimile edition, L. Koenen and C. Römer, *Der Kölner Mani-Kodex* (Bonn: R. Habelt, 1985).

[17] Cameron and Dewey to p. 7.

[18] Ibid., p. 98 line 8 to p. 99 line 9.

[19] A. Henrichs, "'Thou Shalt Not Kill a Tree': Greek, Manichaean and Indian Tales," *BASP* 16 (1979) 85-108. The quote is on p. 99.

[20] *Gen. Rab.* 40(41).1 (ed. Theodor-Albeck 387) emended on the basis of the parallel in *Midrash Tehillim* 92:11 (ed. S. Buber 410). For more on the botanical aspects, see I. Löw, *Die Flora der Juden* (4 vols.; Leipzig: R. Lowit, 1924-34) 2.306-62, esp. p. 318, and pp. 361ff. for our passage. Cf. Pliny the Elder, *Natural History* 13.4,9. For a narrative of the "riding" process see Thomas Mann's description cited in the epigraph to this essay.

[21] R.J. Williams, "The Fable in the Ancient Near East," *A Stubborn Faith: Papers on Old Testament and Related Subjects Presented to Honor William Andrew Irwin* (ed. E.C. Hobbs; Dallas: Southern Methodist University Press, 1956) 3-27; our texts pp. 8ff.

[22] Ibid. *passim.*

[23] (Oxford: Clarendon, 1960) 150-64.

[24] Part VI in *ARW* 17 (1914) 132-33.

[25] *The Testament of Abraham: The Greek Recensions* (ed. M.E. Stone; Missoula: Scholars Press, 1972), and see the more recent translation and bibliography by E.P. Sanders in *OTP* 1.871-902.

[26] Recensions A and B, chap. 3.

[27] Little more than "Holy, holy, holy."

[28] *Gen. Rab.* 40(41).1 (Theodor-Albeck 388).

[29] Col. xix, in J.A. Fitzmyer, *The Genesis Apocryphon of Qumran Cave I* (Rome: Biblical Institute Press, 1966) 50-52. I follow Fitzmyer's transcription and have consulted his commentary (pp. 99-104).

[30] Following Fitzmyer. See his commentary *ad loc.*

[31] "A dream is one-sixtieth part prophecy" (*b. Ber.* 57b). See A.L. Oppenheim, "The Interpretation of Dreams in the Ancient Near East," *Transactions of the American Philosophical Society* 46 (1956) 179-255.

[32] See Fitzmyer's discussion (*Genesis Apocryphon* 14-25).

[33] Thanks to Dianne Esses for research assistance and keen criticism. Thanks as well to my most perspicacious copy-editor and to the Abbell Publication Fund (JTSA) for supporting the leisure to write this essay.

THE COMPOSITIONS OF ABRAHAM

James E. Bowley
Cincinnati, Ohio

Abraham and Books

In the biblical record one finds no indication that Abraham was acquainted with, read, or authored writings of any kind. This of course did not prevent later writers from associating the great patriarch (and many other persons of antiquity) with books, tablets, or other documents. The second or third century BCE author of *Jubilees* wrote that Abraham copied and studied the Hebrew books of his father (*Jub.* 12:27). Several centuries later, in the brief introduction to the compilation *Sefer Ha-Razim* (late third to early fourth century CE), it is said that the "books of the mysteries" were given to Noah by the angel Raziel and passed on to Abraham, Isaac, and eventually Solomon.[1]

As opposed to just a reader or tradent of written materials, there are traditions which make Abraham an author of texts, and it is these which will be considered here. These "Abrahamic" texts can be roughly classified according to the several variant portraits of Abraham current in the Second Temple period and beyond. During

215

the Graeco-Roman period, different authors in their descriptions of Abraham's life and activities presented diverse and sometimes clashing depictions of the Jewish patriarch. The various pseudepigraphic writings attributed to the patriarch, also produced during this period, can be shown to fit the same basic patterns of the narrative portraits of Abraham.

The Familiar Abraham and His Writings

The role played by Abraham as patriarch and exemplar of faith in the developing thought of early Jewish and Christian traditions can hardly be overemphasized. Abraham's image as the inaugural recipient of God's eternal covenant with the Jewish people and as the supreme example of faith, obedience, and zeal hardly varies from the end of Genesis 11 through the writings known as Apocrypha and Pseudepigrapha to later rabbinic, Christian, and Islamic texts.

Samuel Sandmel in his work *Philo's Place in Judaism* surveyed the characterization of Abraham in various Jewish literary works, including the biblical material, apocryphal and pseudepigraphic texts, rabbinic traditions, Graeco-Jewish historians, and Philo.[2] Most of the Second Temple era texts that Sandmel examined emphasize the patriarch's rejection of idolatry and of all the abominations of the Gentiles, including astrology and other matters of Hellenistic culture (e.g., *Jub.* 11-12; 15). Other texts stress his eternal covenant with God (*Jub.* 14), his obedience to the law (*2 Apoc. Baruch* 57; *T. Benj.* 10; CD 3:2), his fidelity to the purity code (*Jub.* 20-21), and the merit of his righteousness for his covenantal children (*1 Enoch* 93; *T. Levi* 15). He is sometimes depicted as the pious recipient of supernatural revelation and wisdom, thus qualifying him as a great sage (*Jub.* 12; *Apoc. Abr.* 7-8).[3] These are the themes which typically dominate the portrayal of Abraham in the pseudepigraphical and extracanonical literature.[4]

It is from out of this general portrait of the righteous and wise Abraham that one finds literary compositions credited to the patriarch himself. Such pseudepigrapha are not surprising in themselves, given the extraordinary popularity of pseudepigraphic compositions in

Second Temple literary history. The intention here is to consider how these compositions ascribed to Abraham relate to the traditional portrait of the pious Abraham just described.

One such work is the *Apocalypse of Abraham*, an originally Hebrew work now preserved only in Slavonic, but whose composition is usually dated to the end of the first or the beginning of the second century CE.[5] The revelations granted Abraham in the *Apocalypse of Abraham* stress God's exclusive choice of an eternal covenant with Abraham and his descendants and their deliverance from the destiny of the wicked (9:1-10; 14:3; 20:5; 33:3-5; 24:1; 31:1-8),[6] a traditional Abrahamic theme reappearing in later Jewish, Christian, and Islamic sources. This "composition" of Abraham thus harmonizes with the character of Abraham as depicted in the Second Temple literature mentioned above.

Another work of the first or second century CE is known as the *Testament of Abraham.* The designation "testament" is puzzling, for the book records neither deathbed scene nor final instructions to assembled progeny. Indeed, an essential motif of this so-called "testament" is that Abraham will *not* make a testament.[7] Aside from the single exceptional use of first-person narrative style (recension A 12:1), the work in its current forms can hardly be said to be pseudepigraphic, since it neither explicitly purports to be, nor does it contain, a composition of the patriarch. However, the singular occurrence of first-person style at 12:1 does suggest that at least at some point much of this material was in the form of a genuine pseudepigraphon. In any case, the overriding concerns of this text are Abraham's piety and the maintenance of a proper relationship with God (*T. Abr.* recension A 9:2, 10:14, 12:15, 14:8-15, 18:1; recension B 4:11, 11:4), and it thus displays affinities with the portrait of Abraham supplied by Second Temple era literature. However, the *Testament of Abraham* also contrasts somewhat with many of those works. On the one hand, in accord with many other apocryphal and pseudepigraphic descriptions, Abraham is primarily a righteous and pious individual, and the author's ultimate concerns are theological and soteriological. Yet on the other hand, as noted by E.P. Sanders, the theology of the

Testament of Abraham is peculiar because of its universality and lack of emphasis upon distinctively Jewish concerns like the Torah and the covenantal relationship.[8] Hence while it is interested in the piety of Abraham, this piety is much more broadly defined.

The Qur'ānic references to Abraham remain within the traditions stressing the patriarch's faithfulness to the one true God and his role as the father of the people displaying true faith (2:124; 3:67-68; 14:35-36; 19:43; 26:70; 37:70). In two early *suras* the Qur'ān also refers to writings of Abraham with these words: "... is one not acquainted with what is in the books of Moses and of Abraham who fulfilled his engagements?" (53:36), and "And this is in the books of the earliest (revelations) -- the books of Abraham and Moses" (87:18-19). S.D. Goitein in the *Encyclopaedia Judaica* attempts no identification of the work(s) mentioned here.[9] R. Paret in the *Encyclopaedia of Islam* merely says that these were "presumably texts of revelation."[10] The English commentary to the Qur'ān prepared by A. Yusuf Ali suggests that the book of Abraham mentioned in these lines is the work known as the *Testament of Abraham*.[11] However, the context of one of these references, when compared to the contents of the *Testament of Abraham* and the *Apocalypse of Abraham*, renders it more likely that it is the latter writing which the author has in mind, if indeed it is either one.

Qur'ān *sura* 87, when referring to Abraham's writings, speaks of the eternal fire awaiting the unfaithful and the prosperity reserved for the faithful. This recompense motif is readily comparable to *Apoc. Abr.* 31-32. *Sura* 87:9-19, referring to Abraham's writing as a revelation of the eschaton, reads:

> Therefore give admonition in case the admonition
>   profits (the hearer).
> The admonition will be received by those who fear
>   (God):
> But it will be avoided by those most unfortunate
>   ones,
> Who will enter the great fire,
> In which they will then neither die nor live.
> But those will prosper who purify themselves,

And glorify the name of their Guardian-Lord, and
   (lift their hearts) in prayer
Nay (behold), ye prefer the life of this world;
But the hereafter is better and more enduring.
And this is in the books of the earliest (revelations),
The books of Abraham and Moses.[12]

While there is no direct citation of the *Apocalypse of Abraham* in this passage, the conclusion of that book (especially chaps. 29-32) finds God revealing to Abraham (32:1, 5-6) that he (God) "will burn with fire those who mocked" his people (31:2), those who "followed after idols" (31:4), and those who "abandoned the Lord" (31:8). However, "those who strive in the glory of my name toward the place prepared beforehand for them ... will live, being affirmed by the sacrifices and the gifts of justice and truth in the age of justice. And they will rejoice forever in me ..." (29:17-19).

Furthermore, the Qur'ānic picture of Abraham as a whole, with its strong emphasis on Abraham's rejection of idolatry (2:135; 6:74; 19:41-50; 21:52-71; *et al.*), mirrors this identical theme in the *Apocalypse of Abraham* (1:1-9:6; 29:1-8; 31:4-8). This is, of course, a recurring theme in the portrait of Abraham found in apocryphal/pseudepigraphic, Christian, and rabbinic writings. Condemnation of idolatry is however conspicuously absent in the *Testament of Abraham*,[13] thus making that work an unlikely candidate as background material for the Qur'ānic image of Abraham and its references to his writings. It thus seems probable that the *Apocalypse of Abraham,* rather than the *Testament of Abraham,* is the text presupposed by Qur'ān *sura* 87, especially given the thematic similarity of both passages.

As for the other reference to Abraham's authorship in *sura* 53:36-37, the context here stresses Abraham's faithfulness to God, a popular motif in much of postbiblical literature, regardless of its origin. For the specific words or phrases of the text, parallels are not readily apparent in the surviving versions of either the *Apocalypse of Abraham* or the *Testament of Abraham*. It is possible that the Qur'ān refers here to a pseudepigraphon which is no longer extant.

Therefore with regard to the Qur'ānic portrait of Abraham, it seems safe to say that it belongs in the same gallery with those apocryphal, Christian, and rabbinic portraits that emphasize Abraham's rejection of idolatry and his unyielding faithfulness to God. Moreover, insofar as it can be determined from the contexts which mention the writing(s) of Abraham (see *sura* 87), the content of these writings also matches this righteous portrait.

In Christian tradition there are some more references to writings from the hand of Abraham. Both the *Synopsis* of Pseudo-Athanasius (ca. 500 CE) and the *Stichometry of Nicephorus* (ca. 850 CE) list a work designated [ἀνάληψις] or [ἀποκάλυψις] 'Αβραάμ.[14] Furthermore, the fourth-century monk Epiphanius (*Panarion* 39.5.1, written 375-378 CE) says that the Sethian sect composed an apocalyptic book ἐξ ὀνόματος 'Αβραάμ. Epiphanius thus indicates that the work used by the Sethians bore a claim of Abrahamic authorship, although he himself is incredulous. Little or nothing is known of these works. M.R. James identified all three of these references with the writing now known to us as the *Testament of Abraham*.[15] However, Sethian theology as described (not so briefly) by Epiphanius has little in common with the *Testament of Abraham*. In fact, one could plausibly argue that Sethian beliefs were antithetical to material contained in the *Testament of Abraham*. According to Sethian doctrine, as related by Epiphanius, Seth is identified with Jesus, and, in typical Christian fashion, this Seth/Jesus presumably acts as the judge of all creation. By contrast, the *Testament of Abraham* presents Abel as the judge of the world (13:1-5). Regardless of the precise identification of the three books mentioned above, it is clear that there was a composition in Abraham's name which Epiphanius considered heretical. As James pointed out, Epiphanius' censure indicates nothing about the contents of the work, save that it was not accepted by Epiphanius.[16] Therefore, aside from accepting James' speculative identification of these works with the *Testament of Abraham*, we are unable to probe the portrait of Abraham presented by these texts to judge whether his image correlates with that found in the extant pseudepigraphic/apocryphal texts or is developed according to a different pattern.

The Other Abraham and His Writings

Another portrait of Abraham was current in the Graeco-Roman era, which while not contradicting the image of the pious, monotheistic, covenant recipient, nevertheless exhibits the patriarch in a quite different light. It appears both in literature about him and in at least one extant composition bearing his authorial stamp. This alternate depiction occurs in Greek compositions of both Jewish and pagan authors of the Graeco-Roman period, who, in the course of their diverse historiographical works, treat the patriarch. To illustrate this "other Abraham," we will consider briefly the portraits rendered by Pseudo-Eupolemus (*apud* Eusebius, *Praep. evan.* 9.17.2-9), Artapanus (*apud* Eusebius, *Praep. evan.* 9.18.1), Josephus (*Ant.* 1.154-242,256), and the anonymous sources used by Alexander Polyhistor (*apud* Eusebius, *Praep. evan.* 9.18.2). These Greek sources are united by their common recognition of Abraham as an expert in celestial affairs.

Before analyzing the portrait of the "Greek Abraham" found in these authors, it is worth noting that Abraham's reputation spread beyond the confines of the Jewish community in the Hellenistic world. While probably not as famous as Moses,[17] Abraham was not completely unknown in non-Jewish circles. Philo, a Jewish epic poet of the second century BCE, labels Abraham κλυτοηχής (*apud* Eusebius, *Praep. evan.* 9.20.1), a unique description best translated "famous" or "renowned" (from the more common κλυτός).[18] There is evidence that this epithet is more than poetic hyperbole, and actually reflects Abraham's status as a relatively well-known personage of Jewish antiquity, at least among lettered persons of the Hellenistic era, many of whom had some knowledge of Jewish traditions.[19]

There is first of all the literary testimony of non-Jewish authors. Apollonius Molon, a famous first-century BCE Rhodian rhetor, knew and repeated traditions concerning Abraham's sons as the first kings and eponymous ancestors of the peoples of Arabia (*apud* Eusebius,

Praep. evan. 9.19.1-3). Nicolaus of Damascus, friend of Julius Caesar and important diplomat of international influence who flourished in the second half of the same century, and a contemporary Latin author from Gaul, Pompeius Trogus, both report independent traditions of the kingship of Abraham in Damascus.[20] In Pompeius' work, thought to be dependent on the Greek author Timagenes (first century BCE), we find Abraham situated near the beginning of Asian civilization, a royal figure of remote antiquity in what Pompeius considered the most important city of the land.

Finally, we should not neglect to mention the first-century BCE scholar Alexander Polyhistor ('Αλέξανδρος ὁ πολυίστωρ), in whose debt we are for the remains of so many otherwise unknown authors. Alexander contributed profusely to historiography and more specifically to ethnography. He composed and compiled books on various lands and peoples, including Αἰγυπτιακά, Περὶ Βιθυνίας, Περὶ Εὐξείνου Πόντου, Ἰνδικά, Περὶ Καρίας, Κρητικά, Λιβυκά, Περὶ Συρίας, Χαλδαικά, and Περὶ Ἰουδαίων.[21]

Eusebius, using Alexander Polyhistor's compilation *On the Jews* for his own *Praeparatio evangelica*, cites no less than seven different sources featuring Abraham, more sources than Alexander provides for any other figure, including Moses.[22] We have no way of knowing to what extent the quantity of quotations preserved by Eusebius reflects the interests of the well-read pagan compiler Alexander, but it is probably not inaccurate to say that Abraham was a figure well represented in Alexander's work on the Jews. The quantity of works dealing with Abraham, as compared to other figures, could also reflect the greater amount of material available to Alexander on this patriarch. We have then, in the historians Alexander, Pompeius, Nicolaus, and Apollonius, pagan witnesses to the diffusion of historical traditions concerning Abraham among non-Jewish authors and readers of histories written in Greek in the last centuries BCE.[23]

In addition to this literary testimony, there is other evidence of Abraham's fame. According to a piece of Spartan royal correspondence which is preserved in 1 Macc 12:19-23 and in Josephus' *Ant.* 12.225-26, official Spartan records held that the Spartans and the Jews were ethnically kindred via Abraham.[24] This letter from the Spartan king Areus (probably Areus I, 309-265 BCE) to the Jewish High Priest Onias (probably Onias I, ca. 300 BCE) is an appendix to a letter carried by ambassadors of the Jewish high priest Jonathan (161-143 BCE) to the Spartans detailing the history of positive relations between Sparta and Jerusalem and appealing for a cordial renewal of those ties.[25] The letter of Areus (1 Macc 12:20-21) begins as follows:

> Ἄρειος[26] βασιλεὺς Σπαρτιατῶν Ονια ἱερεῖ μεγάλῳ χαίρειν. εὑρέθη ἐν γραφῇ περί τε τῶν Σπαρτιατῶν καὶ ᾽ Ιουδαίων ὅτι εἰσὶν ἀδελφοὶ καὶ ὅτι εἰσὶν ἐκ γένους ᾽ Αβραάμ.

> Areus, king of the Spartans to Onias, high priest, greetings. It has been found in a document concerning both the Spartans and the Jews that they are kinsmen and that they are from the family of Abraham.

An essential point which must be made first is that the tradition of Spartan descent from Abraham, while not recorded elsewhere in Greek tradition, is by no means far-fetched in the context of Hellenistic historiography and ethnography. Elias Bickerman has discussed the Hellenistic historical and ethnological models which accepted the antiquity of eastern peoples (as compared to the Greeks). These draw upon foreign traditions to enlighten native history, and posit genealogical relationships among diverse peoples.[27] For example, contrary to the traditional Greek sagas, Hecataeus of Abdera (late fourth century BCE) wrote that Belus, the legendary founder of Babylon, and Danaus and Cadmus, important figures in Greek antiquity, were actually Egyptian colonists, as were many other national founders and certain rulers of Athens, such as Peteus and Erechtheus (Diodorus Siculus 1.28-29). Even more astonishing is the claim by Hecataeus (*apud* Diodorus Siculus 1.17.3, 1.24.1-4) that Heracles, "the greatest and most popular Greek hero,"[28] was an Egyptian general who lived long before the Greek sagas would allow.[29] Despite the revolutionary nature of such assertions, the Hellenistic Greek historians "rarely dared to controvert such claims" of foreign (especially eastern) priority in matters of genealogy and even cultural advancement.[30] Suffice it to say that, in principle, any Greek who could surrender Heracles to the Egyptians, could, without raising an eyebrow, accept Abraham into the genealogy of the Spartans.

It is also important to note that the claim of descent from Abraham is based on a γραφή; i.e., a written document, which was apparently available in Sparta. This generic term could refer to the work of an ethnographer or to an archived document which had been interpreted to refer to Abraham. Even prior to the era of Areus I (early third century BCE), Greek historiography had a marked interest in foreign matters. A. Momigliano writes that "the geographical and ethnological exploration which characterized the beginnings of Greek historiography (the interest in foreign peoples, in differing customs, in geographical discoveries) originated [among Greeks] in the Persian empire and was made easier by the empire itself."[31] More specifically concerning the Spartans, already Plato (*Greater Hippias* 285D) had noted their interest in antiquarian matters, such as city foundations and genealogies.[32] It is therefore completely credible that there existed in Sparta in the days of Areus I a γραφή which enlightened Lacedaemonian history with a ray of foreign tradition.

It is even possible that Hecataeus of Abdera was the source of this assertion concerning the common heritage of Sparta and Jerusalem, since he is known to have visited Sparta during the reign of Areus I and his co-regent Archidamus IV.[33] Hecataeus had written of the similarity between the Spartan and Jewish claims of divine origin for their respective law codes, and he may have been aware of other common features of their manner of life.[34] Bickerman writes that "the Greek ethnological school insisted on the importance of rites for tracing the origins of a people,"[35] so that these cultural similarities may have been interpreted by Hecataeus as evidence of a genealogical relationship. Furthermore, the tradition of Abraham as common ancestor to both Spartans and Jews coheres with what is known of Hecataeus' research regarding the origins of the Spartans and the Jews. Hecataeus (*apud* Diodorus Siculus 40.3.1-3) had written that the foreigners Moses, Danaus, and Cadmus were expelled from Egypt at the same time. Traditional Greek mythology identified the Dorian

Spartans as descendents of Danaus,[36] while Moses is credited by
Hecataeus himself as the founder of Jerusalem. It is a simple matter to
posit a common ancestor; i.e., Abraham, for these two foreigners in
Egypt, Danaus and Moses.[37] One could further speculate that
Hecataeus knew something of the biblical traditions about Abraham's
journey to Egypt. In such a composition one would then find
traditional Greek mythological elements (descent of the Spartans from
Danaus), Egyptian elements (the origin of Danaus in Egypt), and Jewish
elements (Abraham as an ancestor of Danaus).

Regardless of the source and specific author of this γραφή
known to Areus I, the crucial point for our study is simply the fact that
such a tradition was extant in early third-century Greece. Abraham,
the ancestor of the Jews, was known in Sparta and had even become a
Lacedaemonian ancestor in at least one Spartan tradition.[38]

But Sparta was not the only place outside of the Jewish world in
which Abraham had a claim to fame. Josephus reports that during the
reign of John Hyrcanus I (135-104 BCE) a foreign city appealed to
Abraham as the basis of cordial diplomatic relations with the Jews. In
Ant. 14.247-55 Josephus presents the text of a decree from the Ionian
city of Pergamum (Ψήφισμα Περγαμηνῶν) which concludes with this
reminder:

> ... μεμνημένον τε ὡς καὶ ἐν τοῖς κατὰ Αβραμον καιροις,
> ὃς ἦν πάντων Ἑβραίων πατήρ, οἱ πρόγονοι ἡμῶν ἦσαν
> αὐτοῖς φίλοι, καθὼς καὶ ἐν τοῖς δημοσίοις εὑρίσκομεν
> γράμμασιν.

> ... remembering that in the time of Abraham, who is the
> father of all Hebrews, our ancestors were their friends,
> even as we find it in the public records.

One need not repeat the arguments from above that prove that
such a tradition could have been believed in the Hellenistic world. The
principle of friendship is not dissimilar to that of kinship, except that it
is a less audacious claim.[39] The point of emphasis is simply the fact
that this important Anatolian city of the first century BCE knew
Abraham as the ancestor of the Jews and claimed that their own
forefathers were his friends. One can only speculate as to the source

and nature of this tradition, which apparently combined Pergamene historical or mythological lore with Jewish tradition. It should also again be noted that this tradition was enshrined in written form, and in this case, the more specific form of a public record (δημοσίος γράμμασις). The friendship of the ancestral Pergamenes with Abraham was recorded in the official account of their own history.

In light of all of this evidence, it is justified to say that the above-cited boast of Abraham's fame from the pen of the poet Philo was not merely the product of poetic license. Of course measuring a person's fame, whether in antiquity or today, is a perilous task and open to objection, due to the inherent relativity of the claim.[40] Famous compared to whom? The task is furthered hampered by the loss of so much literary material from the Hellenistic world. In any case, the name of Abraham enjoyed currency among several pagan historians and was inscribed in the civic records of Sparta and Pergamum, in addition to its prominent display in the Greek literature of Jewish authors. Where else he may have been known is lost to us except by way of imagination. But it is surely not too much to claim that Abraham could well have been a recognizable name to Hellenistic readers of historiography and ethnography who had some knowledge of the Jews.

A question remains regarding this "famous Abraham." How was he represented and known to Greek readers in the last centuries BCE and the first century CE? The Jewish authors of Greek histories who spoke of Abraham, such as Pseudo-Eupolemus, Artapanus, Josephus, and the anonymous sources used by Alexander Polyhistor, present a different portrait of Abraham than that found in much of the apocryphal/pseudepigraphical literature and the traditions based on that literature.

For our purposes this other portrait of Abraham need only be summarized.[41] It is first of all worth observing that for all authors through Josephus who write in Greek concerning Abraham, the patriarch is a positive figure, found undeserving of criticism.[42] This attitude, of course, is not surprising in Jewish literature. However, non-Jewish authors of the period exhibit the same positive assessment of the Jewish patriarch, in spite of the not uncommon pagan criticisms of the Jews themselves or of Moses their lawgiver.[43] To whatever extent Abraham was known in the ancient world, he bears an overwhelmingly positive image in Greek literature.

Abraham was widely regarded as a great sage. For the several authors who paint Abraham as a learned man, one field of learning stands out from all the rest as his particular expertise -- astrology. We find Abraham as an astrologer *par excellence* in the work of Pseudo-Eupolemus, who declares that Abraham not only discovered astrology but also taught it to the Phoenicians and Egyptians. Similarly Artapanus and the anonymous sources used by Alexander Polyhistor portray Abraham teaching astrology. Josephus (*Ant.* 1.154-56) gives a detailed exposition of Abraham's far-reaching philosophical inferences which were based upon his alleged astronomical prowess.

While this depiction of Abraham as astrologer is absent from Genesis, it is no doubt related to Abraham's Chaldean origins.[44] The Chaldeans were renowned for their astrological skills throughout the Near Eastern and Graeco-Roman worlds.[45] The book of Daniel, in both its Hebrew and Aramaic portions, uses the name כשדים as a title for the learned diviners at the king's court.[46] Already in the mid-first century BCE in Rome the name *Chaldaei* without any further qualification had become a Latin *nomen professionis* for astrologers.[47] So too among Greek authors, perhaps as early as Aristotle, the term "Chaldean" can mean without further qualification "astrologer."[48]

The subject of Abraham and astrology occurs quite often in Jewish literature. In much of this literature Abraham's involvement with this controversial science is denied or in sundry manners excused.[49] Of course a given author's view of Abraham and astrology is directly related to the same author's opinion of astrology in general. It is becoming clearer that among some Jews in the Second Temple period, astrology played a greater role than what biblical, extracanonical, and rabbinic literature reveal.[50] Among the Graeco-Jewish authors (Artapanus, Pseudo-Eupolemus, anonymous sources used by Alexander Polyhistor, Josephus), a negative assessment of astrology cannot be detected. Abraham's role in the development of the discipline is seen in a positive light.[51]

A less prominent feature of Abraham's image in these four Jewish authors is his religiosity. Josephus detected religious and philosophical implications in Abraham's astronomical learning (*Ant.* 1.154-56). Josephus also sees religious faithfulness in Abraham's willingness to offer Isaac as a sacrifice (*Ant.* 1.222-34). Pseudo-Eupolemus says only that Abraham "applied himself to piety and was pleasing to God" (*apud* Eusebius, *Praep. evan.* 9.17.3). Both B.Z. Wacholder and L.H. Feldman have observed that Abraham's piety and religiosity are not points of emphasis for the historians, but are rather matters of secondary concern.[52] Artapanus and the anonymous sources relate nothing of Abraham's faith.

Closely related to Abraham's astrological skills is his role as a member of a class of international intelligentsia. In this setting he is found studying astronomy in a land renowned for that discipline (Chaldea) by Pseudo-Eupolemus, the anonymous sources, and Josephus. Pseudo-Eupolemus (with the anonymous sources) writes of his teaching the Phoenicians and (with Josephus) of his instructing the Egyptian priests. He is presented by Artapanus as an instructor of astrology before the Egyptian king.

The character of this "Graeco-Jewish Abraham" is most interesting in that it differs significantly from the Abraham described in much of the extracanonical literature summarized at the outset of this paper. In those writings, the stress is generally on some aspect of Abraham's righteousness. His involvement in astrology is polemically denied. Such is not the case with this less familiar portrait of Abraham, whose most fascinating and prominent aspect is this astrological prowess. According to Josephus, the patriarch's skill in this field was already mentioned by the Babylonian priest and historian Berossus (early third century BCE). Abraham's reputation as an astrologer can be observed in Greek literature up to the time of Vettius Valens of Antioch (second century CE) and beyond. It was the patriarch's expertise in celestial lore that gave rise to another more obscure pseudo-Abrahamic text -- his astrological treatise. Such a writing was known to Vettius Valens. Two centuries later, Firmicus Maternus (*Mathesis* 4.5) names Abraham among a handful of world-renowned astrological experts and authors (Aesculapius, Petosiris and Nechepso, Orpheus, and Critodemus) whom he had read in order to produce his Latin astrological guide.[53]

Firmicus Maternus gives only a slight indication of the specific contents of Abraham's work, but Vettius Valens claims to recount part of Abraham's composition in his own massive astrological compendium entitled *Anthologiae*, for which he culled material from many ancient sources. In his book two, Valens deals with technical horoscopic material involving the traits of the twelve *loci* (Greek τόποι). The twelve *loci* were an alternative horoscopic system, charted astrologically in a manner similar to the twelve zodiacal signs, and were said to reveal one's destiny in accordance with the placement of one's geniture on the chart.[54] The ninth locus is named "concerning travel" (περὶ ἀποδημίας/ξένης) and deals with matters concerning religion and travel. It is with regard to this ninth horoscopic position that Vettius Valens cites Abraham as an expert.

Preceding his first mention of Abraham, Vettius Valens (*Anthologiae* 2.28) credits the works of a certain Hermippus as his source for the information regarding Abraham's exposition of the ninth *locus* (περὶ ἀποδημίας ἐκ τῶν Ἑρμίππου). Scholars who have studied this citation have referred it to Hermippus of Smyrna, the third-century BCE Peripatetic and Alexandrian student of Callimachus.[55] His vast biographical work was used by Plutarch, and he had some knowledge of the Jews.[56] However, it seems that this citation, if noticed, has not been taken seriously, since there is no mention of this "text" of Abraham in most modern discussions of the patriarch and astrology. Wilhelm and Hans Gundel in their work on Greek astrology do refer to the citation of Hermippus by Vettius Valens and find it credible that by 220 BCE Hermippus knew of an astrological treatise under the name of Abraham.[57]

Long before Hermippus, Greeks had learned of and utilized Babylonian astrology. Aristotle's influential successor at the *peripatos*, Theophrastus (fourth and early third century BCE), knew of the

Chaldeans' ability to predict a person's life and death based on the heavens.[58] The flourishing of astrology in Ptolemaic Egypt (and the Hellenistic world generally) is supported by massive evidence.[59]

Its popularity is also seen in another Hellenistic pseudepigraphic astrological treatise which was ascribed to Nechepso and Petosiris. This astrological handbook, with its formulation of astrological and nativity casting principles, remained the standard of the discipline until the time of Ptolemaeus in the second century CE.[60] According to Manetho (*apud* Syncellus, p. 141), Nechepso (Νεχεψώς) was the second king of Egypt's twenty-sixth dynasty (ca. 597-591 BCE). Petosiris (Πετόσιρις) is usually identified as an Egyptian priest and astrologer. It is exactly into this category of literature that the similar work of Abraham fits. In fact, the excerpt from Vettius Valens provided below refers to the work of Nechepso and Petosiris, and claims that with regard to the *locus* concerning travel, the work of Abraham is superior.

Perhaps the best support for Hermippus' awareness of such a text comes from the other known works of Hermippus. Pliny in his *Natural History* (30.2.2) credits Hermippus with indexing and commenting on the verses of Zoroaster. Diogenes Laertius (*Lives of Eminent Philosophers* 1.8) ascribes to Hermippus a multi-volume work on the Magi, another group widely renowned for their astrological prowess. Felix Wehrli has explained that the availability to Hermippus of genuine Zoroastrian and ancient Babylonian texts is a fiction. However,

> Was Hermippos zur Verfügung stand, können nur Pseudepigrapha hellenistischer Zeit gewesen sein, Produkte jener Literatur, welche nicht allein angeblich pythagoreische Werk, sondern auch solche östlicher Offenbarungsweisheit umfasste; Hauptvertreter derselben waren aber Zoroaster, Ostanes, Hystaspes und andere sogenannte Magier.[61]

To this list of pseudonymous authors must be added Abraham, who stands alongside the other famous eastern sages.

Much work remains to be done upon this testimony of Hermippus as cited by Vettius Valens. The astrological text

(*Anthologiae* 2.28-29) has yet to be analyzed or even translated by a scholar at home in such material.[62] Precisely which words of Vettius Valens' *Anthologiae* 2.28-29 represent the pseudo-Abrahamic writing has not been determined. Moreover, the implications for both pagan and Jewish literature of an Alexandrian scholar's citation of a pseudo-Abrahamic composition already in the early Hellenistic period have not been drawn.

For now it can be said that as early as the third century BCE Abraham had a reputation among some Alexandrian scholars as an astrological authority and author. Thus Abraham's fame as an astrologer, also present in Graeco-Jewish authors,[63] must be dated somewhat earlier than the testimony of Pseudo-Eupolemus, who wrote in the late third to mid-second century BCE.[64]

Here is the first portion of the relevant text of Vettius Valens and a rough translation.

> Vettius Valens *Anthologiae* 2.28.1-3[65]
> Περὶ ἀποδημίας ἐκ τῶν Ἑρμίππου
> (1) Τὸν περὶ ἀποδημίας τόπον δύσληπτον ὄντα οὔτε Πετόσιρις οὔτε ὁ γνώριμος βασιλεὺς ἐν τοῖς ὑπομνήμασιν ἑαυτῶν ἐξεῖπον ἢ μόνον εἰς τὸν τόπον τοῦτον τοῦτο εἰρήκασιν· "εἰς τοὺς χρόνους εἴ τις τῶν κακοποιῶν ἔχει φάσιν, ἐν ἀποδημίαις καὶ σκυλμοῖς ποιήσει τὴν γένεσιν." (2) ὅ ἐστιν ἀληθές, περαιτέρω δὲ τούτων οὐδὲν ἄλλο εἰς τὸν περὶ ξένης τόπον ἔχουσιν. (3) ὁ δὲ θαυμασιώτατος Αβραμος ἐν τοῖς βιβλίοις αὐτοῦ τούτου τοῦ τόπου δέδειχεν ἡμῖν ἄλλων δηλώσεις τε καὶ αὐτοῦ ἴδια, ἄλλα ἐξευρών τε καὶ δοκιμάσας ἐπὶ τῶν ἀποδημητικῶν μάλιστα γενέσεων, αἵτινες ἔχουσι θεωρήματα τάδε.

On traveling from the works of Hermippus:
> (1) Neither Petosiris nor the well-known king in their treatises explain the *locus* concerning traveling which is difficult to comprehend, except having spoken only this in regard to this *locus*: 'In regard to the time-degrees, they said that if anyone is of the maleficent (planets) he will make his geniture in travels and annoyances.' (2) Which is true, but beyond these they have nothing else in relation to the *locus* concerning travel. (3) But the most wonderful

> Abramos in his books about this *locus* has shown us both
> the explanations of others and ideas of his own, both
> originating other things and testing them, especially in
> matters of genitures prone to travelling, which have the
> following theories regarding these things.

The entire text of Vettius Valens *Anthologiae* 2.28-29 raises
many fascinating questions regarding the astrological traditions
associated with Abraham and their extensiveness and availability. One
might speculate as to why Abraham's work was peculiarly helpful with
regard to the travel/religion *locus* of this divinatory system. A.
Bouché-Leclercq explains more fully the ninth position:

> Au IX lieu, le 'Dieu' par excellence, le Soleil, préside aux
> 'sectes, religions et pérégrinations.' ... Pourquoi réunir des
> idées aussi disparates que religions et pérégrinations? Je
> résoudrais volontiers l'énigme en disant qu'il y a là très
> probablement une association d'idées due à la vogue
> exceptionnelle des cultes solaires, c'est-à-dire des religions
> étrangères ou 'pérégrines' sous l'Empire. Ce 'Dieu' est
> encore plus Mithra, le dieu oriental, que le soleil qui luit
> pour tout le monde.[66]

Similarly the oriental Abraham of Greek traditions combines the ideas
of foreignness, travel, and religion, being one who traversed lands from
Chaldea to Egypt and who became the father of a people famous for
their religious traditions. Perhaps it was thought that Abraham was
particularly qualified to instruct his readers in precisely these fields.

Speculation aside, this important text of Vettius Valens, and the
supporting testimony from Firmicus Maternus, clearly show that the
portrait of Abraham depicting him as an eminent astrologer was long-
lived (Hermippus to Firmicus) and widely disseminated. Like the more
traditional and pious portrait of Abraham, this astrological Greek
portrait was supported by pseudepigraphic writings. In fact, with
Hermippus of Smyrna as the first witness, it would appear that the
penning of Abraham's astrological treatise preceded the composition of
any other "Abrahamic" work.

We have then, in the motley collection of texts and testimonies
consisting of the *Apocalypse of Abraham*, the *Testament of Abraham*,

the Sethian work mentioned by Epiphanius, and the statements of Vettius Valens and Firmicus Maternus, evidence for the diverse threads of Abraham's compositions which weave their way through Jewish, Christian, and Muslim religious traditions and through the records of pagan historiography and astrology.

---

1 M. Margalioth, *Sefer Ha-Razim* (Jerusalem: American Academy for Jewish Research, 1966); M.A. Morgan, *Sefer Ha-Razim: The Book of the Mysteries* (Chico, CA: Scholars Press, 1983).

2 S. Sandmel, *Philo's Place in Judaism: A Study of Conceptions of Abraham in Jewish Literature* (reprinted, New York: Ktav, 1971) 30-95.

3 J.J. Collins, "The Sage in the Apocalyptic and Pseudepigraphic Literature," *The Sage in Israel and the Ancient Near East* (eds. J.G. Gammie and L.G. Perdue; Winona Lake, IN: Eisenbrauns, 1990) 347-54.

4 See Sandmel, *Philo's Place* 37-38, 49-52.

5 For discussion of the date, see R. Rubinkiewicz, *OTP* 1.683.

6 Rubinkiewicz, *OTP* 1.681; E. Schürer, *The History of the Jewish People in the Age of Jesus Christ* (ed. G. Vermes, F. Millar, and M. Goodman; Edinburgh: T. & T. Clark, 1973-87) 3/1.288-89.

7 On the relation of the work to the testamentary genre, see A.B. Kolenkow, "What is the Role of Testament in the Testament of Abraham?" *HTR* 67 (1974) 182-84; idem, "The Genre Testament and the Testament of Abraham," *Studies on the Testament of Abraham* (ed. G.W.E. Nickelsburg; Missoula: Scholars Press, 1976) 139-52; G.W.E. Nickelsburg, "Structure and Message in the Testament of Abraham," ibid. 85-88.

8 E.P. Sanders, *OTP* 1.879.

9 S.D. Goitein, "Abraham," *EncJud* 2.119.

10 R. Paret, "Ibrāhīm," *EI*² 3.980-81.

11 A. Yusuf Ali, *The Holy Qur'ān* (Washington: American International Printing Company, n.d.) 1449 (n. 5111), 1725 (n. 6094).

12 Translation of Ali, *Holy Qur'ān* 1724-25.

13 Sanders notes that idolatry is not even mentioned in this book, which is, he says, remarkable for its "lowest-common-denominator universalistic soteriology" (*OTP* 1.876).

14 On the title see M.R. James, *The Testament of Abraham* (Cambridge: Cambridge University Press, 1892) 8-9.

15 Ibid. 26. James provides a thoughtful analysis of these texts (pp. 4-14) and a thorough review of the ancient testimony to *T. Abr.* (pp. 7-29).

16 Ibid. 27-28.

17 J.G. Gager writes that "Moses was by far the best-known figure of Jewish history in the pagan world" (*Moses in Greco-Roman Paganism* [Nashville: Abingdon, 1972] 18).

18 Philo's work was excerpted by Alexander Polyhistor and preserved in scattered quotations in Eusebius, *Praeparatio evangelica* Book 9. On the

identity and date of this Philo, see C.R. Holladay, *Fragments from Hellenistic Jewish Authors* (2 vols.; Chico and Atlanta: Scholars Press, 1983-89) 2.205-209; Schürer, *History* 3/1.559-61. On the translation of the *hapaxlegomenon* (this is the only occurrence appearing in the massive *Thesaurus Lingua Graeca*) κλυτοηχῆς, see LSJ *Supplement* 85. Text and commentary on Philo's work appear in Holladay, *Fragments* 2.205-99. For a conjectured word play on κλυτοηχῆς, which does not alter the basic meaning "renowned," see A. Gutman, "Philo the Epic Poet," *ScrHier* 1 (1954) 52-53.

[19] On the growing knowledge among Greeks of the Jews and other foreign peoples see A. Momigliano, *Alien Wisdom: The Limits of Hellenization* (Cambridge: Cambridge University Press, 1975), esp. pp. 1-21.

[20] Nicolaus of Damascus *apud* Josephus, *Ant.* 1.159-60; Pompeius Trogus from the epitome by Justinus, *Historiae Philippicae* 36.2.1. See M. Stern, *Greek and Latin Authors on Jews and Judaism* (3 vols.; Jerusalem: Israel Academy of Sciences and Humanities, 1974-84) 1.335.

[21] F. Jacoby, *Die Fragmente der griechischen Historiker* (Leiden: Brill, 1964) #273. See also J. Freudenthal, *Alexander Polyhistor und die von ihm erhaltenen Reste jüdischer und samaritanischer Geschichtswerke* (Breslau: Druch, 1874); B.Z. Wacholder, *Eupolemus: A Study of Judaeo-Greek Literature* (Cincinnati: Hebrew Union College Press, 1974) 44-52; C.W. Fornara, *The Nature of History in Ancient Greece and Rome* (Los Angeles: University of California Press, 1983) 190-91.

[22] Abraham (*Praep. evan.* 9.17-20): Pseudo-Eupolemus, Artapanus, "anonymous works," Apollonius Molon, Demetrius, Philo the epic poet, Cleodemus-Malchus; Moses (*Praep. evan.* 9.26-29): Eupolemus, Artapanus, Ezekiel, Demetrius.

[23] Besides these, Berossus, the Babylonian priest and historian of the early third century BCE, may have referred to Abraham and known of his reputed astrological skills. The claim comes from Josephus, *Ant.* 1.158. Some scholars have denied that Berossus referred to Abraham (B.Z. Wacholder, "Pseudo-Eupolemus' Two Greek Fragments on the Life of Abraham," *HUCA* 34 [1963] 102; Stern, *Greek and Latin Authors* 1.155; S.M. Burstein, *The Babyloniaca of Berossus* [Malibu: Undena, 1978] 21). J. Siker argues in favor of Josephus' claim ("Abraham in Graeco-Roman Paganism," *JSJ* 18 [1987] 189 n.3) as do I (*Traditions of Abraham in Greek Historical Writings* [Ph.D. dissertation, Hebrew Union College-Jewish Institute of Religion, 1992]).

[24] The authenticity of this letter is now accepted by many scholars. Important defenses of the genuineness of the document come from M. Ginsburg, "Sparta and Judaea," *CP* 29 (1934) 117-22; S. Schuller, "Some Problems Connected with the Supposed Common Ancestry of Jews and Spartans and Their Relations during the Last Three Centuries B.C.," *JSS* 1 (1956) 257-68; F. Dornseiff, "Echtheitsfragen II," *Würzburger Jahrbücher für die Altertumswissenschaft* 1 (1946) 128-32; Y. Gutman, *Ha-sifrut yehudit ha-hellenistit* (2 vols.; Jerusalem: Bialik Institute, 1963) 1.108-11; J.A. Goldstein, *1 Maccabees* (AB 41; Garden City, NY: Doubleday, 1976) 447-62. See also the notes of R.H. Charles, *APOT* 1.112. For the contrary view see M. Hengel, "Anonymität, Pseudepigraphie und 'Literaturische Fälschung' in der jüdisch-hellenistischen Literatur," *Pseudepigrapha I* (Genève: Fondation Hardt, 1972) 241-42. Bibliographies on

the subject are to be found in Josephus, *Jewish Antiquities, Books XII-XIV* (LCL; ed. R. Marcus; Cambridge: Harvard University Press, 1933) 769; Stern, *Greek and Latin Authors* 1.535.

[25] On the identification of Areus, see Goldstein, *1 Maccabees* 445-62; Schürer, *History* 1.184-85.

[26] The unusual spelling of the name 'Αρεύς and other details of the text are usually explained as due to the process of transmission from the letter's original Greek to the Hebrew of the original book of 1 Maccabees and then subsequent re-translation to Greek. See Schuller, "Some Problems" 265.

[27] E.J. Bickerman, "Origines Gentium," *CP* 47 (1952) 71-74. For other evidence of the official acceptance of such genealogical relationships between peoples, see idem, "Sur une inscription grecque de Sidon," *Mélanges syriens offerts à Monsieur René Dussaud* (2 vols.; Paris: Libraire Orientaliste Paul Geuthner, 1939) 1.91-99.

[28] M. Morford and R.J. Lenardon, *Classical Mythology* (New York: Longman, 1971) 353.

[29] Herodotus (2.43-44, 145) had already shown that the Greeks had borrowed Heracles and other deities from the Egyptian pantheon.

[30] Bickerman, "Origines Gentium" 75.

[31] A. Momigliano, "Eastern Elements in Post-Exilic Jewish, and Greek, Historiography," *Essays in Ancient and Modern Historiography* (Middletown, CN: Wesleyan University Press, 1987) 29.

[32] Schuller, "Some Problems" 261.

[33] Goldstein, *1 Maccabees* 458-59; F. Jacoby, "Hekataios 4," PW 7.2752; Gutman, *Ha-sifrut* 1.110.

[34] Diodorus Siculus 1.94.1-2. Schuller lists the other similarities with references to the work of Hecataeus on the Jews ("Some Problems" 261-62).

[35] Bickerman, "Origines Gentium" 75.

[36] For the genealogy from Danaus to the royal houses of Sparta, see Morford and Lenardon, *Classical Mythology* 343, 355, 374-75.

[37] E. Meyer (*Ursprung und Anfänge des Christentums* [3 vols.; Stuttgart: Cotta'sche, 1921-23] 2.31) and Ginsburg ("Sparta and Judaea" 120) see the work of Hecataeus behind the assertion of kinship between Jews and Spartans. See also Goldstein (*1 Maccabees* 457-58), who suggests that Danaus may have been equated with Abraham's son by Ketura (Gen 25:3) named Δαιδάν.

[38] For another non-Jewish tradition relating the Jews and Spartans, though not through Abraham, see Claudius Iolaus (first century CE?) *apud* Stephanus Byzantius, *Ethnicorum* s.v. 'Ιουδαία (= Jacoby, *Fragmente* #788, F4; Stern, *Greek and Latin Authors* 1.534-35). Similarly, Jason of Cyrene (2 Macc 5:9) wrote of the kinship between the Jews and Spartans.

[39] For discussion of the authenticity of this text, see Schuller, "Some Problems" 261; Schürer, *History* 3/1.18; Goldstein, *1 Maccabees* 458.

[40] Thus Siker's survey of Abraham in pagan literature led him to conclude that Abraham was "not widely known" ("Abraham in Greco-Roman Paganism" 208). However, Siker was only reviewing literary evidence and does not take into account the Spartan and Pergamene traditions.

[41] For more detailed discussions see B. Beer, *Leben Abraham's nach*

Auffassung der jüdischen Sage (Leipzig: O. Leiner, 1859); Sandmel, *Philo's Place*; G. Mayer, "Aspekte des Abrahambildes in der hellenistisch-jüdischen Literatur," *EvT* 1 (1972) 118-27; L. Ginzberg, *The Legends of the Jews* (7 vols.; Philadelphia: Jewish Publication Society, 1909-38) 1.185-308; K. Berger, "Abraham in den paulinischen Hauptbriefen," *TRE* 1.372-82; L.H. Feldman, "Abraham the Greek Philosopher in Josephus," *Transactions of the American Philological Association* 99 (1968) 143-56; J. Siker, *Disinheriting the Jews: Abraham in Early Christian Controversy* (Louisville: Westminster, 1991) 17-27, 202.

42 Siker reaches the same conclusion and gives the earliest and closest criticism of Abraham as that of Celsus (second century CE, *apud* Origen, *Contra Celsum* 4.33), who discredits the Jewish ancestors, the Chaldeans, as sorcerers, though he does not actually mention Abraham ("Abraham in Greco-Roman Paganism" 199, 208).

43 Gager, *Moses* 80-112. For example, Apollonius Molon, who condemned the Jews generally and severely criticized Moses (cf. Josephus, *Ag. Ap.* 2.79, 145, 148, 236, 258, 295), presents a very complimentary description of Abraham, apparently believing that the decline of Jewish civilization came with their legislator, not their patriarch.

44 Wacholder suggests that Gen 15:5, where Abraham is told to count the stars, may have been given an astrological interpretation ("Pseudo-Eupolemus' Two Greek Fragments" 102).

45 Strabo 16.2.39; Philo, *Abr.* 69; Julian, *Contra Galilaeos* 178; Origen, *Contra Celsum* 6.80.

46 Dan 2:2-5, 10; 4:4; 5:7, 11.

47 Edict of Cn. Cornelius Scipio preserved by Valerius Maximus, *Factorum et Dictorum memorabilia* 1.3.3 in the epitome of Paris (ed. Kempf, p. 17). See also Stern, *Greek and Latin Authors* 1.357-60; Servius, *Commentarii in Vergilii Aeneida* 8.187 (= Stern, *Greek and Latin Authors* 2.653-54).

48 Diogenes Laertius (*Lives of Eminent Philosophers* 1.1) refers to Aristotle as one who speaks of the Chaldeans as a philosopher-class among the Babylonians.

49 For surveys of those ancient authors who discuss the subject, see Wacholder, "Pseudo-Eupolemus' Two Greek Fragments" 130; Holladay, *Fragments* 1.180-81; N. Walter, *Der Thoraausleger Aristobulos* (Berlin: Akademie-Verlag, 1964) 226-27; E.M. Yamauchi, *Persia and the Bible* (Grand Rapids, MI: Baker, 1990) 477-80. For a rare positive view of Abraham as an astrologer in rabbinic literature see *b. B. Bat.* 16b.

50 The *Treatise of Shem* (first century BCE?) is one of the most striking examples of a Jewish astrological text. On the issues of Judaism and astrology see the introduction to this text by J.H. Charlesworth (*OTP* 1.473-80); idem, "Jewish Astrology in the Talmud, Pseudepigrapha, Dead Sea Scrolls, and Early Palestinian Synagogues," *HTR* 70 (1977) 183-200; A. Altmann, "Astrology," *EncJud* 1.788-95.

51 Among others writing in Greek who refer to Abraham, Philo (*Abr.* 84) is critical of Abraham's involvement with astrology. See also *Sib. Or.* 3.218ff.

52 Wacholder, "Pseudo-Eupolemus' Two Greek Fragments" 102; Feldman, "Abraham the Greek Philosopher" 155 n.45.

53 Firmicus Maternus mentions Abraham four times in connection with astrology. These texts have been collected by Stern, *Greek and Latin Authors* 2.492-94.

54 On the system of twelve *loci* see A. Bouché-Leclercq, *L'astrologie grecque* (Paris, 1899; reprinted, Darmstadt: Scientia Verlag Aalen, 1979) 280-88; O. Neugebauer and H. van Hosen, *Greek Horoscopes* (Philadelphia: American Philosophical Society, 1959) 7-8.

55 For Hermippus as a Peripatetic and Callimachean, see R. Pfeiffer, *History of Classical Scholarship* (Oxford: Clarendon Press, 1968) 150-51.

56 W. and H. Gundel, *Astrologumena* (Wiesbaden: Franz Steiner, 1966) 52; Stern, *Greek and Latin Authors* 2.174. On Hermippus' knowledge of the Jews see Josephus, *Ag. Ap.* 1.162-65; Origen, *Contra Celsum* 1.15.334; and Stern, *Greek and Latin Authors* 1.95-96. F. Wehrli does not mention this text from the Vettius Valens citation in his collection of Hermippus' writings (*Hermippos*, Supplementband 1 of *Die Schule des Aristoteles* [Basel: Schwabe, 1974]).

57 *Astrologumena* 52.

58 This is according to Proclus' commentary on Plato's *Timaeus* (3.151, ed. Diehl). This reference is cited by O. Neugebauer, *The Exact Sciences in Antiquity* (reprinted, New York: Dover, 1969) 168, 187.

59 See Neugebauer, *Exact Sciences* 53-59, 169-71. See also W. Capelle, "Spuren der Astrologie bei den Griechen," *Hermes* 60 (1925) 395.

60 F.J. Boll, *Sternglaube und Sterndeutung* (ed. W. Gundel; Leipzig: B.G. Teubner, 1926) 24; F. Cumont, *The Oriental Religions in Roman Paganism* (Chicago: Open Court, 1911) 163. On the high repute enjoyed in the Greco-Roman era by Nechepso and Petosiris, see W.M. Gunn, "Petosiris," *Dictionary of Greek and Roman Biography and Mythology* (3 vols.; ed. W. Smith; London: John Murray, 1880) 3.213. The pseudepigraphic handbook has not been precisely dated. 150 BCE is the *terminus ante quem* (see Boll, *Sternglaube* 24), but W. and H. Gundel have suggested a date as early as the third or fourth century BCE (*Astrologumena* 27).

61 Wehrli, *Hermippos* 46.

62 Only the first book of Vettius Valens' *Anthologiae* has been translated and annotated. See Vettius Valens, *Anthologies, Livre I* (ed. J.-F. Bara; Leiden: Brill, 1989).

63 Pseudo-Eupolemus: Eusebius, *Praep. evan.* 9.17.3-4, 8; anonymous sources: *Praep. evan.* 9.18.2 (this text is considered by some as coming from Pseudo-Eupolemus); Artapanus: *Praep. evan.* 9.18.1; Josephus, *Ant.* 1.167-68. It is possible that our oldest reference to Abraham as an astrologer is from the early third century BCE work of Berossus (Josephus, *Ant.* 1.158).

64 This commonly accepted dating of Pseudo-Eupolemus is based on his use of the Septuagint and his reference to the temple on Mount Gerizim, which was destroyed ca. 129 BCE by John Hyrcanus (Josephus, *Ant.* 13.255-56), but which was most likely standing at the time our author composed his work. We have a firm *terminus ante quem* in the mid-first century BCE, the *floruit* of Alexander Polyhistor, who cites this passage in his work *Concerning the Jews* (see Jacoby, *Fragmente* #273, f.19).

65 Text is that of D. Pingree, *Vettii Valentis Antiocheni Anthologiarum libri*

novem (Leipzig: B.G. Teubner, 1986).
66 Bouché-Leclercq, *L'astrologie grecque* 284.

THE TALE OF BULŪQIYĀ AND THE *ALEXANDER ROMANCE* IN JEWISH AND SUFI MYSTICAL CIRCLES

Stephanie Dalley
Oriental Institute, Oxford University

The *Epic of Gilgamesh* was transformed during the period between the latest known version of the Akkadian story in the Arsacid period,[1] after 247 BCE, and the tenth century CE when the Tale of Bulūqiyā emerged from its ancient background into Arabic literature.[2] Despite many difficulties, not least the enormous span of time and the use of different languages (including Babylonian, Aramaic, Persian, Greek, and Arabic), a few threads remain to mark certain aspects of continuity in this particular tale. This study attempts to show a part of the contribution that Babylonian culture made to early Islamic tradition through one story, with clear evidence of some kind of Judaic mediation. However, it must be emphasized that the writer, whose field is cuneiform studies, has pursued the subject far beyond the boundaries of her own expertise into dangerous territory.[3]

Some of the changes and omissions that altered the story during the gap in written sources of over a millennium can be traced to the influence of specific groups of people. Two parts of the story, concerning Humbaba as a giant, and the tale of the Flood, were incorporated in the Aramaic book of *Enoch* found at Qumran, dated during the final century or so of the pre-Christian era. Those two themes were also used in the Book of Giants which the Manichaeans used as holy scripture. Evidence for the Manichaean version of the Flood story has recently been discovered by Professor Reeves, who showed that the survivor of the Flood was named "Atambish" (Utnapishtim), not Noah. The name proves that a Babylonian and not a Jewish version of the story was Mani's source.[4]

This discovery underlines the importance of the Babylonian Flood story, rather than the biblical version, as a source for Enochic and Manichaean traditions. There is evidence, too, that Mani (died 274 or 277 CE) used themes from the *Epic of Gilgamesh* in formulating his religious ideas, and modelled his own spiritual calling to some extent upon the relationship between Gilgamesh and Enkidu.[5] The purpose of this paper is to trace the kinds of circles in which the Tale of Bulūqiyā was popular when it had freed itself from the taint of Manichaean associations, and by analyzing certain elements in the story, to point out a few indications of Babylonian and Assyrian contributions to Jewish mysticism.

Sufi Connections

The first piece of evidence is almost direct. The chain of tradition given by Tha'labī (born 1035 CE) for his version of the Tale of Bulūqiyā runs as follows: "We were told by Abū Bakr Muḥammad ibn 'Abdallāh al-Hazraqī on the authority of 'Abd Allāh ibn Salām al-Isra'ilī."[6] Professor Madelung has drawn the writer's attention to the fact that al-Hazraqī is a corruption for the name al-Jawzaqī, a sage of Nishapur who died in 988 CE. Although none of his own writings are extant, some details of his life are known from short biographies by three authors: al-Sam'ānī, al-Ṣafadī and al-Subkī. All the information is given in the account of al-Sam'ānī, whose text has been translated here by Professor Madelung:[7]

This *nisba* refers to two Jawzaqs, one of them Jawzaq of Naysābūr. From among them is Abū Bakr Muḥammad b. 'Abd Allāh b. Muḥammad b. Zakariyyā al-Jawzaqī, the author of the *Kitāb al-Muttafaq*, the ascetic, pious, learned Imām. He heard Abū l-'Abbās al-Daghūlī, Abū l-'Abbās al-Aṣamm, Abū Hātim Makkī b. 'Abdān al-Tamīmī and their contemporaries. From him related Abū Bakr Aḥmad b. Manṣūr b. Khalaf al-Maghribī, Abū 'Uthmān Sa'īd al-'Ayyār al-Ṣūfī and others. Al-Hākim Abū 'Abd Allāh al-Hāfiẓ mentioned him in his *Kitāb al-Ta'rīkh* and said: Abū Bakr b. Abi l-Hasan al-Mu'addil, i.e. al-Jawzaqī, heard, wrote, and spent much on scholarship. He witnessed while he was a boy and the (great) shaykhs were alive. His maternal uncle Abū Isḥāq al-Muzakkī travelled with him to Sarakhs and he heard much from Abu l-'Abbās al-Daghūlī .... He heard from Abū l-'Abbās al-Sarrāj and Abū Nu'aym al-Jurjānī and he transmitted from them in the year (3)69. He heard in Rayy Abū Hātim al-Wasqandī, in Hamadan al-Qāsim b. 'Abd al-Wāhid, in Baghdad Abū 'Ali al-Ṣaffār, and in Mecca Abū Sa'īd al-A'rābī and Ṭalḥa al-'Umarī.

The details make it clear that the Tale of Bulūqiyā was popular in an ascetic circle in northeastern Iran. One of al-Jawzaqī's teachers, Abū 'Uthmān Sa'īd al-Ayyār, is called "the Sufi."

That the *qiṣaṣ* of Tha'labī in general emerged from a circle of mystics in Baghdad is known, and that they were often attributed to Jews who were Muslims or to Jewish converts to Islam is also clear: 'Abd Allāh b. Salām, Ka'b al-Aḥbār, and Wahb b. Munabbih are three whose names are most frequently credited. The tales appear to have travelled northeast from Baghdad through Khorasan to central Asia, and perhaps this may be seen together with the movement of persecuted Manichaeans away from the exclusive religious groups of western Asia.[8] The *isnād* of the Tale of Bulūqiyā is not only a paradigm for the attribution and propagation of such stories, but gives particular emphasis to its continued popularity in mystical, Sufi circles. The story itself contains distinct features that indicate an integral connection with mystic practices.

In all three main versions of the Tale of Bulūqiyā, the hero is granted an audience with al-Khiḍr at a late stage in his wanderings.

The name and character of al-Khiḍr contain elements that can be traced back to the Babylonian sage Atra-hasis, who lived through three major catastrophes early in man's history; namely, famine, plague, and flood. As sole survivor he was granted immortality by the gods, who settled him at the "mouth of rivers" across lethal waters; there Gilgamesh met him at a late stage in his wanderings beyond the limits of the ordinary world. Al-Khiḍr is an important figure in Sufi tradition. He is the immortal medium between God and the early, great mystics, as well as the sage who acted as Moses' guide in the Qur'ān (18:59-81). The experience of meeting him was like a divinely inspired vision or dream to the great Sufi sages, and was claimed as giving authority to them. The ultimate abode of al-Khiḍr, who had the ability to appear in any place at any time, is variously described as on a green carpet on an island in the middle of the sea, or on Mount Qāf, the cosmic mountain, from which he ruled the emerald sea. Equated with Elijah, he was sometimes referred to by Sufis as "the Jew,"[9] and by means of the name Idrīs he is also partly assimilated with Enoch.[10] His Babylonian origins show that his own authority comes from his distant past as sole surviving link with the earliest civilization.

For the purposes of this study, the importance of al-Khiḍr as a spiritual guide for Sufis, closely connected to a Hebrew tradition, is not only that he meets Bulūqiyā but also that he plays a part in Persian and Arabic versions of the *Alexander Romance*. There he acts as a guide leading Alexander through the Land of Darkness to the Waters of Life in a passage long recognized as containing themes traceable to the *Epic of Gilgamesh*.[11] In Greek versions of the *Romance*, an anonymous old man guides the king through the Land of Darkness, and Alexander's cook Andreas is substituted for him when they reach the Water of Life, where Andreas drinks the water and becomes immortal by accident.[12] The lack of development accorded that character in the Greek *Romance* gives the incident much less significance than it enjoyed in the Persian, Arabic, and Ethiopic versions. In this instance the Greek accounts appear to be secondary to the Near Eastern ones. In both the Greek and Near Eastern stories, the characters are integral to the search for the Water of Life which is itself an ancient

Mesopotamian motif: it occurs in the *Myth of Adapa* in which the sage Adapa, like the survivor of the Flood, bears the epithet Atra-hasis. It is virtually certain, therefore, that this episode in all versions of the *Alexander Romance* comes substantially from the Akkadian traditions of Mesopotamia. The role of al-Khiḍr, quite brief in the Tale of Bulūqiyā, is at its maximum in the Persian prose *Iskandarnāmeh*.[13]

The Tale of Bulūqiyā and the Alexander Romance

The appearance of al-Khiḍr and the search for the Water of Life are not the only threads that join the Tale of Bulūqiyā to the *Alexander Romance*. The adventure stories in the Tale of Bulūqiyā are of the same genre as those in the *Alexander Romance*, and some close comparisons can be made. Apart from resemblances between relatively minor travellers' tales,[14] there is one comparison that is informative about the milieu in which the two works were popular.

The goal which justifies the hazardous adventures for Bulūqiyā is Solomon's tomb, where the body, perfectly preserved, can still be seen in all its splendor on a throne or couch, located on an island which can be reached only after crossing the Seven Seas. The Greek version of the *Alexander Romance* does not provide the most striking parallel, but it is nonetheless instructive: Alexander visited the tomb of Proteus on the island of Pharos where he saw the hero's coffin on the island; in his case the tomb is not the final goal after many dangers. The episode has long been connected by classical scholars with *Odyssey* 4.384ff., where the meeting of Menelaus with Proteus on the island of Pharos is the culmination of a long string of hazardous adventures. S. Eitrem has pointed out the tradition which regards Proteus as a magician, and has connected certain elements in the tale of Menelaus with a Greek initiation ritual found in the Paris Magical Papyrus, also known as the Recipe for Immortality.[15] In this tale Menelaus has also been seen as a doublet for Odysseus.[16] Some of the *qiṣaṣ* of Thaʻlabī were interpreted as mystical stories symbolizing the stages through which a mystic proceeded towards communion with God;[17] since all three heroes -- Gilgamesh, Menelaus, and Alexander -- were worshipped as minor deities long before the coming of Muḥammad, similarities in the structure of these particular narratives show that the interpretation is integral to the structure, and not merely grafted on to it at a later stage.

It was a deliberate move with a specific purpose for Alexander's Greek promoters to link him with that passage in the *Odyssey*. According to Plutarch's *Life of Alexander,* a dream-vision from Homer inspired Alexander to settle upon the site for his famous city of Alexandria in Egypt opposite Pharos where the lighthouse was built. In the city a temple to Homer was erected later by Ptolemy Philopater. The literary prestige of Alexandria was founded upon this association with Homer. However, Pseudo-Callisthenes A seems willfully to have detached the home of Proteus on Pharos from the context of an ultimate goal that it enjoys in the Tale of Menelaus and which is also used in the Tale of Bulūqiyā where Solomon has replaced Proteus. The reason for the deliberate change may be to escape from the mystical Jewish and Sufi associations that are described below, because they belonged to the Semitic world of intuition and mystery rather than to the logical, rational world promoted by Hellenism. Elements of the genre may have been used in other compositions without a purposeful link with theurgy. If so, points of resemblance between the *Odyssey* and the *Epic of Gilgamesh* may be explained as the result of development from a similar background of mystical practices.[18]

There is a Hebrew version of the *Alexander Romance*, not at all closely connected with the Greek versions, in which the context of the ultimate goal has not been detached.[19] The hero makes a long and fabulous journey to reach the sepulchre of a very old king whose mortal remains are preserved in balsam and whose name is given as Alṭinos. In view of the Homeric connection just mentioned, and for lack of alternative interpretations, a corruption from Alkinoos, King of the Phaeacians who lived on a distant island is almost certain, the Hebrew letters ב and ט being quite easy to confuse. Since this is a Jewish version of the *Alexander Romance* and since it begins with Alexander ruling as king in Egypt, its composition can be placed firmly among the Jews of Alexandria, whose contribution to the Greek versions of the *Alexander Romance* was analyzed by Pfister.[20]

Quite close to the Tale of Bulūqiyā and to Gaster's Hebrew *Alexander Romance* is the Ethiopic version of the latter, in which the hero experiences a series of adventures to reach the tomb of Enoch within a temple.[21] Upon leaving it, he undergoes further adventures before arriving in Alexandria. The format for the adventures to and from the tomb is the same; the tomb, like that in the Tale of Bulūqiyā, is set in a garden, and the perfectly preserved remains of the sage recline on a couch with a golden coverlet. Furthermore, before Alexander (called Dhu'l-Qarnayn) reached it, he was warned against trying to acquire forbidden knowledge, a warning which is echoed in the Tale of Bulūqiyā by the giant who guarded the apples in the garden where the tomb of Solomon was situated. Both stories allude, therefore, to humanity's first sin according to the book of Genesis, rather than to ancient Mesopotamian concepts concerning the creation of humankind. In the latter tradition, humanity was created in order to labor on the gods' behalf, and then acquired knowledge through the agency of sages sent for that purpose by the gods, but then the sages angered the gods and were banished.

A very early sequence of the same type as the crossing of Seven Seas by Bulūqiyā and 'Affan (though land-based rather than by sea) in which a series of journeys or trials leads to the ultimate goal is evident in the Sumerian tale of Gilgamesh and Huwawa. The heroes there, Gilgamesh and Enkidu, cross seven mountains to reach the Forest of Pines with its guardian giant Huwawa.[22] The Pine Forest in later tradition exemplified by the Tale of Bulūqiyā was equated with Paradise and the Garden of Eden.[23]

An Arabic version of the *Alexander Romance* from Spain[24] provides unequivocal links between the Alexander tradition and the Tale of Bulūqiyā. As García Gómez pointed out in 1929, the dialogue between the angel and Bulūqiyā on Mount Qāf is a slightly briefer version of the dialogue between the angel and Alexander Dhu'l-Qarnayn on Mount Qāf.[25] There are three explanatory statements made by the angel in response to the hero's questions. Burton's version

of the Tale of Bulūqiyā contains the three parallels; Thaʻlabi's version
contains only the first one.

> Bulūqiyā: 'Know, Bulūqiyā, that this is Jabal Qāf, which
> encompasses the earth …. When God most high wishes to
> bring on that earth any earthquake or famine or plenty or
> war or peace, He bids me to do it.'
> Dhu'l-Qarnayn: 'I must tell you that this mountain
> encompasses the whole earth …. When God desires to
> engulf a town or city or any other place He wills, He
> inspires this mountain to stir its roots -- a single one of
> them moves, and God causes that land to be engulfed.'
>
> Bulūqiyā: 'And He caused to dwell therein (the wasteland)
> angels whose food and drink are glorification and
> hallowing.'
> Dhu'l-Qarnayn: 'The food and drink of the angels is only
> glorification and acclaim and invocation of God.'
>
> Bulūqiyā: 'Behind Jabal Qāf is a mountain with an extent
> of five hundred years' journey. It is composed of snow
> and frost, and is what protects the world from the heat of
> hell; were it not for that mountain, the world would be
> consumed by the heat of hell fire.'
> Dhu'l-Qarnayn: 'Between me and them (the angels who
> support the Throne of God) are seventy thousand veils of
> snow and fog and frost and wind; the qualities of that wind
> are such that were a needle's eye thereof to come forth,
> the whole world would be consumed.'[26]

Another very close comparison can be made from Thaʻlabi's
eleventh-century account of the *Alexander Romance* in Arabic (with
the hero as Dhu'l-Qarnayn) in which the hero, just like Bulūqiyā,
wishes to drink the Water of Life in order to stay alive to greet and
praise the prophet who is destined to come in the future. This gives
the romance the purpose of a pseudo-prophecy, and is the same
purpose as that which leads Bulūqiyā on his wanderings. Tarṣuṣī's
Persian version of the twelfth century likewise contains a pseudo-
prophecy for the coming of Muḥammad, uttered by an angel. Like the
Tale of Bulūqiyā, these versions of the *Alexander Romance* were
popular in Islamic circles, even though Alexander signally failed to visit
Mecca.

The exception to this is the Islamic version of the *Alexander Romance* of Ibn Hishām, which has been studied by Nagel.[27] The story is attributed to a tradition that comes through the tales of Wahb ibn Munabbih,[28] but it is told about the hero Dhu'l-Qarnayn as King of the Yemen, incorporated into a chronicle of the Kings of Yemen, and so can be called a South Arabian version. In it the hero travels to Mecca and then to Jerusalem where he meets Mūsā Al-Khiḍr, who then accompanies him on his travels and conquests, just as Bulūqiyā meets the sage 'Affan when he reaches Jerusalem in the versions of Burton and Tha'labī. The search through the Land of Darkness for the Water of Life, successful for Al-Khiḍr but not for Dhu'l-Qarnayn, is in some respects close to the Greek *Alexander Romance*. Nagel showed that this version was based upon a pre-Islamic Jewish version of the *Romance* from Egypt.

The South Arabian story gives a possible clue to part of the justification by which the story of Gilgamesh might be relocated in Egypt. Gilgamesh, king of Uruk, was essentially a Babylonian hero, and when Babylon replaced Uruk as the leading city in war and politics, Gilgamesh could be considered a Babylonian king. He is actually called "king of Babylon" by the Greek author Aelian. The South Arabian story calls Egypt "Babylon" because there was a Roman garrison called Babylon in Old Cairo,[29] standing at a key position at the junction of a route to the Red Sea along which the Muslim invasion of Egypt largely took place, carried out almost exclusively by South Arabians. Whether Babylon-in-Egypt had an earlier, Mesopotamian connection is not certain; Tiglath-pileser III and Sargon certainly set up trading colonies at key points in lower Egypt.[30] The only overt reference to ancient Mesopotamian involvement in these traditions seems to be Gaster's Hebrew *Romance*, in which the hero meets refugees from the time of Sennacherib. This detail might perhaps be explained by transmission through Jewish mercenaries who are known to have served the Assyrians after the fall of Samaria in 722[31] and who, much later, formed an unorthodox colony in Upper Egypt at Elephantine in the Persian period.[32] But this is very uncertain.

The Jewish Background to the Tale of Bulūqiyā

In describing Bulūqiyā as king of the sons of Israel, the three versions of the tale all place themselves firmly within a Jewish tradition. Tha'labī's version reinforces the Jewish setting by describing Bulūqiyā as son of Ushia (Josiah). Since Josiah did not have such a son, Horovitz suggested that the name was introduced to make a clear comparison between Josiah's discovery of a book of original scripture (as recorded in the biblical book of Kings) and Bulūqiyā's discovery of an early prophecy for the coming of Muḥammad which had been removed from its proper place in the Torah.[33] The beginning of the Tale of Bulūqiyā, in the versions of Burton and Tha'labī, belongs to the category of *taḥrīf* literature. The father of Bulūqiyā had concealed from his son sacred writings which foretold the coming of Muḥammad, and had corrupted holy scripture by excerpting them from the sacred writings. When Bulūqiyā discovered them, long after the death of his father, they came as a revelation, and he ordered them to be reinstated. Muslim tradition considered that the true text of Jewish scripture was preserved in the temple in Jerusalem until it was destroyed by Nebuchadnezzar; the holy scripture was later recomposed by Ezra, but this meant the transmission was faulty.[34] By setting the Tale of Bulūqiyā into the period when the First Temple still stood, the author implied that the uncontaminated, original scrolls contained clear evidence that Muḥammad would come. This gave support to later Muslim exegesis which discovered predictions of Muḥammad's coming and the spread of Islam in various passages of the Bible. The story is remarkable for putting the blame for scriptural corruption on Josiah.

The concept of *taḥrīf*, whether in the sense of deliberate tampering, bogus addition, or deliberate removal, is an ancient one, clearly expressed in the colophon to the Babylonian *Epic of Erra and Ishum*:

> The one who put together the composition about him
> (Erra) was Kabti-ilani-Marduk son of Dabibi.

(The god) revealed it to him in the middle of the
    night, and when he recited it upon waking, he did
    not omit anything,
Nor add a single word to it.
Erra heard and approved it,
And it was pleasing also to Ishum.

The wording implies that a corrupt text would have displeased the
gods, thereby losing authenticity. The work dates from at least the
eighth century BCE.

Another possible reason for including Josiah may have been
that, according to an Arab tradition,[35] al-Khiḍr was originally Jeremiah
the son of Hilkiya during the reign of Josiah. The story described how
al-Khiḍr-Jeremiah doubted God's word and so died, but revived after
one hundred years and then wandered through the world, living among
wild animals. In this respect, he displays one of the main characteristics
of Enkidu, who accompanied Gilgamesh in his quest for fame.

The versions of Tha'labī and Burton both name Jerusalem as the
city from which the hero sets out with 'Affan on his quest, without
ascribing to Jerusalem any temporal power. Evidence for an anti-
Jewish insertion comes from the passage in the versions of Mardrus
and Burton in which two regions of hell are reserved for Jews and
Christians; their description follows closely the one given by al-Kisā'ī
and attributed to Wahb ibn Munabbih,[36] but the names of the third
and sixth hells are transposed.

The theme of an original Torah in which Muḥammad's coming
was specifically foretold, as well as the ascetic milieu in which the Tale
of Bulūqiyā was popular, are both found also in an Arabic legend to
which Professor S. Wasserstrom has kindly drawn my attention. Two
stories of the Yemenite Jew Ka'b al-Aḥbār's belated conversion to
Islam mirror the first part of the Tale of Bulūqiyā with its theme of
taḥrīf.[37] In the first story the explanation given for the late conversion
of Ka'b is that his father had sealed up some writings and told him not
to consult them. Ka'b became suspicious, eventually broke the seal,
and read the contents, despite his filial piety; there he found the good
tidings of the Prophet's coming inscribed, just as Bulūqiyā did in the
versions of Burton and Tha'labī. In the second story Ka'b's delayed

conversion is explained because it took him years to discover why ten passages in the Torah and the Gospels were erased and the text altered. He found out the truth from a Christian monk named Bulukhya who lived on Mount Lukām (Amanus). Both Ka'b and Bulukhya eventually convert to Islam in an elaborate sequel. In the name Bulukhya and in the theme of the tale, connections with the start of the Tale of Bulūqiyā are close, but the episode is set in an ascetic Christian context rather than a Jewish one. The second story of Ka'b gives particular emphasis to the instruction in Tha'labī's version that the announcement of the Prophet's coming is to be appended to the Torah.[38] One manuscript is introduced with a different piece of text written in a different hand, comprising a Sufi sermon, although no specific connection with the tale of the monk Bulukhya which follows has been found.

Another feature of the Tale of Bulūqiyā deserves consideration within the same general context of a Jewish background. The preamble to the story in the versions of Mardrus and Burton sets the scene in a dialogue between the Queen of Serpents and Hasib, son of Daniel. Here Daniel is the archetypal sage who begot no sons until he prayed to God and then succeeded just before his death in fathering Hasib. Although it might be thought that Daniel here is the biblical figure, thus reinforcing the Jewish links, it is probably better to see in him an archetypal Semitic sage to whom many different traditions were attached. A story known outside the Israelite/Hebrew spheres during the late Bronze Age at Ugarit, the *Legend of Aqhat*, features as its title character a son of Daniel's old age.[39] It may also be relevant for the connections with the *Alexander Romance* that, according to Josephus, Alexander when he visited Jerusalem was shown the book of Daniel with its prophecy that he would conquer Persia.[40]

Ascetic Emphases

Certain emphases in the Tale of Bulūqiyā and the *Alexander Romance* confirm the ascetic milieu suggested by the line of tradition which Tha'labī gives. None of the sexual exploits or aggressive encounters of Gilgamesh have been included in the Tale of Bulūqiyā, and this is one reason for the blandness of the characterization. Likewise Alexander's character has been purged of flaws: his wife Roxana has the barest mention, unadorned, without romantic detail, nor are scurrilous stories about his drunken excesses included. The mother of each hero plays an important role: like Gilgamesh, Bulūqiyā is advised by his mother before he sets off, and Alexander's fabulous adventures take the form of letters written to Olympias as well as to Aristotle; no letters to Roxana are included. Both travel beyond the boundaries of the known world and are granted knowledge beyond the scope of other men, though each in a different way. In the case of Bulūqiyā, knowledge of the mysteries of the cosmos is granted through interviews with demons and angels. In the case of Alexander, future events are revealed through oracles, and key philosophical questions are answered by the gymnosophists in India. The dating of those passages is now fairly clear: scholars have agreed that the legend of Alexander's quest for the Land of the Blessed recounted in a letter concerning miraculous adventures was known in the third century BCE[41] when the cuneiform *Epic of Gilgamesh* still existed in Iraq. Another miraculous adventure has been recognized as Manichaean in tone, and so may be no earlier than the late third century CE unless it goes back to an older story used by Mani. It recounts how Alexander tried to have sap collected from cuts made in myrrh-like trees, but the sap-collectors were whipped by an invisible force, and a voice warned them not to continue.[42] The question-and-answer form in which the hero obtains knowledge from super-mortals goes back to Gilgamesh and his dialogues with the Scorpion-man, with Siduri, with the boatman Ur-Shanabi, and with Ut-napishtim.

These characteristics enabled Bulūqiyā and Alexander to be models for aspiring ascetics, and made the tales about them suitable for didactic purposes. But there is more to it than that. Within the format of the Tale of Bulūqiyā one can discern the essential ritual and the states through which the mystic must pass to achieve communion with heaven. The tale is embedded in the story of Hasib Karim ad-din, which Bencheikh has identified in some detail as a ritual of initiation.[43]

The result of the ritual is that Hasib instantly acquires fundamental knowledge of astrology, medicine, and alchemy, as well as coming into contact with supernatural beings. Bencheikh has pointed out that the Tale of Bulūqiyā is integrated into that ritual, and that the pursuit of immortality is the generating scheme for both stories.

Bulūqiyā's Journey to Solomon's Tomb and Hekhalot Mysticism

The format of Bulūqiyā's journey consists of walking over the Seven Seas, landing after each sea upon an island where the supernormal inhabitants testify to a realm beyond the world of everyday reality. The sight of Solomon's tomb, with its golden couch or throne and the extreme danger in approaching it, as well as the presence of the angel Gabriel, are closely comparable to the vision of divine glory beheld by the *Hekhalot* visionary, whose approach is likewise fraught with danger, and who meets angels there.

In the case of Bulūqiyā, the requisite knowledge for reaching the goal is possessed by 'Affan, who is described in Tha'labī's version as a rabbi. He knows of the existence of Solomon's tomb, he knows where it is, and he knows how to obtain the magic plant juice which enables them to walk over the Seven Seas. He also knows the appropriate conjuration that will protect them when they reach the point of ultimate danger. But in teaching it to Bulūqiyā, who does not possess the right training, and whose memory proves faulty at the moment of stress, 'Affan makes a mistake that is fatal to himself.

Likewise the practitioner of *Hekhalot* mysticism must know the precise rules and methods for reaching his goal, and his practices must not be revealed to the uninitiated. He must pass through seven concentric palaces during his visionary journey and invoke the "Prince of the Torah," reciting perfectly various forms of his name, expressed in forty-two letters, for which his memory must be faultless. At any point in the procedure he is likely to fail and to die or go mad.[44] There are two *Hekhalot* texts which imply that the space between the fifth and sixth palaces resembled water but was actually translucent crystal that might be mistaken for water by an ignorant mystic.[45] It seems possible that the Seven Seas of the upper world were conceived of as translucent crystal that only looked like water, but could in fact be walked on.

Two different schemes for the regions of the heavens were at work in Jewish apocalyptic literature: a threefold heaven found in *1 Enoch* 14 and in the *Testament of Levi*, and a sevenfold heaven found in the *Ascension of Isaiah* and in *Hekhalot* texts.[46] Similarly, in the standard cosmology of ancient Mesopotamia there are three heavens (of Anu, Enlil, and Ea) and Gilgamesh seems to visit three regions beyond the known world, whereas the *Descent of Ishtar* and the myth of *Nergal and Ereshkigal* show a sevenfold descent to the Queen of the Underworld.

D.J. Halperin has shown that in *1 Enoch* 14:10 the ground of the divine palace was made of crystal, likewise in Rev 4:6 there was a sea of glass-like crystal before the throne of God; and in the *Vita Adae et Evae* (Latin version, 29:1-3) Michael "touched the waters which were round about Paradise, and they froze hard." He relates their deceptive appearance to extreme danger, also hinted at in R. Akiba's warning that one must not say "water, water" when ascending to the throne of God. These dangerous waters that must be crossed at the last stages before Paradise can be reached are present in the *Epic of Gilgamesh*, where they are indeed water, but lethal water that must not be touched; and in the Tale of Bulūqiyā, where they are crossed on foot thanks to the magical sap rubbed upon the soles of the feet. The hidden writing found by Bulūqiyā in the version of Mardrus warns that these are no ordinary seas: "To cross those seas and to reach that Isle beyond the Seventh Sea no ship avails; he only may succeed who finds the plant with magic juice which, rubbed upon the soles of the feet, makes men capable of walking on the surface of the sea." This echoes the warning of Siduri to Gilgamesh when he expressed the desire to travel to Ut-napishtim on his paradise-island: "There has never been a ferry of any kind, Gilgamesh, and nobody from time immemorial has crossed the sea ... The crossing is difficult, the way of it very difficult, and in between are lethal waters which bar the way ahead." Halperin has drawn attention to early Islamic stories about Solomon which seem to imply that the palace and throne of Solomon, set upon a floor of glass, is a counterpart or Islamic reworking of the theme from *Hekhalot* literature in which Solomon is substituted for the divine presence.[47]

The throne of God in Ezekiel 1 is normally taken to be the inspiration for the vision of God's throne in *Hekhalot* and Merkabah mysticism. A much earlier trace of this is found in the Babylonian myth of the *Descent of Ishtar to the Underworld*, in which the goddess travels through seven gates to meet the Queen of the Underworld, who resides among the chthonic Anunnaki-gods. They perform the judging of the dead, making decisions about the time and manner of each man's death, from golden thrones.[48] Imagery from Ezekiel 1 is found in the Tale of Bulūqiyā: the lion, bull, man, and eagle which support the throne of God as angels there are transferred to the four angels beneath the tree in a heavenly garden in the Burton version, and to the four angels whom the hero meets at the approaches to Mount Qāf in Thaʿlabī's version.

The mystic who wished to see the abode of God and the palaces of the heavenly angels "must ... place his head between his knees,"[49] a deliberate pose with an ancestry that can be traced back to the *Epic of Gilgamesh*. When Gilgamesh wanted to induce a dream-vision, Enkidu drew a magic circle within which Gilgamesh sat "with his chin on his knees," whereupon he experienced an apocalyptic dream of the netherworld.

Some versions (Persian, Syriac, and Ethiopic) of the *Alexander Romance* contain an episode in which the hero is in a garden with talking trees which have the heads of an ox, a lion, an eagle, and a man respectively; the trees foretell his death. It was commonly illustrated in Persian miniatures; in Ferdowsi's version, incorporated into the *Shāhnāmah*, the talking trees that predicted Alexander's death are associated with a topaz palace enshrining a corpse.[50] Therefore connections with Ezekiel 1 in the *Alexander Romance* and the Tale of Bulūqiyā include both the vision of a distant and dangerous tomb with a golden throne, and an episode related to the bearers of the divine throne which referred to them not as living creatures with wings, but as trees.

Babylonian Contributions to Hekhalot Mysticism

A consensus seem to be emerging that *Hekhalot* mysticism originated in pre-Islamic Babylonia rather than in Palestine.[51] Moreover, some connections between kabbalistic Judaism and Sufi literature in the Middle Ages are known.[52] Babylonian ancestry may account in part for some of the similarities.[53]

1. Descriptions of the size and materials of God's body

Cohen has drawn attention to one neo-Assyrian cuneiform text that seems to be a forerunner to the *Shi'ur Qomah* (a text for which close links with the text of *Hekhalot Rabbati* are clear)[54] in describing the different parts of the god's body in terms of precious materials.[55] The *Hekhalot* texts in general can be described as manuals for making the ecstatic journey into the divine presence with the aim of acquiring knowledge and wisdom.[56] It is possible to point to a quite substantial Babylonian and Assyrian component from cuneiform texts which may help to explain some of the links between different branches of mysticism, even though evidence for the latter is so much later in date. A text which describes Marduk as king of the gods in terms of exceptional size and construction is the *Epic of Creation* I:

> He (Anu) made him so perfect that his godhead was
> doubled.
> Elevated far above them, he was superior in every
> way.
> His limbs were ingeniously made beyond
> comprehension,
> Impossible to understand, too difficult to perceive.
> Four were his eyes, four were his ears;
> When his lips moved, fire blazed forth.
> The four ears were enormous
> And likewise the eyes; they perceived everything.
> Highest among the gods, his form was outstanding.
> His limbs were very long, his height (?) outstanding.

The ritual for which the *Epic* was recited was the New Year festival in which the king "took the hands of Bel," and came into direct contact with the deity.[57]

2. Hašmal and the Crystal Floor

Another neo-Assyrian text (VAT 8917) contains not only the same type of description of the god's body as VAT 9739, but also a description of the warrior god Ninurta standing in his chariot, a description of the middle heaven (one of three) with Bel sitting on a lapis lazuli throne surrounded by a shining floor (?) of glass (?) and crystal (?),[58] a description of the size of the visible orbs of the sungod and moongod as 40 double hours and 60 double hours respectively, and a description of the tablet as "a secret of the great gods, a taboo of the great gods," a rubric reserved for writings with magical associations, including medicine and astronomy. The word translated as "crystal" is *elmešu*, for which a connection with Hebrew חשמל has been posited.[59] It is the substance from which the "horns" of Ishtar's chariot are made in the *Epic of Gilgamesh*, and in the *Epic of Erra and Ishum* Marduk as king of the gods declares that he "changed the location of the *elmešu*-stone and did not reveal it to anyone" (I 148).

3. The divine chariot

The idea that a deity might be seen on an awesome chariot is often attested in Akkadian texts, notably in the ritual for the autumn New Year festival at Uruk recorded on a Seleucid tablet which begins by mentioning the gold chariot of Anu and the silver chariot of Anu.[60] In the neo-Assyrian hymn of Assurbanipal to Ishtar of Nineveh (K.286), the chariot of Ishtar at the temple of the New Year festival is described as "too awesome for kings,"[61] and the same king describes with pride the details of manufacture for a new chariot of Bel-Marduk in Babylon: "A lofty chariot, vehicle for Marduk prince of gods, lord of lords, of gold, silver, and choice gemstones, I perfected its form."[62] There are several attestations of the divine chariot receiving offerings of animals and of libations in neo-Babylonian texts.[63] There is thus a possibility that the concept of a terrifying chariot closely associated with an anthropomorphic god has its origin in ancient Mesopotamia, perhaps specifically at the New Year festival. If the glassy throne-room of Bel has been interpreted correctly in VAT 8917, it may be appropriate to mention that a text known as *Marduk's Address to the Demons* contains a line describing "Bel, who sits in the middle of Tiamat (i.e., the sea/primeval chaos) in the Temple of the New Year Festival." Another text describes the procession to that temple: "to the lofty cella, on the rolling sea (= Tiamat) he set his feet." Finally, a topographical list describing the temples in Babylon says that "Tiamat is the seat of Bel, upon which Bel sits."[64] The lapis lazuli throne upon a glass floor, if correctly understood, corresponds closely to details in the vision of Ezekiel (1:22-26), giving rise to the possibility that his own vision was stimulated by witnessing or hearing accounts of some of the ceremonies of the New Year festival while he was in exile in Babylonia. It may be relevant for understanding Ezekiel's vision and its connection with the merkabah that two Akkadian words for "chariot", *magarru* and *mugirru*, also mean "wheel."

4. The Shekhinah

It has been observed that the key word *Shekhinah* is not found in the Bible nor (yet) in the texts from Qumran.[65] In Akkadian the word *šikittu*, construct *šiknat* "form, construction" appears to have the same root and the same meaning.[66] It is first attested in an early second millennium poem describing Ishtar,[67] and is also found in the description of a youth who appears in a dream-vision in the wisdom composition *Ludlul* tablet III,[68] described there as having an exceptional *šikittu*, proud limbs, new clothing, a mantle of radiance, and being clothed in fearfulness.

These indications support the evidence quoted by Cohen for ancient Mesopotamian influence upon the formation of *Hekhalot* mysticism. The New Year festival of ancient Mesopotamia is mentioned in several of the texts quoted above for their similarity to *Hekhalot* concepts. During the several days of ceremonies not only was the *Epic of Creation* recited or enacted, but also the king entered the temple of the New Year festival and "took the hands of Bel," i.e., communed with the deity and perhaps took part in a *hieros gamos*.[69] The foreign kings who ruled Mesopotamia from the Achaemenid period certainly took part, and ritual tablets from Uruk date to the Seleucid kings.[70] But the festival took different forms in different cities, and the king was certainly not the only human protagonist in all of them. To what extent Ezekiel might have witnessed the rituals is unknown. A neo-Assyrian tablet (K 2892) lists different New Year festivals for Marduk, Ninurta, Ishtar, and Sin.[71] However, if the *Epic of Gilgamesh* had a cultic origin or function, it has yet to be discovered from cuneiform records. Perhaps a hint towards it may be found in the facts that Shulgi, king of Ur, claimed divinity during his lifetime and claimed also to be the twin brother of Gilgamesh; but the cuneiform records themselves do not make a direct connection between those two facts.

The scribe whose name is given as the "author" of the Standard Babylonian *Epic of Gilgamesh* is Sin-leqe-unninni, a divination priest or seer.[72] A recent study has drawn attention to the role of the seer in the late Bronze Age, especially in tablets from Emar, as a scribe, a diviner, and as the one who officiated at rites of initiation.[73] Thus there is evidence which might be interpreted to show a link between the *Epic of Gilgamesh* and mystical initiation, but it is arguable; seers are named as authors for other kinds of texts too.

Although cuneiform literary production seems to have ceased not long after the beginning of the Christian era, it is clear from the writings of Damascius (born ca. 480 CE) that some version of the *Epic of Creation* was still known in the fifth century. Whether the survival of the *Epic* should be linked to survival of the ritual is unknown. But in the context of a possible connection between the New Year festival and *Hekhalot* ritual, it should be mentioned that the three (Tablet VI) and the fifty (Tablet VII) names of Marduk, together with the cryptic, complex word-play involved in each name, might be considered to be forerunners of later techniques for mystic meditation.[74]

Bulūqiyā's Departure from the Tomb of Solomon: A Ritual Pattern

A fixed pattern, modelled upon rituals known from texts of the Middle Ages for the practice of magic, forms the framework for events following the death of 'Affan in the Tale of Bulūqiyā. It has the same sequence in all versions, for the sequence itself is significant, and does not allow individual parts to be transposed and the order changed. Bulūqiyā utters an imperfect conjuration; he is transported from the tomb of Solomon and approaches the territory of the demon king Sakhr. Aggressive, armed warriors rush up to him. When he is escorted to Sakhr, the latter is surrounded by his officers or courtiers.

The text from which this pattern can be recognized is the *Clavicula Salomonis*[75] known in Latin from the Middle Ages. Beginning as a testament from Solomon to his son Roboam (Rehoboam), it contains magical instructions for procedures which will summon up demons and exorcise evils of many kinds. Its literary form as a testament, and the pentacles or magic circles which are still inscribed in Hebrew, place much of the material into a Jewish tradition of late antiquity. Features that may be linked with Enochic traditions include Asmodeus as the name for the demon king, Kokabiel as one of the angels invoked, and the *nephilim*-giants among the accursed nations, as well as the names of Anael (Ananel), Daniel (Danel), Samael (Samiel), and Saraiel (Sariel). The prologue to the text is reminiscent of the start to the Tale of Bulūqiyā, and is in fact common to many hermetic writings of late antiquity: secrets written down just before Solomon's death are hidden in an ivory casket in his tomb by Roboam and later discovered there by Babylonian "philosophers." Upon that secret document the elaborate procedures that follow purport to be based.

Revelation Through Secret Writings

The tradition that vital secrets were to be found in hidden writings is, of course, extremely common in hermetic and revelatory texts of late antiquity. Not surprisingly, therefore, the Tale of Bulūqiyā

makes use of it. In early antiquity, however, secret writings are
scarcely attested, certainly not in Homer, nor in the Babylonian *Epic
of Creation*, nor in early Egyptian literature. Their presence in the Tale
of Bulūqiyā points to one early attestation that may be crucial to
understanding the origin of the tradition, namely the Babylonian *Epic
of Gilgamesh.*

> Look for the copper tablet-box,
> Undo its bronze lock,
> Open the door to its secret,
> Lift out the lapis lazuli tablet and read it,
> The story of Gilgamesh, who endured all kinds of
>   sufferings.

The prestige of Gilgamesh rested in part upon his ability to bring
back an account of times before the Flood. The Ptolemaic story of
Setne Khamwas, set in the time of Ramses II (1290-1224 BCE),
attempts to retroject the tradition into ancient Egyptian history, but in
using the reign of Ramses II fails to establish priority over the
Babylonians by a margin of more than a millennium.[76]

In Greek hermetic tradition it was the emerald tablet of Hermes
Trismegistos which contained the secrets needed by mystics and
initiates, including details of the cosmos and very early history, such as
are told to Gilgamesh by Ut-napishtim, to Bulūqiyā by Sakhr and the
angels, and to Enoch by God and his angels. The origins of hermetic
tradition, once pronounced a bogus creation of Egyptian Hellenism,[77]
are now being seen at least in part as a native Egyptian phenomenon
that was transferred into Greek with much expansion and adaptation.[78]
A fundamental claim for a Babylonian component, advanced thirty-
eight years ago,[79] has received strong support from two recent
developments. The fragment of cuneiform text which gave the
prologue to the *Epic of Gilgamesh*, including the passage quoted
above, was published only seventeen years ago. Also quite recently
cuneiform evidence has emerged for the Mesopotamian tradition of
Seven Sages and their connection with traditions about Enoch.[80]
Precisely how cuneiform Babylonian traditions passed to Egypt and
emerged in Hellenic guise is extremely difficult to document. But the

Tale of Bulūqiyā, from its Babylonian ancestry, passing through unorthodox Jewish tradition and into the *Alexander Romance*, gives one thread that can be traced.

Different versions of the medieval "Emerald Tablet" are known: a Latin text of it has been shown to comprise the conclusion of an ancient cosmological composition used by Arab alchemists, and an Arabic version called *Kitāb dakhirat Aliskandar* associates the tradition with Alexander. The latter states that a treasure-book of gold, written in Greek, was found concealed in the cloister of Armorium by the 'Abbāsid caliph al-Mu'taṣim (833-842 CE), renowned founder of Samarra; its text was said to contain the knowledge of Aristotle and of Great Hermes, with whose seal it was sealed. It had belonged to Dhu'l-Qarnayn son of Filiqus in the time of Antiochus.[81] In Sufi traditions conveyed by Suhrawardi, the initiate may see Hermes-al-Khiḍr seated on a throne holding the emerald tablet.[82] Mardrus' version of the Tale of Bulūqiyā specifies Greek as the language in which the hidden text was written; this may be a reflection of the story which would have been popular in Tha'labī's day.

The *leit-motif* of a precious scripture containing secret revelation is found in other contexts attached to Alexander. In Greek versions of the *Alexander Romance*, the magician-king Nectanebo visited Olympias and foretold the divine conception and birth of Alexander, using a tablet made of precious materials engraved with astrological designs. Some details concerning the Arabic book of the *Mystery of Mysteries* may be mentioned. Like the *Alexander Romance* in Greek, which has proved to be composed using "letters" ostensibly written by leading characters in the narrative, the *Mystery of Mysteries* begins with an exchange of letters between Aristotle and Alexander.[83] The earliest date for it comes from a manuscript of 941 CE, a century or so before Tha'labī's version of Bulūqiyā was written.

In connection with *Hekhalot* mysticism, Halperin has shown that some Judaic traditions linked it to the revelation of the Torah on Mount Sinai.[84]

There appears to be a case for suggesting that revelation through hidden or secret writings has its origin in ancient Mesopotamian rituals of initiation, although the motif in literature presumably spread into wider contexts. This suggestion may be supported by colophons to certain types of texts containing esoteric information, which forbid access to the uninitiated. Such instructions are first attested on neo-Assyrian tablets of the late eighth and seventh centuries BCE, and they are connected with the profession of seers.[85] A prayer to Bel recited by a priest at the New Year festival in Babylon is included in this category, as well as a description of Marduk's shrine in Babylon.[86]

A Literary Genre Rooted in Theurgy

3 Enoch, the Hebrew and Aramaic compilation, is normally regarded as *Hekhalot* literature. *1 Enoch* 17-36 contains the account of Enoch's travels, like those of Bulūqiyā, through the regions of heaven and hell, where at the seventh mountain he sees the throne of God together with a wonderful tree, fragrant and fruitful; he goes on to visit the "garden of righteousness." Scholem has pointed out "the clear tendency toward asceticism as a way of preparing for the reception of the mystical tradition, which is already attested to in the last chapter of the Book of [I] Enoch, becomes a fundamental principle for the apocalyptics, the Essenes, and the circle of Merkabah mystics who succeeded them."[87] In Greek mystery cults too, asceticism accompanied the attempt to commune with the gods,[88] and many parallels are agreed to exist between Greek theurgy and the theurgy of the Merkabah mystics.[89]

A genre of literature may be discerned, even if diverse languages and cultures have led to wide variety within the genre. Menelaus, Gilgamesh, and Alexander were all born mortal but ended up as gods who received sacrifices. All travelled through strange lands and either met an immortal sage -- Proteus, Ut-napishtim, al-Khiḍr -- or the tomb of a sage -- the tomb of Proteus, of Enoch, of Solomon, etc. -- or both. Enoch had a special status as one who had communed with god, although no actual worship of him is known; and certain other works such as the *Testament of Levi* and the *Apocalypse of Zosimos* share some of the same features even though their heroes are not immortalized in any way by their experiences. Another difference is that whereas Menelaus, Gilgamesh, and Alexander pass through a series of adventures which take place on this earth and can thus be described as travellers' tales, Enoch, Levi, and Zosimos experience celestial adventures where they meet angels, not sages who lived long ago. Essentially, however, the adventures reflect the initiation of the mystic who can commune with heaven only at the last stage. Revelation through hidden writings often plays a crucial part in the genre.

Obviously the rise of monotheism did not allow mortals to attain immortality, and so the genre was adapted for new prophets and for saints. But the stories of fantastic travels and difficulties overcome, often told in a perfunctory manner, were selected from a large corpus which crossed the boundaries of different languages. The means by which the genre crossed such boundaries may be seen in terms of the wandering seer known from the Bible and from ancient Greek literature,[90] and the peripatetic holy man of early Islamic times. This explanation may help to show why adventures or specific details within them are sometimes found attached to more than one hero.[91]

Evolution of both the ritual and its accompanying myth might explain not only increasing complexity in the genre, but also why a report from the underworld seems to have been added secondarily both to the *Odyssey* and to the *Epic of Gilgamesh*.

Conclusion

The ascetic milieu identified for remnants of the *Epic of Gilgamesh,* first at Qumran and later among the Manichaeans, developed through Gnostic groups of late antiquity into new groups during the early Middle Ages. These new groups, Sufis on the one hand and Jewish mystics on the other, used modified versions of the Babylonian *Epic* in the Tale of Bulūqiyā. Since a strong Babylonian component for mystical practice and literature can be demonstrated, arguments over whether one group drew upon the literature of the other[92] can be tackled in a clearer light. The pattern of construction in certain parts of the *Epic of Gilgamesh*, the *Alexander Romance,* and the Tale of Bulūqiyā seem to reflect the rituals and the stages through which initiates must pass, rather than giving rise to them through an exegetical development.

The goal is expressed clearly in the prologue to the *Epic of Gilgamesh*, that "he who searched lands everywhere, he who experienced the whole gained complete wisdom ... he brought back a tale of times before the Flood, he had journeyed far and wide, weary and at last resigned." To read or listen to such a tale allowed the hearer to partake of the wisdom of the hero and provided him with a model.[93]

The authority of the genre among different religious groups came ultimately from the antiquity and prestige of the *Epic of Gilgamesh*.

Postscript

The gap in time between *Hekhalot* mysticism and the Babylonian New Year festival at which the *Epic of Creation* was recited is narrowed by evidence from Palmyra. There the great temple of Bel, rebuilt from 32 CE onwards with partial funding from the city of Babylon,[94] was inaugurated in that year on the sixth day of Nisan, its dedication thus taking place during the New Year festival. Sculpted in the main doorway of the temple was a frieze showing Bel dispatching Tiamat in a scene some five meters long.[95] One of the largest temples in the world when completed, it remained in use for centuries. Another very large temple dedicated to the Babylonian deity Nabu has recently been identified at Palmyra. Palmyra therefore was a center where Babylonian cultic traditions were maintained during the Roman period, long after cuneiform writing died out.

---

[1]   J. Oelsner, "Ein Beitrag zur keilschriftlichen Königstitulaturen in hellenistischer Zeit," *ZA* 56 (1964) 262-64 redated BM 35174 + 35628 (Tablet X) to that period. See also idem, *Materialen zur babylonischen Gesellschaft und Kultur in hellenistischer Zeit* (Budapest: Eotvos Lorand Tudomanyegyetem,

1986) 206.

2 S. Dalley, "Gilgamesh in the Arabian Nights," *JRAS* (1991) 1-17. The different versions and their relationship to the *Epic of Gilgamesh* are described there. Muslim sources are detailed by J.E. Bencheikh, *Les mille et une nuits ou la parole prisonnière* (Paris: Gallimard, 1988) 181-85.

3 Several colleagues have given help and advice at different stages, but they are not responsible for the pitfalls into which she may unwittingly have fallen. Particular thanks are due to Professor A.F.L. Beeston, Professor W. Madelung, Dr. R. Nettler, and Peter Kingsley.

4 J.C. Reeves, *Jewish Lore in Manichaean Cosmogony: Studies in the Book of Giants Traditions* (Cincinnati: Hebrew Union College Press, 1992) 116-121; idem, "Utnapishtim in the Book of Giants?" *JBL* 112 (1993) 110-115.

5 S. Dalley, "The Gilgamesh Epic and Manichaean Themes," *Aram* 3 (1993) 23-33.

6 I thank Prof. A.F.L. Beeston for translating the whole of Tha'labī's version into English for me.

7 I am grateful to him for his help. The three accounts contain the same information.

8 W.M. Thackston, *The Tales of the Prophets of Al-Kisā'ī* (Boston: Twayne Publishers, 1978), introduction.

9 *EI²* *s.v.* al-Khaḍir. The Jewish legend of Elijah and Rabbi Joshua ben Levi is essentially the same tale as told by al-Kisā'ī about Al-Khiḍr and Moses.

10 W. Scott, *Hermetica* (4 vols.; Oxford: Clarendon, 1924-36) 4.254, quoting Mas'ūdī.

11 I. Friedländer, *Die Chadhirlegende und der Alexanderroman* (Berlin and Leipzig: B.G. Teubner, 1913) 247.

12 Thackston, *Tales* xxv has suggested that the name Idrīs is taken from the Greek Andreas, but Babylonian ancestry for the episode suggests that the reverse is the case.

13 M.S. Southgate, *Iskandarnameh: A Persian Mediaeval Alexander Romance* (New York: Columbia University Press, 1978) 54-59.

14 For example, in the former sea-monsters land on one of the islands carrying torch-like, luminous stones in their mouths; in the latter a huge fish leaps out of a lake displaying a lantern-like stone in its belly. In Jami's Persian version (1485-91) Alexander walks over water as one walks over land, which is reminiscent of Bulūqiyā's progress over the sea when he has rubbed juice from the magic plant upon the soles of his feet.

15 S. Eitrem, "Die vier Elemente in der Mysterienweihe," *SO* 4 (1926) 46-49.

16 E.V. Rieu, in his introduction to the translation of Homer's *Odyssey* (Harmondsworth: Penguin, 1946) x.

17 Thackston, *Tales* xviii. Numenius gave a similar interpretation to the *Odyssey*. See Numenius, *Fragments* (ed. E. des Places; Paris: Société d'édition "Les Belles Lettres", 1973) frg. 33.

18 Details for the points of resemblance are given by W. Burkert, *The Orientalizing Revolution: Near Eastern Influence on Greek Culture in the Archaic Age* (Cambridge: Harvard University Press, 1992) 88, 200 n.1.

19 M. Gaster, "An Old Hebrew Romance of Alexander," *JRAS* (1897) 485-549;

I.J. Kazis, *The Book of the Gests of Alexander of Macedon* (Cambridge, MA: Mediaeval Academy of America, 1962) 33.

20 F. Pfister, *Alexander der Grosse in den Offenbarungen der Griechen, Juden, Mohammedaner und Christen* (Berlin: Deutsche Akademie der Wissenschaft zu Berlin, 1956).

21 E.A.W. Budge, *The Alexander Book in Ethiopia* (Oxford: Oxford University Press, 1933) 91-92.

22 D.O. Edzard, "Gilgameš und Huwawa," *ZA* 80 (1990) 165-203, esp. p. 181. The Akkadian version of the story is too badly broken at this point to be useful.

23 See Dalley, *Aram* 3 (1993) 31-32, with reference to 2 Kgs 19:23.

24 MS 5379 Biblioteca Nationale Madrid.

25 E. García Gómez, *Un texto arabe occidental de la leyenda de Alejandro* (Madrid: E. Maestre, 1929) cxlvii.

26 I am grateful to Prof. A.F.L. Beeston for supplying the English translations of these passages.

27 T. Nagel, *Alexander der Grosse in der frühislamischen Volksliteratur* (Walldorf-Hessen: Verlag für Orientkunde H. Vorndran, 1978), whose conclusions were independently confirmed; see the review of H.T. Norris in *BSOAS* 43 (1980) 595-97.

28 R.G. Khoury, *Wahb b. Munabbih* (Wiesbaden: Otto Harrassowitz, 1972) 237ff. Tha'labī's version of the *Alexander Romance* cites the authority of Ali b. Abi Talib, although the story has important differences.

29 See *Lexikon der Ägyptologie* (Wiesbaden: Otto Harrassowitz, 1975-) *s.v.* Babylon.

30 H. Tadmor, *Inscriptions of Tiglath-Pileser III* (forthcoming); idem, "The Campaigns of Sargon II of Assur," *JCS* 12 (1958) 34, Annals line 18, and Nimrud Prism lines 46-48.

31 S. Dalley, "Foreign Chariotry and Cavalry in the Armies of Tiglath-Pileser III and Sargon II," *Iraq* 47 (1985) 31-48.

32 J.A. Soggin, *Introduction to the Old Testament* (London: SCM Press, 1976) 485ff.

33 J. Horovitz, "Bulūqjā," *ZDMG* 55 (1901) 519-25. See also Bencheikh (cf. n.2 *supra*) 183-87.

34 H. Lazarus-Yafeh, *Intertwined Worlds: Medieval Islam and Bible Criticism* (Princeton: Princeton University Press, 1992), esp. chap. 3; *EI[1]* s.v. *tahrīf*.

35 Related by Ibn Hajar. See Friedländer, *Chadhirlegende* 269-71.

36 Thackston, *Tales* 18.

37 M. Perlmann, "A Legendary Story of Ka'b al Ahbār's Conversion to Islam," *The Joshua Starr Memorial Volume: Studies in History and Philology* (New York: Conference on Jewish Relations, 1953) 85-99.

38 A further story with this emphasis was studied by Perlmann, "Another Ka'b al-Ahbār Story," *JQR* 45 (1954) 48-58.

39 J.C.L. Gibson, *Canaanite Myths and Legends* (Edinburgh: T. & T. Clark, 1977) 103-122; Bencheikh (cf. n.2 *supra*) 165 is doubtful about this.

40 Josephus, *Ant.* 11.337.

41 R. Merkelbach, *Die Quellen des griechischen Alexanderromans* (München: C.H. Beck, 1977) 65.

42 Ibid. 69-70. The (pre-)Manichaean tone of a Babylonian elegy mourning the death of Tammuz may be noted; see A. Livingstone, *Court Poetry and Literary Miscellanea, State Archives of Assyria III* (Helsinki: Helsinki University Press, 1989) 39-41. See also Dalley, *Aram* 3 (1993) 23-33.

43 Bencheikh 166-70.

44 G. Scholem, *Kabbalah* (Jerusalem: Keter, 1974) 17-18.

45 D.J. Halperin, *The Faces of the Chariot: Early Jewish Responses to Ezekiel's Vision* (Tübingen: J.C.B. Mohr, 1988) 200.

46 I owe this observation to the seminar paper given in Oxford in 1991 by Dr. C.R.A. Morray-Jones.

47 Halperin, *Faces* 487-90.

48 S. Dalley, *Myths from Mesopotamia* (Oxford: Oxford University Press, 1989) 159.

49 D.J. Halperin, *The Merkabah in Rabbinic Literature* (New Haven: American Oriental Society, 1980) 3.

50 Ferdowsi, *The Epic of the Kings* (trans. R. Levy; rev. by A. Banani; London: Routledge and Kegan Paul, 1985) 248; Southgate, *Iskandarnameh* 172-73.

51 Halperin, *Faces* 362; M.S. Cohen, *The Shi'ur Qomah: Liturgy and Theurgy in Pre-Kabbalistic Jewish Mysticism* (Lanham, MD: University Press of America, 1983) 66-67.

52 Scholem, *Kabbalah* 35-37.

53 Parallels between Ezekiel's vision and Babylonian imagery in general have recently been discussed by Peter Kingsley, "Ezekiel by the Grand Canal: Between Jewish and Babylonian Tradition," *JRAS* (1992) 339-46.

54 Cohen, *Shi'ur Qomah* 171.

55 VAT 9739 + STT II 118. Cohen quoted the extract translated by T. Jacobsen, *The Treasures of Darkness: A History of Mesopotamian Religion* (New Haven: Yale University Press, 1976) 235.

56 Halperin, *Faces* 367, 407.

57 S.A. Pallis, *The Babylonian Akītu Festival* (Copenhagen: A.F. Host, 1926).

58 Translations of the latter vary; this is the interpretation given in *CAD* B (1965) *s.v. bušu*, and followed by A. Livingstone, *Mythical and Mythological Explanatory Works* (Oxford: Clarendon, 1986) 83, but in a more recent publication (*State Archives of Assyria III* 100) the same author has followed the earlier *CAD* E (1958) *s.v. elmešu* in emending the text and translating: "and has made a lamp of electrum shine there." Cf. Kingsley (n.53 *supra*) who translates "amber"; and BDB *s.v.* חשמל, "evidently some *shining* substance."

59 *CAD* E 108a.

60 F. Thureau-Dangin, *Rituels accadiens* (Paris, 1921; reprinted, Osnabrück: Otto Zeller, 1975) 89.

61 Livingstone, *State Archives of Assyria III* 19.

62 M. Streck, *Assurbanipal und die letzten assyrischen Könige bis zum untergange Nineveh's* (Leipzig: J.C. Hinrichs, 1916) 300 iv 12 and 148 x 32.

63 *CAD s.v. narkabtu*.

64 A.R. George, *Babylonian Topographical Texts* (Leuven: Peeters, 1992) 44.

65 G. Scholem, *On the Mystical Shape of the Godhead: Basic Concepts in the Kabbalah* (New York: Schocken, 1991) 147.

[66] The thorough account of the *shekhinah* in E.E. Urbach, *The Sages: Their Concepts and Beliefs* (Jerusalem: Magnes, 1975) 40-65 has been very useful.

[67] V. Scheil, "Le poème d'Agušaya," *RA* 15 (1918) 175 i 22.

[68] W.G. Lambert, *Babylonian Wisdom Literature* (Oxford: Clarendon, 1960) 48 lines 9-12.

[69] J. Renger, "Heilige Hochzeit," *Reallexikon der Assyriologie* (Berlin: W. de Gruyter, 1928-   ) 4.251-59; J.N. Postgate, *Early Mesopotamia* (London: Routledge, 1992) 123-24, 130, and 266-67.

[70] There is evidence that Antiochus III (222-187 BCE) probably celebrated the festival; see S. Sherwin-White and A. Kuhrt, *From Samarkand to Sardis* (London: Duckworth, 1993) 130-31.

[71] Livingstone, *Mythical Works* 157.

[72] W.G. Lambert, "A Catalogue of Texts and Authors," *JCS* 16 (1962) 66 line 10.

[73] D. Fleming, "The Voice of the Ugaritic Incantation Priest," *UF* 23 (1991) 147.

[74] J. Bottéro, "Les noms de Marduk," *Essays on the Ancient Near East in Honor of Jacob Joel Finkelstein* (ed. M. de J. Ellis; Hamden, CT: Archon Books, 1977) 5-28.

[75] S.L.M. Mathers, *The Key of Solomon the King* (London: Kegan Paul, 1909); E.M. Butler, *Ritual Magic* (Cambridge: Cambridge University Press, 1949); and in general, E. Schürer, *The History of the Jewish People in the Time of Jesus Christ* (3 vols. in 4; ed. G. Vermes, F. Millar, and M. Goodman; Edinburgh: T. & T. Clark, 1973-87) 3/1.375-79.

[76] G. Fowden (*The Egyptian Hermes: A Historical Approach to the Late Pagan Mind* [Cambridge: Cambridge University Press, 1986] 59-60) uses the text to show that Egyptian tradition is prior to the Greek.

[77] F. Yates, *Giordano Bruno and the Hermetic Tradition* (London: Routledge & Kegan Paul, 1964), largely accepting the polemical denunciation of Isaac Casaubon in 1614.

[78] Fowden, *Hermes* (see esp. xiv); Peter Kingsley ("Poimandres: The Etymology of the Name and the Origins of the Hermetica," *Journal of the Warburg and Courtauld Institutes* 56 [1993] 1ff.) shows that *Poimandres* is a Greek rendering of an originally Egyptian title.

[79] M. Plessner, "Hermes Trismegistos and Arab Science," *Studia Islamica* 2 (1954) 52ff.

[80] J.C. Vanderkam, *Enoch and the Growth of an Apocalyptic Tradition* (Washington: Catholic Biblical Association, 1984).

[81] J. Ruska, *Tabula Smaragdina* (Heidelberg: C. Winter, 1926) 68.

[82] Ibid. 109ff.

[83] L.L. Gunderson, *Alexander's Letter to Aristotle About India* (Beiträge zur klassischen Philologie, Heft 110; Meisenheim am Glan: Hain, 1980), compared with M. Manzalaoui, "The Pseudo-Aristotelean Kitāb Sirr al-asrār," *Oriens* 23 (1974) 147-257.

[84] Halperin, *Faces*, esp. pp. 109-114 and chap. VIII.

[85] R. Borger, "Geheimwissen," *Reallexikon der Assyriologie* 3.188-91.

[86] Borger, ibid., texts nos. 18 and 34. For no. 18 see now George,

Topographical Texts 414.

87 Scholem, *Kabbalah* 11.

88 W. Burkert, *Greek Religion* (Cambridge: Harvard University Press, 1985) 276ff. Note that a Semitic etymology for the *Kabarnoi* and *Kabeiroi* has been proposed, and that the servant-god Kasmilos/Kadmilos has a name formed like the angels of late antiquity as, e.g., in *1 Enoch.*

89 Schürer, *History* 3/1.363; Halperin, *Faces* 195.

90 Burkert, *Orientalizing Revolution* 41ff.

91 M. Asin Palacios, *La escatologia musulmana en La Divina Comedia* (Madrid: E. Maestre, 1919) has collected a wide variety of relevant material.

92 Scholem suggests that Jewish mystics drew upon Sufi literature. See his *Kabbalah* 35.

93 One wonders whether the early part of Gilgamesh's life may have provided a model for libertine groups of Sufis.

94 J. Cantineau, *Inventaire des inscriptions de Palmyre IX* (Beirut: Impr. catholique, 1933) nos. 1 and 11.

95 R. du Mesnil du Buisson, "Le bas-relief du combat de Bel à Palmyre," *Annales archéologiques de la Syrie* 26 (1976) 83ff. The information about this decoration came too late to be included in such standard works as H. Seyrig, R. Amy, and E. Will, *Le temple de Bel à Palmyre* (2 vols.; Paris: Librairie orientaliste P. Geuthner, 1975); H.J.W. Drijvers, *The Religion of Palmyra* (Leiden: Brill, 1976); or even J. Teixidor, *The Pantheon of Palmyra* (Leiden: Brill, 1979). It is discussed by M. Gawlikowski, "Les dieux de Palmyre," *ANRW* II.18.4 (1990) 2614-15.

INDEX OF CITATIONS

I. HEBREW SCRIPTURES

George the Monk
Chronicon
1.57.1-9 - 168
1.92.17-94.21 - 169

Hegemonius
Acta Archelai
5 - 202
8 - 201

Hippolytus
Refutatio
9.13-17 - 80 195
9.16.4 - 195
10.29 - 80 195

Irenaeus
Adversus haereses 1.20.1 - 63 67 86

Jerome
Liber hebraicarum quaestionum in Genesim
Gen 9:27 - 168
Gen 12:4 - 170
Gen 32:28 - 30

John Chrysostom
In Genesim sermo ix - 168

John Malalas
56.1-9 - 167

Justin Martyr
1 Apology 20 - 64

Dialogue with Trypho
72 - 64
120 - 64

Leo Grammaticus
Chronographia 13.4-16 - 168

Origen
Comm. in Joh.
2.31[25] - 65

Comm. in Matt.
13:57 - 65
23:37 - 65 66
27:9 - 66

Contra Celsum
1.15.334 - 237
4.33 - 236
5.54-55 - 65
6.80 - 236

Hom. in Luc. 35 - 65

In Genesim 41:45-46 - 66

Syncellus
3.6-18 - 124 138
3.19-22 - 167
4.19-22 - 167
4.21-23 - 167
5.12-25 - 123
27.11 - 167
27.33-28.9 - 128
47.14-29 - 122
55.22-56.5 - 168
90.11-12 - 170
106.16-22 - 170
107.16-24 - 169
107.27-29 - 169
107.30-108.5 - 170
111.13-15 - 169
112.4-6 - 168
112.7-12 - 170
112.17-21 - 168
120.22-28 - 126
121-124 - 126
124.1-14 - 167

Tertullian
Cult. fem. 2-3 - 66

Theodoret
Quaest. in Gen. 9.10 - 168

INDEX OF ANCIENT AND MEDIEVAL AUTHORITIES

INDEX OF MODERN AUTHORS